THE TEACHING OF THINKING

THE TEACHING OF THINKING

Raymond S. Nickerson
Bolt Beranek & Newman Inc.
Cambridge, Massachusetts
David N. Perkins
Harvard University
Edward E. Smith
Bolt Beranek & Newman Inc.
Cambridge, Massachusetts

LEA LAWRENCE ERLBAUM ASSOCIATES, PUBLISHERS
1985 Hillsdale, New Jersey London

Lawrence Erlbaum Associates, Inc., Publishers
365 Broadway
Hillsdale, New Jersey 07642

Library of Congress Cataloging in Publication Data

Nickerson, Raymond S.
The teaching of thinking.

Bibilography: p.
Includes index.
1. Thought and thinking—Study and teaching.
2. Reasoning—Study and teaching 3. Problem solving—Study and teaching. I. Perkins, D. N., 1942–
II. Smith, Edward E., 1940– . III. Title.
BF455.N53 1985 153.4'2'07 85-15887
ISBN 0-89859-539-8

Printed in the United States of America
10 9 8 7 6 5 4 3

Table of Contents

PREFACE xi

PART I: THE CHALLENGE OF TEACHING THINKING

1. INTRODUCTION 3

2. ASPECTS OF INTELLECTUAL COMPETENCE 8

1. What is Intelligence? 8
   The ability to classify patterns *9*
   The ability to modify behavior adaptively—to learn *9*
   The ability to reason deductively *10*
   The ability to reason inductively—to generalize *10*
   The ability to develop and use conceptual models *11*
   The ability to understand *12*
2. Some Conceptions of Differential Intelligence 14
3. The Assessment of Intelligence 23
   Some sociological factors behind the idea and practice of mental testing *23*
   Forerunners and pioneers of mental testing *24*
   Components of early tests *27*
   Summary *27*
4. Cognitive Development 29
5. Efforts to Increase Intelligence Through Training 36
6. Summary 42

3. SOME PERSPECTIVES ON THINKING 44

1. Thinking Ability as a Skill or Collection of Skills 45
2. Bartlett's View 46
3. Thinking Skills versus Knowledge 48
4. Some Dichotomies 50
5. What Limits Thinking? 51
Encoding, operations, goals *51*
Style, know-how, load, abilities *52*
Rule-based versus model-based behavior *54*
Implicit and explicit know-how *56*
Generality versus context-boundedness *57*
6. Can Thinking Skills be Taught? 59
7. Summary 61

4. PROBLEM SOLVING, CREATIVITY AND METACOGNITION 64

1. Problem Solving 64
What is problem solving? *65*
The identification of problem-solving strategies *68*
Some problem-solving heuristics *74*
Implications for the teaching of thinking *85*
2. Creativity 86
Definitions of the creative and creativity *87*
Components of creativity *89*
Implications for the teaching of thinking *100*
3. Metacognition 100
Some examples of metacognitive skills *103*
Accessibility as a metacognitive skill *107*
Implications for the teaching of thinking *109*
4. Summary 109

5. ERRORS AND BIASES IN REASONING 111

1. Errors in Deductive Reasoning 111
Nature of deductive reasoning *111*
Using criteria other than validity *112*
Errors due to difficult terms *115*
Altering the representation *116*
Summary *118*
2. Errors in Inductive Reasoning 118
Nature of inductive thinking *118*

Biases in drawing a sample *119*
Biases in relating a sample to a hypothesis *124*
Biases in forming new hypotheses *127*
Summary *129*
3. Reasoning Errors Due to Social Factors 130
Favoritism in evaluating hypotheses in which one has a vested interest *131*
Evaluating people rather than hypotheses *134*
Summary *135*
4. Failures to Elaborate a Model of a Situation 136
Measuring the quality of informal reasoning *136*
Common errors in informal reasoning *137*
Failures of elaboration *138*
5. Summary 140
6. Summary for Part I 140

PART II: APPROACHES TO TEACHING THINKING

6. COGNITIVE OPERATIONS APPROACHES 147

1. The Instrumental Enrichment Program 147
Feuerstein's concept of intelligence and its assessment *148*
Cognitive modifiability and the importance of mediated learning *149*
Cognitive structure, deficient cognitive functions and cognitive maps *151*
Specifics of the program *153*
Evaluation of the program *155*
2. The Structure of Intellect Program 161
The theoretical basis for the program *161*
Content of the program *163*
Evaluation *166*
3. Science ... A Process Approach 169
Specifics of the program *169*
Klausmeier's work with SAPA material *170*
4. ThinkAbout 172
Content of the program *173*
A program cluster *174*
Evaluation *175*
5. BASICS 176
Content of the program *176*

Evaluation *179*
6. Project Intelligence 181
Background *181*
The course *182*
The teacher's manual *182*
Evaluation *185*
7. The Cognitive Operations Approach in General 187

7. HEURISTICS ORIENTED APPROACHES 190

1. Patterns of Problem-Solving 191
The course *191*
The book *193*
2. Schoenfeld's Heuristic Instruction in Mathematical Problem Solving 195
Instruction in heuristics *196*
The importance of a managerial strategy *197*
A further evaluation study *200*
3. A Practicum of Thinking 203
Contents of the program *203*
Evaulation studies *205*
4. The Cognitive Studies Project 206
The Whimbey and Lochhead approach *206*
Observations about the project *207*
5. The Productive Thinking Program 209
The program *209*
Formal tests *211*
6. Lateral Thinking and the CoRT Program 214
Overview of the CoRT program *215*
Evidence for the effictiveness of CoRT *217*
7. Problem-Based Self Instruction in Medical Problem Solving 220
8. The Heuristics Approach in General 225

8. FORMAL THINKING APPROACHES 227

1. ADAPT (Accent on the Development of Abstract Processes of Thought) 231
Description *231*
Evaluation *233*
2. DOORS (Development of Operational Reasoning Skills) 234
Description *234*
Evaluation *235*
3. COMPAS (Consortium for Operating and Managing Programs for the Advancement of Skills) 237

Description 237
Evaluation 238
4. SOAR (Stress on Analytical Reasoning) 239
Description 239
Evaluation 240
5. DORIS (Devlopment of Reasoning in Science) 241
Description 241
Evaluation 242
6. Formal-Thinking Programs in General 245

9. THINKING THROUGH LANGUAGE AND SYMBOL MANIPULATION 248

1. Language in Thought and Action 248
2. Writing as an Occasion for Thinking 251
The demands of writing 251
The pedagogy of writing 254
3. Writing as a Means of Thinking 258
4. Universe of Discourse 260
Instructional approach 261
Evaluation 263
5. Modeling Inner Speech and Self Instruction as a Means of Teaching Thinking 265
6. LOGO and Procedural Thinking 269
The LOGO language and early uses 269
Turtle geometry 271
LOGO with the handicapped 273
Evaluation 274
7. The Language Approach in General 278

10. THINKING ABOUT THINKING 280

1. The Philosophy for Children Program 280
Children as natural philosophers 281
The general approach 282
The program 283
Evaluation 286
2. The Anatomy of Argument 290
3. Metacognitive Skills 294
Self monitoring for reading comprehension 295
Metamemory 296
Metacognition and transfer of training 299

Summary 302
4. The Complete Problem Solver 302
5. The "Thinking About Thinking" Approach in General 306
6. Summary for Part II 308

PART III: PROSPECTS FOR TEACHING THINKING

11. EVALUATION 313

1. Purposes of Evaluation 313
2. Obstacles to Evaluation 315
3. Performance Measures and Tests 316
4. Some Neglected Issues 318
Statistical versus practical significance 318
Direct versus indirect, or primary versus secondary, effects 319
Short-term versus long-term effects 319
The need to assess goals 320
The need to assess negative effects 321
The possibility of premature closure 321

12. PROSPECTS FOR TEACHING THINKING 323

1. Is the Teaching of Thinking a Legitimate Educational Objective? 323
2. Ingredients of Success 326
The Teacher 326
Teacher acceptance of the program 327
Objectives, instructional procedures, and evaluation procedures 329
Time on task 333
Transfer 335
Conducive Environments 336
Motivation 337
Attitudes 339
3. Some Recommendations 340
On selecting programs 341
On implementation of any program 342
4. Risks 343

REFERENCES 346
INDEXES 367

Preface

This book began through our involvement in an effort to develop a course to enhance thinking skills. In connection with that effort, which was funded by Petróleos de Venezuela, we began reviewing whatever documentation we could obtain of other attempts to develop methods and programs for teaching thinking skills, in the hope of learning enough from the literature to guide our work. While this review was still in process, we began working on a related project, funded by the U.S. National Institute of Education, one objective of which was to determine what is known about the the teaching of thinking from the research literature and from the results of efforts to develop cognitive enhancement programs. With the consent of both sponsors, we decided to broaden the review we had begun under the Venezuela project so that it would meet also this objective of the NIE project, and the book took shape.

We are aware that our coverage of programs is not exhaustive; we believe, however, that the programs we describe are a representative sample of the work that is being done. We are aware also of the speculative or conjectural nature of some of our discussion of these programs and the theoretical and pedagogical issues that relate to them. However, we see not only a need for more accessible information regarding what has been done, but the desirability of involvement of a larger segment of the educational community in thought and discussion regarding the general objective of teaching thinking and the host of issues that relate to it. Our hope is that this book will, to some degree, facilitate that thought and discussion. We offer no definitive answers, but try to articulate some of the issues and to provide glimpses of the opinions, objectives, and products of several of the people who have been working most actively in this area.

Our thanks are due to many people for their encouragement and various types of support. We owe a special debt of gratitude to Luis Alberto Machado, former Minister of State of Venezuela for the Development of Human Intelligence. It was as a consequence of his invitation to Harvard University to undertake an educational project in Venezuela that the three of us became involved in the effort mentioned above. Not only are we grateful for the fact that Minister Machado's initiative provided us an opportunity to work in this area, but we have also been inspired by his tireless championing of the idea that people have the right to develop their intellectual potential and that governments have a responsibility to provide them the opportunity to do so.

We owe special thanks also to many other friends and colleagues in Venezuela who supported the project in which the work on this book originated. We mention in particular Paul Reimpell, First Vice President of Petróleos de Venezuela, for his consistent and congenial support throughout the life of that project, and Margarita de Sánchez, Commissioner of the Minister of Education, whose skills as a teacher and administrator were invaluable to the project in numerous ways.

It was our very good fortune to have first Joseph Psotka and then Patricia Butler as Project Officers on our project with the National Institute of Education. They not only made it a pleasure to do the work required by that project, but their insightful guidance was most helpful and greatly appreciated. We are grateful also for the encouragement and supportive feedback that we received from other members of the NIE staff, notably, Susan Chipman and Judith Segal.

We are indebted to our colleagues from Bolt Beranek and Newman and Harvard University who worked with us either on the Venezuela Project, the NIE Project, or both. These include Marilyn Adams, Bertram Bruce, José Buscaglia, Allan Collins, Jorge Dominguez, Carl Feehrer, Dedre Gentner, David Getty, Mario Grignetti, Richard Herrnstein, Catalina Laserna, William Salter, Brenda Starr, and John Swets. It is impossible, happily, to have such colleagues without being influenced by their thinking. Our thanks to them for much intellectual stimulation.

We owe special thanks to the people who typed the manuscript and shepherded it through a seemingly endless series of edits and revisions. The bulk of this chore was done with amazing patience and good humor by Anne Kerwin and Diane Flahive.

Raymond S. Nickerson
David N. Perkins
Edward E. Smith

TO OUR PARENTS

RAYMOND AND VELMA NICKERSON

DAVID AND LEONE PERKINS

HARRY AND BESSIE SMITH

I THE CHALLENGE OF TEACHING THINKING

1 Introduction

"Think!" Who has not received this admonition many times? From parents, from teachers, from employers, from politicians, and from other promoters of ideas, ideals, and ideologies.

Good advice, no doubt. But good advice presumes that the person given it knows how to follow it. And what evidence is there that this is so? One can imagine a motivated recipient of such advice sincerely responding "How?" One has more difficulty imagining what a helpful answer would be. Clearly it is much easier to admonish people to think than to tell them how to do so.

Perhaps part of the difficulty stems from the fact that the word "think" is commonly used in a variety of ways. Consider the following examples: "What do you think about X?" "I think this is the one I saw, but am not sure." "When I think about my childhood, I get nostalgic." "I did not think about that." "One should think carefully before deciding what to do." The first example might be paraphrased: "What is your opinion about, or attitude toward, X?" In the second case "think" is synonymous with "believe," in the third with "reminisce." In the fourth example "think about" means "consider," and in the fifth "think" could be replaced by "reflect," "ponder," "reason," or "deliberate."

The last two examples best represent what we mean by thinking in this book. That is not to say the others are of no concern; indeed attitudes, beliefs, and memory processes are of considerable interest, and will be mentioned in several contexts in what follows. Our primary focus, however, will be on intentional, purposeful, goal-oriented thinking—thinking, if you will, for the express purpose of realizing some specific objective.

Undoubtedly most people would readily acknowledge the importance of being able to think effectively. We suspect that few would challenge the assertion that a primary objective of education ought to be to teach people how to think. One might expect less unanimity about whether education has been successful in this respect. A wide range of attitudes could probably be found regarding the extent to which the explicit teaching of thinking is possible, and certainly, among those who believe that it is, there would be many differences of opinion regarding how best to do the teaching.

The ability to think effectively has surely always been an important one. Individuals who have had it undoubtedly have been better able to cope and to prosper than those who have not. There are reasons to argue, however, that thinking skills are more critical today than ever before. The world is more complex and so are the challenges it presents. Meeting those challenges will require not only considerable knowledge but the skill to apply that knowledge effectively. Change today is more rapid and the need to accommodate to it more pressing that in the past. No longer is it possible, as it once was, to learn enough during 12, or even 16, years of formal schooling to prepare oneself for a lifetime vocation. Moreover, if recent history is any indication of things to come, many of the most significant changes in the future will take us by surprise, in spite of our best efforts to anticipate them. Survival in the midst of rapid change will require the ability to adapt, to learn new skills quickly, and to apply old knowledge in new ways.

Among the more obvious effects that technology has had on us as individuals is that of increasing our personal degrees of freedom in many ways. Most of us who live in developed countries in the free world have a much greater range of options than did our grandparents, whether we are choosing what to have for dinner, what to do for entertainment, where to go for a vacation, or how to spend a life. It seems reasonable to expect this freedom of choice to continue to increase. But options imply the burden of making decisions and living with them; and the ability to choose wisely assumes the ability to assess the alternatives in a reasonable way.

All of us today are exposed on all sides to arguments and efforts to persuade. These arguments take many guises, come through many media, and serve many purposes. They include efforts to convince us to purchase specific products, to vote for particular political candidates, to support specific philosophical or ethical positions, to accept certain ideologies, to interpret particular events in suggested ways. Never before in history have so many voices clambered simultaneously for the attention of the individual and sought his acceptance of their claims. Clearly, figuring out what to believe, in a wide variety of contexts, is an especially important aspect of modern life. And to do that in a rational way requires the ability to judge the plausibility of specific assertions, to weigh evidence, to assess the logical soundness of inferences, to construct counter arguments and alternative hypotheses—in short, to think critically.

While common sense convinces us of the importance of effective thinking, many researchers and educators are asserting the need for new approaches to education in general and to the problem of teaching thinking in particular. One of the strongest pleas for new approaches to education in general comes from Botkin, Elmandjra, and Malitza (1979) in their recent Club of Rome report. Botkin et al. argue that there is a great disparity between what is being accomplished toward realizing the potential of human beings for learning and what could be accomplished. This, they suggest, is the fundamental issue that confronts us on a worldwide scale today. The old perspective on education will no longer do: what is needed is a change not in degree but in kind.

Botkin et al. distinguish between *maintenance learning*, which they claim has sufficed in the past but will not in the future, and *innovative learning*, which they believe is needed for long-term survival. Maintenance learning, by their definition is "the acquisition of fixed outlooks, methods, and rules for dealing with known and recurring situations. It enhances our problem-solving ability for problems that are given. It is the type of learning designed to maintain an existing system or an established way of life" (p. 10). Innovative learning questions assumptions, even those of long standing, and seeks new perspectives. While maintenance learning has been, and will continue to be, indispensable, it will not be enough; innovative learning is required if we are to cope with the problem of anticipating and dealing effectively with turbulence and change. If one accepts the idea that a fundamental challenge for education today is to prepare people to anticipate change—to shape the future rather than accommodate to it—the need for a better understanding of how to teach thinking skills becomes apparent.

Another, and more explicit call for greater emphasis on the teaching of thinking skills comes from investigators who have concluded that many high school students are unable to deal effectively with problems that require abstract thinking (Karplus, 1979; Lawson & Renner,1974; Renner & Stafford, 1972). Others have reported test results suggesting that a large percentage of college students, as many as 50% of incoming freshmen in some cases, are not operating at the level of formal thinking in the Piagetian sense (Gray, 1979; Renner & McKinnon, 1971; Tomlinson-Keasey, 1972). Such observations have prompted some educators, especially science teachers, to ponder what can be done about the situation. Collea and Nummedal (1980) pose the challenge very well:

> What kinds of concepts, courses, experiences, and programs in science are likely to enhance intellectual development in college students? How can science instructors at the college level develop teaching strategies that ease the

> transition from concrete to formal thinking? What kinds of experiences are necessary and how many? Can we measure this intellectual growth? How do you make college professors aware of the intellectual growth patterns of their students? Can a science curriculum be reorganized around specific thinking skills rather than scientific content? If so, will as much subject-matter learning take place? Could the function of general education in science be designed to teach the nonscience major abstract thinking skills systematically?

In short, the need for greater educational emphasis on thinking skills is, we believe, very substantial, and there is evidence of an increasing awareness among educators and educational researchers of that need. This book deals with the problem of teaching such skills. It is addressed primarily to educational administrators and teachers who are interested in the teaching of thinking skills in the classroom and researchers who are involved, or intend to be involved, in the development or study of approaches to the teaching of such skills. We suspect that most educators recognize the fundamental importance of thinking ability and that many teachers do an inspiring job of instilling in their students a spirit of inquiry and reason in the process of teaching conventional content courses. Nevertheless, it is an indisputable fact that many students do not acquire the ability to think very effectively as a consequence of their educational experience, and, until recently, relatively little attention had been given to the possibility of making the teaching of thinking skills a primary educational objective, in the sense in which the teaching of reading, writing, and mathematics are primary educational objectives. Many of the programs reviewed in this book represent efforts to give the teaching of thinking skills this status.

The book is organized in three major Parts. In Part I we discuss several concepts and conceptual distinctions by way of providing a background against which to view various approaches to the teaching of thinking skills. We begin this part with an informal consideration of the concept of intelligence, inasmuch as the concept relates rather directly to the concept of thinking, and one's understanding of what intelligence is may predispose one to one or another bias regarding the teachability of thinking skills. We consider a variety of perspectives on thinking and, in particular the usefulness of the notion of "thinking skills." We discuss problem solving, creativity, and metacognition because there is an experimental literature around each of these topics that is highly relevant to our general subject. We end this part with a review of a variety of common reasoning deficiencies. The fact that the commonality of these deficiencies is easy to document helps make the case for the need of more effective methods for the teaching of thinking.

In Part II we review several attempts that have been made to develop thinking-skills programs. This review is not exhaustive—we are aware of many programs that are not described and there undoubtedly are others of which we are unaware—however we believe that the programs included are a representative sample of those that exist. Our review is more descriptive than critical, primarily because in most cases compelling evaluation data have not been obtained. We venture opinions regarding strengths and weaknesses of specific programs; however, we urge readers to seek out original sources for programs of special interest, so as to form their own opinions of their merits. Our hope is that this review will provide a broad context within which individual programs may be viewed and useful pointers to more complete information.

In Part III we discuss the issue of program evaluation and we consider the question of what the evidence, on the whole, indicates regarding the teaching of thinking skills. What do the results of the various efforts described in Part II suggest regarding the legitimacy of the teaching of thinking as an educational objective? What guidance do they provide to teachers and researchers who wish to teach thinking or to work on the development of new and more effective techniques for doing so?

2 Aspects of Intellectual Competence

1. WHAT IS INTELLIGENCE?

Probably most people would agree that there is some relationship between thinking ability and intelligence. It seems appropriate therefore to consider the concept of intelligence, if only in a cursory way.

"Intelligence" is one of those words we use as though we understood what it means, but also one that nobody has been able to define to everyone's satisfaction. Before considering some of the definitions that have been proposed, it may be instructive to indulge a fantasy.

Imagine that you were to sit down at a computer terminal one day and before you had a chance to do as you had planned, the machine said to you "I am an intelligent machine." You probably would not accept such an assertion at face value, but, if you had an open mind about the possibility of machine intelligence, you might be inclined to reply, "Prove it." Suppose then that the machine responded, "What will you take as evidence of my intelligence?"

The question is an eminently fair one, but one that you might find your self hard-pressed to answer in a completely satisfactory way. The question of whether machines can be intelligent will not concern us much in this book because it would take us too far afield from our primary purpose. However, in thinking about what we mean by the word "intelligence," it may be worth considering the question of what one would be willing to take as evidence of intelligence in a machine. Scientists working in the area of machine intelligence are fond of pointing out that more has been learned about the aerodynamics of flight as a result of efforts over a relatively few years to build flying machines than during centuries of watching birds in flight. One way to learn about human intelligence is try to build machines with the ability to behave in an intelligent way.

But what does it mean to behave in an intelligent way? What would we take as evidence of intelligence on the part of a machine? The following list of abilities is offered not as a complete answer to the question, but as representative of the kinds of abilities without which a machine probably could not be considered intelligent.

The Ability to Classify Patterns

All higher organisms display an ability to deal with variability in sensory stimulation. That is, they can assign nonidentical stimuli to classes, the members of which are more or less equivalent in terms of their implications for the organism's behavior. This ability is basic to human thought and communication. Indeed, it is doubtful whether anything worthy of the name of either thought or communication could exist without conceptual categories. Suppose that there were no such concept as "chair," and that each one of those patterns of sensory experience that we now classify as instances of "chair" had to be treated as a unique thing. Whenever one had occasion to refer to such a thing, one would have to describe it in terms of its features. But now we find ourselves thinking in terms of backs, and seats, and legs, which is to say in terms of other conceptual categories. If we disallow these, we push ourselves back to other categories that are perhaps somewhat closer to the sensory data—contours, colors, sizes, textures—but are conceptual categories still. To divest ourselves of the use of categories is to divest ourselves of thought.

The Ability to Modify Behavior Adaptively—To Learn

The ability to adapt one's behavior on the basis of experience, making it more effective for coping with one's environment, is usually considered a sine qua non of intelligence. Many organisms, ants and bees for example, display complex behavior patterns, but are not considered intelligent because these patterns resist change. Thus, an ant will engage in an involved behavior sequence under certain conditions, even when the sequence no longer serves a useful purpose.

In general it appears that the adaptability of an organism depends on its position on the phylogenetic scale: the higher the organism the greater the degree of adaptability. But even within a given species—for example, human beings—individuals differ considerably on this dimension; inflexibility and an inability to modify one's behavior are usually taken to be indications of relatively low intelligence.

The Ability to Reason Deductively

The distinction is often made between deductive and inductive reasoning. Both types of reasoning are pervasive in our daily lives, both are essential to intelligent behavior, and both are susceptible to various types of reasoning deficiencies.

Deductive reasoning involves logical inference. When one reasons deductively one does not go beyond the information at hand. One draws a conclusion from premises, but the information that is stated explicitly in the conclusion was—if the logic is sound—contained in the premises already, albeit only implicitly. Thus, there is no information in the assertion "Mr. Peabody likes seafood" that is not implicit in the two assertions "All Bostonians like seafood" and "Mr. Peabody is a Bostonian." The first statement follows logically from the other two, which is to say, if they both are true, it also must be true; but it adds no information to what was there in the first place. Of course deductive inferencing need not be as simple and as transparent as this example; sometimes the information that is implicit in a set of assertions may not be obvious at all, and explicating it can serve a very useful purpose.

Our use of deduction is much greater than is apparent. Much of what each of us "knows" about the world we never learned explicitly, but is deducible from other things we know, or have deduced in turn. One knows, for example, that Lake Victoria contains water, not necessarily because one has learned this fact explicitly, but because one knows that all lakes, by definition, contain water and that Lake Victoria is a lake. If our knowledge were limited to what we had learned explicitly, it would be impoverished indeed.

Although it serves us well, deductive reasoning can and does go astray. We find it very easy to violate rules of inference and to derive invalid conclusions; that is, we often deduce conclusions that are *not* implicit in the premises. Moreover even if one's deductive logic is sound, one is not guaranteed to reach true conclusions, unless the premises from which the conclusions are derived are themselves true.

The Ability to Reason Inductively—To Generalize

Inductive reasoning involves going beyond the information given. It has to do with the discovery of rules and principles, with arguing from particular instances to the general case. When, from the fact that one has had greater success in catching trout on cloudy days than on sunny days, one concludes that trout generally are more obliging to fisherman when the sun is not shining than when it is, one is engaging in inductive reasoning. Induction is as pervasive and important in our daily lives as is deduction. If we were unable to generalize, to go beyond the information in hand, we would not be able to discover the lawfulness of the world. We would be unable to make universal statements except those that are true by definition or that pertain to small—exhaustibly observable—universes. Thus one might be able to say something about the cats in one's household, but one could say nothing about cats in general, except what would be true by definition.

While the ability to reason inductively is a critically important one, inductive reasoning, like deductive reasoning, can and often does lead to conclusions that turn out to be inconsistent with the facts. If, for example, one concludes that two events are causally related because they have always occurred together in one's limited experience, one may or may not be right. Overgeneralizing and imputing stronger relationships than actually exist are risks inherent to inductive reasoning. They are a price that must be paid for an immensely useful capability.

In deciding whether a machine is intelligent in the same sense in which human beings are intelligent, we should not demand that it never make an invalid inference or arrive at an untrue conclusion. We would want evidence, however, that it could reason both deductively and inductively and that in doing so it arrived at defensible conclusions with roughly the same degree of consistency as do people.

The Ability to Develop and Use Conceptual Models

Each of us carries around in his head a conceptual model (or models) of our world and the things in it, including himself. It is only because of such models, which are elaborated over many years, that we can interpret the sensory data with which we are continually bombarded, and can maintain the integrity of perceptual and cognitive experience. When you see a ball roll under one end of a couch and then emerge at the other end, how do you know that the ball that came out is the same one that went in? In fact you do not really know for sure that it is, but your conceptual model of the world leads you to make such an inference. This model incorporates, among other things, certain assumptions about the relative permanence of physical objects and the invariance of their properties even when they are out of sight. That an inference is involved is clear. Moreover, had the ball, on emerging, been a different color, or a different size, than on entering, you would have had to infer either that the ball that came out was not the one that went in, or that something peculiar was going on under the couch.

The development and use of conceptual models involve both inductive and deductive reasoning. Induction plays a major role in the development of such models, deduction is essential to their use. The process is circular, however, and insofar as a model leads to deductions that prove to be empirically false it must be modified—if it is to be useful—and the modification will undoubtedly involve further inferences of an inductive kind.

It is interesting to speculate about how much of what an individual knows was ever learned explicitly. Certainly every human being knows many facts that he has *not* learned explicitly. For example, you have probably never learned explicitly that kangaroos have teeth, or that there are 24 hours in every Tuesday, or that your mother was once six years old. You know these things and countless others, only because you deduce them from other facts that you have learned explicitly, and from the models of the world that you carry around in your head.

The Ability to Understand

What does it mean to say that a machine, or a person for that matter, understands? This is a much easier question to ask than to answer; indeed, perhaps there is no generally acceptable answer. We all know when we understand—or think we understand—something, but to define the term without resorting to synonyms is a different matter.

We may be willing to take as evidence that one understands an assertion, the ability to paraphrase it, to say the same thing in other words. However, there are times when we discount this evidence, such as when one party to an argument insists that he understands the other's point of view, while the other insists that he does not. Sometimes the ability to carry out a procedure is considered evidence that the instructions were understood. But understanding can occur at different levels; it is one thing to understand *how* to carry out the steps of a procedure, but quite another to understand *why* the procedure works.

Sometimes one has the experience of suddenly "seeing" a relationship, or understanding a concept, which one was unable to see, or understand, before that time. We usually refer to this "Aha," or "Of course, now I see," experience as insight. It often seems to involve a reformulation of one's thought space, a viewing of things from a new perspective. Insight is difficult to evoke intentionally; it often seems to occur at the least likely moments. But the following problem may illustrate how a change of perspective can facilitate understanding.

Consider two containers, A and P. Container A has in it 10 ounces of water from the Atlantic Ocean; P contains an equal amount of water from the Pacific. Suppose that 2 ounces of Atlantic water are removed from container A and put into P. After the liquid in P is mixed thoroughly, 2 ounces of the mixture are removed and added to the contents of container

A. Which container now has the greater amount of foreign water, the Atlantic water being foreign to P, and the Pacific to A?

One way to solve this problem is to track the interchange of liquids step by step: After 2 ounces of the Atlantic from A are added to 10 of the Pacific in P, P contains 12 ounces of water in the proportion 10-parts Pacific to 2-parts Atlantic. When 2 ounces of this thoroughly-mixed mixture are returned to A, P is left with 2/ 12 x 10 or 1.67 ounces of foreign (Atlantic) water. Container A, on the other hand, receives 2 ounces mixed in the proportion 10-parts Pacific to 2-parts Atlantic, so the amount of foreign (Pacific) water that goes into A will be 10/12 x 2 or 1.67 ounces. Thus, each container ends with the same amount of foreign water.

Another way of viewing this problem makes the answer obvious. Consider the fact that both containers end up with exactly the same amount of *liquid* as they had initially. It follows that whatever amount of the Atlantic is missing from A (and thus is in P) must have been replaced by an equal amount of the Pacific (which is missing from P). Notice that viewing the problem this way makes it clear that the "equal amounts of foreign water" answer holds irrespective of how many transfers are made, what amounts are involved in each transfer, or how thoroughly the mixing is done, provided the containers hold the same amount of liquid in the end as in the beginning.

The ability to "see" relationships such as those represented by this problem and to appreciate the implications of these relationships in determining the problem solution would seem to require some intelligence. One would not expect an unintelligent machine, or organism, to have that ability. More generally, while we perhaps cannot say to everyone's satisfaction what it means to understand, we know intuitively the difference between believing that we understand something and realizing that we do not. Moreover, we know too from personal experience that some things are more easily understood than others; and it is consistent with our ideas about intelligence to assume that the understanding of more complex relationships requires more intelligence than does the understanding of simpler relationships.

We have not, of course, done justice to the question of what intelligence is, but perhaps the point has been made that intelligence does have many aspects or dimensions. Thus, we may expect that attempts to build intelligence into machines will take many different forms, and we should not be surprised to see research approaching this task from a variety of avenues.

We do not mean to suggest that the above list of abilities that one might take as evidence of intelligence in a machine represents a model of intelligence in any sense. The abilities mentioned, however, are representative of things we expect an intelligent organism or artifact to be able to do. One might argue that, given the conception of intelligence implicit in this list, we would have to conclude that all normal human beings have it, and indeed that is the case. All people classify patterns, learn, make inductions and deductions, develop and use conceptual models, have insights, and so on. That is not to suggest that all people do all these things equally well. The considerable effort that has been devoted to the development of machine intelligence has made us aware, however, of how very impressive "normal" or "average" human intelligence really is. Individuals who lack any formal schooling can do easily many tasks that have proven to be exceedingly difficult to program for machines. It may be that the difference between what the most intelligent people can do and what people of average intelligence can do is very small when compared with what people of average intelligence can do. Moreover, the fact that people of average intelligence are manifestly capable of extremely complex cognitive performance even without the benefit of formal training lends credibility to the hypothesis that the untapped intellectual potential of most of us may be very much greater than is generally assumed.

2. SOME CONCEPTIONS OF DIFFERENTIAL INTELLIGENCE

The preceding comments were made in the spirit of characterizing intelligence as a property of human beings as a species, without necessarily implying that human beings have it exclusively. But while we may recognize intelligence as a property of the species, it has not escaped notice that individuals differ considerably with respect to their ability to perform intellectually demanding tasks. Much of the interest in intelligence on the part of researchers and educators has been motivated by the desire to understand better how and why people differ from each other in this respect.

In the context of this interest, intelligence has been defined in a large variety of ways. Resnick (1976a) has recently illustrated this fact by noting the diversity of definitions given to the term by contributors to the 1921 Journal of Educational Psychology symposium on the topic as follows:

> Intelligence was defined variously as: the ability to "carry on abstract thinking" (Lewis Terman); "the power of good response from the point of view of truth or fact" (E. L. Thorndike); "learning or the ability to learn to adjust oneself to the environment" (S. S. Colvin); "general modifiability of the nervous system" (Rudolf Pintner); a "biological mechanism by which the effects of a complexity of stimuli are brought together and given a somewhat unified effect in behavior" (Joseph Peterson); an "acquiring capacity" (Herbert Woodrow); and a "group of complex mental processes traditionally defined ... as sensation, perception, association, memory, imagination, discrimination, judgment, and reasoning" (M. E. Haggerty) (p. 2).

We may add to this list numerous other recent definitions: the ability to direct oneself and to learn in the absence of direct and complete instruction (Brown & French, 1979); a learned habitual approach to problem solving (Whimbey, 1975); skill in the analysis and mental reconstruction of relations (Bereiter & Engelmann, 1966); the ability to use knowledge effectively: "what you can do with what you know" (DeAvila & Duncan, 1985).

Debates about the nature of intelligence have sometimes focused on quite specific issues. One such debate that started almost with the introduction of the concept of intelligence and that continues to the present day concerns the question of whether intelligence is best considered a general cognitive ability or a collection of individual abilities. The earliest writers on the subject, including Spencer and Galton, viewed intelligence as a general ability that would manifest itself in a wide variety of contexts. Other writers, including many contemporary investigators, have favored the view that intelligence is a collection of special abilities and that different people can be intelligent (or unintelligent) in different ways. Still other writers, Spearman among the first of them, have presented a conception of intelligence that includes a general ability and a collection of special abilities as well . In Spearman's (1923) influential view, the general ability, which he identified as "g," is involved to a greater or lesser degree in the performance of most of the types of tasks that are used to assess intelligence. In addition to this general factor, however, performance of a given task is determined, in part, by a particular factor specific to it. Somewhat reminiscent of the distinction between "g" and specific abilities is R. B. Cattell's (1963) more recent distinction between fluid and crystallized intelligence. According to this view, fluid intelligence is assumed to be innate, nonverbal, and applicable in a wide variety of contexts. Crystallized intelligence reflects the skills and specific abilities that one acquires as a result of learning.

Thurstone (1924) deemphasized the pervasive involvement of a general factor, and stressed the importance of several more specific abilities. He also contrasted intelligence with impulsiveness. Impulsive behavior is behavior that is carried out relatively thoughtlessly to satisfy, in the most obvious and immediately feasible way, the desires, motives, and incentives of the individual; "impulsive and unintelligent satisfaction of a want takes for granted any solution which seems handy, and fails to discover the possible solutions which might have appeared by stating the motive in its most abstract and generalized form" (p. 126). However, the most obvious and immediately feasible action is not necessarily what is most satisfying in the long run, so impulsive behavior is not, in any very general sense, optimal behavior.

A key aspect of intelligence, in Thurstone's view, is the inhibition of impulsiveness. By inhibiting impulses before they develop into overt behavior, and focusing on them consciously while they are still relatively general, one gains latitude of choice with respect to the different ways in which one's needs or desires might be satisfied . "Intelligence is therefore the capacity for abstraction, which is an inhibitory process. In the intelligent moment the impulse is inhibited while it is still only loosely organized" (p. 159). It is the ability to consider and evaluate possible courses of action without actually engaging them that distinguishes between intelligent and unintelligent life forms, and the more intelligent the individual the higher the level of abstraction and the greater the degree of flexibility of choice attained.

An interesting, and perhaps paradoxical, aspect of Thurstone's view is the idea that intelligence can, in theory at least, lead to inaction. The greater the urgency of a situation, Thurstone suggests, the more difficult will be the exercise of intelligence; intelligence is most readily shown when the urgency for quick action is minimal. Thurstone's own statement of the extreme to which this view can be pushed is somewhat startling: "If it were possible for a human being to be of perfect intelligence, it would be impossible for him ever to move. He would die of intelligence because he would be so deliberative that no decision could ever be made about anything" (p. 101).

Perhaps the most extreme emphasis on specific abilities appears in the structural model of intelligence proposed by Guilford (1967). This model distinguishes three major components of intelligence: operations, contents, and products. Each of these components is represented by several types. The types of operations that the model postulates are cognition, convergent operations, divergent operations, memory operations, and evaluative operations. The contents are behavioral, figural, semantic, and symbolic. The products are units, classes, relations, systems, transformations, and implications. The 120 possible combinations of types of five operations, four contents and six products are viewed as representing the complete "structure of intellect." Any intellectual activity is assumed to be reducible to one or more of these combinations.

It is clear from this brief consideration of several influential characterizations of intelligence that a definition that would satisfy everyone would be very difficult to produce. Indeed, Neisser (1979) has suggested that a satisfactory definition of intelligence is impossible not only because of the nature of intelligence but also because of the nature of concepts. The concept "intelligent person," Neisser argues, is an example of the kind of natural concept (or category) that Rosch and her colleagues (Rosch, 1978; Rosch & Metuis, 1975) have called attention to in recent years. A "Roschian" concept, to use Neisser's term, lacks decisively defining features and is best described by means of "prototypical" instances. "Chair" is an example of such a concept, as are most of the concepts by which we categorize the common objects of our environment.

> In my opinion, then, *intelligent person* is a prototype-organized Roschian concept. Our confidence that a person deserves to be called 'intelligent' depends on that person's overall similarity to an imagined prototype, just as our confidence that some object is to be called 'chair' depends on its similarity to prototypical chairs. There are no definitive criteria of intelligence, just as there are none for chairness; it is a fuzzy-edged concept to which many features are relevant. Two people may both be quite intelligent and yet have very few traits in common—they resemble the prototype along different dimensions. Thus, there is no such quality as *intelligence*, any more than there is such a thing as *chairness*—resemblance is an external fact and not an internal essence. There can be no process-based definition of intelligence, because it is not a unitary quality. It is a resemblance between two individuals, one real and the other prototypical. (p. 185)

While he questions the possibility of defining intelligence, or of measuring it adequately, Neisser (1979) does list some of the characteristics of the prototypical intelligent person: "not only verbal fluency, logical ability, and wide general knowledge but common sense, wit, creativity, lack of bias, sensitivity to one's own limitations, intellectual independence, openness to experience, and the like. Some of these characteristics," he points out, "manifest themselves only in unique or practical situations; others cannot be evaluated except by considering the individual's life as a whole" (p. 186).

We find ourselves in general agreement with Neisser's reservations about the possibility of defining intelligence acceptably, at least at the present time. That is not to say that it is difficult to come up with definitions: the plethora that have been proposed attests to the ease with which they can be produced. What is difficult is to come up with *a* definition that everyone, or even a sizeable subset of the people working in the area, may agree really captures the essence of the concept. Moreover, without denying the possibility of a general intelligence factor, we concur also that intelligence manifests itself in many ways and that people whom we typically consider to be especially intelligent are likely to give evidence of possessing a variety of intellectual skills.

Apparently, most designers of intelligence tests have accepted the idea that intelligence is a multi-faceted thing. Present-day tests vary considerably in details; however, most of them have in common the fact that they are composed of many different types of items. That is to say, they are designed to assess one's ability to perform numerous different types of cognitively demanding tasks: some items require an ability to memorize, others require that one be able to detect patterns (for example, in sequences of letters or numbers), others assess vocabulary or facility with words, others depend on an ability to visualize spatial relationships, and so on.

As Horn (1979) points out, however, in spite of this tacit acknowledgment of the multidimensional (or multi-component) nature of intelligence, no technology for multidimensional assessment of intelligence has yet been developed. Although intelligence tests sample performance on a variety of tasks with differing cognitive demands, they typically are designed to yield a single score that is taken as an indication of intelligence level in a general sense. Horn predicts that this situation will change and that intelligence tests of the future will put decreasing emphasis on a single score and will increasingly focus on the measurement of separate capacities that fall under the general heading of intelligence.

One indication of this trend is seen in the development of factor-referenced cognitive tests, such as the one recently published by the Educational Testing Service (ETS) of Princeton, New Jersey. The Kit contains 72 factor-referenced tests for 59 aptitude factors and is accompanied by a Manual for the administration of the tests (Ekstrom, French, Harman, & Dermen, 1976). The tests are intended for research use only and not for purposes of counseling, selection, or individual prediction.

Table 2.1 lists the 23 factors addressed in the 1976 edition of the tests and gives for each both the factor label and the definition provided in the Manual. Research leading to the preparation of the 1976 Kit is summarized in a final report of a four-year project by Harman (1975). Details regarding research results may be found in a series of technical reports (Carroll, 1974; Dermen, French, & Harman, 1974; Ekstrom, 1973; Ekstrom, French, & Harman, 1974; Ekstrom, French, & Harman, 1975; French, 1973; French & Dermen, 1974; Harman, 1973).

It is of some interest to compare this list of factors with a list of fundamental traits, or mental capacities, proposed by Kraepelin in 1895, as basic factors by which an individual might be characterized. Kraepelin's list included: ability to be influenced by practice; persistence of practice effects, or general memory; special memory abilities; fatigability, and capacity to recover from fatigue; depth of sleep; capacity for concentration of attention against distraction; and ability to adapt oneself to effective work under distracting conditions. Comparison of the two lists points out the fact that the concept of intelligence has become somewhat more complex over a period of roughly 80 years.

The main analytical tool that was used to identify factors in the ETS list is factor analysis. A factor was considered established when the underlying construct was found in at least three factor analyses performed in at least two different laboratories or by two different investigators (Ekstrom et al., 1976). Preparation of each edition of the Kit, of which there have been three, has been preceded by a conference of individuals interested in multiple factor analysis.

TABLE 2.1
Factors Addressed by the 1976 ETS Kit of Factor-Referenced Cognitive Tests

Flexibility of Closure	The ability to hold a given visual percept or configuration in mind so as to disembed it from other well defined perceptual material.
Speed of Closure	The ability to unite an apparently disparate perceptual field into a single concept.
Verbal Closure	The ability to solve problems requiring the identification of visually presented words when some of the letters are missing, scrambled, or embedded among other letters.
Associational Fluency	The ability to produce rapidly words which share a given area of meaning or some other common semantic property.
Expressional Fluency	The ability to think rapidly of word groups or phrases.
Figural Fluency	The ability to draw quickly a number of examples, elaborations, or restructurings based on a given visual or descriptive stimulus.
Ideational Fluency	The facility to write a number of ideas about a given topic of exemplars of a given class of objects.
Word Fluency	The facility to produce words that fit one or more structural, phonetic or orthographic restrictions that are not relevant to the meaning of the words.
Induction	This factor identifies the kinds of reasoning abilities involved in forming and trying out hypotheses that will fit a set of data.
Integrative Processes	The ability to keep in mind simultaneously or to combine several conditions, premises, or rules in order to produce a correct response.
Associative Memory	The ability to recall one part of a previously learned but otherwise unrelated pair of items when the other part of the pair is presented.
Memory Span	The ability to recall a number of distinct elements for immediate reproduction.
Visual Memory	The ability to remember the configuration, location, and orientation of figural material.
Number Facility	The ability to perform basic arithmetic operations with speed and accuracy. This factor is *not* a major component in mathematical reasoning or higher mathematical skills.
Perceptual Speed	Speed in comparing figures or symbols, scanning to find figures or symbols, or carrying out other very simple tasks involving visual perception. It may be the centroid of several subfactors (including form discrimination and symbol discrimination) which can be separated but are more usefully treated as a single concept for research purposes.
General Reasoning	The ability to select and organize relevant information for the solution of a problem.
Logical Reasoning	The ability to reason from premise to conclusion, or to evaluate the correctness of a conclusion.

(continued)

TABLE 2.1
(continued)

Spatial Orientation	The ability to perceive spatial patterns or to maintain orientation with respect to objects in space.
Spatial Scanning	Speed in exploring visually a wide or complicated spatial field.
Verbal Comprehension	The ability to understand the English language.
Visualization	The ability to manipulate or transform the image of spatial patterns into other arrangements.
Figural Flexibility	The ability to change set in order to generate new and different solutions to figural problems.
Flexibility of Use	The mental set necessary to think of different uses for objects.

The authors of the 1976 Kit note the improbability of the existence of truly "pure" factors, and the difficulty of classifying such factors as exist in terms of any rigid taxonomy. This observation is consistent with the fact that the 1976 Kit differs from its two predecessors (French, 1954; French, Ekstrom, & Price, 1963) not only with respect to details of test design but with respect to the factors addressed as well. In particular, several of the factors represented in the 1943 edition are not included in the 1976 edition; and conversely, a few factors are included in the latter edition that were not in the former. The ETS effort adds credence to the idea that intelligence is multi-faceted, but it also demonstrates how difficult it is to partition it into a set of clearly delineated factors.

In contrast to the factor-analytic approach to the study of intelligence, another trend that has become apparent in recent years is an increasing focus on process. The need that seems to have been increasingly felt among investigators is that of identifying the basic processes that underlie intelligent performance. Two examples of this trend are the views of Feuerstein and of Sternberg. Feuerstein's conceptualization of intelligence is described in Chapter 6, in the context of a discussion of his Instrumental Enrichment Program. Sternberg's (1985) conceptualization of the nature of intelligence distinguishes five different kinds of "components" into which intelligence can be analyzed: metacomponents, performance components, acquisition components, retention components, and transfer components. Components are thought of as processes. "A component is an elementary information process that operates upon internal representations of objects or symbols.... The basic idea is that components represent latent abilities of some kind that give rise to individual differences in measured intelligence and in real-world performance, and to individual differences in factor scores as well" (p.225).

Metacomponents are control processes involved in planning and decision making in problem solving. Performance components are processes that implement the plans and decisions of the metacomponents in carrying out actual tasks. Acquisition, retention, and transfer components deal with learning new information, retaining or retrieving previously learned information, and carrying over retained information from one context to another.

Intellectual development occurs as a result of a dynamic interplay among all the components. Conversely, one aspect of intellectual development is an increased effectiveness and sophistication of the component processes. For example, acquisition, retention, and transfer components provide the means for increasing knowledge; conversely, increased knowledge allows for more sophisticated forms of these components. "There is thus the possibility of an unending feedback loop: the components lead to an increased knowledge base, which leads to more effective use of components, which leads to further increases in the knowledge base, and so on" (p. 2).

Although all five types of components, and interactions among them, are important to intellectual growth, a key role is assumed for the metacomponent processes: "There can be no doubt," Sternberg says, "that the major variable in the development of the intellect is the metacomponential one. All feedback is filtered through these elements, and if they do not perform their functions well, then it won't matter very much what the other kinds of components can do. It is for this reason that the metacomponents are viewed as truly central in understanding the nature of human intelligence" (p. 228).

In one recent paper, Sternberg (1981) has presented a view of intelligence as a set of thinking and learning skills that are used in academic and everyday problem solving, and that can be separately diagnosed and taught. As representative of the types of skills involved, he lists:

- Problem identification: "Perhaps the most important prerequisite to successful problem solving."
- Process selection: Selection of processes that are appropriate to the problem or task at hand.
- Representation selection : Selection of useful ways of representing information pertaining to the task both internally (in one's head) and externally (for example, on paper).
- Strategy selection: Selection of sequences in which to apply processes to representation.
- Processing allocation: Efficient allocation of time to various aspects or components of task.
- Solution monitoring: Keeping track of what has been done, what remains to be done, and whether satisfactory progress is being made.
- Sensitivity to feedback: Necessary if one is to improve one's performance.

- Translation of feedback into action plan: Necessary not only to know what one is doing incorrectly, but how to express that knowledge in a plan of corrective action.
- Implementation of the action plan: Unimplemented plan does no good; a motivational issue, in part.

Thus we see that intelligence has been conceptualized in many ways. In attempting to analyze it people have used such concepts as skills, capacities, abilities, operations, factors, and processes. There does seem to be general agreement on the point that whatever intelligence is, it has many aspects. How best to characterize those aspects and their interrelationships must be considered an open question. It is not clear that any one of the currently held views is more useful and better supported by empirical data than the others. Thomas (1972) has observed that "the models of intellect that are to be found in the literature tend to be constructed for specific psychometric, educational, or clinical purposes" and should therefore not be considered to be theoretical alternatives. We agree with his suggestion that they are more appropriately thought of as heuristic devices that researchers or practitioners may find useful for purposes of organization.

Before leaving the subject of how intelligence has been conceptualized, we should acknowledge that any conceptualization that did not deal with the relationship of intelligence to knowledge and culture would be incomplete. Any attempt to do justice to either of these relationships could easily yield a book-length discussion, however. We mention them here only in passing.

A distinction is often made between knowledge and intelligence; knowledge being information that one has stored in one's memory and intelligence being the ability to use that information effectively. The distinction is seen in some discussions of intelligence tests. The usual intent of test designers is to make intelligence tests as independent as possible of the knowledge that an individual has acquired. Ideally, one wants to measure intellectual potential as opposed to achievement. The extent to which this ideal has been realized (or is, in principle, realizable) is a matter of some controversy. It seems clear that for most purposes intellectual performance must depend on both the information one has stored in one's head and the effectiveness of the various processes one can apply to the utilization of that information.

The extent to which—or the way in which—intelligence is dependent on cultural or societal variables remains an unanswered question. It is clear that certain abilities that may represent evidence of intelligence in some cultures may be of little use or interest in others (Cole, Gay, Glick, & Sharp, 1971; Goodnow, 1976; Horn, 1979; Laboratory of Comparative Human Cognition, 1982). The ability to recognize many different types of snow is a useful skill to an Eskimo, for example, and how good one is at doing this might be taken as one indication of intelligence among inhabitants of arctic regions. The skill is of little use, and undoubtedly is not found within equatorial cultures. Whether skills of the snow-recognition type can be shown to be dependent on more abstract abilities that are common across cultures and environments is a question that has not yet been resolved.

3. THE ASSESSMENT OF INTELLIGENCE

The assessment of intelligence has proven to be as controversial as the concept of intelligence has been difficult to define. It is not our intention to enter that controversy here. The purpose of this section is simply to provide a cursory account of the chronology of some of the major ideas and events that played a role in the development of intelligence testing and to note some of the key contributors to this development. The information in this section has been gathered from a variety of sources, notably Peterson (1926), Pintner (1931), and Anastasi (1954).

Some Sociological Factors Behind the Idea and Practice of Mental Testing

Mental testing is a relatively recent idea. Several factors contributed to its emergence. A general growth in humanitarian values in the 19th century, and, in particular, some positive changes in attitudes toward persons with mental deficiencies provided some motivation for trying to understand better why people seemed to differ so greatly in their intellectual abilities. The assumption seemed to be that if the bases of the differences were better understood, training techniques could be developed to suit the individual's capabilities and limitations. There was also a growing interest during the 18th and 19th centuries in educating people with communication disorders, especially children who were deaf or blind. These interests are illustrated by several developments:

- The founding in the late 18th century of the Institute for Deaf Mutes in Paris by the Abbe de l'Epee.
- The founding in 1817 of the first school for the deaf in America, located in Hartford and headed by Gallaudet.
- Establishment of the Perkins Institute for the Blind around 1833.
- Commencement of training of a few mentally retarded individuals in France by Sequin in 1837. Sequin came to the United States in 1848 and stimulated work there.
- Establishment of the first state school for retarded persons in America (Fernald) in Massachusetts in 1849.

- Opening by Witner of a psychological clinic at the University of Pennsylvania in 1896. Witner emphasized the necessity of careful psychological diagnosis of the nature of mental defects as a prelude to treatment.

The demands that society places on individuals became more complex as a consequence of the industrial revolution. This may also have called more attention to individual differences in mental abilities, inasmuch as such differences are more obvious in more complicated and intellectually demanding environments than in simpler settings. Interest emerged in identifying extremes on both ends of the ability continuum: Terman was particularly interested in identifying exceptional talent; the first use of Binet's testing methods in the United States was in institutions for persons with mental retardation.

The increasing importance of public education and the need of educational systems to determine capabilities and limitations of students stimulated the development of methods for classifying students according to mental abilities. Tyler (1976) identifies the emergence of systems, during the late 19th and early 20th centuries, of universal compulsory education as one of the major, albeit typically overlooked, factors in establishing the need and setting the stage for the widespread use of intelligence tests.

> The historical fact is that demand for intelligence tests arose everywhere in the period after school attendance was made compulsory. Obviously what the legislation did was to assemble in one place, probably for the first time in human history, almost the full range of human intellects, and to make it necessary for educators to struggle with this diversity. (p. 14)

World War I was a very significant factor in increasing the use of mental testing. Large numbers of men had to be inducted into the armed forces and trained quickly for a variety of military functions. It was important under these circumstances to insure, insofar as possible, that inductees not be selected for training programs for which they lacked the aptitude. The realization by the military of this fact led to the close coupling of "selection and training" as two aspects of the single objective of filling the wide variety of military job slots with people qualified to do those jobs. The operating assumption was that the more sophisticated the selection process is, the more efficient and effective the training can be. The selection function was accomplished primarily through the development and use of tests of intelligence and aptitude.

Forerunners and Pioneers of Mental Testing

One of the first scientists to discuss the possibility of measuring intelligence was Galton, who was interested in individual differences and in the relationship between heredity and mental ability. In 1882 he established an anthropometric laboratory in London, at which he studied traits, sensory acuity, and reaction time, and gathered considerable data on individual differences. Galton published *Inquiries into Human Faculty and its Development* in 1983, and *Hereditary Genius: An Inquiry into its Laws and Consequences* in 1869. Impressed by the fact that a measure of something may be expressed not only in terms of such physical properties as inches and pounds, but also in terms of the frequency with which the measure may be expected to occur in a population, Galton saw that a meaningful comparison of measures of different types (e.g., height and weight) could be made by expressing both in terms of frequency distributions. He also noted the importance to intelligence testing of the development of various mathematical methods for statistical treatment of data, and he applied the method of correlation to psychological measures. He constructed an imaginary scale for the measurement of general ability based on the theory of a normal distribution. The fact that his scale ranged continuously from the lowest to the highest levels was contrary to the prevailing idea of the existence of specific types. It is also worth noting that Galton expected a relationship between sensory acuity and intelligence, such that a person with keen senses would be more intelligent than one whose senses were dull.

Interest in the measurement of individual differences was stimulated in the United States by Cattell, who was the first to use the term "mental tests." In 1890 he published *Mental Tests and Measurements*, in which he promoted the importance of standardization of methods and urged the establishment of norms. Cattell's tests emphasized sensory and perceptual tasks, often involving visual and auditory discrimination. It is perhaps not surprising that early tests of intelligence emphasized sensation and perception rather strongly, inasmuch as much of the earliest experimental work in psychology, in the beginning of the latter half of the 19th century, focused on sensation and perception, and especially on vision.

In 1891, Boas made perhaps the first attempt to compare test scores with independent subjective estimates of individuals' abilities. He tested 1500 children as to vision, hearing, and memory, and obtained teachers' judgments of intellectual acuteness. Bolton introduced a digit memory-span test in 1892. The following year, Jastrow had a booth at the Columbian Exposition in Chicago at which people could take mental tests composed of sensory, sensory-motor, and memory tasks.

Gilbert gave a battery of eight tests to 1,200 children in 1893 and tried to correlate his results with teachers' estimates of general ability. He reported slight correspondence between intelligence (as judged by teachers) and memory, somewhat greater correspondence between intelligence and sensory discrimination of weights and shades, and the strongest relationship between intelligence and simple reaction time. None of the relationships, however, was especially strong.

A sentence-completion test was introduced by Ebbinghaus in 1897. Ebbinghaus experimented with three types of tests—rapid calculation, memory for digits, and sentence completion—only the third of which he considered successful. His view of intelligence stressed "combination ability," or synthesis.

A significant innovation was introduced by Norsworthy, who expressed performance of each child on intelligence tests in terms of variability of the group. Norsworthy's test of feeble-mindedness, introduced in 1906, is sometimes viewed as second in importance only to the Binet scale in early test developments in the United States.

Perhaps the best-known name among the pioneers of intelligence testing is that of Binet. Having received his early training in medicine, Binet founded a psychology laboratory at the Sorbonne in 1889, and took a Doctor's degree in natural sciences in 1892 with a thesis on the psychic life of microorganisms. In collaboration with Simon he developed the Binet-Simon scale, for use in identifying mentally deficient students, in 1905. The scale was revised in 1908 and again in 1911. This scale was adapted by Terman of Stanford University for use in the United States, and the resulting test became known as the Stanford-Binet test of intelligence. The Stanford-Binet, which was widely used in the U.S., is noteworthy also as the test that introduced the idea of an intelligence quotient (IQ), the ratio of one's mental age (as indicted by performance on the test) to one's chronological age.

Binet was impressed with the importance of *attention* and *adaptation* as components of intelligence. He produced the first real standardization in terms of norms for evaluating mental tests, and emphasized the importance of validating test items. Unlike many of his predecessors, he, along with Henri, advocated the measurement of higher mental processes rather than sensory-motor reflexes, and he believed that it was with respect to the higher mental processes that the greater individual differences would be found.

Other events, trends, and publications during the latter half of the 19th century that influenced the beginnings of the intelligence testing movement included the following:

- The publication by Titchener of *Elements of Psychophysics* in 1860.
- The publication by Wundt of *Vorslegen uber die Menschen un Tierseele* (Lectures on the Human and Animal Mind) in 1863.
- Experiments during the 1860's by Helmholtz, Wundt, Jaeger, and Donders, using reaction time measures to estimate speeds of neural or mental events. Later work during the 1880's by Lange and Cattell also using reaction times to measure the speed of mental processes.

- The publication by Darwin of *The Descent of Man* in 1871 and *The Expression of Emotion in Man and Animals* in 1872. Some scholars consider some of Darwin's ideas to have served as points of departure for many aspects of psychology, including the work of Galton on the measurement of intelligence.
- The publication of *Intelligence* by Taine, a book said to have had a considerable influence on Binet, which supported the view that the normal mind can be understood by studying the abnormal mind.
- Publication by Preyer in 1882 of *The Mind of a Child* (detailed observations of his own child's development), which is often considered the first book published on child psychology.
- The founding of numerous psychological laboratories, especially in Germany, France, and the United States, during the 1880s.

Components of Early Tests

Among the earliest mental tests were those published by Oehrn (1889), under the direction of Kraepelin. These tests involved: perception (letter counting from a printed page; search for, or cancellation of, particular letters; and noting of errors in proofreading); memory (learning series of digits and series of nonsense syllables); association (adding of single-digit numbers); motor functions (writing from dictation; reading as fast as possible).

We have already noted that Cattell's tests, which he published in 1890, emphasized sensory and perceptual tasks. More specifically, they involved: keenness of vision and hearing, reaction time, afterimages, color vision, perception of pitch and weights, sensitivity to pain, color preferences, perception of time, accuracy of movement, and imagery.

In 1891 Munsterberg described various tests he had made on school children, which included the following tasks: stating as quickly as possible the colors of ten objects whose names were written on a sheet, such as "white" for "snow"; reading ten names of animals, plants, or minerals, and giving as quickly as possible the classification of each; giving as quickly as possible when the objects were seen the names of 58 simple designs and of 10 squares of colors; adding ten single-digit numbers; giving, as quickly as possible, the number of angles in 10 different irregular polygons; judging how many times one length is contained in another. The 15 tests used by Jastrow at the Columbia Exposition in 1893 included five of touch and cutaneous sensibility, five involving touch and vision, and five of purely visual tasks.

In 1895, Binet and Henri published an article on the psychology of individual differences in which they critically reviewed much of the contemporary work on testing. They proposed the study of the following ten mental processes or functions: memory, nature of mental images, imagination, attention, the faculty of comprehension, suggestibility, aesthetic appreciation, moral sentiments, muscular force and force of will, motor skill, and judgment of visual space.

Summary

We may see from this abbreviated review of the early history of the development of intelligence testing that the notion of intelligence has evolved over the years and is still evolving. Several points are clear:

- Interest in the assessment of intelligence stems from the observation that people seem to differ greatly in their effectiveness at performing intellectually demanding tasks and from the assumption that these differences in performance are the consequences, at least in part, of differences in underlying cognitive abilities.
- Interest in intelligence testing also stems in part from the assumption that the results of such testing should be useful for purposes of predicting performance on intellectually demanding tasks, whether in school, on the job, or elsewhere in everyday life.
- Even scientists who have been most interested in intelligence and most influential in the development of ways of assessing it are not entirely agreed on what it is.
- There seems to be fairly general agreement that whatever intelligence is it is a multifaceted thing. People who have been most interested in developing techniques for assessing it have typically designed tests that include an assortment of tasks. Some writers have predicted that during the next few decades we will see an increasing effort to develop tests that will assess separate cognitive skills rather than yield a composite measure of intelligence.

With respect to the last two points, Herrnstein (1980) summarizes the current status of the concept of intelligence and its implications for assessment this way:

> First, "intelligence" is not yet a concept that has been pinned down by a scientific discipline, the way "force" has been by physics. When we consider whether tests measure intelligence, we can only mean whether the scores correlate with what people generally understand by the word. Since people are unlikely to mean precisely the same thing, the correlation can only be approximate. But if there is any sort of correlation, then as a practical matter the test measures intelligence to some extent, however obliquely. Second, as a one-dimensional scale, the IQ cannot fully represent a multidimensional conception of intelligence. There are, consequently, many measurement procedures that yield not a single number like an IQ, but multiple scores, such

as the verbal and quantitative tests used for college entrance. The objective measurement of intelligence can be made as multidimensional as the data and the occasion warrant (p. 44).

In recent years the practice of intelligence testing has come under considerable fire. Test results have unquestionably been effective predictors of performance in school, at least in a statistical sense. That is to say, students who score relatively highly on intelligence tests tend, as a group, to do relatively well in school, and perhaps beyond. Herrnstein (1980) suggests that this fact accounts for the durability of intelligence tests in spite of the criticisms they have received. Such tests have been less useful in predicting the performance of individuals or in diagnosing the reasons for poor performance for the purpose of prescribing remedial training. Critics of intelligence testing have been particularly concerned about its use for categorizing or labeling individuals, especially when the purpose is to set long-term educational goals and select educational tracks matched to the individual's presumably-fixed abilities as indicated by test results. Support for this criticism has come from Resnick (1979) who has suggested that people who do well on IQ tests are people who have a facility for learning, and that the reason test performance is a good predictor of performance in school is because school performance also depends on an ability to learn. That is to say, in her view, IQ tests do not measure skills that are essential to learning; they measure the extent to which one has already learned to perform certain types of tasks. A question that should be of interest to educators is that of *how* people learn to perform the kinds of tasks that tend to appear on IQ tests—analogies, vocabulary tasks, quantitative reasoning and the rest.

There is some evidence that a consensus may be forming among researchers in the area of intelligence and its assessment concerning the proper use of tests. One suitable use is determining *current* capabilities and limitations for the purpose of aiding short-term educational planning (Resnick, 1979; Sternberg, 1979; Turnbull, 1979). This view does not require the assumption that intelligence tests measure something inherent and unchangeable, and it is antithetical to the practice of using such tests to place children on educational tracks from which they cannot hope to diverge. On the other hand, it acknowledges their ability to measure something that has considerable educational utility, and it provides no support for the idea of altogether discontinuing their use.

4. COGNITIVE DEVELOPMENT

If we want to teach people additional thinking skills, we should probably try to understand how people acquire the impressive array of cognitive skills that they typically do in the normal course of development. The most influential source of current ideas about cognitive development is Jean

Piaget, although contemporary research has lead to a number of qualifications about Piaget's theory in its original form that have implications for our purposes. Piaget distinguishes three stages of development: a sensorimotor stage (0 to 2 years), a pre-operational stage (2 to 7 years), and an operational stage (7 to 16 years). Each stage is marked by the ability to do certain things and not others and to deal with one's experience of the world in certain ways. Of particular relevance to the development of thinking skills is Piaget's further breakdown of the operational stage into two substages: concrete operations and formal operations. The concrete operations stage, according to Piaget, is characterized by the ability to deal effectively with concrete concepts and operations but not with abstract ones. During this stage the ability to generalize learning is limited; what is learned in one context does not readily transfer to other contexts. Only when one has reached the stage of formal operations can one deal effectively with abstract concepts and demonstrate the ability to apply reasoning and problem-solving skills in contexts different from those in which they were acquired.

Table 2.2 gives a list of mathematical tasks that an individual at Piaget's stage of concrete operations would be expected to be able to do and a corresponding list of tasks that he probably could not do. The lists are taken from Thornton (1980) who credits Herron (1975) and Copes (1975) as the sources of the first six items on each list.

Fuller (1980) characterizes formal reasoning in terms of three properties: (a) the inversion of reality and possibility; (b) hypothetico-deductive reasoning; and (c) operations on operations (p. 8). Regarding the first of these properties, Fuller argues that an essential difference between the pre-formal and the formal thinker lies in the ability to generate possibilities and to rethink reality in light of those possibilities. The pre-formal thinker, he suggests, can imagine how things might be different from what they are, but tends to perceive these differences as unorthodox, peculiar or deviant. The formal thinker, in contrast, can construct a variety of possibilities and evaluate reality relative to them.

In a similar vein, formal thinkers have a better grasp than pre-formal thinkers of the difference between empirical truth and logical validity. They can pursue a line of reasoning that begins with a hypothetical, or even obviously false, assertion to see where it leads. Pre-formal thinkers have difficulty in accepting an assertion that they recognize to be false as a point of departure for a line of thought to be explored. Finally, formal thinkers can deal with second-order relationships, relationships between relationships, more easily than can pre-formal thinkers.

With respect to the distinction between concrete and formal reasoning in the social sciences, Duly (1978) describes the concrete thinker as one who sees only limited, immediate relationships and has little awareness of interrelationships, whereas the formal thinker is better able to integrate

TABLE 2.2
Mathematical tasks that individuals at the concrete-operations stage of development can or cannot do (Thornton, 1980)

Can	*But Can't*
make routine measurements and observations	measure "indirectly" quantities such as speed and acceleration, perhaps even area and volume
answer acceptably the question, "Are there more squares or rectangles in the diagram?" (if they realize that all squares are rectangles)	respond correctly to the choice, "If all squares are rectangles, then: 1. All rectangles are squares. 2. Some rectangles are squares. 3. No rectangles are squares."
order a collection of sticks according to length	decide who is tallest if told that Bill is taller than Tammy and shorter than Sheila
count and perform elementary arithmetic operations	systematize counting procedures well enough to understand permutations and combinations
manipulate algebraic expressions including fractions	given the equation $y=3x^2$ or $y=1/x$, decide what happens to y as x increases
generalize simply from given data: all quadratic equations (in x) represent parabolas	perform a "once-removed" generalization; since quadratic equations in x represent parabolas, so do quadratic equations in y
solve $x/3=7/5$ for x	find the shadow of a three foot child when his five foot mother has a seven foot shadow
change a number from base ten into base two using a memorized procedure	use the analogous process to write numbers in base three
write numbers in scientific notation	solve linear equations with coefficients written in scientific notation
apply memorized formulas to find the mean and standard deviation	decide whether the computed mean and standard deviation are at all reasonable for the data
find the intersection of two given finite sets	draw a Venn diagram to represent "some A are also B"
list all possible outcomes of flipping two coins	easily list the outcomes for three and certainly not for four coins
work through a flowchart with a given set of data points	discover that the flowchart just counts the positive data
write simple truth tables involving implication	give a specific example of the denied antecedent falacy
compute what percent 6 is of 8	find the percent change from 8 to 6

generalizations, to have insights and to see the interplay of ideas and actions. To Duly's characterization, Corzine (1980) adds that the concrete thinker relies more on stereotypes than on empirical observations and experiments as a basis for decision making and that his acceptance or rejection of information is more likely to be based on its source than on an assessment of its merits.

How does Piaget's account of cognitive development relate to the question of teaching thinking? Whether or not one accepts his notion of developmental stages and his account of the normal progression through them, the distinction between concrete and formal operations takes on considerable practical educational significance in the light of two claims: (1) that much of the thinking that is required by conventional college courses is formal thinking by Piaget's definition (Prosser, 1979); and (2) that a significant percentage of adolescents, and even of college students, has not acquired the ability to engage in this type of thinking (Carpenter, 1980; Chiapetta, 1976; Dulit, 1972; Jackson, 1965; Karplus, 1974; Kohlberg & Gilligan, 1980; Kolodiy, 1975; Lawson & Renner, 1974; Lovell, 1961; McKinnon, 1971; McKinnon & Renner, 1971; Renner & Lawson, 1973; Tomlinson-Keasey, 1972; Towler & Wheatley, 1971; Wason, 1968; Wright, 1979).

The inability of many adolescents and college students to engage in formal operational thinking becomes especially serious in light of another aspect of the Piagetian view: a person's level of cognitive development represents a constraint on what he can and cannot learn. In particular, an individual who has not reached the stage of formal operations cannot be expected to learn particular concepts that require such operations. This means that much instruction in science and other disciplines would be problematical for a substantial percentage of students.

Accordingly, instruction to improve thinking based on Piaget's theory typically seeks to promote transition to more advanced stages of development, which means, in most cases, to the formal operational stage. Various examples of this approach are reviewed in Part II of this volume. For the present, it will suffice to make a general point: although experience of the physical world is, in the Piagetian view, one of several factors that contribute to development, development is not equated with learning in the traditional sense; instruction based on a Piagetian view may mean a deemphasis on traditional learning.

Narveson (1980) addresses just this point explicitly. However, the deemphasis is justified in his view by the longer-lasting nature of developmental gains. "Whatever developmental gains students make will remain with them after specific learning is forgotten and will furthermore permit qualitatively more advanced kinds of learning in the future" (p. 83). The assumption is that students may "learn" enough of course-content material by rote to get them through college exams even if they have not attained a sufficiently advanced developmental stage to understand what it is they have "learned." However, the results of such learning will soon evaporate and not provide a useful basis for further learning or for performance outside of school. In contrast, developmental gains should equip the students for fuller understanding of the concepts with which advanced education deals and give them a solid basis for real learning in the indefinite future. Whatever one may think of this argument, there is compelling evidence that students sometimes do learn enough to get passing grades in school without acquiring a good understanding of some of the fundamental concepts with which they are dealing (Nickerson, 1982b).

We mentioned earlier that certain qualifications about Piaget's theory also may have implications for education. For one point, it is important to note that the Piagetian stages are not always viewed as being separated by precise boundaries that an individual crosses in one leap. Piaget himself has acknowledged that a person may well display formal operations in matters familiar to him while functioning at a lesser level with unfamiliar matters. Pursuing the same theme, Narveson (1980) points out that people may think formally on some tasks and concretely on others depending on such factors as motivation, familiarity, and social conditioning. It is risky, therefore, to assume that because a student shows evidence (or lack thereof) of thinking formally in one class or discipline that he will necessarily also do so in others.

McShane (1980) notes that speaking of "the concrete thinker," at least at the college level, is probably an oversimplification. It is unlikely that anyone enters college with no capacity for formal operations whatsoever, which is not to deny that many students may not be "formally operational" with respect to the requirements of some of the disciplines they will encounter. McShane goes on to suggest that the degree to which individuals operate at a formal level may depend strongly on their familiarity with the discipline: professors who are highly formal in their approach to their own disciplines may well function at a concrete level, at least initially, when encountering a new field.

At the least, these points question a "formal operations first, then content" approach to instruction, because they suggest that formal operations may take care of themselves, to some degree, once students are sufficiently familiar with the content of a discipline. That is, perhaps the problems with many students is not that they lack the structure of formal operations, but have not yet extended it to various unfamiliar domains. This is not to say that learning considerable conventional content from, say, physics, is a sufficient condition for such an extension to physics, but it may be a necessary condition.

However, the mixing of different Piagetian levels in the same individual might have another, more far-reaching implication: maybe the Piagetian construct is simply wrong. Perhaps there is no general formal-operations ability that empowers an individual to grasp advanced concepts and reasoning in all disciplines. Perhaps, instead, what Piaget views as an integrated structure is a collection of thinking strategies, some more context dependent and some less. Inasmuch as Piaget's formulation allows for a mix of levels in the same person, it is not easy to design a critical experiment to distinguish between the view of formal operations as a highly integrated structure and a "conglomerate" interpretation of formal reasoning abilities.

Whatever the case, Piaget's studies still have import. For example, consider such aspects of formal operations as understanding control of variables or being able to generate all possible combinations. These abilities have a manifest importance in the sciences, regardless of whether they derive from one underlying construct or several. Accordingly, instruction might be, and in fact has been (see Part II), designed to foster an understanding of such concepts, independently of the "unity" issue. To the extent that one believed in an integrated structure for formal operations, one would expect to achieve a general advance providing one could impart understanding of a few, perhaps even one, of the concepts. To the extent that one believed in the conglomerate view, one would expect to have to teach the diverse concepts separately, and design the instruction accordingly.

The challenges to the details of Piaget's formulation have led to various efforts to account for his observations by quite different theories. For example, Case (1985) argues that Piaget's stages reflect a mix of gradually increasing processing capacity with age and the learning of discipline-specific schemata that reduce effective cognitive load. Employing his model, Case has carried out a number of persuasive instructional experiments, without, however, attempting to teach general thinking skills. In general, Case's position suggests that general thinking skills of great power do not exist.

An alternative view is represented by Gholson and Beilin's (1979) developmental model that blends some aspects of Piaget's stage-development theory with conventional developmental learning theory and some of the concepts that come from information-processing views of cognition. Cognitive capabilities are seen as stage-dependent and reflecting different forms of cognitive organization. The model assumes a "processor" that operates on information, transforming it and integrating it with existing cognitive structures, and a set of cognitive sub-processes that control the flow of information to and from the processor. The processor is likened to an executive system, which uses various sub-processes to accomplish specific tasks. The sub-processes available to the processor include stimulus differentiation, directed attention, verbal and nonverbal coding processes, and memory-storage and retrieval processes. The model assumes two types of developmental effects, "qualitative changes in the functioning of the processor, and quantitative changes in the functioning of the various cognitive subprocesses involved in the flow of information to the processor" (pp. 50-51). The capabilities available to the processor, which determine the kinds of solution plans the individual may generate and execute, are assumed to be roughly comparable to the cognitive operations assigned by Piaget to preoperational, concrete operational, and formal operational thought. The efficiency with which the various subprocesses function is assumed to change quantitatively with development.

Not all developmental psychologists subscribe to the view that development proceeds through a succession of stages. Bruner (1966) presents one notable countervailing view. He explicitly rejects the notion of developmental stages; however, he does hold that different modes or processing and representing information are emphasized during different periods of a child's life. During the first few years, the important function is physical manipulation. "Knowing is principally knowing how to do, and there is minimum reflection" (p. 27). During the second period, which hits its high point between the ages of 5 and 7, the emphasis switches to reflection, and the individual becomes able to represent internal aspects of the environment. During the third period, which coincides roughly with adolescence, thinking becomes increasingly language-dependent and abstract. At this time, the individual acquires an ability to deal with propositions as well as objects. From Bruner (1966):

> What comes out of this picture, rough though I have sketched it, is a view of human beings who have developed three parallel systems for processing information and for representing it—one through manipulation and action, one through perceptual organization and imagery, and one through symbolic apparatus. It is not that these are "stages" in any sense; they are rather emphases in development. You must get the perceptual field organized around your own person as center before you can impose other, less egocentric axes upon it, for example. In the end, the mature organism seems to have gone through a process of elaborating three systems of skills that correspond to the three major tool systems to which he must link himself for full expression of his capacities—tools for the hand, for the distance receptors, and for the process of reflection (p. 28).

Bruner (1966) lists the following factors as characteristics of the nature of intellectual growth:

a. Growth is characterized by increasing independence of response from the immediate nature of the stimulus.
b. Growth depends upon internalizing events into a "storage system" that corresponds to the environment.

c. Intellectual growth involves an increasing capacity to say to oneself and others, by means of words or symbols, what one has done or what one will do.
d. Intellectual development depends upon a systematic and contingent interaction between a tutor and a learner, the tutor already being equipped with a wide range of previously invented techniques that he teaches a child.
e. Teaching is vastly facilitated by the medium of language, which ends by being not only the medium for exchange but the instrument that the learner can then use himself in bringing order into the environment.
f. Intellectual development is marked by increasing capacity to deal with several alternatives simultaneously, to tend to several sequences during the same period of time, and to allocate time and attention in a manner appropriate to these multiple demands (pp. 5, 6).

It is clear from this brief excursion into developmental psychology that there exists a variety of opinions among researchers regarding how development occurs and what can and cannot be taught to children and young people at different ages. So if one wants to design a program that has a theoretical basis, one can choose among several theoretical points of view. There are three points, however, that we believe deserve emphasis. First, there can be no question about the fact that Piagetian ideas have greatly influenced several of the programs to enhance thinking skills that have been developed. We review some of these programs in Chapter 8. Second, there is no theory the validity of which is sufficiently well established to permit one to assume that a program true to that theory would necessarily produce the desired results. While theoretical issues are of unquestioned interest, the major concern of most potential users of a program to enhance thinking skills is probably a practical one, namely the question of whether or not the program works; and given the state of theory in cognitive development, it seems safe to assert that that question will not be resolved on purely theoretical grounds. Third, it is undoubtedly the case that the acquisition of some types of thinking skills is dependent on the pre-existence of certain types of knowledge and more elementary skills. The extent to which the acquirability of any knowledge or skills is age dependent, however, appears to us to be an open question.

5. EFFORTS TO INCREASE INTELLIGENCE THROUGH TRAINING

If intelligence is defined as genetically endowed intellectual potential, then, of course, by definition it cannot be increased. Intelligence typically is not defined this way, however, and the question of whether it can be raised by deliberate efforts is an empirical one.

Of at least passing interest here is John Stuart Mill's assessment of the importance of early training on his own intellectual development. Mill is often considered to have had one of the keenest minds that the world has produced. In his autobiography he recounts the unusual early training he got at the direction of his father. Mill later attributed his remarkable intellectual achievements to this training rather than to an extraordinary intellectual endowment.

Even Schopenhauer, who had a rather depressing view of the capabilities of humankind in general, and who believed strongly that genius is a rare and inborn quality, asserted that we are capable of learning how to do better than we otherwise might in such intellectually demanding situations as disputations and debates—of learning, in other words, how to win arguments. Indeed, he provides us with some thirty-eight specific tactics, or "stratagems," that, he suggests, should be useful to that end (Schopenhauer, undated). He is careful to point out that the purpose of these stratagems is not to help establish the truth or falsity of any given proposition, but only to help one get the best of it in a dispute. Schopenhauer's point of departure for his discourse is the assumption that real disputes seldom are won or lost on logical grounds. (The stratagems are well worth reading and thinking about, if not for the purpose of increasing one's ability to win arguments without speaking to the point, at least for the sake of lessening one's chances of losing arguments on other than logical grounds.)

What is the evidence that intelligence, or at least measures thereof, can be raised by training? Whimbey (1975) reviews several attempts to increase the IQ of preschoolers, including attempts by Bereiter and Engelmann (1966), Blank and Soloman (1968), Klaus and Gray (1968), and Karnes (1973) all of which produced positive results. The programs differed from each other in many respects; but most tended to use relatively low student-to-teacher ratios, and they focused on the teaching of language and specific reasoning skills, emphasizing the importance of involving the student actively in the learning process.

For example, the Bereiter–Engelmann program for preschoolers listed the following 15 specific "minimum goals":

1. Ability to use both affirmative and *not* statements in reply to the question "What is this?" "This is a ball. This is not a book."

2. Ability to use both affirmative and *not* statements in response to the command "Tell me about this———[ball, pencil, etc.]." "This pencil is red. This pencil is not blue."

3. Ability to handle polar opposites ("If it is not———, it must be———") for at least four concept pairs, e.g., big-little, up-down, long-short, fat-skinny.

4. Ability to use the following prepositions correctly in statements

describing arrangements of objects: on, in, under, over, between. "Where is the pencil?" "The pencil is under the book."

5. Ability to name positive and negative instances for at least four classes, such as tools, weapons, pieces of furniture, wild animals, farm animals, and vehicles. "Tell me something that is a weapon." "A gun is a weapon." "Tell me something that is not a weapon." "A cow is not a weapon." The child should also be able to apply these class concepts correctly to nouns with which he is familiar, e.g., "Is a crayon a piece of furniture?" "No, a crayon is not a piece of furniture. A crayon is something to write with."

6. Ability to perform simple *if-then* deductions. The child is presented a diagram containing big squares and little squares. All the big squares are red, but the little squares are of various other colors. "If the square is big, what do you know about it?" "It's red."

7. Ability to use *not* in deductions. "If the square is little, what else do you know about it?" "It is not red."

8. Ability to use *or* in simple deductions. "If the square is little, then it is not red. What else do you know about it?" "It's blue *or* yellow."

9. Ability to name the basic colors, plus white, black, and brown.

10. Ability to count aloud to 20 without help and to 100 with help at decade points (30, 40, etc.).

11. Ability to count objects correctly up to ten.

12. Ability to recognize and name the vowels and at least 15 consonants.

13. Ability to distinguish printed words from pictures.

14. Ability to rhyme in some fashion to produce a word that rhymes with a given word, to tell whether two words do or do not rhyme, or to complete unfamiliar rhyming jingles like "I had a dog, and his name was Abel; I found him hiding under the———."

15. A sight-reading vocabulary of at least four words in addition to proper names, with evidence that the printed word has the same meaning for them as the corresponding spoken word. "What word is this?" "Cat." "Is this a thing that goes 'Woof-woof?'" "No, it goes 'Meow.'" (Whimbey, 1975, 31–32)

In the Bereiter-Engelmann program, the student-to-teacher ratio was 5 to 1 (three teachers for a class of 15 students). Several 20-minute teaching sessions were distributed over two hours.

> The teaching format consisted of intensive repetitive attention demanding highly structured drill; discipline was strict and pertinent to the task being practiced; errors were pointed out explicitly rather than glossed over in vague terms; and most important, emphatic and overt response was required of each child (p. 33).

One of the more provocative findings reviewed by Whimbey involved differences in attitude and thinking styles of low- and high-aptitude college students. Low-aptitude students, these investigators reported, were mentally careless and took a superficial approach to solving problems, making mistakes because they had failed to read instructions carefully, or to make the effort a problem deserved. The tendency to rush superficially through a problem, rather than making an extended serious effort to understand it, the researchers referred to as "one-shot thinking."

In addition to one-shot thinking, another factor that characterized the low-aptitude students was an attitude of indifference toward their performance. Low-aptitude students tended to place relatively little value on reasoning as a way of solving a problem, and showed more interest in what the right answer to a question was than in how it was obtained.

Bloom and Broder (1950) developed a remedial training program designed to correct some of these deficiencies and implemented it as a pilot project. They reported positive results in that grades of participating students on comprehensive examinations were higher than those of a control group. They also reported improved academic performance.

Although intelligence manifests itself in many forms, Whimbey claims there is one expression of it that is especially important in scholastic pursuits: the ability to read comprehendingly. The basic cause of poor comprehension among unskilled readers, he contends, is failure to attend carefully to meaning. Moreover, how to attend to meaning is a skill that can be taught. Whimbey suggests that within elementary and secondary schools, the teaching of overall academic thinking ability could be effectively organized around training in reading comprehension.

The studies reviewed by Whimbey have not gone uncriticized. As a group, however, they represent highly suggestive, if not incontrovertible, evidence that the kind of intellectual performance that is measured by IQ tests can be improved as a result of training.

More recent evidence comes from two programs designed to raise the intelligence of preschool students. Detterman (1982) characterizes these programs as "The most extensive, most methodologically sophisticated attempts to increase intellectual ability and subsequent school achievement yet undertaken." One of these programs is the Carolina Abecedarian Day-care Program (Ramey, MacPhee, & Yeates, 1982). This program addresses preschool children determined to be at risk of mild psychosocial retardation. Such children tend to show a profile of declining mental abilities from about age one through the first few years of schooling: they fall farther and farther behind other children from more favored backgrounds. The aim of the Abecedarian Program was to investigate a way to rescue at-risk children from this fate.

In the Abecedarian Program, the "at-risk" designation depended on a number of measures, including parent IQ, family income, parent education, and intactness of family. These factors have been shown to be predictive of mild retardation. Families having an at-risk infant and who agreed to participate were assigned at random to a treatment group or a control group. Both treatment and control group families received certain benefits: social services for the family, and medical and nutritional attention for the participating child. Only the treatment group children attended the day-care program itself. There was no special guidance for treatment group parents (nor, of course, control group parents) about fostering intellect development in the home.

The program's schedule was intensive. Children began as early as six weeks of age, and had to begin by the age of three months . The children, transported to and from the day-care center, attended from 7:45 a.m. to 5:30 p.m. every weekday, 50 weeks per year. The program offered a stimulating environment and toys appropriate to the children's ages. The authors characterize the setting as one designed to be "predictable and promote self-help; supportive and facilitate social-emotional adjustment; reflective of the child's age, ability, and interest; and varied in activities" (p. 86). The teacher/student ratio ranged from one-to-three to one-to-six.

The instructional component of the program featured careful attention to language development in both play and work contexts. Whenever there was a motivating occasion to communicate, the teachers tried to take this as an opportunity to boost skills of effective discourse and social interaction. Besides the general emphasis on language, instruction for the infants and toddlers, up to 3 years of age, was guided by an array of over 300 objectives in the language, social, motor, and cognitive areas. Each was represented by a worksheet that helped the teacher guide the student toward mastery of a particular skill. For children of ages 3 and 4, instruction was based on a variety of materials designed to prepare the youngsters for reading and to acquaint them with simple aspects of the arts, science, and math. The authors summarize the intervention this way: "The infant and early childhood curricula, in toto, provide a systematic yet individually responsive experience for at-risk children such that relevant domains of development are enriched and sustained, and so that the children are prepared to cope with the educational and social demands of public school" (p. 89).

Ramey, MacPhee, and Yeates present findings representing the first two cohorts to be admitted to the program, which initiated four cohorts between 1972 and 1977. They address the impact of the program with a variety of measures, but, in the present context, we limit our summary to the question of IQ. The experimental group quickly established and maintained over the control group an advantage of roughly seven or eight IQ points. At age five, the mean IQ of the experimental group was about 98, the mean of the control group about 90. The authors treat 85 as a cut-off point below which a youngster might be considered handicapped. At five years of age, 39% of the children in the control group fell below this cut-off, but only 11% of the children in the treatment group.

In summary, it seems clear that the Carolina Abecedarian intervention had an impact on IQ, an impact that although not dramatic, sufficed to keep a fair number of children from being classified as handicapped. The authors report no information about subsequent school performance of the children, which is unfortunate inasmuch as the gains produced by interventions of this sort often diminish as the students proceed through the normal curriculum.

Garber and Heber (1982) discuss the Milwaukee Project, one with ambitions similar to the Carolina Abecedarian Program. The Milwaukee Project focused on 40 economically disadvantaged mothers of IQ less than 75 with infants ranging in age from three to six months. Half were assigned to a control group and half to a treatment group at random. Like the Abecedarian Program, the Milwaukee Project provided the children in the treatment group with preschool virtually year-round until they entered school. Unlike the Abecedarian Program, the Milwaukee Project also worked with the mothers to try to alter the home environment.

Garber and Heber offer few details about the actual treatment. In general, they say that the preschool program emphasized problem solving and language skills. The teachers, mostly paraprofessionals, worked with the students in large and small groups and "utilized an open-ended questioning approach to teaching, trying to expand beyond the immediate" (p. 123). The mothers received attention primarily during the first two years of the preschool that included remedial education, guidance in home management, and job training.

Garber and Heber discuss the impact of the program from a number of perspectives, but again we limit our review largely to the question of IQ. By age 22 months, an impressive difference had developed between the experimental and the control children, the former having a mean IQ of 120, the latter of 94. This difference of about 25 IQ points was maintained throughout the duration of the preschool program. After the children graduated from the preschool program, seventeen experimental and seventeen control students were tracked for four years of normal schooling. At ten years of age, the treatment group had a mean IQ of 104, range 93–138, while the control group had a mean IQ of 86, range 72–106, a sustained difference of 18 points.

The actual school performance of the treatment group was less encouraging. On the plus side, the treatment group maintained a significant difference in academic achievement over the control group. However, the performance of both groups steadily declined. In the first year, the experimental group performed in accordance with national norms; in the next years it declined to the lower than normal level of the city schools in general, and then to the typical level of the inner city schools. Considering that the treatment group children in the fourth grade still had an average IQ of over 100, their gradual drop to an inner-city-level academic performance seems to reflect the effect of the school system.

Why the Milwaukee Project achieved more than twice the IQ difference of the Carolina Abecedarian Day-care Program is an interesting question. One possible explanation is that the Milwaukee Project included an instructional component for the mothers. In support of this possibility, Garber and Heber present evidence that other siblings of the treatment children showed a modest benefit also, presumably via the mother.

In summary, there seems to be considerable evidence that IQ scores can be modified by training. Furthermore, the findings from the Milwaukee Project show that substantial differences can survive for several years after training. The most notable gap in this picture is that these studies address groups with initially low to average IQ. We know of no experiments on whether training can raise significantly the IQ of individuals who begin with IQs already well above average. Unfortunately because such individuals are not seen as having a problem in the first place, this sort of research tends not to get done.

6. SUMMARY

We have discussed several aspects of intellectual competence: What intelligence is or is thought to be, how it is measured, how it relates to cognitive development, and whether it can be increased by training.

Regarding what intelligence is or is thought to be, we noted that efforts to define it have not been highly successful. Many definitions have been proposed but none has been widely accepted. The argument has been made that this concept, like many others that we use, cannot really be defined satisfactorily except by way of pointing to or describing behavior that is prototypical of what would be expected of individuals who are considered to be intelligent. One point on which there seems to be increasing agreement is that intelligence, whatever it is, is multi-faceted. It has many aspects, and that being the case, people can be intelligent or unintelligent in different ways.

The history of mental testing illustrates both the difficulty that researchers have had in converging on a conceptualization of intelligence that everyone can accept and also the persistence of the idea that intelligence is a multi-faceted thing. Attempts to assess intelligence have included measurements or indicants of a large number of variables ranging from sensory acuity to vocabulary size.

These complexities notwithstanding, psychologists have spent a substantial amount of time developing and refining instruments to measure intelligence or specific aspects of it. Clearly, these instruments might be employed to measure gains in thinking ability, or even as guides to the de sign of instruction to improve thinking ability. One's attitude on this matter is likely to depend strongly on one's view of the relationship between intelligence and thinking ability. If one believes that thinking ability is a simple consequence of intelligence—the more intelligent an individual the greater his ability to think will be—then the implication is clear. The only way one can hope to improve thinking ability is to increase intelligence, and then the question of whether intelligence is modifiable through training becomes key.

On the other hand, at least two other possibilities deserve serious consideration: (1) intelligence as measured is more a consequence of thinking ability than a cause, or (2) thinking ability and intelligence are only partially related; either one might be modified somewhat independently of the other.

In our judgment, the second position is the more sensible one, all things considered. This position leads to two kinds of plans for enhancing thinking. First, since it seems sound to view thinking ability as at least somewhat reflective of intelligence, one might try to improve intelligence and reap the benefits in improved thinking. Moreover, this route appears viable, inasmuch as some efforts to increase intelligence, as reflected in performance on intelligence tests, have seen some success. This is not to suggest that intensive training for better performance on one particular type of instrument improves thinking in general, or even intelligence in general; such a tactic risks all the hazards of "teaching to the test." But at least some of the cases reviewed appear not to have been subject to this reservation.

But, according to position (2), there is another route. Imperfectly correlated with intelligence, thinking ability involves something else besides. A common way of describing this "something else" refers to how people use their intelligence. Just as an athlete with a certain musculature and bone structure can learn to use it more or less skillfully, so, perhaps, a person with certain mental capacities can learn procedures for utilizing them effectively. By far the majority of programs designed to enhance thinking skills adopt the latter perspective, rather than trying to improve intelligence as such. According to this view, even if intelligence cannot be improved at all by instruction, thinking ability still might be enhanced in this way.

3 Some Perspectives on Thinking

As we have noted, the concepts of intelligence and thinking clearly are closely related. Probably most of us assume that the more intelligent one is, the more effective a thinker one is likely to be; or conversely, we are apt to accept particularly good thinking ability as evidence of high intelligence. But "intelligence" and "thinking ability" are not, in our view, synonymous terms. "Thinking ability" appears to be a less controversial concept than "intelligence." Moreover, although some investigators have been willing to consider intelligence to be teachable, there seems to be a greater reluctance among psychologists to accept this idea, or to talk in these terms, than to refer to thinking ability as something that can be acquired or improved at least to some degree.

We might well view thinking ability as, in part, a matter of good strategy. If we do, there is nothing self contradictory about the idea of a person of high intelligence who has not learned good strategies, perhaps because of an inadequate education. Another individual of more moderate intelligence, but who had had the opportunity to learn powerful strategies, might, in many contexts, "outthink" the first. In short, from some perspectives, intelligence relates more to the "raw power" of one's mental equipment, and here, as in other contexts, raw power is one thing and the skilled use of it something else.

In exploring the concept of intelligence, we have not addressed what is distinctive about thinking in general or skilled thinking in particular. Much of that discussion takes place in the following chapters, in association with particular themes such as problem solving, creativity, or reasoning. But a few general points are made here before turning to those specific topics.

1. THINKING ABILITY AS A SKILL OR COLLECTION OF SKILLS

Thinking ability is sometimes viewed as a complex skill or collection of skills. Given this view, it is natural to consider thinking to be something that may be done well or poorly, efficiently or inefficiently; and to assume that how to do it better is something one can learn.

Viewing thinking ability as a complex skill also invites the drawing of parallels with other complex skills. One parallel that we find particularly suggestive is the distinction between general and specific skills. Many athletic activities require both intensive physical conditioning and the development of fine-grained motor control. Any exercise that develops the cardiovascular system is likely to be helpful toward getting one in shape to play basketball, to swim, to engage in track events, and so forth. However, to remain in peak condition for a specific activity, one must practice that particular activity; thus, running is not as effective in preparing for swimming as is swimming itself.

We suspect that a distinction similar to the one between general conditioning and the development of the ability to execute finely controlled motor activities may be appropriate in the case of thinking. It may make sense to assume that one's general ability to engage in intellectually demanding tasks can be increased simply by frequent vigorous mental exercise, as it were. It is also undoubtedly true, however, that in order best to prepare oneself for certain types of cognitive problems, one needs practice in dealing with those particular types of problems. While an alert and energetic mind is an asset for solving geometry problems, it also helps to have some specific mathematical skills. We suspect, in short, that intellectual performance may be enhanced, in part, by the cultivation of habitual thoughtfulness and certain general strategies for approaching cognitive tasks, and, in part, by the mastery of skills specific to particular types of problems.

In athletics, practice of a specific activity often accomplishes two things. It produces the physical conditioning appropriate for that activity, and it gives the athlete the ability to expend energy efficiently when engaged in the activity. These two effects may be difficult to distinguish in particular cases, but there can be no doubt that they are both there. Trampolining provides an example that illustrates the point. When an individual tries bouncing on a trampoline for the first time, he is likely to be amazed at how quickly he tires and at how wobbly his legs feel when he gets back on the ground. In contrast, even a moderately proficient trampolinist can bounce for very long periods of time without tiring noticeably. Certainly practicing on the trampoline strengthens the particular muscles that are involved in its use. However, just as certainly the novice user wastes a great amount of energy because of a lack of "feel" for how to couple with the device. He waves his arms a great deal in order to maintain his balance, and wastes much effort jumping instead of letting the trampoline do the work. A large component of acquiring skill in an activity such as trampolining is that of learning how to expend energy efficiently.

Here again, we see a possible analogy with the learning of thinking skills. On the one hand, practice with a particular kind of intellectual task should strengthen specific abilities that serve that task. On the other hand, one may learn also how to expend intellectual energy on the task more appropriately, and by minimizing the mental analogs to the unnecessary hand waving and ineffective jumping of the novice trampolinist, to approach the task in a way that is not only effective but efficient.

Another idea that relates to the learning of complex motor skills, and that is suggestive with respect to thinking skills is the following one. A common assumption regarding the learning of psychomotor skills is that a primary effect of training is to enlarge an individual's repertoire of precoded response sequences. Thus a key difference between the skilled and semi-skilled player of a game, such as tennis, that requires complex movements is the number of precoded motor programs that the player can call upon to meet the demands of the moment. Such precoded response patterns facilitate performance in two ways: to the extent that a motor sequence has been practiced as a whole, it is more likely to be executed smoothly; to the extent that it is already coded and can be run off with a minimum of conscious control, more of the individual's limited processing capacity is available for other uses.

If thinking skills are really learned behavior patterns, we might expect an an alogous effect of training, namely an enlarging of one's repertoire of precoded intellectual performance patterns that function relatively automatically in appropriate contexts. We do not mean to suggest that there is nothing more to the development of thinking skills than this, but that this may be one aspect of it.

2. BARTLETT'S VIEW

Bartlett's (1958) view of thinking deserves comment for its historical significance, if for no other reason. He wrote eloquently about thinking and memory during a time when the vast majority of psychologists were assiduously avoiding the use of such mentalistic terms. His contribution is especially worthy of mention here because he was a forceful spokesman for the view that thinking should be thought of as a "complex and high-level form of skill"; indeed he was as responsible as anyone for establishing this tradition.

Bartlett (1958) placed great emphasis on one dominant characteristic of thinking, namely, the tendency to go beyond the evidence at hand, to engage—in his terms—in "gap filling." All thinking, he claimed, appears to illustrate one or another of three kinds of gap-filling processes: interpolation (gap filling in the most literal sense, involving the filling in of information that is missing from a logical sequence), extrapolation (extension of an incomplete argument to a terminus) and reinterpretation (rearrangement of evidence—change of perspective—to effect a new interpretation).

Extrapolation he considered to be somewhat more representative than interpolation of thinking "as it most frequently occurs in experimental science, in daily life, and in artistic construction" (p. 33). Extrapolation in the experiments Bartlett conducted typically required the discovery of a rule of structure that would allow one to extend an incomplete series.

Bartlett summarized his view of thinking this way:

> The process begins when evidence or information is available which is treated as possessing gaps, or as being incomplete. The gaps are then filled up, or that part of the information which is incomplete is completed. This is done by an extension or supplementation of the evidence, which remains in accord with the evidence (or claims to do so), but carries it further by utilizing other sources of information besides those which started the whole process going, and, in many instances, in addition to those which can be directly identified in the external surroundings. Between the initial information and the terminal stage, when the gaps are alleged to be filled, or completeness achieved, theoretically there are always a succession of interconnected steps. These steps may be described either before or after the terminal point is reached. They, more than anything else, are what makes an experimental approach to thinking possible, and they confer upon thinking its character of necessity. We are not to suppose that this necessity implies that, given the initial information, the steps through which a terminus is reached must always be the same steps, or the same number or order of steps; or that the terminal point reached must be the same in all cases.
>
> More briefly, thinking can be defined as: The extension of evidence in accord with that evidence so as to fill up gaps in the evidence: and this is done by moving through a succession of interconnected steps which may be stated at the time, or left till later to be stated. (p. 75)

The process of "reinterpretation," as Bartlett conceived it, has much in common with what might be called alogical approaches to thinking, which several other writers have discussed under a variety of rubrics. Reinterpretation occurs in situations in which all the information needed is at hand, but the fact may not be obvious to the problem solver. In Bartlett's terms, the evidence is "in disguise." Solving the problem requires that one rearrange the evidence and examine it from an unusual point of view.

Bartlett drew several parallels between thinking and bodily skills and believed that, in both cases, expertness is acquired, in large measure, "by well-informed practice." He fully expected that thinking would prove to be more complicated than bodily skills and would reveal unique characteristics, but he argued that approaches that had been effective in the experimental investigation of bodily skills provide a reasonable point of departure for the experimental study of thinking.

We use the term *thinking skills* throughout this book much in the spirit of Bartlett's precedent. In that spirit we give the term a relatively broad connotation. In particular, it does not suit our purposes here to draw a sharp distinction between skills and strategies, although for other purposes such a distinction is useful (Nickerson, Salter, Shepard, & Herrnstein, 1984).

3. THINKING SKILLS VERSUS KNOWLEDGE

Traditional approaches to education have focused on the teaching of "course content" material, which is to say on imparting factual knowledge. By comparison, relatively little attention has been given to the teaching of thinking skills—or at least to the teaching of the skills involved in such higher-order activities as reasoning, creative thinking, and problem solving.

In focusing on thinking skills, one need not deny the importance of acquiring knowledge. Indeed, we question whether a strong distinction between thinking skills and knowledge—a distinction that has sometimes been drawn quite sharply—is really defensible. At the very least, we would argue that the two are interdependent. On the one hand, thinking is essential to the acq uisition of knowledge, and, on the other, knowledge is essential to thinking. Regarding the first point, some educators have questioned whether factual knowledge can be assimilated effectively unless the student actively processes it in a thoughtful way. Dewey (1974) expressed this view as follows:

> No thought, no idea, can possibly be conveyed as an idea from one person to another. When it is told, it is, to the one to whom it is told, another fact, not an idea .... What he (the person) directly gets cannot be an idea. Only by wrestling with the conditions of the problem at first hand, seeking and finding his own way out, does he think (p. 159).

Nor is the dependence of thinking on knowledge less apparent; indeed skillful thinking might even be defined as the ability to apply knowledge effectively. Clearly, thinking involves thinking about something; thinking about nothing is an exceedingly difficult thing to do. And presumably the more knowledge one has—the more food one has for thought—the richer one's mental life, and the more impressive one's intellectual performance, are likely to be. However, recognizing the interdependence of thinking and knowledge does not deny the reality of the distinction. It is at least conceivable that people possessing the same knowledge might differ significantly in how skillfully they apply what they know.

A fairly conspicuous trend in the recent literature on problem solving research also highlights the interdependence of thinking skill and knowledge, namely the increasing emphasis on the role of domain-specific knowledge in problem solving (e.g., Greeno, 1980; Hayes, 1980). In Greeno's terms "one of the consequences of recent fundamental research in problem solving has been a serious erosion of the distinction between knowledge-based performance and problem solving" (p. 10). "A cause of this erosion," he notes, "is the fact that researchers have been increasingly able to identify the knowledge that is used in the solution of specific problems." Greeno acknowledges that it is possible to distinguish between situations in which the possession of specific knowledge makes the problem easier to solve and those in which one must resort to more general knowledge, but he suggests that the specificity of the available knowledge is a matter of degree and not of kind. One of the practical implications that follows from this new emphasis on the role of knowledge in problem solving is the advisability, in teaching problem solving, of first analyzing the knowledge that is needed by a class of problems and then providing the instruction that will convey that knowledge.

Several other investigators have increasingly emphasized the central importance of large amounts of knowledge in the performance of intellectually demanding tasks (e.g., Goldstein & Papert, 1977; Hayes, 1980; Simon, 1980). But while Simon stresses the importance of knowledge in problem solving, he rejects the notion put forward by Goldstein and Papert (1977) that the fundamental problem of understanding intelligence relates to the question of how to represent large amounts of knowledge rather than in the identification of a few powerful techniques. Both knowledge and general methods for operating on that knowledge are essential to successful problem solving, Simon (1980) claims:

> The evidence from close examination of AI [artificial intelligence] programs that perform professional-level tasks, and the psychological evidence from human transfer experiments, indicate both that powerful general methods do exist and that they can be taught in such a way that they can be used in new domains where they are relevant. We reassert our earlier conclusion that the scissors does indeed have two blades and that effective professional education calls for attention to both subject-matter knowledge and general skills (p. 86).

Our position on whether the primary purpose of education should be to impart knowledge or to develop thinking skills is that education should address both objectives. Moreover, we believe it would be very difficult to attain either objective to a significant degree without making some headway on the other. In this book our focus is on thinking skills, but as we attempt to identify ways in which such skills may be taught, we are neither surprised nor disappointed when it proves convenient or necessary to touch also upon the topic of the acquisition of knowledge.

4. SOME DICHOTOMIES

Numerous writers about thinking have contrasted two types of thought processes. The distinctions are not all identical, but they have more in common than the fact that they divide thinking into two types. The distinction between rigorous logical reasoning and exploratory experimental groping for insights, for example, is fairly common. Polya's (1954a, b) distinction between the psychology of mathematics and the logic thereof is a case in point. He notes that the typical textbook shows the reader the deductive rigor of mathematical proofs, but fails to reveal the dynamics of the exploratory behavior that originally led, often by complex routes, to the development of those proofs.

A closely related distinction is that between hypothesis testing and hypothesis generation. Hypothesis testing is seen as prototypical of deductive and analytical processes, and hypothesis generation as prototypical of inductive and analogical processes. Deductive and analytical skills are more common, we suspect, than is the ability to generate useful hypotheses, or to impose structure on data that are not related in an obvious way. In other words, the ability to test theories seems to be more prevalent than the ability to construct them.

Other dichotomous distinctions that seem to be similar in spirit include the following: closed versus adventurous thinking (Bartlett, 1958), right-handed versus left-handed thinking (Bruner, 1962), convergent versus divergent thinking (Guilford, 1963), problem solving versus problem finding (Mackworth, 1965), vertical thinking versus lateral thinking (de Bono, 1968).

In short, while different writers use different terminology, the view that there are two qualitatively different types of thinking is widely shared. Among the terms that are used to describe one type are analytic, deductive, rigorous, constrained, convergent, formal, and critical. Representative of the terms used to describe the other type are synthetic, inductive, expansive, unconstrained, divergent, informal, diffuse, and creative. No doubt the partitioning of thinking into two types involves something of an oversimplification, but possibly a useful one. There certainly does seem to be a difference between rigorously following a chain of inferences to its logical conclusion and trying to back off and look at a problem from an entirely fresh perspective. We suspect too, however, that most substantive problems with which life presents us represent opportunities for both types of thinking. Any program to enhance thinking skills that focused on one type of thinking and ignored the other would, in our view, be an incomplete and unbalanced program. That is not to say that it would be useless, a half loaf *is* in many cases better than none; however, acknowledgment of the importance of both types of thinking and an effort to enhance each of them is greatly to be preferred.

5. WHAT LIMITS THINKING?

What do skilled thinkers have, or do, that distinguishes them from unskilled thinkers? This question puts in a nutshell the problem faced by the many investigators currently pondering the nature and nurture of thinking skills. A survey of efforts to answer the question quickly reveals that no consensus exists. Different researchers interpret the resources of the effective thinker differently.

It is not that one investigator imagines the mind to use mechanisms that another investigator denies outright. The contrasts are better understood in terms of limiting factors. Most would agree, for example, that thinking involves encoding information about a situation, operating on the information in some way, and deriving results in accordance with guiding goals. But while some may see inept thinkers as limited by their repertoire of operations, others may find their encoding impoverished, while still others locate the difficulty in inadequate goals, or inadequate monitoring of them.

Ultimately, considerable research will be needed to sort the empirical facts from the plausible conjectures. Our present aim is to spell out some of the alternatives that appear in the literature. An orderly map of the theoretical terrain may prove to be an aid in matching it to the realities of laboratory experiment and practical experience. Below, current positions on the factors that limit effective thinking are organized into five aspects or dimensions, each with two or more levels. Different writers emphasize different dimensions, and locate the problem on different levels within a dimension. We should note, however, that the alternative levels are not always mutually exclusive. Although authors tend to choose one level rather than another as the problematic level, in principle, limits of performance could arise on several levels at once.

Encoding, Operations, Goals

As noted above, it is useful to view thinking as involving *encoding* the matter thought about and *operating* on the encoded representation to achieve some *goal*. However, different investigators emphasize one or another of this trio as the limiting factor in effective thinking. Sometimes encoding is identified as the problem. Siegler (1981), in studies of Piagetian tasks, has concluded that children often fail to recognize the inadequacies of their current strategy because they do not encode the relevant features of the situation—in a weight balancing problem, for example, they may notice the number of weights but fail to take account of the distance of weights from the balance point. Depending on the task, they also may encode too much information so that the relevant data get lost among irrelevancies.

In contrast, the literature on heuristic problem solving stresses the importance of a repertoire of operations (Polya, 1954 a, b, 1957; Schoenfeld, 1978, 1979, 1980; Wickelgren, 1974). The effective thinker must be ready to divide problems into subproblems, relate a problem to analogous problems, work backwards from the solution or a characterization of it to produce the proof or derivation. According to this formulation, even if the thinker has an adequate encoding of the problem, performance may be limited by lack of the operations needed to move toward the goal effectively.

But sometimes the goal itself may be the limiting factor. Although they emphasize operations, writers on heuristics also acknowledge that the problem solver should be sure the problem is thoroughly understood—a matter, in part, of grasping the goal clearly. In certain studies, problem understanding has emerged as the most critical factor. Johnson (1972) reviewed several experiments in which subjects were asked to perform inventive tasks such as devising titles for story plots. The results suggested that understanding of the criteria was the most influential determinant of effective performance. Perkins (1981, Chapter 4) identifies several respects in which professional level production in the arts and the sciences is clearly goal limited: artists sometimes fall short for failing to recognize weaknesses in their products rather than because of any failure in inventiveness. In short, limits to thinking sometimes lie in encoding, sometimes in operations, sometimes in goals, depending on the task. And, no doubt, limits occur in all three aspects for many complex tasks. It follows that efforts to improve thinking skills might benefically address any one of these three aspects—encoding, operations, and goals and that any program developer who aspires to develop a comprehensive approach cannot safely ignore any of them.

Style, Know-How, Load, Abilities

Where limits appear—in encoding, operations, or goals—is one question, but what limits are is another. Style, know-how, load, and abilities represent four different types of limitations that might arise. Style refers to cognitive style. Baron (1981), among others, has proposed that thinking skill may be largely a matter of an effective cognitive style. He suggests that the effectiveness of a person's thinking on nearly any subject depends on cognitive-style traits such as precision, efficiency, and originality. Certainly, many ineffective thinkers seem to think with insufficient thoroughness and precision, rather than being fundamentally incapable of the required course of thought. Some instructional programs may be roughly characterized as efforts to foster thorough, precise thinking in general.

Cognitive style usually is considered a pervasive trait, equally relevant to encoding, operations, or goals. In principle, however, it is possible that some individuals might be less precise, thorough, or inventive with one of these factors than with the others. According to research by Getzels and Csikszentmihalyi (1976), thorough attention to goals is a characteristic that distinguishes more from less creative thinkers.

Know-how, in contrast to style, concerns what sorts of encoding, operations, or goals the thinker is able to apply in various situations. Effectiveness is seen as a strategic matter, a matter of knowing what to do when. Siegler (1981), for example, argues that encoding suffers not from a general lack of thoroughness, something that could be considered a matter of cognitive style, but from failing to distinguish between relevant and irrelevant features in particular instances. Nisbett and Ross (1980) identify a number of problems in reasoning that could be ascribed to the absence of appropriate reasoning heuristics and goals that reflect the realities of probabilistic inference. As these examples suggest, problems of know-how can arise in association with encoding, operations, or goals.

Other authors emphasize cognitive load as the factor that limits performance. If only the thinker had sufficient working memory and other capacities, cognitive style and appropriate know-how would take care of themselves, at least to a considerable extent. Case (1981), for example, describes experiments suggesting that increases in cognitive capacity are responsible for the improvement of performance on Piagetian tasks with age. When children were taught strategies for decreasing cognitive load, they were able to master tasks that otherwise would have been beyond them. Bereiter (1980) and Flower and Hayes (1980) argue that cognitive load is the single most important reason why writing proves to be such a difficult task for youngsters. The activity requires doing several things at once, and until some of these activities are automated, the learner cannot manage the whole performance very well.

There is yet another view of limiting factors that contrasts with all three of the foregoing: perhaps the ineffective thinker lacks the abilities required to perform well, or at all, some of the basic mental activities involved in encoding, operating on encoded representations, or monitoring progress toward the goal. Guilford's structure of intellect (Guilford & Hoepfner, 1971) identifies an array of operations on which more complex intellectual performances are assumed to be based. Deficits in any of these should limit the thinker. According to this view, reducing cognitive load, inducing a thorough, precise, inventive style, and supplying the right know-how in the form of procedures to fit the occasion will not suffice, simply because the person lacks the component abilities necessary to execute the procedures required. Meeker (1969), working from Guilford's theory, has developed an instructional program that provides exercises attuned to the individual student. The exercises are chosen to strengthen component mental abilities that testing shows to be weak in the student.

Here there is a temptation to conclude, as in the previous section, that any program designed to teach thinking skills in a comprehensive way needs to take all four of these aspects into account—style, know-how, cognitive load, and component abilities. However, to say that would be to miss some significant subtleties. Style seems complementary to the other three as well as important in its own right, and hence deserves attention in any program. However, many programs probably impart cognitive styles simply by virtue of the sorts of tasks and standards they pose, without style ever being mentioned as such.

As to cognitive load, for certain types of tasks it may be useful to teach strategies for reducing load. However, in general, increasing one's cognitive capacity appears to require maturation. At least, we know of no investigators who propose that cognitive capacity can be enhanced by any sort of "mind-stretching" exercises. Accordingly, the question to ask about an instructional program is not whether the program tries to increase cognitive capacity, but whether it takes account of and helps students to deal with whatever capacity limitations they may have.

Regarding know-how and abilities, we favor instruction based on know-how, for the following reasons. Virtually all substantive tasks appear to involve a significant strategic component. Accordingly, instruction based on improving constituent information processing abilities alone does not suffice. On the other hand, if one is teaching relevant know-how and providing practice in using it, whatever constituent abilities are involved will receive plenty of exercise in any case. In short, an abilities approach may be useful, but we would be less enthusiastic about a program based on abilities that does nothing explicit about know-how than we would be about a program based on know-how that does nothing explicit about underlying abilities.

Rule-Based versus Model-Based Behavior

Suppose a person does employ certain procedures, abide by certain goals, encode certain factors, manifest a certain cognitive style, use certain strategies to control cognitive load, and so on. The question remains what mechanism keeps people behaving in accordance with whatever principles they follow. Usually, we think of people as following rules—the rules of grammar, heuristic strategies, or whatever. Accordingly, instruction becomes, at least in part, a matter of teaching the appropriate rules.

Johnson-Laird (1981), writing on the nature of human reasoning, offers an alternative viewpoint, arguing that people reason in terms of models rather than by means of rules of inference. Roughly speaking, a person will construct an internal model of the world, and "run" it to find out what will happen in given circumstances. An alert thinker will attempt to construct alternative models or run the same model in alternative ways, to explore what consequences the initial conditions really force. The seeming observance of principles of inference does not reflect the application of principles as such, but the operation of the model manipulator. Accordingly, Johnson-Laird concludes, teaching rules of inference probably will do little to improve everyday reasoning, the power of which depends on the artful use of the models available to the reasoner.

Some support for this view comes from a recent experiment by Perkins, Allen, and Hafner (in press), who conducted an investigation of informal reasoning, collecting samples of arguments on social issues from over 300 subjects of widely varying degrees of education. The arguments were analyzed to determine the nature of the reasoning process and to define what kinds of lapses in reasoning occurred. The authors concluded that, by and large, the reasoning process could not be considered one of manipulating logical structures, nor could the lapses be considered lapses in formal reasoning. Instead, the subjects were best viewed as evolving models of the situations under discussion. The most common lapses were failures to test or elaborate the model in various ways. For instance, subjects overlooked counterexamples or alternative causal chains that might lead to different consequences.

The same interpretation could apply to many other aspects of effective thinking besides principles of inference. For example, to a considerable extent the management of cognitive load depends not on increased capacity but on larger chunks—models, as it were—in terms of which more can be done with the same cognitive capacity (cf. Simon & Chase, 1973). Similarly, the strategies that skilled mathematicians use (Polya, 1952 a, b, 1957) include attention to diagrams and to similar problems solved previously, both models in different senses. The importance of analogical models in scientific thinking—the atom as a miniature solar system or a gas as a swarm of small elastic balls—is well attested to by history. We find this a persuasive argument that instruction in terms of bare rules and formal systems is likely to be less effective than instruction that emphasizes models and their use. Of course, many programs designed to enhance thinking skills do use models and encourage thinking in terms of models, whether those programs are described as doing so or not. However, it is also our impression that many programs could encourage thinking in terms of models more than they do. The opportunities are numerous—diagrams, mental imagery, analogies, use of mental simulations, paradigmatic cases and limiting cases, to name a few.

Implicit and Explicit Know-How

Sometimes it is held that rules, models, or other possible factors that contribute to thinking limit performance when they are too explicit and consciously controlled. Only when such elements become automated can the thinker proceed effectively. Furthermore, effective performance may not even develop by way of explicit elements that become automated. Acquisition may occur implicitly in the first place. The most familiar example of this is initial language learning, whereby the child acquires a "working knowledge" of syntax without ever explicitly knowing the rules. Some advocates of the audiolingual method of language instruction hold that this serves best for second language learning, too. The learner should simply drill with the language and assimilate the rules covertly.

However, others maintain the opposite position. Some contemporary research on second language learning suggests that explicit learning of the rules leads to more rapid mastery (Smith & Baranyi, 1968; Von Elek & Oskarsson, 1973). Where thinking skills are concerned, Campione and Armbruster (1981) hold that many instructional efforts fall short in leaving to the students the job of implicitly or explicitly abstracting the general principles from the exercises they must do. Often, these authors suggest, when the instruction does not make the principles explicit for students, the students fail to abstract them in any form, implicit or explicit.

According to some, explicit know-how in the form of a procedure to be followed by rote may not suffice. The Piagetian position emphasizes that formal operational thinkers appreciate the compelling necessity of the rules they follow. The individual who is taught to follow such rules by rote behaves quite differently from the one who genuinely understands the operations involved. While the former's belief in the rule may falter under various pressures, the latter's will not, because he perceives its necessity.

Klausmeier (1980) adopts a related position regarding what he calls "process concepts." Process concepts are concepts that allow not only identification of instances versus noninstances, but also execution of the process the concept represents. For example, *observing, inferring*, and *predicting* are process concepts important in *Science: A Process Approach*, the program (See Chapter 6 of this book) that Klausmeier uses as a context for testing his theory. Klausmeier maintains that, although students can learn to execute rote procedures relating to such concepts, the most effective performance comes only when they can distinguish instances from noninstances, list criteria, and otherwise deal with process concepts in a formal way. Klausmeier provides some experimental evidence consistent with the position that instruction designed to enhance the formal grasp of process concepts increases students' ability to use the concepts in practice, although the gains might simply reflect the considerably greater instructional time on problems of a similar kind.

We know of no writer who advocates outright that lack of understanding is preferable to understanding. However, many authors concerned with the nature of thinking skills and instruction designed to improve thinking skills place no particular stress on a refined understanding of the rationale behind the skills. Rather, a certain repertoire of recipes is to be learned, much as addition or subtraction are often learned as rote procedures.

Certainly the options presented above can be debated. However, in the balance we are inclined to think that instruction built around explicit presentation of rules and models, and instruction which conveys an appreciation of their motivation, is to be preferred over implicit or rote instruction. We see no evidence that in general students learn more slowly by the former route; if anything, they learn faster. Furthermore, instruction designed in such a way has a clear content that facilitates evaluating, comparing, and improving programs.

Generality versus Context-Boundedness

Perhaps the single most controversial question regarding skilled thinking is this: To what extent is there such a thing as generally skilled thinking versus thinking that is skilled in various specific contexts? Very likely, the power of principles of thinking varies inversely with their generality. The more general the rule, the less leverage the rule provides in any specific application. Various studies of performance in particular problem domains argue persuasively that expertise depends on a collection of schemata specific to the domain (Larkin, 1981; Simon & Chase, 1973). Siegler (1981), in his studies of encoding, concludes that encoding difficulties vary from situation to situation. As discussed earlier, many writers now find Piaget's position—that there are general overarching formal operations—to be wanting, and see instead development of skills within each performance domain. Such positions as these argue that skilled thinking encounters the ultimate limit of context-boundedness: there are no or few general skills of thinking to be learned, only expertise within particular domains.

However, other views balance these. Baron (1981) and other writers point out that cognitive style traits seem reasonable candidates for an important component of skilled thinking that cuts across fields. Certainly below-par academic performers seem to suffer from bad habits of attending that limit their performance in a general way.

Also, no matter to what extent experts may depend on a repertoire of schemata in handling routine problems, they must spend much of their time working at the edge of their competence on fresh types of problems not so well covered by their repertories. It may be that there, general principles, which admittedly are not that powerful in comparison with the more particular knowledge and skills applicable to specific familiar problems, make the difference between skilled and unskilled performance. They are all that the expert has to fall back on.

Also, although the more powerful principles may be somewhat context-bound, there may be few enough contexts each covering enough ground so that the concept of general thinking skills is not empty. If there are powerful principles specific to, say, probabilistic reasoning, mathematical problem solving, writing, and other such performance domains, then perhaps skillful thinking would be fostered by ingraining the appropriate principles in a dozen or so key domains (Perkins, 1981).

In summary, the accumulating evidence that skilled thinking is often more context bound than one might suppose cannot be ignored. This sounds a warning that efforts to teach very general know-how may not help students as much as one would like. It sounds another warning that people can easily deceive themselves about the generality of skills exercised by instruction. For instance, lessons thought to improve writing may only enhance short story narrative writing; lessons thought to improve reasoning may only facilitate formal deductive inference, and so on.

At the same time, however, there are arguments for the general importance of cognitive style and the existence of know-how of moderate generality and significant utility. What remains uncertain is how much such know-how empowers the thinker. We suspect we are talking about a potential gain more than negligible but short of spectacular. Indefinite though that is, it is sufficient to say that such instruction should be pursued.

In this discussion, we have defined several dimensions that characterize different ways in which thinking might be limited. Taken together, the dimensions make room for the theoretical positions of a number of contemporary investigators. To summarize, instruction might need to supply: (1) better encoding, operations or goals; (2) cognitive style, know-how, cognitive load, or component information-processing abilities; (3) formal rules or models; (4) implicit or explicit guidance; (5) general or context-bound guidance.

We suggest that, in the balance, efforts to teach thinking skills ought to address all three of the aspects—encoding, operations, and goals. Also, such efforts should have an impact on know-how and cognitive style; cognitive load and component information processing abilities are less clearly improvable. Efforts to teach thinking should encourage thinking in terms of models rather than rule systems when possible, and should stress explicit over implicit guidance. Finally, inasmuch as extremely general know-how and pervasive cognitive style may help significantly but not powerfully in specialized contexts, know-how should be provided that is appropriate to important specialized contexts, for instance, mathematical problem solving or writing.

These preferences are not sufficient grounds in themselves for rejecting programs that do not match some of them or for wholeheartedly approving those that match all of them. Quality and quantity of exercises, clarity of objectives, the degree to which a program motivates students and fosters productive attitudes, are among other factors that are likely to influence the effectiveness of a program. Nonetheless, the preferences noted provide a rough guide that may be useful to keep in mind in considering efforts to teach thinking skills.

6. CAN THINKING SKILLS BE TAUGHT?

Crutchfield (1969) suggests that the neglect of the teaching of thinking skills is due to two ill-founded assumptions: (1) that these skills cannot be taught, and (2) that they need not be taught. Evidence is accumulating, Crutchfield claims, that both assumptions are wrong: high-level thinking skills can be improved by training, and it is not safe to assume that such skills will emerge automatically as a matter of development or maturation.

The alternative to the assumption that thinking skills can be taught is the assumption that thinking ability is innate and not subject to modification by training. According to the latter view, the purpose of education should be to provide students with a great deal of information. Those with the intelligence to assimilate it and use it effectively will do so; those without it will not. Or perhaps more adaptively, the goal should be to expose students to that type and amount of information that they are able to assimilate and use, given their individual intellectual endowments.

Our own position on the question of whether thinking skills can be taught is strongly biased by two considerations: the first involves a form of Pascal's wager, and the second relates to the notion of unactualized potential.

With respect to the first consideration: Let us suppose, for the moment, that it is impossible to tell whether the assertion that thinking skills can be taught is true or false. One could then be wrong in either of two ways: by believing it to be true when it is really false, or by believing it to be false when it is really true. In our view, one of these mistakes is greatly preferable to the other. The assumption that thinking skills can be taught, if they cannot, should, at worst, lead to unsuccessful attempts to teach them. In time the futility of the quest would become apparent, and the only loss would be the effort that had been devoted to the task. But suppose we reject the assumption that thinking skills can be taught when in fact it is true. How profound might be the consequences of failing to attempt to teach what so obviously should be taught.

With respect to the issue of unactualized potential: We begin with the assumption that potential cannot develop in a vacuum, but that its development must be stimulated. Further, we assume that very few people develop anything close to the full potential they have. Finally, while we believe that people do differ with respect to potential, we suspect that these differences are small relative to differences in accomplishments. We cannot support this suspicion empirically, but we can perhaps make it plausible with another reference to the acquisition of psychomotor skills.

People often ascribe the attainment of virtuoso or championship performance in the performing arts or athletics to a combination of extraordinary native ability and single-minded adherence—over many years—to an extremely demanding training discipline. We have in mind the type of skill that is displayed by a Jascha Heifetz with a violin, by a Van Cliburn at the piano, and by a Nadia Comaneci on the horizontal bars. Clearly, individuals who do attain virtuoso or championship skill levels differ as a group from the rest of us in terms of the amount of time they spend developing their virtuosity. It is equally clear that the acquisition of such skills must depend on the existence of certain native capacities or potentialities. What is *not* so clear is whether these native capacities are unique to the virtuosos or are relatively common to most human beings.

We are touching upon an old bone of contention in psychology—the so-called "nature-nurture" question—and we want to speculate that the differences are perhaps not so great with respect to the former factor as with respect to the latter. To give some credence to that speculation, we would suggest that anyone who can talk has demonstrated beyond any doubt the capacity to acquire an extremely complex psychomotor skill. It is not clear that any of the skills alluded to above—impressive as it may be—demands much more of the organism than does the nearly universal but immensely complex skill of speech. Speech fails to amaze us only because nearly everybody talks. Skill on the violin would undoubtedly also amaze us less if everyone had it. Perhaps the difference between violin playing and talking is not that the former is more difficult to learn than is the latter, but rather that almost everybody gets the enormous amount of practice needed to acquire and maintain the latter skill, but not the former. This is not hard to understand: The ability to talk has considerable survival value for a human being, whereas most of us manage reasonably well as musical incompetents.

If anyone doubts that speech is an acquired skill, he need only familiarize himself with the immense difficulty that prelingually deaf children have in learning to talk. These are children whose speech production apparatus is perfectly normal, but who, because of deafness, have been unable to take advantage of the auditory feedback that hearing children use to determine how close their speech production efforts are to the sounds that they are trying to make.

Regarding the claim that speech is a complex skill, consider what one must do with the speech-production apparatus to say a simple thing like "construct." One must, within a period of about a second, produce a string of nine phonemes, each of which requires a complex articulatory gesture determined by the positioning and behavior of several quasi-independent components of the speech production apparatus—jaw, lips, tongue tip, tongue body, vocal cords, velum. And the timing of the transitions from one articulatory posture to another must be quite precise if perceptual confusions are to be avoided. Furthermore, in order to talk intelligently and intelligibly one must be able to produce any given articulatory gesture in a large variety of contexts, indeed to modify the gestures to accommodate the context, and to be able to move smoothly from one gesture to another within rather precise time constraints and without thinking much about the process.

It has been estimated that an average speaker produces phonemes at the rate of about 12 per second in conversational speech. For whatever it is worth, this is approximately the rate at which a pianist would have to emit discrete responses (counting each combination of simultaneously struck keys as a discrete response) in order to play Chopin's Minute Waltz in one minute flat. (The more typical time is closer to two minutes.) We suspect, although we cannot substantiate the suspicion, that in terms of the complexity of the motor coordination that is involved, producing the phonemes is the more demanding task.

The point is this: It may be that people are rather alike not only in terms of their native capacities to acquire very complex skills, but also in terms of the complexity of the skills that they have acquired. Focusing on the differences between the Heifitzes, the Cliburns, the Comanecis and the rest of us is focusing on the tip of the iceberg. Perhaps the difference between the unusually skilled and the "average" human being is minuscule compared to the skill potential of the average human being, much of which, unfortunately, is never realized by most of us.

7. SUMMARY

It is reasonable, in our view, to think of thinking as a form of skilled behavior, after the tradition of Bartlett (1958). Doing so invites the drawing of parallels with other complex skills, and speculation regarding how much of what we know about the acquisition of motor skills is transferable to the cognitive domain. One parallel involves the distinction between general physical conditioning and fine-grained control of specific motor skills on the one hand and the distinction between habitual thoughtfulness and the application of specific cognitive skills that are appropriate to specific task situations on the other. Other parallels were also drawn.

We noted the interdependence of thinking and knowledge. Clearly the substance of thought, if not the process of thinking, is constrained by what one knows. Thinking means thinking about something. Indeed, as Papert (1980) has reminded us, even thinking about thinking requires thinking about thinking about something. The vast majority of people who have made great and original contributions to their fields have not only been effective thinkers, they have known a lot about their areas; their heads have contained, as it were, much food for thought. The objective of teaching thinking skills should not be viewed, therefore, as in opposition to that of teaching conventional content, but as complementary to it. Thinking ability and knowledge are the warp and woof of intellectual competence, and the development of either to the neglect of the other will produce a less than superb fabric.

We noted also that many writers have distinguished two types of thinking, one characterized by such descriptors as analytic, deductive, rigorous, constrained, convergent, formal, and critical, and the other by synthetic, inductive, expansive, unconstrained, divergent, informal, diffuse, and creative. An implication of this distinction is that efforts to teach thinking skills should take cognizance of both types. That is not to suggest that there is no place for approaches that emphasize only the one type or the other, but they should be viewed as focusing on a limited aspect of the general problem.

We considered the question of what limits thinking and organized a tentative answer around five sets of concepts: (1) where limits appear—in encoding, operations, or goals; (2) what sorts of limits appear—limits in cognitive style, know-how, encoding of situations, or cognitive abilities; (3) whether thinking is best guided by complex rule systems such as the rules of logic or by mental models; (4) whether rules and models are best exercised implicitly, or explicitly and consciously; and (5) the reciprocal limits of the weakness that comes from lack of specificity in very general know-how, and the weakness that comes from lack of breadth in specific know-how that serves a particular context powerfully.

With these limits in mind, we suggested that ideally instruction to enhance thinking skills should address all three of the aspects—encoding, operations, and goals; concentrate on fostering cognitive style and know-how; focus on mental models more than rule systems when possible; emphasize explicit over implicit models and rules; and teach both general, although perhaps not very powerful know-how, and specific powerful, know-how for important kinds of thinking situations.

Can thinking skills be taught? Or, more importantly, can they be learned? Of course analogies prove nothing; however, one of the reasons we find the analogy between thinking skills and motor skills attractive is our belief that, like the latter, the former can indeed be taught, practiced, and learned. This does not mean that there is nothing innate about intellectual potential, or that all individuals could develop the same degree of intellectual competence if only given the same training experience. We do strongly suspect, however, that most people have the potential to develop far more effective thinking skills than they do, and that the disparity between the potential and what is typically actualized is so great that the question of genetically-based differences is, in most cases, of secondary importance. If our conjecture is false, it is not demonstrably false at present. Indeed, as we discuss in Part II, there are a number of encouraging findings. In any case, the mere possibility that thinking skills might be taught dictates that efforts to teach them should be made. If we try, and discover that it cannot be done, the cost is only a bit of wasted effort. If it can be done, but we choose not to try, the cost, in wasted intellectual potential, could be enormous.

4 Problem Solving, Creativity, and Metacognition

The literature dealing with thinking is immense. An attempt at even a cursory review of all of it is well beyond our level of aspiration in this book. Certain aspects of thinking seem to have attracted more attention among researchers than others, however, and research activities have tended to cluster around certain topics. Four of these are of particular interest in a discussion of teaching thinking: problem solving, creativity, metacognition, and reasoning.

This partitioning of the subject matter should not be taken as evidence that we consider these topics to be independent or that we espouse a view of thinking that recognizes these and only these components. There is, however, an identifiable literature on each of these topics, so this partitioning reflects one that already exists, and we adopt it as a matter of convenience. In this chapter, we consider the first three topics in turn. In the chapter that follows, we focus on reasoning, and in particular, on the various ways in which reasoning often proves to be deficient.

1. PROBLEM SOLVING

In this section we review selectively research on problem solving and the teaching of problem-solving skills. Particular attention is given to several writers who have explicitly considered how to improve problem-solving skills in a general way.

What is Problem Solving?

The term problem solving, as used in the psychological literature, usually refers to behavior and thought processes directed toward the performance of some intellectually demanding task typified by the following examples:

1. Substitute the ten decimal digits for the ten different letters in the following three words so that the sum is correct.

   Given: D = 5

   ```
    DONALD
   +GERALD
   -------
    ROBERT
   ```

2. Imagine a common sixty-four square checkerboard from which two squares, one from each of two diagonally opposite corners, have been cut out. Suppose you had thirty-one dominos, each of which would cover exactly two squares of the checkerboard. Determine whether it is possible to arrange the dominos in such a way that all sixty-two squares are covered.
3. Consider two containers, A and P. Suppose A has in it 10 ounces of water from the Atlantic Ocean, while P contains an equal amount of water from the Pacific. Suppose that 2 ounces of Atlantic water are removed from container A and put into P. After the liquid in P is mixed thoroughly, 2 ounces of the mixture are removed and added to the contents of container A. Which container now has the greater amount of foreign water, the Atlantic water being foreign to P, and the Pacific to A?
4. Figure 4.1 shows a simple and familiar children's puzzle. Fifteen squares, numbered 1 to 15, are arranged in a 4 × 4 array leaving one empty position. The problem is to rearrange the squares so that the numbers are in some specified order, for example, 1 through 4, across the first row, 5 through 8 across the second, etc. The array is so constructed that the only admissible change that one can effect in a single move is that of interchanging the hole with one of the squares adjacent to it.

One may question whether these problems are representative of those confronted in our day-to-day lives, and whether techniques effective with the former will be so with the latter. Is it reasonable to assume that procedures that are useful in to solving problems such as those described above will apply to such problems as diagnosing why an automobile will not start, finding one's way to a new destination, budgeting one's time and finances, organizing one's thoughts for a paper or talk, finding a job, writing a computer program, and staying sane? There is room for a range of opinions here. The important point, for present purposes, is that these problems are representative of those used to study problem solving in the laboratory. We do assume that such problems have some properties in common with those encountered outside the laboratory, and that

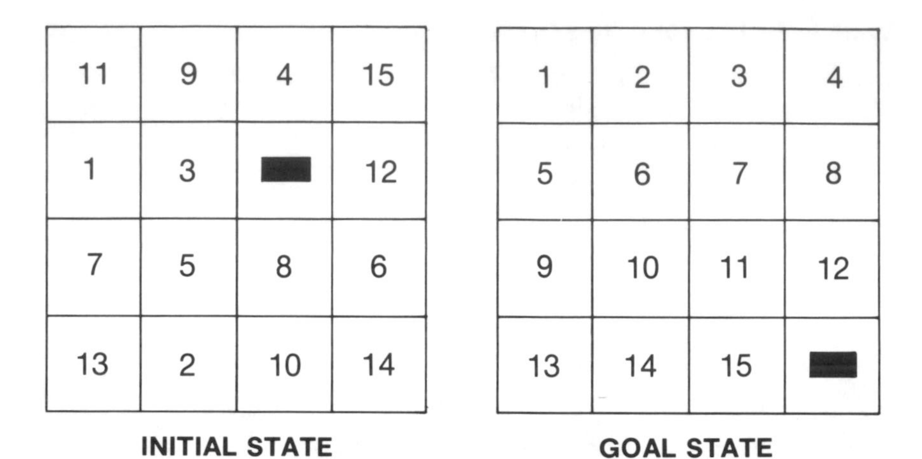

FIG. 4.1. The 15-square puzzle. See Nilsson (1971) for an analysis of this problem and a state-space search approach to solution.

approaches that work well in the one context are likely also to have some utility in the other.

Problems differ both in difficulty and in the nature of the skills required to solve them. Both jigsaw puzzles and crossword puzzles can be made arbitrarily simple or complex; however, they differ considerably with respect to the intellectual demands they place on the problem solver. The jigsaw puzzle is primarily a visual search task that requires an ability to remember and match visual patterns. Good visual memory and pattern-matching capabilities are of little value to the doer of crossword puzzles, however; the need here is for a rich store of associatively linked verbal concepts and an ability to spell.

Problems also differ in terms of how apparent an appropriate approach to solving them may be. Consider, for example, problems 1 and 2 above. Each is sufficiently difficult that the reader is likely to need a few minutes to solve it. However, most readers will know immediately how to attack the first; whereas many will not have any clear idea as to how to approach the second. In the first case, one begins a series of inferences of the sort: inasmuch as D equals 5, T must equal 0; and since there is a carry into the next column, R must be an odd number; furthermore, from the leftmost column it can be seen that R must be greater than 5 (inasmuch as D is 5), so it must be either 7 or 9, ... One assumes that persistence in this type of behavior will eventually reveal the value of every letter. The approach to the problem is apparent, and for most people it probably would not even involve a conscious choice.

(The problem is taken from Bartlett, 1958, and has been extensively used in the work of Newell & Simon, 1972; both sources contain step-by-step accounts of several attempts—both successful and unsuccessful—to solve it.)

In contrast, what would be an effective approach to the second problem is not at all obvious. One might try visualizing various configurations of dominos on the board, but probably would give this up in frustration, failing to find a configuration that works, and also not being able to demonstrate that there is no such configuration. It is in fact not possible to cover the board exactly with thirty-one dominos and the demonstration of this is shorter and easier to follow than the solution of the DONALD + GERALD problem. Seeing the method for solving this problem is almost tantamount to solving it. The required insight is that two diagonally opposite corners are the same color. Therefore, when they are eliminated the board has two more squares of one color than of the other. And, inasmuch as there is no way to cover two squares of the same color with a single domino, there is no way that thirty-one dominos can be used to cover the entire board.

The A&P problem (Problem 3) described above has already been considered (Chapter 2) in the context of a discussion of insight. We mention it here again to make the point that a problem sometimes can be solved in radically different ways. Both of the solutions that were given for this problem are correct; they differ, however, in some important respects. The first, or analytic, approach is somewhat laborious, and it produces a solution that suffices to answer the specific question that was asked, but does not generalize readily to related cases. Moreover, the answer that is obtained seems to lack intuitive force; one's belief in its accuracy rests on one's confidence that the sequence of calculations was performed without error. The appeal of the approach is its obviousness; tracking the results of the individual transactions seems like a reasonable way to figure out the ultimate outcome of any series of transactions.

The second approach produces a solution that has considerable generality. It holds no matter how thoroughly the mixtures are mixed, and no matter how many exchanges between containers are made. It applies beyond the immediate problem to a whole class of problems that share the critical constraint that the containers begin and end with the same amount of liquid. The drawback to the approach is that people typically do not think to look at the problem this way. Something of an insight seems to be required. Indeed, not everyone is able to see the problem from this perspective even when it is explained to them.

Problem 4 will be considered presently in a discussion of problem solving by computer.

The Identification of Problem-Solving Strategies

It seems safe to assume that most nontrivial problems can be approached in a variety of ways. Some approaches work; some do not. Among those that do succeed, some are more efficient than others.

Investigators have used two quite different methods for identifying effective problem-solving strategies that work. One has been to study the performance of experts; the other has involved attempts to give problem-solving abilities to computers.

Study of Expert Performance. Among the less surprising findings from research on problem solving is the fact that experts differ from novices in their problem-solving performance; not only are experts generally more effective, but their performance is qualitatively different. Of greater interest than the fact that differences exist, however, is the nature of those differences. Several investigators have studied differences between expert and novice performance in the hope of discovering what might be done to help transform novices into experts. Much of this work has focused on strategies.

Schoenfeld (1980), for example, notes that expert mathematicians are not only more likely to be able to solve mathematical problems than non-experts but that they approach the problems in qualitatively different ways. Experts apply strategies that novices either do not know or sometimes know but fail to apply when they should. Such strategies include: (a) For complex problems with many variables, consider solving an analogous problem with fewer variables. Then try to exploit either the method or the result of that solution. (b) Given a problem with an integer parameter n, calculate special cases for small n and look for a pattern.

Probably few people would question the merits of studying the behavior of experts in order to learn how to behave like an expert in a particular area of expertise. It does not follow, however, that observing expert behavior is a good way to learn about strategies that are applicable across different domains. The idea that the study of how experts solve problems is a useful way to identify *generally* effective problem-solving strategies involves the assumption that experts apply such strategies across domains. If the assumption is valid, we would expect to find a considerable degree of commonality in at least some of the strategies used by experts, independently of their areas of expertise.

There are, perhaps, two types of expertise that should be distinguished. There is the expertise that is based on knowing a lot about a subject area; there can be no question of the importance of domain-specific knowledge for problem solving. The second kind of expertise relates to the ability to manage one's intellectual resources and to use whatever domain-specific knowledge one has most effectively. Schoenfeld (1983 a, b) has emphasized the latter type of expertise. He suggests that expert problem solvers are better at problem solving generally than are novices even when they are dealing with problems outside their areas of domain-specific expertise. In particular, what they are better at is managing their resources. Without denying the importance of domain-specific knowledge, Schoenfeld argues that the quality and success of problem solving are also very much dependent on the presence or absence of effective management behavior. The second type of expertise is particularly important when the first type is lacking. In Schoenfeld's words, "it is precisely when the expert's problem-solving schemata (or 'productions') do not work well that the managerial skills serve to constitute expertise" (1983 a, p. 39).

Experts are more likely than novices to conduct an "executive review" of a process in which they are engaged, perhaps especially when the process seems to be getting bogged down. It appears that experts have "monitors" that trigger such reviews, whereas novices do not. It is almost as though the expert has developed the ability to assume simultaneously the roles of doer and observer. He works on solving the problem, and watches himself critically as he does so. The observer role is not a passive one but rather that of an overseer, critic, director, who sets goals, continually evaluates performance, and redirects it as necessary. (We return to these types of notions in Chapter 10.)

One difficulty associated with the study of expert performance in order to obtain insights to guide instruction is that there is no guarantee that the most important aspects of the expert's performance will be visible to the observer. Self management or control processes of the type emphasized by Schoenfeld, for example, typically are invisible in the classroom. And when a student sees a teacher explain a problem, he sees the results of the teacher's thinking but seldom witnesses the thought process itself. That is to say, the teacher typically has thought the problem through before explaining it to the students. Polya (1954 a) makes a similar point in noting that mathematics textbooks present the logic of mathematics by way of elegant well-structured theorems or proofs but seldom reveal much about the often messy ways in which those proofs were originally discovered. That is, they show much about the logic of mathematics but very little about the psychology of doing mathematics. Thus, while observing the performance of experts is an obvious way to investigate what constitutes expertise, it is essential to bear in mind that much of what is most important may be very difficult to see.

As a counterpoint to the idea that expert behavior is the best place to look for generally useful strategies, Scriven (1980) has distinguished sharply between the goal of producing descriptive theories of how people go about solving problems and the development of prescriptive approaches to problem solving. He rejects the notion that descriptive theories are either necessary or sufficient to the development of useful prescriptions. Moreover, he argues strongly for the application of more resources to the objective of prescription. It is possible, he believes, to learn and teach something useful about problem solving without fully understanding how people naturally go about performing problem-solving tasks.

Our own attitude on this question is that the study of expert performance is indeed an effective way to identify generally useful problem-solving strategies, but not the only one. The point that prescriptive approaches need not be descriptive of the approaches that people take spontaneously is well taken. Conversely, descriptions of how people, including experts, spontaneously approach problems are not always assured of providing the best bases for the development of prescriptions for success. Decision theorists and investigators of human decision making have made a sharp distinction between prescriptive and descriptive models of decision making, and the large empirical literature in this area documents the many ways in which actual decision making falls short of the optimality represented in prescriptive models. It would be surprising if what had proven true in decision making would not hold also, at least to some degree, in other areas of cognitive performance as well.

Programming Computers to Perform Problem-Solving Tasks. An approach to the identification, or invention, of strategies that need not start with descriptions of strategies that people use is that of trying to program computers to perform intellectually demanding tasks. To be sure, these attempts have often tried to represent in computer programs the strategies that people, and in particular experts, use, but this is not an essential aspect of the approach. The goal is to develop a program that will perform some particular task—play master-level chess, prove mathematical theorems, diagnose medical problems, write poetry—and produce the desired results—skillful play, proved theorems, diagnoses, interesting poetry. Except for the investigator who wishes to use such programs as descriptive models of human behavior, whether the program uses the same strategies as do people to accomplish these objectives is of secondary concern; the critical issue is whether the approaches that are built into the program—whatever they are—work and yield the desired results.

Larkin (1980) identifies a few general problem-solving strategies that appear repeatedly in computer programs that are useful in solving logic and arithmetic puzzles and in some aspects of playing chess. These include: (1) means-ends analysis, which involves determining the difference between the current state of knowledge about a problem and the state required to produce a solution, and selecting some action that will reduce the difference between these two knowledge states; (2) the kind of planning that involves replacing the original problem with a simplified version that retains only its central features, solving this abstracted problem and using its solution to guide the search for a solution to the original problem; and (3) the replacement of temporarily unattainable goals with simpler sub-goals. Larkin suggests that there is some evidence to indicate that these strategies are useful not only for well-defined tasks such as puzzles and games but also for solving problems of the types found in classroom mathematics and science.

The problem represented in Figure 4.1 is useful for illustrating some concepts that have emerged from attempts to develop computer programs that can engage in "intelligent" problem solving behavior. It also can be used to illustrate how one's approach to solving a problem is conditioned by how one represents it. We discuss this problem at some length, not because we are interested in problem solving by computers per se, but because of our belief that some of the concepts and methods from the literature on computer problem solving, or machine intelligence more generally, may facilitate our understanding of human problem solving as well.

Usually a problem can be represented in a variety of ways; however, some will be more suggestive than others of a path to a solution. The representation that one chooses will influence strongly the way in which one thinks about a problem and the strategy that one uses to try to solve it. As many writers on problem solving have noted, sometimes when one is having unusual difficulty with a problem, the most effective thing one can do is to attempt to find a radically different way of representing it.

A useful way of representing some problems is in terms of a "state space." This type of problem representation has been discussed at length by Nilsson (1971) who points out that to use it one must specify three things: "(a) the form of the state description, and, in particular, the description of the initial state, (b) the set of operators and their effects on state descriptions, and (c) the properties of goal state description" (p. 22).

The number-square problem described above (and analyzed by Nilsson) is readily represented in this way. Every possible configuration of numbers within the square is a state; any configuration can be an initial state; and the desired configuration is the goal state. The board is changed from one state to another by the operation of interchanging the hole with one of the numbers adjacent to it. Thus, there are four operators in this representation, corresponding to whether the hole is filled by the number above it, below it, to the left of it, or to the right of it. Any sequence of operations that transforms an initial state into a goal state is a solution of the problem, and the intermediate states that result from this sequence of operations are said to lie on a solution path. The objective of the problem solver is to find a solution path that has an acceptably small number of steps.

The state-space representation often may help the problem solver to solve the problem. But it has a significance beyond that: it is of interest to the theoretician as a general way of formulating what a problem is. Problems radically different from this relatively well defined one can be discussed in terms of a state space representation. Consider, for example, the very open-ended problem of writing a poem. One can take the states to be configurations of words on the page, with the initial state the blank page. The operations are additions or deletions of words. Goal states are determined by the "black box" of the poet's judgment. The poet's task is to generate a series of operations that leads him to a goal state.

Clearly this representation is not much of a "how to do it" guide to poetry writing. Too much of that art is buried in the knack for generating appropriate operations and the "black box" of the poet's judgment. Nonetheless, as a framework for discussing problems in general, the state-space representation still proves useful. This becomes more apparent as we explore the various characteristic dilemmas and tactics of problem solving in the context of a state space representation. These dilemmas and tactics—the limitations of exhaustive search, combinatorial explosions, the need for restricted search, evaluation functions, the role of heuristics, and so on—apply as much to poetry writing as to number-square problems.

In many kinds of problems, parsimony is important: a short solution path is wanted. One way to guarantee finding the shortest solution path would be to explore all possible paths and select the shortest one that terminates in a goal state. This strategy is called *exhaustive search*. One might develop an exhaustive solution tree by beginning with a node representing the initial state and branching to each of the states that could be realized by application of one of the four admissible operators. Each of these nodes could be expanded in turn, again by application of each of the operators, and the process continued until one or more goal states is reached. Nilsson distinguishes between breadth-first and depth-first search methods: the former expands nodes in the order in which they occur; the latter follows some branches all the way to termination before other branches are expanded at all.

For all but the most trivial problems, exhaustive search is possible in theory only; the number of paths that could be generated is too large to make such an approach practicable. It may make sense, however, to conduct a search that is limited in one or more ways. For example, only a fraction of the nodes of a tree might be expanded, or the expansion might be carried only a limited number of steps ahead. Obviously, such *restricted search* and limited look-ahead procedures will be no better than the rules that are used to distinguish promising nodes for expansion and for evaluating the intermediate states at the end of the look-ahead.

The rules and measures that are used for narrowing a search and for evaluating intermediate states are referred to as *evaluation functions*. Usually they assess the similarity of an intermediate state to a goal state, and typically they are developed empirically, often by a combination of guesswork and trial and error exploration. Consider, for example, the problem of the 8-tiles puzzle, which is identical to the 15-tiles puzzle above except that the square is 3×3 instead of 4×4. One plausible evaluation function for this puzzle is the number of tiles that are in the wrong place (or the number of those in the right place). In general, one would expect (although one cannot be sure) that a solution would be more easily found for a configuration that had many tiles in their goal-state positions than one that had few there. Another possible evaluation function is the sum of the distances from each tile to its goal-state destination. An even better function for evaluation, as it turn out, is $P(n) + 3S(n)$, where $P(n)$ is the sum of the distances from each tile to its destination, and $S(n)$ is the score obtained by assigning 2 for every non-central tile not followed by its proper successor, 0 for every other non-central tile, and 1 for a tile if it occupies the center position (Nilsson, 1971, p. 66). This evaluation function is not based on a theoretical analysis of the puzzle and has not been shown to be an optimal one. The justification for using it is that it works.

How does one know that this evaluation function works better than any other? One does not. Presumably, it works as well as any *known* function; otherwise, the better function would be used. But there is no guarantee that someone will not invent another function that improves upon the performance of this one.

More generally, we might ask how one tells how well any given search procedure works compared to other possibilities. The efficiency of any search technique depends both on the length of the solution path that it finds, compared to the minimum length possible, and on the cost (in terms of time and resources required) of finding that path. Sometimes, it is possible to specify the minimum length of a solution path analytically, in which case one can judge relative efficiency of the search technique directly. More often, the minimum path is not known, and one must then resort to a less direct means of assessment.

One measure that has been suggested for judging the power of a search technique is the ratio of the length of the solution path found to the total number of nodes generated during search. The measure is called *penetrance* (Nilsson, 1971). A large penetrance value (close to 1) is obtained when a search tree has few branches that are not in the solution path. This indicates an efficient search procedure. A small value is obtained if the tree is very bushy, indicating a blind, or at least a not very efficient, search.

There is no generally applicable procedure for generating evaluation functions. Indeed, what makes the whole area of problem solving by machine so intriguing to the researcher is the paucity of formal procedures (excepting the generally impractical exhaustive-search techniques) that are guaranteed to come up with problem solutions. There are, however, numerous methods, principles, and rules of thumb that work reasonably well in many instances. These approaches that are not guaranteed to work, but often do, are referred to as *heuristic procedures*, or simply *heuristics*.

Some Problem-Solving Heuristics

The word "heuristic," comes from the Greek *heuriskin*, meaning "serving to discover." It appears sporadically in the literature of philosophy and logic as the name of a branch of study dealing with the methods of inductive reasoning. Polya (1957), in his classic treatise on problem solving, used the word to connote inductive and analogical reasoning leading to plausible conclusions, as opposed to the deductive developments of rigorous proofs.

More recently the term has been used by researchers in the field of machine intelligence to sharpen a distinction between two types of procedures that can be realized as computer programs. One of these types of procedures, called an algorithm, is a step-by-step prescription for accomplishing a particular goal. By definition, an algorithm is guaranteed to accomplish what it is intended to accomplish. In contrast, a heuristic is only a good bet, a procedure believed to have a reasonable likelihood of yielding a solution, or at least of bringing one closer to a solution. But it is not guaranteed to work. Not surprisingly, heuristic procedures are used instead of algorithms either when an algorithmic solution to the problem is not known or execution of an algorithm is precluded for practical reasons (e.g., it would consume too much time or require too much in the way of resources). One oversimplifies only a little in saying that the general goal of research on problem solving by machine is the discovery or development of effective heuristic procedures. And, of course, the more generally applicable the heuristic discovered, the more successful the quest.

Problem solving by machine is not the focus of this book. The effort to develop general problem solving techniques that may be programmed on computers is relevant, however, to the task of teaching problem solving skills to human beings. A controversial question relating to this task is whether there are effective problem-solving strategies that are general enough to be applicable to a wide variety of problem types. Some investigators have argued that there probably are not, and that the best one can hope to do is to teach people how to deal with specific problems. To the extent that computer scientists are successful in developing heuristic procedures that prove to be effective across a variety of problem types, they will have demonstrated that the idea of effective general strategies is a valid one, and provided one good reason to assume that generally useful strategies might be taught to human problem solvers.

While many writers have discussed heuristics, and many computer scientists have developed programs that make use of heuristic approaches to solving complex problems, two treatments of the topic have been particularly influential, and consequently will be given special attention here. These are the treatments by Polya (1957) and by Newell and Simon (1972).

Polya's Work. Polya, himself a mathematician, was much interested in the teaching of mathematics, and his work on heuristics grew out of a desire to teach students that which would be of general use to them in solving different kinds of mathematical problems. Many of the heuristics he described are applicable more generally than to mathematics alone, however, and, not surprisingly, some thinking skills programs that we later consider are based on Polya's work. Polya's heuristics are most conveniently discussed within the framework of his prescriptive model of problem solving, which distinguishes four stages:

- Understand the problem.
- Devise a plan. This involves formulating a general strategy, not a detailed proof. Formulation of such a strategy is an inductive process, not a deductive one. This is important because Polya claims that, contrary to appearance, even mathematics is partly an inductive process.
- Carry out the plan. This is the detailed proof, and here is where deductive reasoning comes in.
- Look back, i.e., check your results.

Heuristics for representing or understanding the problem:

- Make sure you understand the *unknown*, the *data* (i.e., the *givens*), and the *conditions* that relate the data.

The use of terms such as *unknown* and *data* are particularly well suited for mathematical problems (Polya's main concern); but this heuristic may be stated more generally by using the computer-science terminology we introduced earlier:

- Make sure you understand the nature of the goal state, the initial state and the permissible operations.

The main purpose of this prescription is to insure that the problem solver has represented all the important aspects of the problem, and that he clearly understands the goal state.

- Draw a graph or diagram and introduce suitable notation.

The intent of this heuristic is to concretize the problem. Part of such concretization has to do with visual thinking: once a graph or diagram is drawn, the problem solver can bring perceptual processes to bear on it. Also, a visual representation of a problem can make apparent certain relations among parts that might otherwise go unnoticed. However, there is probably more to concretization than visualizing. Much work in cognitive psychology demonstrates that people understand text better when it is made more concrete even when they do not report using visual imagery. Moreover, Polya himself stresses the importance of notation, which is purely symbolic (as opposed to isomorphic, as is an image), and if symbolic notation facilitates problem solving, it probably does not do so via imagery.

Another general heuristic for understanding is:

- If one way of representing a problem does not lead to the solution, try to restate or reformulate the problem.

This heuristic highlights the importance of an appropriate problem representation. Every problem must be represented in *some* way, and how it is represented is very important. Sometimes a poor representation can inhibit or preclude a solution, and when one comes to an impasse in problem solving, one often does well to take a completely fresh and novel look at the problem—to attempt to view it from a different perspective.

Heuristics for devising a plan:

Most of Polya's heuristics in this category involve bringing to bear related problems that one already knows how to solve. Some examples follow.

- Think of a known problem that is structurally analogous to the present one and try to solve that.

Some psychologists have considered the ability to see similarities and to engage in analogical reasoning to be among the most reliable indicators of general intelligence. Hence it is not surprising that researchers in problem solving should emphasize this ability. But although the analogy heuristic can be powerful, it is not always easy to see the critical analogy between two problems. Indeed, recent work indicates that the surface form of a problem may have a substantial effect on how it is represented (e.g., Gick & Holyoak, 1980; Simon, 1979), and surface similarities or dissimilarities between two problems can obscure deeper relationships that may have greater significance.

- Think of a known problem that has the same kind of unknown but is simpler.

A common, and very effective, approach to problems in solid geometry is to solve an analogous problem in plane geometry and then try to generalize the method to the three-dimensional case. More generally, a useful heuristic for problems involving hyperspaces is to consider an analogous problem in a space of two or three dimensions so that the solution, or at least the problem, can be visualized. Often the solution that is found for the two- or three-dimensional problem readily generalizes to the space of higher dimensionality. The usefulness of reverting to plane or solid geometry may again be partly due to concretization. A closely related heuristic is:

- If you cannot solve the problem on which you are working, see if you can transform it into a problem whose solution you know.

Of course, whether this strategy is a reasonable one to try depends on how close the problem whose solution is known is to the problem you have to solve. (One form of this strategy is well known to students and used with abandon on the problem of taking exams: if you do not know the answer to a question on the exam, think of a question whose answer you do know, pretend that this is the question that was asked, and answer it. Sometimes the strategy works!)

The potential risk in the use of this strategy is apparent. Some writers have pointed out the danger of problem solvers "bending" problems so they can make use of the tools at their disposal (e.g., Stewart, 1976). This approach may constrain the problem solver to think about the problem in terms of the capabilities and limitations of available tools rather than in terms of the problem itself. Moreover, by bending a problem one may qualitatively change it so that one ends up solving a problem that one is able to solve but not the problem that was originally posed for solution. In spite of these caveats, however, there seems little doubt that the transform-the-problem heuristic can be effective in many cases.

- Simplify the problem by looking at special cases.

A good example of this heuristic is given in Polya's *Patterns of plausible inference* (1954b). There the heuristic is tailored to problems involving integer variables, for which it can be restated in the following more particularized form.

- Substitute specific values for the integer variable (e.g., 0,1, and 2) and see if any generalization appears; If it does, try to prove the generalization by mathematical induction.

Another way to implement this heuristic is to substitute extreme values (e.g., zero or infinity) for the unknowns, and see if a solution suggests itself.

- Make the problem more general, and see if you can solve that.

Our familiar A&P problem can be used to illustrate this heuristic. Recall that the solution involved an insight regarding the fact that what was missing from one container must have been replaced by an equal amount of liquid from the other one. This solution was more general than the more conventional solution, because it made the answer independent of the amount of liquid exchanged, the thoroughness of the mixing, and number of exchanges. As the problem was presented in Chapter 2, these facts came to light after the solution had been found. It would have been possible, however, to reverse the process and begin the search for a solution by intentionally generalizing the problem at the outset. In other words one might have begun by saying to oneself: Suppose half the contents of A were poured into P initially, and then an equal amount were poured back, or suppose that *all* the contents of A were poured into P and then half of the mixture were poured back. Or suppose the contents were poured back and forth several times. The hope is that generalizing the problem in one or another of these ways might evoke a solution. If a solution for a more general case is discovered, that solution should, of course, be applicable to the special case, unless in attempting to generalize the problem one changed it qualitatively. In any case, one can, and should, check any general solution against the specific problem to be sure it does indeed apply.

- Break the problem into parts. If the parts are not manageable, break those into smaller parts, continuing in this fashion until you arrive at problems of manageable size.

As Polya (1957) points out, this heuristic can be doubly beneficial: having solved a component problem, one can sometimes use both the method and the result of the simpler problem to solve the more difficult one. This heuristic seems to be a fore-runner to Newell and Simon's *Subgoal Analysis*, which is described later.

Heuristics for executing a plan:

In mathematical problems, which are Polya's main concern, this stage is the deductive one, so Polya offered no true heuristics here, except perhaps for "Check each step."

Heuristics for checking results:

Having found what appears to be a solution to a problem, there is a natural tendency to consider oneself done. The careful problem solver will not do that, however, but will look for ways to confirm the solution, or show it to be wrong, as the case may be. Heuristics for checking results include the following:

- Try to solve the problem a different way.
- Check the implications of your solution.

Finding a second way to solve a problem, and determining that it yields the same solution, obviously should increase one's confidence that the solution is correct. Checking the implications of a solution involves considering what else should be true if the solution is correct. This is a one-sided test, but useful nevertheless. That is, if one notes that if the solution is correct X must be true, then determining that X is true does not demonstrate conclusively that the solution is correct, but determining that X is false does demonstrate that the conclusion is incorrect. Determining that X is true may well increase one's confidence in the solution somewhat, however.

The Newell-Simon Approach. Newell and Simon (e.g., 1972) have been concerned with a broader domain than has Polya; essentially, they have attempted to use the methods of computer simulation to develop a general theory of human problem solving. Much of their work has focused on heuristics for solving mathematical problems and puzzles, however, and so is readily related to Polya's approach. In what follows, we discuss some of their heuristics within the context of Polya's 4-stage model. The material is taken mainly from Wickelgren (1974), who offers a lucid account of most of the Newell-Simon heuristics.

Heuristics for representing a problem:

- Draw inferences about the initial and goal states, and add them to your representation.

The idea here is to bring to bear as much of one's prior knowledge as possible on the task of representing the problem. Sometimes what can be inferred about initial states and goal states can fundamentally alter the character of a problem so that it becomes easy to solve. This seems to happen often with so-called *insight* problems: insight often amounts to a radical reorganization of the representation that simplifies the rest of the problem-solving process. A good example is the checkerboard problem mentioned earlier; here the critical insight hinges on the realization that the two missing squares must be the same color.

To discuss the next few heuristics, we again need the computer-science terminology introduced earlier. Recall that in this terminology, solving a problem involves applying to the initial state a sequence of operators that will yield the goal state. The intermediate states that result from these operations are said to lie on a solution path. The difficulty in solving many problems is this: when confronted with the initial state, several different operators can be applied, each leading to an intermediate state; and once at an intermediate state, several different operators can again be applied, yielding more intermediate states; and this sequence may be repeated many times before culminating in the goal state. Moreover, there are many possible paths emanating from the initial state only a few of which are likely to be solution paths, and an exhaustive search of all such paths typically is, for practical purposes, impossible. The heuristics that follow are essentially rough short-cuts for finding solution paths among the many possible alternatives.

Heuristics for devising a plan:

- Organize the paths into classes that are equivalent with respect to the final solution; then systematically try one sequence from each class.

Wickelgren (1974, pp. 49–51) illustrates the use of this heuristic in a "six-arrow" problem. The initial state is six arrows in a row, the left three pointing up, the right three pointing down; the goal state is six arrows in a row with an alternating sequence of up and down arrows. The only permissible operators are simultaneously to invert (turn upside down) any two adjacent arrows. In applying the Equivalence Class heuristic, Wickelgren first notes that the order in which any two operators are applied makes no difference, e.g., first inverting the third and fourth arrows and then inverting the fourth and fifth ones is equivalent to applying the two operators in the reverse order. This means that only unordered combinations need be considered, not ordered permutations. Wickelgren then notes that an optimal solution path will contain no more than one occurrence of a specific operator. For instance, if the third and fourth arrows were inverted twice, they would be back in their original position. These two observations mean that all solutions that differ only in the order in which their operators apply or only in how many times each operator is applied, can all be treated as members of the same (equivalence) class; since just one solution need be tried from each class, the consequence of these observations is to reduce greatly the number of solutions that must be considered.

The next heuristic goes as follows:

- Define an evaluation function over all states including the goal state; then, at any state, choose an operation to achieve a next state with an evaluation closer to that of the goal state.

Recall that an evaluation function essentially assesses the similarity of an intermediate state to the goal state. Hence we may paraphrase this heuristic by saying that at any choice point one should select that intermediate state that seems most similar to the goal state. This strategy is sometimes called *hill-climbing*.

Wickelgren shows how this hill-climbing heuristic can be applied to the six-arrow problem we just described, as well as to numerous other problems including the famous missionaries-and-cannibals problem (now often referred to as the *hobbits-and-orcs* problem). These applications illustrate two interesting points. First, successful use of the heuristic depends on coming up with a good evaluation function, which often seems to involve changing one's initial representation of the problem. Thus, it may sometimes be difficult to abide by Polya's distinction between the stage of representing the problem and that of devising a plan. Second, even with a viable evaluation function, some problems require the problem solver to apply at least one operator that temporarily decreases the similarity between the present intermediate state and the goal-state. This is called a *detour*, and the presence of a detour seems to be a major source of difficulty in human problem solving. (See Greeno's, 1974, and Thomas', 1974, studies of the hobbits-and-orcs problem; the one step in this problem that contains a detour is by far the most difficult step for the problem solver to take.)

Perhaps the most well-known heuristic in Newell and Simon's work (as in Polya's) is:

- Analyze a problem into subproblems, then solve each of these.

This is often referred to as *subgoal analysis*, and it seems to have the broadest applicability of any heuristic. By setting up subgoals one restricts attention to a limited number of solution paths in the problem space, so again the heuristic involves shortcutting search. Subgoal analysis can be applied to mundane problems (e.g., "What's the best route to take from Boston to Salt Lake City?"), as well as to standard mathematical puzzles (e.g., the Tower of Hanoi problem).

The remaining heuristics emphasize the goal state rather than the initial state.

- Work backwards from the goal to the initial state.

This is particularly useful when there are many possible operators that could be applied to the initial state (and hence many solution paths to be considered), but few operators that could lead from the last intermediate state to the goal state. In this case, the search of the problem space is more constrained when we start with the goal state.

- Assume the goal state is false, and show that this leads to a contradiction.

In mathematics, this is called the *method of indirect proof*. Sometimes considering what the implications would be if the goal were false suggests some fruitful operations to apply.

The heuristics developed by Newell and Simon, along with those of Polya, are among the best examples we have of general-purpose thinking skills, which is to say processes or approaches that seem applicable in many domains.

Some General Observations about Heuristics. Polya's heuristics were developed primarily with mathematical problems in mind. Those of Newell and Simon were motivated in large part by an interest in providing computers with the ability to solve intellectually demanding problems. Some of the problems in the latter case were mathematical in nature and some were not. However, all of them were relatively well defined and had precise identifiable solutions. Many of these problems were highly structured and more in the nature of puzzles or games than in that of the practical problem situations that people are likely to face in everyday life. It is reasonable to ask to what extent the heuristics developed in these contexts are likely to be applicable in other contexts as well.

It is clear that many of these heuristics are, or can be, stated in terms that are sufficiently general to be prima facie applicable to nearly any problem domain, e.g., find an effective way to represent the problem; break the problem into subproblems, then solve each of these. Moreover, the above heuristics have a great deal of face validity; one would be hard pressed to argue against them. However, stating principles in the abstract may be much easier than implementing or instantiating them in practice. For example, it is one thing to recognize the desirability of finding a way of representing a problem that facilitates the development of a solution. It is quite another thing to find that representation. In the *most* abstract form some of these heuristics are a bit reminiscent of the classical advice to investors to "buy low and sell high." It is obviously wonderful advice if only one knew how to follow it.

Probably, if training with respect to such heuristics is to be effective, it must focus not only on the heuristics themselves but on their implementation in a variety of contexts. Discussions of these principles by Polya, by Newell and Simon, and by others, always include examples of their application to specific problems. One might argue that it is the applications of the principles in context that are useful to the problem solver rather than the principles themselves.

However, even very general advice, such as "work backwards" or "divide the problem into subproblems," might have some point in a fresh problem domain. If a beginner cannot always apply such advice immediately, at least it might help to clarify the task of mastering the domain. That is, the beginner can ask himself, "What would a subproblem *be* here," or "what would it be like to work backwards?" While such questions might not solve any problems at the outset, having them in mind might help the learner to gauge progress and to seize opportunities when they occur.

It is clear the influence of computer science on researchers in the area of problem solving has been strong, and we think it has been a healthy one. Computer science provides a language that is rich enough to describe many things of interest, yet precise enough to pinpoint critical issues. In particular, the language captures some of the important points that have been made by psychologists, especially the Gestaltists. Thus insight problems are those whose solution is obvious only with a non-obvious representation, and detour problems are difficult because they require a temporary decrease in the evaluation function. It is not apparent that any of the critical principles of the Gestaltists are lost in moving to the computer-science approach.

Another advantage of this approach is that it helps to clarify what we do and do not know about problem solving. People often can solve problems without knowing how they do so. In attempting to program computers to do what people do naturally, one is forced to try to make explicit what one otherwise might take for granted. Even when such attempts fall short of their goal, they have the beneficial effect of making what we do not know abundantly clear; and finding out where our ignorance lies is an important step toward overcoming it.

We want to emphasize the importance that the heuristics approach attributes to finding a good representation of the problem. A case can be made that every heuristic essentially works by altering one's problem representation. This emphasis on representation fits well with the findings from many experimental studies of difficulties in human problem solving.

To illustrate, in one early and well-known study of problem solving, Duncker (1945) had people attempt to solve problems of the following sort: "Given a human being with an inoperable stomach tumor, and rays which destroy organic tissue at sufficient intensity, by what procedure can one free him of the tumor by these rays and at the same time avoid destroying the healthy tissue which surrounds it?" (p. 28). An analysis of the protocols he obtained led Duncker to the conclusion that people often first state a principle that the solution should obey, and then attempt to find a way to implement it. In the case of the tumor problem a principle that was often stated was: "Avoid contact between rays and healthy tissue." If the principle proved to be unusable—as this one did—the problem solver would eventually have to discard it and search for another.

The critical point that Duncker notes is that finding a new principle is tantamount to reformulating the original problem. Having stated a principle, one has, in effect, represented the problem in a particular way; and in discarding a principle one admits that this representation was not helpful and should be replaced by one that is. This line of thought brought Duncker to the point of view that the process of solving a problem can be described either as a development of the solution or the development of the problem. One solves a problem, at least sometimes, by reformulating—and in so doing—sharpening it.

One last point about representing a problem. Often it is possible to view a problem in more than one way, to see it from more than one perspective, or to represent it with more than one formalism. Moreover, as noted earlier, not all representations of the same problem are necessarily equally conducive to solutions. The point is nicely illustrated by the following problem (adapted from Adams, 1974).

> One morning, exactly at sunrise, a monk began to climb a mountain. A narrow path, a foot or two wide, spiraled around the mountain to a temple at the summit. The monk ascended at varying rates, stopping many times along the way to rest. He reached the temple shortly before sunset. After several days at the temple he began his journey back along the same path, starting at sun rise and again walking at variable speeds with many pauses along the way. His average speed descending was, of course, greater than his average climbing speed. Prove that there exists a particular spot along the path that the monk will occupy on both trips at precisely the same time of day.

Many people initially try to represent this problem in algebraic equations involving distance and speed. Such efforts typically end in a snarl. One effective way to solve the problem is to represent it visually. In particular, visualize the upward journey of the monk superimposed on the downward journey. No matter what the upward and downward speeds, at some time and at some point along the paths of the two journeys, they will cross. Thus there must be a spot along the path that the monk occupied on both trips at precisely the same time of day.

The same problem also may be used to illustrate the effectiveness of other heuristics that have been mentioned. Consider, for example, Polya's heuristic:

- If you cannot solve the problem on which you are working, see if you can transform it into a problem whose solution you know.

Some people have trouble with the monk-on-the-mountain problem because they find it difficult to try to imagine where the monk would be at different times on different days. Now suppose that instead of asking us to consider the whereabouts of one monk on two different days, the problem asked us to consider whether two monks, one starting at the bottom of the mountain and climbing to the top and the other starting at the top at the same time and descending to the bottom would be at the same place some time during the day. It is our conjecture, although we cannot substantiate it with data, that most people would find this version of the problem much easier than the first one. But the problems are, in all relevant respects, analogous. Solving the second problem in this case, can be an effective, if roundabout, way of solving the first.

Another heuristic that this problem helps to illustrate is that of making a diagram. If we look for a way to represent the situation diagrammatically, one natural idea is that of a graph showing position (say distance from the bottom of the mountain) as a function of time. Thus the upward and downward journeys of the monk might be represented as shown in Figure 4.2. This representation makes it clear that if both journeys start at the same time of day, then indeed there is some spot that the monk will occupy at the same time of day. That spot could be at any of many places, depending on the relative speeds of the ascending and descending journeys, but there obviously must be one: there is no way to draw one line from the bottom to the top of the graph and another from the top to the bottom without having the lines cross.

Implications for the Teaching of Thinking

Our discussion of problem solving has emphasized general strategies or heuristics, for such heuristics seem to be excellent examples of what people sometimes mean by "thinking skills." By way of review, we noted that two

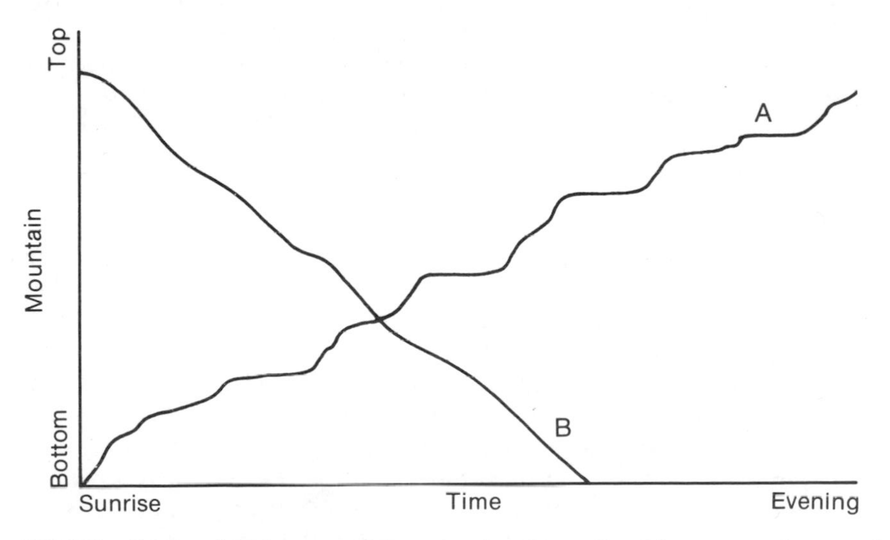

FIG. 4.2. Graphs of the journeys of the mountaineering monk: (a) represents the upward journey, and (b) shows the downward journey.

methods for identifying such strategies are (1) studying expert problem solvers, and (2) programming computers to solve problems; Polya's approach rests mainly on method (1), while the Newell-Simon approach is based more on method (2). Happily, both bodies of work seem to converge on compatible, and in some cases, identical, proposals about useful heuristics. Thus, both approaches emphasize the importance of effectively representing a problem and of devising a plan of attack, and both propose numerous heuristics for representation and planning.

On the face of it, heuristics like these seem to be prime candidates for a course on thinking skills. For one thing, the heuristics seem *worth* teaching: they have great range of applicability and hence should often be beneficial. Many of the heuristics are relatively well specified in the sense that they can be programmed in a computer and therefore should be communicable to students. Furthermore, there is some consensus that the heuristics we have reviewed are the ones that expert problem solvers really do use. And lastly, we note that there are sufficiently few heuristics that it is feasible to teach them.

These good points notwithstanding, there also seem to be difficulties in teaching heuristics. For one, there is the managerial problem of knowing *when* to apply a particular heuristic: in what contexts should one try breaking a problem into subproblems. For another, there is the matter that while the heuristics are specific enough to be programmable, they may not be concrete enough to be implementable in an unfamiliar domain: if you have very little knowledge about hydraulics you are unlikely to have a good idea of what constitutes a subproblem in this domain. Though these two difficulties are real ones, we believe they can be overcome by specific teaching techniques, and that problem-solving heuristics should rank high on any list of aspects of thinking that can be taught.

2. CREATIVITY

Problems can be solved in more or less creative ways, and some problems are unlikely to be solved at all without a fair degree of inventiveness. The ability to look at things in new and unconventional ways is undoubtedly an important problem-solving skill. Indeed, many of the methods that have been proposed for the improvement of problem-solving skills, especially for the breaking away from constraining approaches to problems, emphasize alogical or even non-rational styles of thinking.

Given that creativity is such an important aspect of problem solving, it might seem inappropriate to discuss the two concepts separately. But a similar point might be made with respect to most of the major concepts on which we are focusing: reasoning ability is an important determinant of problem-solving ability, as is metacognition; and all three topics relate closely to the concept of intelligence. Partitioning is primarily matter of convenience, and the one we have chosen reflects the way the research literature is organized.

We note too, however, that creativity has been viewed by many authors as a rather special—perhaps somewhat mysterious—attribute. Whereas the ability to reason and to solve problems requiring analysis and deduction are generally considered highly correlated with intelligence, there is fairly general agreement that high intelligence, at least as it is represented by conventional test results, does not guarantee unusual creativity. Moreover, we conjecture that most investigators who have made a distinction between critical and creative thinking would consider the former to be more likely to be improvable by training than the latter. So the notion of creativity deserves some focused attention in any general discussion of thinking skills and their teaching.

Definitions of the Creative and Creativity

The concept of a creative product seems to be the primary notion in the family *creative product/creative person/creativity*. "Product" as used here includes, but is not limited to, the sorts of products usually thought of as occasions for creativity—works of art or philosophy, scientific theories, and so on. A creative product also might be an inventive conversation, an innovative garden, a lifestyle. Creative persons are persons who, by virtue of their creativity, frequently make creative products, so "creative" with reference to products is definitionally primary.

Creative products are usually defined as original-plus-appropriate products (Jackson & Messick, 1973). Both conditions are necessary. A perfectly fashioned product that lacked originality would not be considered creative. A product inappropriate to the context, however original, would not be considered creative, or at least not creative relative to that context. Originality and appropriateness are highly context-relative, of course, but that seems to be the nature of the concept of creative in general, so this schematic and somewhat open formulation is difficult to improve.

Although a passing joke or a solution to a minor problem may be creative, significant creative products acknowledged by the culture typically possess features more specific than originality and appropriateness. In the arts, and to some extent elsewhere, these features include unity, intensity and complexity (Beardsley, 1958), abstractness and symbolic significance (Getzels & Csikszentmihalyi, 1976; Welsh, 1977), transcendence of constraint, and summary power (Jackson & Messick, 1973).

Creative products add insight, invention, and perspective to competence. Sound judgment, effective problem solving, and acute perception all figure in the making of creative products, but also in products the making of which requires great skill, but not invention. Creative products stretch or break boundaries. What then is creativity? Creativity is that collection of abilities and dispositions that lead to a person frequently producing creative products.

We noted earlier that many authors make a distinction between creative and critical thinking. However, in what sense is there a dichotomy here? In particular, are we talking about opposing and incompatible qualities, or orthogonal but compatible dimensions, or what? The definition of creativity in terms of creative products suggests that neither of these accounts is adequate. Rather, it would seem that critical thinking is a necessary, but not sufficient, condition for creativity, necessary on psychological if not logical grounds.

Why? Creative products of note must be highly appropriate and original. The creator can achieve this either in one stroke, without any critical filtering of possibilities, or piecemeal, by generating possibilities and filtering them so as to construct gradually a creative product. To make this more concrete, we can imagine a poet who, without hesitation, dashes off impressive finished poems, versus a poet who edits a lot. Everything we know about human thought and problem solving suggests that the "filtering" view is much more realistic, in the majority of cases, than the "one stroke" view. Moreover, process-tracing research and other investigations of poets and artists (Perkins, 1982) have disclosed overwhelming evidence of critical filtering. So it is clear that creativity requires critical thinking.

One might defend an opposition between critical and creative thinking, while granting that both critical and creative thinking are necessary for creativity, as follows. One would say that these are two distinct kinds of thinking that occur during different phases, perhaps even in rapid alteration. For instance, the poet might generate and filter, generate and filter, until the poem was complete.

However, this picture is not really adequate either. First, in a cycle of generating possibilities and filtering, the product is the joint consequence of both operations. Were it not for both operations, the product would not be judged creative. Nor is it even safe to say that the generating process provides the originality while the filtering process only selects for other factors. Clearly, the output of the generating process may be a mix of more and less original options, and the filtering process may select for originality among other properties. All of this argues that we cannot identify the generating process as "the creative part" and the filtering process as "the non-creative part." Both are responsible for the ultimate originality and appropriateness of the product.

Moreover, critical response often, perhaps typically, is much more than a matter of filtering. The creator finds an option inadequate, but adequate options are not at hand. Instead, the characterization of the situation yielded by the critical response defines a direction—to find an option not subject to such and such a defect, or an option having such and such an aspect that was missing (Perkins, 1982). This is itself a generative, not just a critical, process—it generates subgoals. Furthermore, such subgoals might foster the creativity of the product. For instance, sometimes a subgoal might include the specific requirement: "find a more original, and equally appropriate, option."

In summary, we have argued that both critical filtering and critical characterizations contribute to the creativity of a creative product. Accordingly, it is somewhat misleading to posit two completely separate styles of thought—critical and creative—because the former is necessarily a part of the latter. To be sure, critical thought can be uncreative. But creative thought cannot be uncritical. Imbedded in it must be a critical component that fosters the creativity of the product by critical filtering and by critical characterizations that lead to subgoals.

Components of Creativity

The best evidence suggests that creativity is a highly complex trait that involves several qualities in the creative person. Although some of these qualities may be primary and the others consequential, it seems useful to address each of them. Indeed, creativity may be an emergent property of the ensemble. With this in mind, we discuss in turn four plausible components of creativity: abilities, cognitive style, attitudes, and strategies.

Abilities. Creativity often is thought of as inventiveness. However, it is important to distinguish between creative abilities specifically and abilities that merely enable inventing in particular fields. The creative painter, for instance, needs a good eye for color, a sense of visual form, a flair for craftsmanship. However, a painter might have all those abilities and yet paint very uncreatively, while an inventive person in physics or drama might benefit little from them. To generalize, a creative ability should in itself make a person more inventive in diverse ways.

Researchers have proposed various creative abilities to account for human inventiveness. Here, we consider three of the most interesting and assess briefly the case for them.

Ideational fluency:

Ideational fluency refers to the ability to produce large numbers of appropriate ideas quickly and easily. A classic example of a task demanding ideational fluency is the "uses of a brick" problem. How many uses of a brick can you list in a limited period of time? A person's response to this question can be scored for number of appropriate ideas, unusualness of ideas, and variety in the kinds of ideas, sometimes called "flexibility."

The theoretical rationale for fluency as a creative ability is straightforward. People who can think of more ideas supposedly are in a better position to invent and to do so in diversified fields. They can devise many candidate solutions and choose the best among them, while less fluent persons will be limited to fewer options. This sensible rationale has been encouraged by a series of seeming successes in teaching creativity. A number of instructional efforts have shown gains on pretests and posttests measuring ideational fluency (Torrance, 1972).

However, such results by themselves provide no evidence that ideational fluency is a creative ability. The real question is whether increased fluency on tests predicts better performance in meaningful creative activities. Here, the evidence is unpersuasive. Crockenberg (1972), and Wallach (1976a, b), himself the co-author of a well-known creativity test emphasizing ideational fluency, concluded that ideational fluency showed little relation to real-world creative achievement. Mansfield and Busse (1981), reviewing the relationship between supposed tests of creativity and demonstrated creative achievement by scientists, concluded about ideational fluency tests that "Commonly used measures such as the Unusual Uses tests and the Consequences tests have shown almost no evidence of criterion-related validity with scientists" (p.46).

Furthermore, the conception of how fluency contributes to inventiveness seems mistaken. Johnson (1972, pp. 300–338), surveyed a number of studies in which investigators instructed some subjects to generate many solutions and other subjects to generate just one or two good ones. He concluded that the generate-many-and-select strategy was not optimal. Subjects trying to think of the best one or two solutions they could at the outset did just as well. This was partly because the other subjects lowered the average quality of their solutions in trying for longer lists—making a tradeoff between quality and quantity—and partly because they did not choose the best options from among those they generated. Perkins (1981, Chapter 5) found that poets who were judged better by experts indeed proved to be more fluent on certain word generating tasks than poets who were judged worse. However, in think-aloud studies of the poets actually writing, the more and less fluent poets alike made relatively short searches for words, usually considering only one or two options on a given pass through the poem-in-progress (although they sometimes returned to edit the same passage many times). Thus, the better poets were not using the generate-many-and-select strategy their fluency allowed. Perkins concluded that in real creative activities, as in the laboratory tasks reviewed by Johnson (1972), the quantity-quality tradeoff and problems of judgment made the strategy inefficient.

Remote associates:

Mednick (1962) suggested that creative ability reflects the retrieval of information only remotely associated with the problem at hand. He argued that conventional thinking relies mostly on the close associations reinforced by everyday life—dog with cat, day with night, and so on. However, creative people might have a "flat associative hierarchy," meaning that they retrieve remote associates more readily than do less creative, plodding thinkers. Mednick formalized his notion with the Remote Associates Test (RAT), an instrument that poses problems supposedly more readily solved by a person with a flat associative hierarchy. The problems were trios of disparate words that had another word in common. For example, faced with "rat, blue, and cottage," a person might retrieve the common associate "cheese."

Mednick's concept, like the concept of ideational fluency, gives a plausible account of creativity. However, again the evidence is unpersuasive. Do people who score high on the RAT exhibit superior creative achievement? Sometimes a positive association has been found, and sometimes it has not (Blooberg, 1973; Mansfield & Busse, 1981, pp. 23–25; Mendelsohn, 1976). The reasons for the inconsistency are not entirely clear, a matter we will not explore further, inasmuch as the research has also disclosed difficulties in the theory of remote associates. According to Mendelsohn (1976), reports from subjects about how they go about solving such problems reveal not an associative blitz, but a methodical exploration of possibilities. Furthermore, investigators have been able to measure the flatness of associative hierarchies by more direct means than the RAT, and have found that the results do not relate to scores on the RAT. In short, whatever allows people to perform well on the RAT, flat associative hierarchies do not seem to be involved.

Intuition:

An appeal to intuition often is the last resort of a person having difficulty explaining something. This is regrettable, since the remark that "It's all intuitive," however true, is singularly unhelpful. However, Westcott (1968) proposed a clarification and test of intuition that gives the concept some explanatory value. Westcott suggested that intuition could be understood as the ability to reach sound conclusions from minimal evidence. Certainly this fits well with many informal anecdotes about creative insight. For example, on numerous occasions in the history of science, discoveries seem to have been made because an investigator noticed and thought about some subtlety most people would never have registered or would have dismissed as unimportant.

Westcott devised a test to assess intuition in this sense. He adopted the sorts of series and analogy problems familiar to psychometrics, but with a twist: instead of receiving all the available information at the outset, test-takers can control how much of the information they see before offering a solution. They are instructed to try to reach a solution with as little information as possible. The following simple verbal series and verbal analogy problems illustrate Westcott's technique. The materials are designed so that one can expose the terms of the series or the sample analogies individually, providing an answer as soon as one feels secure in doing so.

Example 1:
BC CD DE EF FG
Sixth term?

Example 2:
over/under in/out short/long up/down black/white
high/what?

Administering his instrument to Vassar college students, Westcott found two factors that varied independently of one another: the amount of information a person called for, and the likelihood of her being correct. Thus, some people reached sound conclusions requesting relatively little information. These, Westcott identified as highly intuitive. Westcott found that such individuals did not score substantially higher on standard measures of intellectual ability and school performance. However, they tended to be unconventional and comfortable in their unconventionality. They involved themselves in nonsocial pursuits and abstract issues. Also, they were inclined to participate in activities with an obvious creative character, such as writing.

These results suggest that intuition, as operationalized by Westcott, could be considered a creative ability. However, other data confuse the picture somewhat. Westcott found that students involved in the visual arts tended to score high on correctness but also high on information demand. Thus, according to his measure, they were not especially intuitive, even though we think of the visual arts as attracting creative people and personality studies of student visual artists have confirmed their creative personality traits (Baron, 1972; Getzels & Csikszentmihalyi, 1976). Also, Westcott prepared a pictorial version of his instrument that asked the test taker to identify the subject of a drawing with as little information as possible, as additional lines of the drawing were revealed one by one. Westcott found that scores on this test did not correlate well with scores on the original verbal version of his intuition test, even though he had expected they would measure the same underlying trait. For both these reasons, intuition as defined by Westcott cannot be considered a creative ability without further research that clarifies the ambiguities, even though it seems a reasonable candidate for such an ability.

The case for creative abilities:

In general, the case for specific cognitive abilities underlying creativity is not strong. Mansfield and Busse (1981) reviewed a number of instruments designed to measure such abilities. They found that the relevance of most could not be assessed adequately because they had not been evaluated for their relationship to professional creative achievement, the only truly safe criterion in Mansfield and Busse's view. (Westcott's intuition test would fall into this category, although Mansfield and Busse do not mention it.) The several tests that had been adequately evaluated did not show consistent relationships with professional creative achievement. Instead, personality factors, which we discuss under "attitudes" later, had more predictive value, while most predictive of all was biography: those that had already demonstrated accomplishments in a field at some level were likely to continue to do so.

Cognitive Style. While attempting to account for creativity in terms of abilities emphasizes what people can or cannot do, trying to account for creativity in terms of cognitive style emphasizes people's habits of information processing. There are several traits related to creativity that might be considered cognitive style traits.

"Problem finding" refers to a pattern of behavior identified by Getzels and Csikszentmihalyi (1976) in studies of student artists. The authors observed how the artists approached a predefined studio task, and found that certain behaviors characterized the more creative performers, as judged by expert assessment of the products. Some subjects explored many alternatives early on, before deciding what to draw, instead of quickly adopting an arrangement of objects. Some subjects readily changed directions in the course of rendering their chosen arrangements, while others proved less flexible. This tendency to explore and readiness to change direction Getzels and Csikszentmihalyi termed *problem finding*, in contrast with problem solving. They argued that, in the visual arts and in general, creativity depends not so much on special skill in solving defined problems as on attention to what problems should be addressed. At least in the case of the student artists, the problem finding concept proved remarkably predictive. A follow-up study disclosed that the artists most successful in the highly competitive world of galleries and exhibits seven years later tended to be those who earlier had shown the problem finding pattern of behavior.

Other investigators have identified other traits that might be considered cognitive styles. MacKinnon (1962), investigating creativity in science, concluded that the more creative individuals tended to withhold judgment on whatever they encountered. They aimed to penetrate and understand, judging only later if at all, while less creative individuals tended quickly to accept or reject and pass on to other matters. Rothenberg (1979) has gathered evidence that creative people tend to think in terms of opposites. Starting from one idea or concept, they jump to a contrary idea or concept more often than do less creative people. Rothenberg terms this trait "Janusian thinking," after the Greek God Janus who looked both ways at once from faces on both sides of his head.

Investigators also have examined whether a classic dimension of cognitive style, field dependence/independence (Witkin, 1976), relates to creativity. Field independence, the ability and tendency to apprehend things imbedded in and partly concealed by a context, might well foster inventive thinking by helping thinkers to discover hidden patterns. Studies have found associations between field independence and high achievement by gifted children (McCarthy, 1977), logical and insightful problem solving (Noppe, 1978), and choice of a more versus less creative field of study—architecture versus business (Morris & Bergum, 1978). However, these results cannot be viewed as decisive for several reasons. None relates field independence to professional creative accomplishment. Field independence is a component of IQ as often measured, but these studies included no independent measure of IQ that would allow assessing whether the differences found reflected creativity specifically rather than greater intelligence in general.

Finally, it should be recalled that a field-independent style of thinking serves better in some situations and a field-dependent style in others (Witkin, 1976). Perhaps creative tasks present such a range of circumstances that no generalization about the advantages of field independence versus field dependence can be made. In our view, the evidence regarding the relationship of field independence to creativity is, so far, inconclusive, plausible though such a relationship seems.

Attitudes. Various investigators have found consistent associations between creativity and attitudes. Inasmuch as originality is a necessary condition for creativity, it is not surprising to discover attitudinal traits directly connected with originality. However, empirical confirmation is needed, because creativity might just be the consequence of exceptional intellectual skill, rather than a specific disposition toward originality. Welsh (1977), taking a personality approach to creativity, used psychometric techniques to identify two dimensions important in creative activities: "origence" and "intellectance." We discuss intellectance later. Origence refers to a predisposition toward originality. Writing of cognitive style rather than attitudes, Baron (1981) also emphasizes the importance of such a predisposition. Mansfield and Busse (1981), in reviewing research on the traits of creative scientists, report that creative scientists have a need to be original and deliberately seek originality.

Originality as such aside, several personality studies have documented the orientation of creative people toward autonomous judgment independent of social influences (Barron, 1969, 1972; Getzels & Csikszentmihalyi, 1976). Remember that this was a conspicuous trait among individuals who scored high on Westcott's intuitiveness test also, which suggests that sensitivity to subtle patterns may indeed have a connection with creativity.

It might be that everyone values originality, but that creative people are better at distinguishing originality from conventionality. Some evidence against this possibility comes from the research of Getzels and Csikszentmihalyi (1976). They found that a panel of people not involved in the arts did about as well as a panel of art critics at differentiating more from less original student works. However, the participants in the first panel did not *like* the more original works, while the critics did. This suggests that some people may recognize originality but find it disagreeable or alarming, a factor that may limit their own creativity.

Other related attitudes also seem to characterize creative people. Such people tend to value complexity, they encounter ambiguity and uncertainty with equanimity and enjoy resolving it (Barron, 1969, 1972; Roe, 1963). However, according to Mackworth (1965), they have an unusually strong need to find order where it is not apparent to the casual observer. Some studies employing the Barron-Welsh Art Scale (Barron & Welsh, 1952), a preference test using mostly abstract line drawings, have found that creative people tend to prefer imbalance and asymmetry, although other studies have not confirmed this trend (Mansfield & Busse, 1981, pp. 28–29). Welsh (1977) concluded that creative people preferred an abstract, general perspective on problems, a trait captured in his "intellectance" scale. This was also a trait Westcott (1968) identified in individuals who scored high on intuition. Getzels and Csikszentmihalyi (1976) discovered that the more creative of the student artists in their sample tended to base works on matters of deep personal concern that also reflected some of the grand problems of human existence—love and death, for instance—even when such themes were not apparent in the finished product. Pelz and Andrews (1976), in a large-scale study of the productivity of scientists in organizations, also found that wide breadth of interests was characteristic of the more creative scientists.

Commitment is another consistent trait of highly creative individuals. Roe (1951a, b, 1963, 1965) and others have commented upon the extreme commitment often found in creative scientists, reflected in their long hours and total engagement with theoretical problems. Barron (1972), studying students in an art school, found that the male students expressed great commitment to the arts and already thought of themselves as artists for life, although the female students were less certain of their futures. Perkins and Gardner (1978) documented the commitment of amateur and professional poets, some of whom expressed the importance of poetry in their lives in the strongest possible terms.

Attitude toward feedback is another interesting theme, especially in view of the stereotype of creative people as loners, pursuing their own subjective visions. The available results suggest that indeed creative people tend not to defer to social pressures and conventional values, but that they nonetheless may value feedback. Burkhart (1962), in studies of student artists, identified two personality types he labeled "deliberate" and "spontaneous." The worst of the deliberate students were merely incompetent, while the best produced conventional works of great technical skill and precision. The spontaneous students worked more creatively, but also with a range of results. Those Burkhart termed "low spontaneous" produced erratic but imaginative works, while remaining closed to criticism and lacking in perspective. The "high spontaneous" artists valued and selectively used criticism, while following their own final opinion. Their products were the most genuinely creative, in Burkhart's judgment. Perkins (1981), studying the work of professional and amateur poets, found that criticism was greatly valued by both.

We also suggest that certain general beliefs about the world of ideas may relate to creativity. Such beliefs would constitute a "reality" through which creative people navigate in dealing with their work. These might include a sense of the abundance of good ideas in certain "problem spaces" (Newell & Simon, 1972) and a recognition of the ambiguity of experience and the possibility of multiple perspectives (Goodman, 1978; Perry, 1970). Certain aspects of "ego development" (Loevinger, 1976) can be viewed as involving the construction of a reality, and some of the resulting apprehensions of "the way things are" would seem to favor creativity.

Strategies. Strategies that might aid creative thinking have been suggested by a number of authors. A few of the more common of these strategies are: making analogies, "brainstorming," effecting imaginative transformations such as "magnifying," "minifying," or "reversing," listing attributes, challenging assumptions, defining the problem, seeking a new entry point, setting a quota of ideas. Such writers as de Bono (1970) and Koberg and Bagnall (1974) identify a number of strategies for inventive thinking.

De Bono, for example, suggests two techniques that he considers to be useful in helping one to break out of the constraints imposed by dominant ideas and fixed ways of perceiving things and to look at a problem from a fresh perspective: (1) making oneself acutely aware of the idea that seems to be dominating a given situation, perhaps by writing it down; or (2) deliberately distorting the idea, perhaps by carrying it to an extreme. Both of these approaches assume that one can in fact identify the dominant idea.

De Bono argues that a certain degree of rigidity in thinking is the price we pay for the convenience of naming objects and the parts thereof. While names facilitate communication among people, they may constrain thinking. If an object has named parts, the frequent use of those names can reinforce the notion that the organization implied by the names is the only one through which the object can be perceived or conceived. As one way of avoiding such rigidity, de Bono recommends cultivating the practice of thinking in terms of visual images—lines, diagrams, colors—rather than in terms of words.

De Bono notes the role that chance has played in several major discoveries and argues the importance to problem solving of being able to capitalize on what chance has to offer. With respect to whether there are ways to foster the chance generation of new ideas, he suggests such possibilities as nonstructured play, brainstorming, exposing oneself to a variety of stimulating environments, deliberately juxtaposing disparate lines of thought, and interruption of concentrated work with unrelated activities.

Most of the common strategies for inventive thinking sound plausible. Few have been subjected to empirical validation, and efforts to check whether creative people in fact use such strategies are rare. Many strategies seem likely not to be involved in what creative people usually have done while creating, although this does not mean that these strategies have nothing to offer. Here we comment on three strategies that have been investigated to some extent.

Long searches:

One standard recommendation in many sources on creative thinking is to defer closure and consider many alternatives before making a final choice. We have already discussed some results regarding this strategy in connection with the ideational fluency view of creativity, and confine ourselves here to mentioning a few of the pertinent points. Johnson (1972) reviewed a number of experiments investigating the effectiveness of this strategy in contrast to one in which subjects simply try to list the best one or two ideas they can at the outset. Johnson concluded that the long search strategy was no more effective, although certainly more time consuming. Rather than length of search, the critical factor appeared to be subjects' understanding of the solution requirements. Perkins (1981, Chapter 5) reported results indicating that more creative poets do not in fact use longer searches than less creative ones. De Groot (1965) found master chess players did not, in general, search for a longer time than did middle level players.

In summary, there is little evidence that lengthy search is an effective strategy for inventive thinking in general. Two qualifications are in order, however. First, this refers to long searches resulting from a deliberate effort to generate a large number of candidate solutions, not to long searches forced by a problem that refuses to yield. Second, Getzels and Csikszentmihalyi's (1976) results regarding problem finding should be remembered: long searches in the early stages of a creative task, in which initial commitments are made and directions taken, may be very important to creative behavior. Less creative people seem to slight this phase of work, quickly settling on a fairly conventional direction and then concentrating their efforts on following through with it.

Analogy:

Bronowski (1965) has emphasized the importance of analogical reasoning in both science and the arts. The ability to see likenesses that most of us miss is the hallmark of the truly creative person, he suggests. "All science is the search for unity in hidden likenesses" (p. 13). "Poetry, painting, the arts are the same search, in Coleridge's phrase, for unity in variety" (p. 16). Again, "I found the act of creation to lie in the discovery of a hidden likeness. The scientist or the artist takes two facts or experiences which are separate; he finds in them a likeness which had not been seen before; and he creates a unity by showing the likeness" (p. 27).

Gordon (1961) and others have recommended the use of seemingly far-fetched analogies in creative problem solving. History seems to sanction this advice. Many scientific discoveries have involved analogies, sometimes analogies connecting matters quite remote from one another, as with Kekule's well-known discovery of the benzene ring through a dream in which he saw snakes dancing and curling around to bite their own tails (Koestler, 1964). Gordon coined the word *synectics* as a name for such connection-making, and devised a general method for group problem solving that emphasized generating several kinds of analogies. Gordon (1961) reviewed cases in which the method led to inventive solutions to difficult problems.

Less clear, however, is the frequency with which such analogical thinking pays off. Perkins (1981) concluded that "novel, remote" analogies rarely led to insights. By "novel" he meant an analogy that was generated for the occasion, rather than a stock analogy. By "remote," Perkins meant an analogy that, like Kekule's, bridges domains we intuitively would consider remote from one another. Perkins reviewed a number of cases in which people had reported the sequence of thoughts leading up to an insight, including episodes from the history of science, psychiatric interviews, protocols of students solving physics problems, and protocols of students solving insight problems. In this review, novel, remote analogies rarely appeared. Rather, thinkers arrived at their insights by more straightforward means—deduction, recognition of patterns, trial-and-error, close rather than remote analogies, and in other ways.

Perkins suggested that, in fact, *powerful* novel remote analogies were rarely there to be found, however clever the thinker. Such analogies amount to deep fundamental parallels between superficially dissimilar domains, and there seems to be no intrinsic reason why such parallels should be frequent. Close analogies probably are a more useful tool for the thinker than remote analogies, although remote analogies have a dramatic quality that has attracted attention in the literature.

Brainstorming:

Brainstorming is a group problem solving technique devised by Osborn (1963). It was designed to avoid the inhibiting critical attitude that often pervades formal meetings. The basic strategy is to generate a long list of options and then to select from among them. While generating the list, the participants are encouraged to freewheel and build on others' ideas. Criticism is forbidden. Stein (1975, Chapter 13) reviews the research on brainstorming, noting that this is the most investigated of any strategy for inventive thinking. Stein's conclusion is a telling comment on the difficulties and pitfalls of investigating such strategies: he concludes that the benefits of brainstorming have not been adequately demonstrated or disconfirmed. Here are some of the conclusions: Brainstorming sometimes leads to listing many ideas of low quality. The inhibiting effects of criticism coupled with idea generating apparently can be avoided simply by separating standard-setting phases from idea-getting phases, without the latter necessarily coming first. Sometimes having people think separately and pool ideas later appears to yield better quality ideas than having people work together from the outset, but sometimes the opposite result is obtained. The effectiveness of brainstorming depends somewhat on personality characteristics of the participants.

Stein also complains that much of the research has been done with groups introduced to brainstorming by the experimenter, working on problems that lack ecological validity, rather than with experienced practitioners, working on bona fide problems of some practical significance. It seems reasonable to conclude that brainstorming works better for creative group problem solving than the hide-bound kind of meeting it was intended to loosen up, but may well not be the best of several alternate procedures.

The case for strategies:

The cases of long searching, analogy-making, and brainstorming suffice to show that the effectiveness of a strategy for inventive thinking is a complicated question. In none of the three cases did a strategy turn out to be useless, but in all, important qualifications needed to be made. This serves warning that the many untested strategies offered in the literature need to be met with a critical attitude. Very likely, few of the popular strategies serve the objective of inventive thinking in quite so straightforward a way as they might seem to do. Some may even be counter-productive. More research and practical experience are needed to accumulate the evidence that will allow a better appraisal of the strategies' strengths and weaknesses.

Implications for the Teaching of Thinking

In the foregoing discussion, we have tried to make sense of the complex trait of creativity by discussing four possible components or aspects of creativity: abilities, cognitive style, attitudes, and strategies. By way of review, the case for abilities that endow a person with creativity is not strong: Westcott's interesting operationalization of intuition as the ability to reach conclusions with minimal evidence comes the closest, but even in that case there are conflicting and ambiguous results. Certain cognitive styles, for instance a disposition toward problem finding and toward deferring judgment, seem likely to bear a relation to creativity. Very strong connections with creativity appear in studies of attitudes: creative people value and seek originality, practice autonomy, tolerate ambiguity, and so on. Finally, many strategies recommended by "how to do it" books on creative thinking seem not to be used that much by creative thinkers. Some of these strategies may be helpful, but results concerning the few strategies that have been investigated suggest that it is hard to gauge by common sense which ones are effective and to what extent.

With this picture in mind, what are the prospects for teaching creativity? If we take as the goal of "teaching creativity" not producing Beethovens and Einsteins on an assembly line, but rather moderate but useful improvement in creative work, that goal seems attainable judging from the foregoing analysis. In particular, instruction should foster the profile of attitudes characteristic of creativity. By exhortation, providing good role models, noting attributes of well-known creative figures, and reinforcing signs of creative attitudes when they occur, programs should be able to encourage a questing and questioning attitude. Instruction should also foster relevant cognitive styles. For example, such instruction should stress problem finding over the completion of predefined tasks, while providing encouragement and advice about problem finding. In addition, selected strategies that appear to be good bets can be taught.

Note that such an instructional approach diverges both from conventional education and many contemporary efforts to teach creativity. As to the former, the point has often been made that conventional education does little to foster creative attitudes, and may even work against them. As to the latter, many efforts to teach creativity have emphasized strategies of doubtful effectiveness and abilities like ideational fluency. A shift of balance toward more attention to attitudes and cognitive styles, as well as more careful selection of, and more formal testing of, strategies is desirable.

3. METACOGNITION

Perhaps the most obvious way in which experts differ from novices is in the fact that they know more about their area of expertise. However, there are other important differences as well. Experts not only know more, they know they know more, they know better how to use what they know, what they know is better organized and more readily accessible, and they know better how to learn more still.

There is a difference between having some information in one's head and being able to access it when it is needed; between having a skill and knowing when to apply it; between improving one's performance on some particular task and realizing that one has done so. It is in part the recognition of such differences that has led to the notion of metacognition, or more specifically, metacognitive knowledge, experiences, and skills.

Metacognitive knowledge is knowledge about knowledge and knowing, including knowledge about the capabilities and limitations of human thought processes, about what human beings in general might be expected to know, and about the characteristics of specific people—and especially oneself—as knowing and thinking individuals. Metacognitive skills may be thought of as cognitive skills that are necessary, or helpful, to the acquisition, use, and control of knowledge, and other cognitive skills. They include the ability to plan and regulate the effective use of one's own cognitive resources (Brown, 1978; Scardamalia & Bereiter, 1985).

Flavell (1978) defines the substance of metacognitive knowledge in terms of three types of variables and their interactions: person variables, task variables, and strategy variables. The first category—person variables—encompasses all that one might believe about the nature of oneself and other people as cognitive beings. The knowledge that one can fail to understand something either by failing to achieve a coherent representation of it, or by achieving a coherent—but incorrect—representation, is an example of metacognitive knowledge that fits in the person-variable category. The second category—task variables—includes knowledge of what the characteristics of a cognitive task imply regarding the difficulty of the task and how best to approach it. An example is the knowledge that to recall the gist of a narrative is easier than to recall its exact wording. The third category—strategy variables—involves knowledge about the relative merits of different approaches to the same cognitive task.

While this tripartite taxonomy provides a convenient way of thinking about metacognition, Flavell points out that most metacognitive knowledge probably involves interactions between, or combinations of, two or all three of these types of variables. Moreover, metacognitive knowledge, like other kinds of knowledge, may be accessed intentionally or automatically, may be more or less accurate, and may be influential with or without entering consciousness.

Metacognitive experiences, in Flavell's conceptualization are conscious experiences that are focused on some aspect(s) of one's own cognitive performance. The "feeling of knowing" (or feeling of not knowing) experience that has received considerable attention from researchers in recent years would qualify as a metacognitive experience, as would the feeling that one is (or is not) likely to be able to solve a particular problem on which one is working. The line between metacognitive knowledge and metacognitive experiences is not drawn very sharply.

Much of the work on metacognition has been designed to make individuals more knowledgeable about their own abilities and limitations and about how to use those abilities and to work around the limitations effectively. An important aspect of skilled performance is the ability to determine whether one is making satisfactory progress toward the objectives of a specified task and to modify one's behavior appropriately if progress is not satisfactory. It is also important in many professions or vocations to be able to assess one's general level of expertise This is especially true in fields in which knowledge continues to accumulate. The physician, for example, must continually judge whether his knowledge and skills are current and adequate to the demands of his practice. The researcher must be able to tell whether his knowledge base includes the latest findings that are relevant to the research problems on which he is working. The lawyer must be able to determine whether his knowledge of the law and of precedent-setting cases is current. The automobile mechanic must be able to judge whether his knowledge of automotive technology is sufficiently up-to-date and encompassing to justify an attempt to undertake a specific repair task.

Several writers have pointed out that possession of a body of knowledge that is relevant to a particular task domain does not guarantee that that knowledge will be effectively applied in that domain. Miller (1962), for example, notes that while task relevant knowledge is necessary for the best performance it is not sufficient to guarantee it. Barrows and Tamblyn (1980) claim that possession of a large body of knowledge in medicine provides no assurance that the possessor knows when or how to apply that knowledge in the care of patients. Citing Wingard and Williamson (1973), they note that there is little evidence of a correlation between amount of factual knowledge possessed by a medical student, as scored by objective examinations, and clinical competence. The implication is that one needs to have not only the domain-specific knowledge that is essential to skilled performance, but the knowledge of when and how to apply that knowledge in specific contexts.

Evidences of failure to apply knowledge effectively have been obtained with children as well as adults. Davis and McKnight (1980), for example, found that third and fourth grade students often possess knowledge that is sufficient to show that an answer they have produced on an arithmetic problem (e.g., $7002 - 25 = 5077$) is wrong, but they fail to use that knowledge to correct the error. That is, they know that subtracting 25 from

7002 should produce a number that is not very much smaller than 7000, but they fail to use this knowledge to conclude that an answer that is close to 6000 must be wrong. Davis and McKnight concluded that the algorithmic behavior of their third and fourth graders was not influenced at all by their semantic knowledge. Apparently, they suggest, students learn to do mathematics by rote and do not think about what they are doing or the answers they are obtaining. The practical question that these results raise, and one that Davis and McKnight ask, is how the curriculum might be changed so as to increase the likelihood that students not only will acquire knowledge but will learn to apply it effectively to detect and correct errors in mathematical calculations.

Use of the term metacognitive *skills* is consistent with the general emphasis throughout this book on thought *processes*, and more especially on those aspects of thought processes that might be improved by training. What is true of cognitive skills is true of metacognitive skills as well: whether or not one can improve the processes of thought without affecting the content, it would seem silly to try. It seems likely that any effective approach to improving thinking will provide an individual with some new knowledge and some new ways of applying both the old and new knowledge he has. In the case of metacognition the objective is to make one a skillful *user* of knowledge; and the utilization of the term metacognitive skills serves to remind us that more is undoubtedly involved in doing this than simply giving one some new information about cognition.

The notion of metacognition has been implicit in the learning literature for some time. One familiar illustration is the distinction between learning and learning to learn. Until quite recently, however, the types of knowledge and skills that are now being subsumed under the rubric of metacognition were seldom if ever made explicit objectives of training. People did not learn how to learn as a consequence of efforts to teach them this skill explicitly and at a conscious level; they did so spontaneously as a consequence of their experience in situations in which they were being taught other things. The fact that people learned not only what they were being taught but also something about the learning process per se was an interesting finding and one that received considerable attention. But only recently have investigators begun to isolate a class of skills that could be considered metacognitive and that one might try to teach explicitly.

Some Examples of Metacognitive Skills

Examples of metacognitive skills that have been identified by various writers include: planning, predicting, checking, reality testing, and monitoring and control of one's own deliberate attempts to perform intellectually demanding tasks.

Brown notes that such skills are characteristically lacking in the performance of retarded children on laboratory learning tasks, and their absence is often implicated when the effects of training fail to transfer (Brown, 1974, 1978; Campione & Brown, 1974, 1977, 1978). The training of such skills, if it could be done effectively, should have considerable payoff. In particular, inasmuch as these skills are very general, a successful effort to improve them should beneficially affect performance on a wide range of tasks.

Effective Planning and Strategizing. The performance of experts on problem solving tasks differs not only in the fact that it is more likely to be successful but in approach as well. Brown, Bransford, and Chi (1979) point out, for example, that expert physicists are likely to differ from novice physicists in the extent to which they plan and try out potential problem solutions in qualitative terms before making any calculations. Several investigators have noted that experts show a greater tendency than do novices to analyze a problem qualitatively before attempting to represent it in quantitative form (Chi, Feltovich, & Glaser, 1981; Larkin, McDermott, Simon & Simon, 1980; Simon & Simon, 1978). According to McDermott and Larkin (1978), experts dealing with physics problems typically construct a sequence of successively more abstract representations, beginning with representations that show the critical relationships in qualitative terms and proceeding to quantitative expressions of those relationships. Novices, they suggest, are more likely to try to represent a problem quantitatively straightaway.

Wright (1979) makes the following observation based on discussions with "methods" students who had been unsuccessful as problem solvers:

> Most think that the probability of success would have been enhanced if they had first taken the time to identify carefully and sort out the relevant details (or variables) embedded in the problem before they went about attempting solution. It seems as if the students attempt to approach each "new" problem situation from a holistic viewpoint. Rather than first carefully analyzing all aspects of the problem, their first impressions tend to direct their thinking in one direction. In most cases this leads to an oversight of relevant variables. (p. 381)

Monitoring and Evaluation of Own Knowledge and Performance. If the ease with which one acquires new knowledge depends strongly on the knowledge one has to begin with, accurate assessment of the latter is of considerable importance. Effective tutors recognize this fact and devote much attention to determining what a student already knows so as to assure that new information is presented in a way that builds effectively on what already exists. Similarly, they are careful to select tasks that represent a challenge to the student, but do not impose demands that exceed his ability to meet.

The ability to assess one's own capabilities and limitations vis-a-vis the cognitive demands of a specific task, the ability to monitor and evaluate one's performance on the task, and to decide whether to persevere, to modify one's strategy or to quit are clearly valuable skills for people to have. Consider, for example, the task of committing some specific information to memory. When we undertake such a task, we limit the amount of effort that we devote to the "stamping-in" process. We do not continue to study the to-be-remembered material indefinitely. Presumably the decision to stop is based on one's confidence that the material is sufficiently well ingrained to ensure remembrance later. Presumably, too, confidence typically increases with the amount of effort devoted to the task, but with diminishing returns; at some point confidence is high enough that the gain that could be realized from further study does not seem worth the effort.

How accurately can people judge the likelihood that something they are currently studying will be retrievable at some specified later time? The question is of both theoretical and practical interest. Also important for our purposes is the question of whether people's ability to predict their own memory performance can be improved by training. Not surprisingly there is some evidence that this type of memory assessment ability seems to be greater in older than in younger children. Flavell, Friedrichs, and Hoyt (1970), for example, had children ranging from kindergartners to fourth graders study a set of items until they were sure they would be able to recall them perfectly, the recall test to be given as soon as a child said he was ready to have it. When the older children said they were ready, they typically were; that is they typically recalled all the items they had studied. However, the younger subjects typically were not able to recall all the items when they said they were ready to do so.

While much of the research on self-monitoring has been concerned with monitoring memory performance (e.g., Brown, 1974, 1978; Flavell, 1978, 1979), some recent work by Flavell (1981) and by Markman (1977,1979) focuses on the monitoring of comprehension. This is a particularly important domain of study. The ability to comprehend spoken and written language is fundamental to the major way we learn new things; and to the extent that comprehension skills can be improved through training, it should be possible to increase one's knowledge acquisition ability and general intellectual performance. Among the skills that seem to be involved in many instances of comprehension are those needed to *monitor* comprehension—in particular, the ability to determine that one does not understand some portion of what one has heard or read, and the knowledge of what to do about that.

Markman (1977) has demonstrated a surprising insensitivity among elementary-school children to inherent incomprehensibilities in language. She asked children to help evaluate verbal instructions in terms of their communicative accuracy, and in particular to indicate any omissions and unclarities. The instructions that were used had, in fact, many omissions and unclarities, but the younger subjects often failed to detect them; they erroneously thought the instructions were understandable and could be followed.

Much of Markman's research (see also Flavell, 1980) is directed at the question, "What cues do we use to signal a temporary breakdown in our comprehension process?" Or, to put it another way, "What danger signals should we monitor for in metacomprehension?" The suggested cues are of two types, those given by a failed attempt to comprehend a single statement or proposition, and those arising from a failure to relate two or more statements in the same text. Cues derivable from processing a single statement include:

- An unfamiliar word;
- A syntactic irregularity that makes it difficult to determine the sentence's meaning;
- A statement that the text assumes to be true that the comprehender has reason to believe is false;
- A statement for which the comprehender fails to determine any interpretation;
- A statement with more than one interpretation.

The cues derivable from processing multiple statements include:

- An explicit inconsistency, i.e., two statements mentioned in the text that are inconsistent with one another;
- An implicit inconsistency, i.e., inferences from one statement in the text that are inconsistent with either another statement in the text or with inferences from that other statement; and
- A failure to determine any relations between a pair of statements.

The above list provides a taxonomy of comprehension-failure cues. Once a cue is classified with respect to this taxonomy, metacomprehension heuristics can be specified for how to correct things. To illustrate:

- If there is an unfamiliar word, wait and see if it is explained in the next statement; if it is not, ask for its meaning or look it up in a dictionary.
- If a single statement can be interpreted in more than one way, ask the speaker to resolve the ambiguity (if you are reading, retain both interpretations and try to use the next statements to resolve the ambiguity).
- If you detect an implicit inconsistency, check the plausibility of the inferences that led to the inconsistency.

A more complete listing of these heuristics for the case of reading comprehension is given in Collins and Adams (1979) and Collins and Smith (1982).

The metacomprehension skills of an expert include a diagnostic taxonomy of possible comprehension failures as well as a set of remedies for each failure. The critical point is that many people lack some of these skills; consequently their comprehension suffers. Moreover, novice readers may be more likely to overlook comprehension-failure cues that derive from processing multiple statements than those that derive from processing a single statement.

This is indicated by two findings by Markman (1979). First, when third- and sixth-grade children were asked to evaluate an essay, they generally failed to detect an inconsistency if it was implicit, even when the inferences involved were highly plausible. They also sometimes failed to notice even explicit inconsistencies. Second, when informed that there was something wrong with an essay, "a sizeable portion of the children (mainly third graders) still failed to notice inconsistencies even after being set to search for a problem. However, these children did question the (empirical) truth of individual (statements) more." Thus, when pushed to search for comprehension-failure cues of the between-statement type, young children instead focus on possible within-statement cues. It is as if they do not realize that consistency per se is a critical standard for evaluating one's own comprehension.

Recognition of the Utility of a Skill. Brown (1978) points out that one reason for a child not maintaining a newly acquired behavior is that he may be unaware of its value. That is to say, he may not appreciate that the behavior could improve performance. Brown concludes, therefore, that an important component of training is explicit feedback to the student regarding the effectiveness of the behavior that is being acquired. One should be taught not only how to do something but the value of doing it. One wonders how far teachers could go toward motivating children to learn by simply making the effort to explain clearly why what they are learning is important to know. It is not surprising when a child, or adult for that matter, shows little interest in acquiring skills for which he sees no use.

Accessibility as a Metacognitive Skill

Some writers (e.g., Brown & Campione, 1978; Tulving & Pearlstone, 1966) have made a distinction between having knowledge and being able to retrieve it from memory when it is needed. This distinction has important practical implications, because it suggests that the acquisition of knowledge is an inadequate educational objective. One needs to acquire not only knowledge but the ability to access that knowledge at appropriate times and for appropriate purposes.

Flavell (1976, quoted in Flavell, 1978) suggests that in the normal course of events people learn "certain specialized cognitive activities which we call memory strategies" that can be used either to facilitate memorization of information (storage strategies) or the retrieval of information from memory (retrieval strategies). Such strategies, Flavell believes, are normally acquired later than are the automatic, passive types of memory processes: "children may have to learn what it means to make an active, persistent, goal-instigated and goal-directed effort either to recall something now or to memorize something for later recall" (p. 5).

In keeping with his tripartite taxonomy of metacognitive knowledge, Flavell distinguishes three types of metacognition relating to variables affecting performance on memory-dependent tasks: (1) person metacognition (knowledge about the memory capabilities and limitations of people, including self, and the ability to monitor one's own immediate memory experiences); (2) task metacognition (knowledge of how the difficulty of a memory problem relates to the specifics of the task); and (3) strategy metacognition (knowledge of things one can do to affect memory performance). Flavell illustrates this taxonomy with a hypothetical example of an individual trying to understand directions to a person's house:

> Past experience with such problems may have built up a fund of metacognitive knowledge that the presence of this goal evokes. Examples might include the knowledge that you are particularly inept at generating spatial representations from verbal directions (person metacognition), that the number and nature of the steps in his directions will affect the difficulty of your comprehension and memory task (task metacognition), and that verifying your grasp of the instructions by repeating them back to him before driving off into the night might be a useful thing to do (strategy metacognition). (p. 11)

Brown and Campione (1980) consider accessibility to, and flexible use of, knowledge stored in one's head as the hallmark of intelligent activity.

> Given the pervasiveness of the concept of accessibility we are convinced that no theory of intelligence can be complete without ceding it a central place. No serious discussion of what intelligent behavior is could occur without mention of the difficult issues elicited by the family of ideas implied by the term, i.e., awareness, intentionality, consciousness, automatic vs. deliberate processing, etc. (p. 11)

Restricted access to knowledge—for example, inability to access knowledge obtained in one context so as to apply it in another—is, they note, a distinguishing characteristic of the performance of mentally retarded persons.

A distinction has also been made between multiple access and reflective access (Brown & Campione, 1980; Pylyshyn, 1978; Rozin, 1976). Multiple-accessible knowledge is knowledge that can be used in a variety of contexts in addition to the one in which it was acquired. Reflective access to knowledge implies awareness at a conscious level; it means, in Pylyshyn's terms, being able to talk about knowledge as well as to use it. That the two kinds of access are really different is fairly clear in the case of complex motor skills. The production of speech, for example, requires multiple access to skills involving the manipulation of various components of the articulatory apparatus. While people with normal speech exercise those skills effectively, they may be aware only marginally, if at all, of some of them (e.g., the skill of raising and lowering the velum to distinguish between nasal and plosive consonants). Even in the case of more intellectual or cognitive skills the distinction seems to be relatively clear: researchers in the field of artificial intelligence, for example, have long recognized the fact that people are often able to solve cognitive problems effectively without being able to specify how they do so.

Implications for the Teaching of Thinking

Metacognition has only quite recently become a focus of research attention. Relatively little is yet known about this type of knowledge and skills. What is being learned from research in this area is consistent with the view that expert performers tend to differ from novices not only by virtue of their greater knowledge of their specific area of expertise but also in the ways in which they apply that knowledge and these approaches to intellectually demanding tasks more generally. More emphasis on planning and strategizing, better management of time and resources, more careful monitoring and evaluation of progress seem to be characteristics of expert performance that are independent of subject area.

How successfully such skills can be taught remains to be determined. The little empirical work that has been done on this question, while not conclusive, is encouraging. In our view, the area is a particularly promising one for further research. Metacognitive skills have a face validity that is very compelling: who can argue against the desirability of carefully managing one's time and resources, or of monitoring the effectiveness of an approach to a demanding task? If such things can be taught, and in such a way that they generalize across tasks, one would be surprised if intellectual performance were not enhanced as a consequence.

4. SUMMARY

We have tried to summarize the relevant research in three of the major areas of the psychology of thinking: problem solving, creativity, and metacognition. In our discussion of problem solving, we emphasized heuristics, particularly those for representing a problem and devising a plan. Such heuristics are relatively specific processes, and their development and articulation have been aided by attempts to program computers to solve problems. Our discussion of creativity suggested that useful as such specific processes are, they alone may not be sufficient to result in original problem solving and thinking. One may also need attitudes that favor originality and complexity, as well as a commitment to the problem and an openness to explore nonorthodox approaches to a problem. Certain cognitive styles—e.g., a flexible, problem-finding style—may be more conducive than other styles to creative thinking.

Still other components of "good thinking" were suggested by our consideration of metacognition. Problem solving can be enhanced by a number of metacognitive skills, including knowing *when* to apply specific heuristics or knowledge, and monitoring one's performance to insure one is on the right track. Research on metacognition is like that on problem solving in that it has led to some relatively specific skills for improving thinking. However, research on metacognition is also similar to that on creativity in suggesting the importance of more global factors like the need to make one's knowledge as accessible as possible.

The three areas of research thus provide compatible and complementary ideas about the components of good thinking. Most, or all, of these components seem eminently teachable, and, in any case, whether they are is an empirical question that deserves further research. The complementarity of these areas is worth emphasizing. The teaching of problem-solving heuristics should be accompanied by the teaching of the metacognitive knowledge of when to apply these heuristics and of how to tell whether they are working. The cultivation of attitudes and skills that lead to the expansive unfettered creative thought must be balanced by the ability to be analytical and critical. A well rounded program is likely to place some emphasis on all of these aspects, or types of thinking.

5 Errors and Biases in Reasoning

One major kind of thinking ability is the ability to reason inferentially, that is, to evaluate and generate arguments in accordance with the principles of deductive and inductive inference. Though reasoning often is of substantial importance in everyday activities as well as in academic situations, all of us make errors when engaging in this kind of thinking. Some of these errors are systematic, and in what follows we review examples of them in detail. Our motives for focusing on such errors are two. First, the nature of the errors provides valuable insights into how people actually reason; that is, errors in inferential thinking may be the most sensitive indicators of underlying reasoning processes. Second, if common reasoning deficiencies can be identified and organized, there is then the possibility that training techniques can be developed for the express purpose of correcting those deficiencies.

In the following survey, we classify reasoning errors into three groups. The first consists of errors that seem specific to *deductive* reasoning; the second contains errors specific to *inductive* reasoning; and the third group focuses on errors that appear to be partly motivational or social in nature, and are as likely to show up in one form of reasoning as another.

1. ERRORS IN DEDUCTIVE REASONING

Nature of Deductive Reasoning

Deductive reasoning is the ability to reason in accordance with the principles of deductive logic. Deductive logic is concerned with the validity of arguments: an argument is deductively valid if and only if its conclusion follows from—is a logically necessary consequence of—its premises. And this is independent of the truth or falsity of the premises or of the conclusion. The argument, "All fish fly; all guppies are fish; therefore all guppies fly," is perfectly valid, although the conclusion is empirically false (as is the first premise). Conversely, the argument "No mammals are invertebrates; no invertebrates are birds; therefore no mammals are birds" is invalid even though its premises and its conclusion are all true. Validity, is a matter of the form of an argument, not of its content; presumably this fact lies behind a number of the errors that people make when trying to reason deductively.

In detailing these errors, we first consider cases in which people appear to be using some criterion other than validity in evaluating deductive arguments. Then we briefly mention some of the errors that probably arise because some of the terms or concepts in the arguments are particularly difficult. Third, we consider cases in which the errors appear to arise because people misrepresent the argument. As we shall see, it is often difficult to distinguish such misrepresentation errors from those that may arise because of using a criterion other than validity.

Using Criteria Other than Validity

Confusion Between Truth and Validity. The need for training in symbolic logic is testimony to the difficulty that people have in judging the logical validity of an argument independently of its empirical content. The difficulty has been demonstrated by many experiments, which generally show that people are more apt to judge a conclusion to be valid if it is believed to be empirically true than if it is believed to be empirically false (Feather, 1965; Gordon, 1953; Janis & Frick, 1943; Kaufman & Goldstein, 1967; Morgan & Morton, 1944; Wason & Johnson-Laird, 1972; Wilkins, 1928). Other results suggest that it is not a matter of people simply mistaking truth for validity. Revlin, Leirer, Yopp, and Yopp (1980) obtained the usual finding of lower accuracy on deductive reasoning problems when the valid conclusion was false than when it was true; but their detailed analysis revealed that the dominant error subjects made when belief and logic were in conflict was not to select the conclusion corresponding to their belief, but rather to decide that no conclusion could be drawn. It is as if people appreciate the distinction between truth and validity, but fail to appreciate that in evaluating the logical soundness of a deductive argument validity alone is relevant.

Confusion between Consistency and Validity. Consider the following line of reasoning: "The salt deposits at Natrium, which are at a depth of 6,800 feet, are in the same stratum that runs under Cleveland at a depth of

1,000 feet. This stratum gradually deepens in a southeasterly direction from Cleveland. Therefore Cleveland lies to the northwest of Natrium." The first two sentences comprise Item 9 of an Inference Test developed by the Educational Testing Service and the third is an erroneous (from the viewpoint of deductive logic) conclusion that is commonly selected from among five alternatives (Dickstein, 1980). The conclusion is consistent with the given information, but it does not constitute a valid deduction from it: the fact that the stratum deepens in one direction from Cleveland does not rule out the possibility that it deepens also in the opposite direction.

It is important to recognize that while the inference in this example is not deductively determined—in that the conclusion does not necessarily follow from the information given—the reasoning is a respectable form of induction, inasmuch as a conclusion that is consistent with the information available is more likely to be empirically true than one that is not. Of course it is important that the reasoner appreciate the distinction between a conclusion arrived at deductively and one arrived at inductively, in that only in the case of the former does the truth of the premises insure the truth of the conclusion. The next set of problems shows even more graphically how we tend to substitute inductive for deductive reasoning.

Confusion Between Inductive and Deductive Argument Forms. Two common valid forms of deductive reasoning are called *modus ponens*—If A then B; A; therefore B—and *modus tollens*—If A then B; not B; therefore not A. Related to these valid forms are two deductively invalid forms. One is termed *affirming the consequent*—If A then B; B; therefore A—and the other is called *denying the antecedent*—If A then B; not A; therefore not B.

While the latter two forms of argument are incompatible with deductive logic, they can constitute viable inductive arguments. Indeed, affirming the consequent is a prototype of inductive reasoning in science. A scientist has the hypothesis that A leads to B; he performs an experiment in which he sets up the conditions specified in A and then observes that B results; consequently he increases his belief in the hypothesis. Similarly, denying the antecedent can be a perfectly respectable inductive argument. If a scientist has a hypothesis that A is a sufficient condition for B, the observation that B does not occur in the absence of A would probably increase his degree of belief in the hypothesis.

Also, Perkins, Allen, and Hafner (in press) argue that steps in informal arguments that some might interpret as cases of affirming the consequent should not be so simply understood. For example, a person might argue, "Football players have thick necks. John has a thick neck so very likely he's a football player." Now certainly this does not follow by strict logic. On the other hand, it is not a bad conjecture. Furthermore, for practical purposes, the real issue is not so much the logical form as the likelihood of the claim "If

John has a thick neck, then he's a football player." Perhaps there are few common ways of acquiring a thick neck other than being a football player, or perhaps there are many. The plausibility of the argument hangs on this point of judgment, as assessed by the reasoner and his audience. In general, according to Perkins et al., the real issue in informal argument is the reasoner's testing of the plausibility of the "converted" form against his world knowledge. Adequate attention to this testing process, rather than the shunning of conversions, is a sound strategy of informal reasoning. After all, if one never considered converted forms, one's flexibility in constructing everyday arguments would be seriously impaired.

Still, the use of inductive reasoning when deduction is called for constitutes an error of thinking. And in some cases, affirming the consequent seems less like mistaking induction for deduction and more like an all out attempt to support a hypothesis at any cost. Such a case is illustrated nicely by an experiment by Wason (1974). Subjects were shown four cards placed on a table so that their visible sides contained respectively a vowel, a consonant, an even number, and an odd number. Subjects were told that each card had a letter on one side and a number on the other, and were asked to indicate which cards would have to be turned over to determine the truth or falsity of the following hypothesis: "If a card has a vowel on one side, then it has an even number on the other."

Most subjects indicated either the card showing the vowel and the one showing the even number, or just the card showing the vowel. The correct answer is the card showing the vowel and the one showing the odd number. This is because only by (1) finding an odd number on the back side of the card showing the vowel, or (2) a vowel on the back side of the card showing the odd number, would the statement be shown to be deductively false.

Subjects' errors here—selecting the card with the even number and ignoring the one with the odd number—indicated they were trying to confirm the hypothesis, not refute it. This does not mean, of course, that the subjects "wanted" the implication to hold. After all, why should they care? Rather, they appeared to be trying to match the pattern of the implication to the data. Either a vowel or an even number provided a partial match, and the subjects sought to check if the match was complete. Unfortunately, this pattern matching strategy, useful in many contexts, does not test the truth of an implication, because it overlooks a case that could disconfirm the implication as well as including a case that could not.

Confusion Between Polarity and Validity. Pollard and Evans (1980) presented subjects a conditional statement of the form "If P, then Q," and had them say whether they thought each of a number of statements followed deductively from it, including the inverse ("If not P, then Q"), the converse ("If Q, then P") and the contrapositive ("If not P, then not Q"). The results suggested that subjects' responses were little influenced by deductive validity but strongly influenced by a response bias: subjects tended to accept as valid those statements that had affirmative antecedents or negative consequents. Pollard and Evans refer to this tendency as a "polarity bias" and attribute it to a caution heuristic that may facilitate the making of effective decisions under uncertainty in real-life situations. They make the important point that the fact that subjects failed to make valid deductions on abstract reasoning tasks does not necessarily mean that they are incapable of making effective decisions in real-world situations. The specific polarity effects observed by Pollard and Evans may, the investigators suggest, have the effect in real life of maximizing the individual's chances of making statements that are unlikely to be proved wrong. Again, then, we have a case of people using something other than validity in the evaluation of deductive arguments. And again, what they use is by no means irrational. It is just not validity.

Errors Due to Difficult Terms

The Troublesome Or. In evaluating deductive arguments, people make more errors (or take longer) when the premises or conclusion involve a disjunction, *or*, than when they involve a conjunction, *and* (Neisser & Weene, 1962). Unlike the previous cases we considered, this failure does not seem to be due to substituting some process for the determination of validity; rather this problem may simply reflect that *or* is more difficult to understand than is *and*, i.e., our mental processes are such that *or* requires more computational resources than *and*.

This suggestion is strengthened by a number of related facts. For one, most natural concepts are roughly expressible as a conjunction of attributes while few seem to be expressible as a disjunction of attributes (Smith & Medin, 1981). Similarly, in their classic work on the acquisition of artificial concepts, Bruner, Goodnow, and Austin (1956) found that concepts defined in terms of disjunctions of attributes ("red or square") were more difficult to discover than those defined in terms of conjunctions of the same attributes ("red and square"). And finally, computer program statements that involve disjunctive operators are more susceptible to error and less easily debugged than similar statements involving conjunctive operators (Miller, 1973; Thomas & Miller, 1974).

Ineffective Use of Negative Information. People seem to have undue difficulty in using negative information when evaluating deductive arguments. Thus, mention of either explicit or implicit negatives in the premises or conclusion of a deductive argument increases the chances of an error in reasoning (e.g., Clark, 1971). The problem does not seem to be due to a failure to consider validity, but rather to the computational complexities involved in understanding and using negatives. Indeed, there is a considerable body of literature attesting to the fact that negatives are harder to process than positives in numerous contexts (see Clark & Clark, 1977, for a review).

Altering the Representation

There seem to be a number of problems in deductive reasoning that arise because people do not form an adequate representation of the argument they are attempting to evaluate. An illogical argument can sometimes be made to conform to the laws of deductive logic, either by restating premises or conclusions or by deleting premises from, or adding them to, original forms. Such maneuvers, which are found in examples of human reasoning (Henle, 1962), may produce a deductively valid form at the expense of modifying the substance of the argument.

Premise Conversion. A special case of argument modification is the interchanging of terms in a premise. Apparently many college students interpret "A implies B" as "A is equivalent to B," and they do not recognize the difference between "All A are B" and "All B are A" (O'Brien, 1973; Thornton, 1980). Indeed, premise conversion seems to be such a common problem that Revlis (1975b) has argued that some of the reasoning errors that have been attributed to the confusion of logic and truth can also be explained in terms of premise conversion.

Some tend to view premise conversion as just an encoding error. Such a view allows one to believe that the reasoner arrives at an invalid conclusion without violating any of the rules of deductive logic. In changing the meaning of a premise, the conversion also transforms the argument or syllogism, and the reasoner appears to be making a logical error only because he is solving a syllogism other than the one actually written down. But dismissing premise conversion as a simple encoding error is open to question. If "All A are B" gets encoded as "All B are A" as a result of careless reading, perhaps encoding error is the right term for it. But if the conversion is based on a l ack of understanding that "All A are B" and "All B are A" are different assertions, or that "All A are B" does not imply "All B are A," this can be viewed as a serious logical problem itself.

Unlike the conversion of "All A are B" into " All B are A," some conversions will not affect the logic of an argument. For example, converting "No A are B" into "No B are A" has no effect on the validity of the argument. The two negative universal statements are equivalent in meaning, whereas the two positive universals are not. The important question is whether one who converts such assertions realizes this distinction. If one does, the conversion might be considered an encoding error; if one does not, it goes deeper than that.

Revlin, Leirer, Yopp, and Yopp (1980) point out that the conversion error may sometimes be prevented by one's knowledge of the relationship involved. One is unlikely, for example, to reverse the terms in the assertion "All horses are animals" simply because one knows that not all animals are horses. The same investigators have shown that people who believe the converse of a positive universal statement are more likely to make an error in deductive reasoning that can be attributed to premise conversion than are people who do not hold that belief. For example, a person who believes that "All artistic people are unconventional" is more likely than someone who does not believe this to make an error in deductive reasoning that can be attributed to a conversion of the assertion "All unconventional people are artistic." This result strongly suggests that both premise conversion and a confusion between truth and validity can play a role at the same time.

Adding Pragmatic Inferences. People often read more into assertions than is really there. Thus upon reading "John pounded the nail" people are very likely to infer that John did the pounding with a hammer (e.g., Bransford & Johnson, 1972). Inferring that the instrument was a hammer is an example of a pragmatic inference.

If the original sentence had been a premise in an argument, then clearly the addition of the pragmatic inference would change the kinds of conclusions that could be deduced validly. For example, with the added inference, one could deduce that John did an action with a hammer, whereas this is an invalid deduction from the original sentence. So here we have another case of an error in deductive reasoning arising from a misrepresentation of the premises, though in this case the misrepresentation results from an addition to the premises rather than a reversal of them.

Again we need to point out that while pragmatic inferences can lead to errors in deductive reasoning, use of them is often a sound practice in inductive reasoning. That is, pragmatic inferences often (perhaps usually) constitute reasonable inductions. Pragmatic inferences play a particularly useful role in our interpretation and use of language: indeed we would have a difficult time using language without them. When, for example, in the context of a baseball game, we interpret the statement "John hit the ball" to mean "John hit the baseball with a baseball bat," the interpretation is likely to be correct. Or if when told that David's new working hours permit him to spend more time with his children, we infer that as a consequence of the new working hours, David in fact spends more time with his children, we may be inferring no more than the speaker intended that we infer. (Of course, sometimes the speaker may be out to mislead us, as when a commercial advertisement is constructed so that the listener is likely to encode and remember it as a claim favorable to the product even though such a claim was not explicitly made.)

Fallacy of the Undistributed Middle. Another way to misrepresent a deductive argument is to assign different meanings to the same term when it appears in different premises of the argument. We can illustrate with the following syllogism: "All famous twentieth-century mathematicians are doctors," "all doctors have a medical degree," "therefore all famous mathematicians have a medical degree." One could arrive at this false conclusion if the doctor in the first premise were interpreted in the Ph.D. sense while that in the second premise were interpreted in the medical sense. The argument would be invalid in this case, however, because the "middle" term—the term that is common to the two premises—is not really one term but two. Since many words in everyday language are ambiguous, there is a substantial potential for misrepresenting a natural-language deductive argument in this manner.

Introducing Circularity in the Argument. Finally, we should note that sometimes people add information to a premise that essentially amounts to the conclusion. That is, the conclusion is literally assumed in the premise, which results in what is called a circular or question-begging argument.

Summary

The general picture that emerges from the above cursory review is this. Most people seem to have available the processes that can check the deductive validity of an argument, but they make errors in deduction primarily because (1) they do not exclude criteria other than validity and (2) they do not confine their representation to exactly what was presented. Both types of errors are hardly irrational. Using criteria like truth, consistency, and inductive support clearly help us understand our world and negotiate in it. Similarly, adding plausible inferences to given information is also an indispensable heuristic for much that goes under the heading of understanding. The problems we have in deductive reasoning, then, seem to stem, in part at least, from the difficulty of curtailing these useful heuristics and attending only to the form of the argument.

2. ERRORS IN INDUCTIVE REASONING

Nature of Inductive Thinking

Though we may be little aware of it, we are constantly in the business of generating and evaluating inductive hypotheses. Every time we move from some specific observations about the world to a generalization, we have made an induction; thus, much of what we call learning is really induction.

The literature on induction and learning is far too vast for us to review, and much of it is irrelevant to our purposes. Our interest is in the kinds of inductive situations that occur frequently in everyday life; and we are particularly concerned with the errors and biases that people manifest in these everyday inductive situations. Even this relatively constrained topic has an extensive research literature associated with it, much of which has recently been reviewed by Kahneman and Tversky (e.g., 1972, 1973, 1974, 1980) and by Nisbett and Ross (1980). In what follows, frequently we rely on these major sources.

Generating and/or evaluating an inductive argument involves a number of distinct components, each of which has its own associated potential errors or biases. Nisbett and Ross (1980) provide an extensive list of these components and their associated biases, and we use a shortened version of this list to structure our discussion. Induction, then, may be broken into the following three components:

1. Drawing a sample. Every inductive situation involves making some observations about the world, where such observations constitute a sample. For example, if we are interested in divorce rates among physicians, we might contact several physicians at random and inquire about their marital status; more likely, we might try to retrieve from memory cases of divorced physicians.
2. Relating a sample to a hypothesis. Given a sample, one may relate it to a hypothesis or generalization in various ways. In one case, there may be a specific hypothesis of interest, and one uses the sample to alter one's belief in the hypothesis. In another, there may be no specific hypothesis of interest, and one's job is to generalize some aspect or parameter of the sample. The first case can be illustrated by the situation in which one tries to evaluate the specific hypothesis that physicians are more likely to get divorced than elementary school teachers; the second case can be illustrated by the situation in which one tries to estimate the proportion of physicians that are divorced. Both of these cases will figure in our discussion.
3. Forming new hypotheses. We are not always given specific hypotheses to test; and even when we are, sometimes they must be abandoned. In such cases, one has to use sample data to generate a new hypothesis.

In what follows, we review the best known biases or errors that are manifested in these three components of induction.

Biases in Drawing a Sample

Failure to Sample Enough Information. It is an intuitively attractive notion that one should sample as much relevant information as possible before attempting to evaluate a hypothesis or draw a generalization. People are biased, however, toward samples much smaller than optimal. There seem to be two general reasons for this bias. First, there is some evidence that one may be "overloaded" with information when there are too many factors to consider in complex situations (Ackoff, 1967; Hayes, 1964; Hoepfl & Huber, 1970). When this happens, people may ignore some subset of those factors (Slovic & Lichtenstein, 1971); or, if they attempt to consider all the factors, the quality of their performance may actually suffer (Hayes, 1964; Kanarick, Huntington, & Petersen, 1969; Rigney & DeBow, 1966).

Second, in non-laboratory situations, information usually is acquired only at some cost, and there may be a point at which the cost of additional information exceeds its worth. Laboratory experiments designed to evaluate the ability of people to calibrate their information-seeking behavior to the cost or value of the information sought have shown that performance often is suboptimal in this regard. The results of these studies are not easily summarized in a sentence, inasmuch as sometimes too much information has been sought and sometimes too little. A tentative generalization that seems warranted, however, is the following: Too much information often is sought when the a priori uncertainty of the situation is small, and too little when the a priori uncertainty is large (Nickerson & Feehrer, 1975).

Failure to Sample in an Unbiased Way: The Availability Heuristic. In many inductive situations, our sample must be drawn from memory. If asked for our belief in the hypothesis that college professors tend to be politically radical, for example, we retrieve from memory some information about professors and then use this sample to determine our degree of belief in the hypothesis. Kahneman and Tversky (1972) have noted that in situations like this, the more available the critical information in memory (e.g., instances of radical professors) the greater the frequency we will attribute to the relevant event and consequently the greater our belief in the hypothesis of interest. The use of availability in memory to estimate frequency in the world has been called the availability heuristic.

By and large, the availability heuristic serves us well: since frequency of experience is itself a major determinant of availability in memory, one can often safely infer high frequency from high availability. However, there are a number of cases in which use of the availability heuristic can lead to errors in inductive reasoning. The cause of the error can readily be illustrated with our previous example. To get an unbiased sample or estimate of radical professors, one should retrieve an unbiased sample of professors and count how many are radical. What people actually do, however, is retrieve a biased sample, one that is heavily weighted toward radical professors, perhaps because such professors are more salient (and hence available), or perhaps because people are using *radical* as well as *professors* as a retrieval cue in entering memory. Either way, the availability heuristic has produced a biased sample, and given this, the evaluation of the hypothesis will almost certainly be in error.

Another example of such biased sampling is illustrated by a well known study of Kahneman and Tversky (1972). Subjects were asked to estimate which is more frequent in English, words that start with k or words that have k as their third letter (only words at least three letters long were of interest). Most subjects choose k-initial words, even though there are in fact far more English words that have k as their third letter. The reason for the error appears to be that it is easier to retrieve words from memory by their initial letter than by their third one; thus a biased sample is produced. Again, the problem is that availability in memory is a function of more than just frequency, and consequently availability can be responsible for a biased estimate of frequency.

This same kind of reasoning also explains why people rather consistently overestimate the frequency of events that seem to have some shock value, such as murders and fatal accidents (Lichtenstein, Slovic, Fischhoff, Layman, & Coombs, 1978; Tversky & Kahneman, 1973), as the availability of such events in memory should be relatively high. Similarly, people tend to overestimate the probability of spectacular or catastrophic rare events and underestimate the probability of less spectacular but more common events (Bar-Hillel, 1980; Kahneman & Tversky, 1972).

Failure to Sample in an Unbiased Way: The Confirmation Bias. For cases in which people are trying to evaluate a specific hypothesis, a major bias is to sample selectively information that is consistent with the hypothesis and to ignore information that is inconsistent with it. The result is that people tend to accept hypotheses for which corroborating evidence exists but that have never been put to a conclusive test. That is, no effort has been made to find disconfirming evidence. The problem is caricatured by the neurotic Bostonian who persists in snapping his fingers to keep elephants out of his living room because the procedure has proved to be so effective in the past. Narveson (1980) suggests that not only do students writing compositions typically evaluate their claims by considering supporting evidence only, but that standard methods for teaching compositions foster this strategy.

Wason (1974) has studied this problem experimentally with "discover the rule" type tasks. His basic finding is that when people succeed in discovering a rule or hypothesis that works for the samples given, they often fail to subject the hypothesis to the kind of test that might demonstrate its invalidity. For example, given the task of discovering the rule by which the number triads (8, 10,12), (16, 18, 20), were generated, subjects were likely to hypothesize "successive even numbers," and then to test this hypothesis by generating sample triads that conformed to this rule. Subjects rarely attempted to test the adequacy of the hypothesis by generating a sample triad that failed to conform to the working hypothesis but did conform to a more inclusive one. Thus, if the true rule in this example happened to be "any three numbers in increasing magnitude," subjects would be unlikely to discover it because of their willingness to accept the more restrictive rule on inconclusive evidence.

Even when told of the incorrectness of their hypothesis, and shown conclusive disconfirming evidence, Wason's subjects often insisted that their rule was validated by the fact that the samples they generated all proved to be consistent with it. In other words, they failed to recognize the logical requirements of a conclusive validating test. Wason also noted that, when informed of the invalidity of a hypothesized rule, subjects often tended to generate other candidate rules that were more complex and restrictive. This suggests that the induction of a general rule is sometimes impeded by the induction of a more specific rule that fits the data equally well.

Bartlett (1958) has also reported a result that illustrates the problem of failing to look for disconfirming evidence. Subjects were given the task of inducing the rule(s) by which certain actions had been performed on a set of visual stimuli and of applying the rule(s) to continue the actions. Having found a single (necessary but insufficient) rule, the subjects neglected to seek others that were also necessary to prescribe the continued action unambiguously.

Particularly disconcerting examples of the tendency to neglect seeking disconfirming evidence have been found by social psychologists. For example, Snyder and his colleagues (Snyder, 1981; Snyder & Cantor, 1979; Snyder & Swann, 1978) have demonstrated a kind of confirmation bias in testing hypotheses about people's personality attributes. The basic paradigm in Snyder's experiments goes as follows. Subjects are told that they are about to meet another person, referred to as the target person, and that their job is to find out whether or not the target person has a specific type of personality. For one group of subjects, the personality type is specified as extravert; for another group the type is introvert. Both groups are given personality sketches of a typical type: for the extravert group, the sketch mentions general traits such as "outgoing," "sociable," and "talkative"; for the introvert group, the general traits mentioned include "shy," "timid," and "quiet." All subjects are given a list of specific beliefs, attitudes, and actions, from which they are to choose a subset of items about which to question the target person, some of these items having been previously rated as typical of extraverts, and others having been prerated as typical of introverts.

The basic finding is that the subjects who are to test the extravert hypothesis choose more items typical of extraverts—that is, they sample more items that would confirm an extravert hypothesis—while subjects testing the introvert hypothesis choose more items typical of introverts. Thus both groups of subjects tend to sample items for which a *yes* answer would count as confirmation of their hypothesis, and to neglect items for which a *yes* answer would count against their hypothesis.

While this finding demonstrates a bias toward sampling evidence that would confirm the original hypothesis, it is important to note two critical differences between the items used in these experiments and those employed in studies concerned with hypotheses about objects rather than people. One difference is this: while an object cannot, be, say, both large and small, a person may be both outgoing and shy, depending on the situation. Subjects in Snyder's experiments apparently failed to appreciate this fact of human behavior and treated hypotheses about people the way they would treat hypotheses about objects.

A second critical difference is that the classification of people, unlike that of objects, may affect the way they behave. This is clearly demonstrated in a follow-up study by Snyder, in which it was shown that people actually acted more extraverted (e.g., more sociable and outgoing), as determined by independent judges listening to a tape of the interview, if they were questioned by a subject testing the extravert hypothesis than if they were questioned by a subject testing the introvert hypothesis. Similarly, people appeared more introverted when questioned by a subject testing for introversion than when questioned by one testing for extraversion. In short, the situation illustrates the operation of an uncertainty principle in a psychological context, wherein the sample is modified by the act of measurement (and in this case by the attitude of the measurer.) The confirmation bias in social situations is doubly pernicious: it not only leads to a biased sample that can confirm what might have been a false hypothesis, but it can alter reality and turn the false hypothesis into what appears to be a true one.

One would like to make students aware of this confirmation bias, with the goal of helping them to become more resistant to sampling only potentially confirmatory evidence, especially when the hypothesis of interest is about another's personality. Some of Snyder's experiments identify ways that will not work. It appears to do little good, for example, to point out that any particular social hypothesis may have a small chance of being true, for Snyder showed that the prior probability of the hypothesis had no effect on the bias to sample only confirming evidence. Similarly, Snyder obtained no effect on the confirmation bias of payoffs-for-accuracy which suggests that simply emphasizing the seriousness and importance of testing social hypotheses probably will not suffice. (A possible approach might involve a kind of "therapy." Students could perform something like Snyder's task on one another; then, with some subsequent discussion of what transpired, the targets among the students might come to understand that they have been misclassified, and perhaps also that this misclassification actually affected their subsequent behavior.)

Biases in Relating a Sample to a Hypothesis

Ineffective Use of Negative Information. When a hypothesis concerns class membership, then samples that are not instances of the class can of course be used in evaluating the hypothesis. To illustrate, suppose we are interested in this hypothesis: in order to be good teacher, the only attribute one needs is a high level of motivation. If we come across someone who is highly motivated but a poor teacher (i.e., a non-instance of "good teacher"), we should use this sample to disconfirm the generalization. It appears, though, that people have difficulty using such negative information effectively.

This failure to use negative information effectively is well illustrated in the studies of Bruner, Goodnow, and Austin (1956) on the induction of artificial concepts. In these studies it was possible to establish rigorously the information content of sampled non-instances, and to demonstrate that even when this content equalled that of positive instances, negative instances were used less effectively than positive ones in evaluating hypotheses.

It is possible that part of the problem in relating non-instances to hypotheses is that the processing must involve negatives. We have already noted that processing negatives may require more computational resources than processing positives.

Conservatism in the Use of Probabilistic Information. A fairly large volume of data has been accumulated over the past couple of decades on the question of how effectively people process probabilistic information when compared to an ideal Bayesian decision maker (i.e., a decision maker that relates data to hypotheses via application of Bayes Theorem, and makes no errors in calculation). For example, given two urns, one with 80% red balls and the other with 70% red balls, and a sample that is 90% red, what do people think the probability is that the sample was drawn from the 80% urn, and what would an ideal Bayesian decision maker think?

Perhaps the basic conclusion to emerge from the research is that people generally are more conservative in their use of probabilistic information than an ideal Bayesian would be. In particular, posterior probabilities (the probabilities of hypotheses after data have been sampled) typically attain more extreme values and reach asymptote faster when calculated according to Bayes theorem than when estimated by people (Edwards, Lindman, &

Phillips, 1965). Another way to characterize this result is to say that people tend to extract less information from samples than does the application of Bayes theorem. The latter presumably represents an optimal way of aggregating probabilistic data for the purpose of determining the relative certitude of each of a set of competing hypotheses.

More recent research on this topic suggests that the reason why people deviate so substantially from an "ideal" decision maker is that the computations they make are in fact nothing like Bayes theorem. Rather, they use what Kahneman and Tversky (1973) have termed the "representativeness" heuristic, to which we now turn.

Failure to Consider Abstract Statistical Information: The Representative Heuristic. If, when asked to judge "How probable is this sample given this hypothesis," one considers only how representative or similar the sample is to the hypothesis, we would say that one is using the representativeness heuristic. The following example from Kahneman and Tversky (1973) illustrates this heuristic. Subjects were given a brief personality sketch of a man and asked to estimate the likelihood that he was an engineer or a lawyer. The sketch was written so that the man seemed more representative of our concept of an engineer than of that of a lawyer, but subjects were also informed that (in this experiment) only 30% of the people were engineers while the remaining 70% were lawyers. The statistical information, which gives the base rates or prior probabilities for the hypotheses of being an engineer and being a lawyer, was totally ignored by subjects. They made their decisions solely on the basis of how representative the personality description was of their concept of engineers and lawyers, and so in this case overwhelmingly judged the man to be an engineer.

Thus, use of the representativeness heuristic makes one insensitive to the critical factor of the prior probability that a hypothesis or generalization is true. Since this factor figures centrally in Bayes Theorem, we can now see one reason why people appear suboptimal when compared to a Bayesian decision maker. The representativeness heuristic also leads people to be insensitive to other statistical information, particularly the size of the sample. Again we can illustrate with an example from Tversky and Kahneman's (1974) work. Subjects were told that on a particular day 60% of the babies born in a hospital were boys; they were then asked whether this aberrant result is more likely in a small hospital (only 15 babies born per day) or in a large hospital (50 babies born per day). Subjects showed no preference between the two hospitals (they should have favored the smaller one, inasmuch as large percentage deviations are more likely in small samples). Apparently, if the proportion of boys born in a small and a large hospital were the same, both hospitals would be judged to be equally representative (or equally unrepresentative) of the proportion of baby boys in the population at large. Subjects showed no sensitivity to the importance of sample size.

There is another consequence of the representativeness heuristic that deserves mention. Since the heuristic amounts to determining the similarity of a sample to a concept or category, when the category is about a personality type (or about a racial or ethnic type) it may amount to little more than a stereotype. A stereotype is a loose category, one whose properties apply to few rather than most instances, and many person categories tend to be stereotypes. Representativeness applied to person categories can yield the extreme overgeneralizations that are the hallmark of stereotyping.

Failure to Discard Unlikely Hypotheses: Counterproductive Persistence. Holding on to a hypothesis when it no longer fits the sampled data well is an extremely common problem in induction. It has recently been highlighted by the work of Ross, Lepper, and Hubbard (1975) and Nisbett and Ross (1980), but many classic studies of induction reveal the same persistence.

In their work on concept attainment, Bruner, Goodnow, and Austin (1956) had subjects attempt to generate hypotheses about concepts defined in terms of conjunctions or disjunctions of specific attributes (e.g., "red and square," "blue or yellow," and "not circular"). Subjects acquired the information they needed to identify the concepts either by being shown instances of the target concept or by selecting items and being told whether in fact they were instances. Bruner et al. considered their subjects' performance, which they were able to classify in terms of four different types of information-seeking strategies, to be quite good on balance. However, one of the major suboptimal aspects of performance was a tendency to persist in focusing on once-useful cues after their usefulness had evaporated. Thus, subjects might originally hypothesize that color was critical to the target concept, and persist in this hypothesis even after they had accumulated clear-cut evidence to the contrary.

A similar tendency to persist on a course after contradictory data has been received was reported by Bartlett (1958). Subjects were asked to select a route that would get them from one geographical location to another. They were shown a sequence of maps, each map being somewhat more inclusive than the preceding one. The first map in the series showed the location of the point of departure; whereas only the last one showed both origin and destination; however, the subjects were initially told the destination's general direction. As an increasingly greater portion of the final map was revealed, it became apparent that routes that initially were headed in the right direction had turned so as now to be going away from the destination, while other routes that initially did not look promising now did so. Subjects often persisted with the routes they had originally chosen even after it became apparent that those routes were less likely than some others to get them to the desired destination.

In one of the many recent studies reviewed by Nisbett and Ross (1980), subjects were tricked into forming a misleading hypothesis about themselves, perhaps that they were unusually inept at some task. Then, in a debriefing session, subjects were informed that they had been tricked, that the task had been completely rigged, and that their poor performance had nothing at all to do with their ability level. When subsequently asked to estimate their ability on the task and on related ones, subjects persisted in their initial negative assessments. The same persistence also occurred when the initial misleading hypothesis was positive (e.g., subjects were led to believe they were unusually good at some task). The power of persistence seems particularly important for teachers to recognize, because of the influence they can exert, by means of it, on students attitudes about themselves.

Biases in Forming New Hypotheses

Having considered problems in relating data to prespecified hypotheses, let us move to the problems that people have when they must construct a new hypothesis.

Considering Too Few Alternatives. When we have to construct a new hypothesis, often we restrict ourselves to too few alternatives. Instead of considering all relevant hypotheses, we prematurely limit the "hypothesis space." A particularly compelling illustration of this bias is our tendency to oversimplify many situations by presenting them as dichotomous. We consider only two alternatives when in fact there may be many possibilities. We often think of people, for example, in polar terms: black or white, rich or poor, educated or uneducated, liberal or conservative. Such dichotomizing grossly distorts reality, and can have unfortunate behavioral consequences.

Problems in Detecting Covariance. To create a new hypothesis that relates factors A and B, one must be able to detect how A and B covary with one another. If, for example, we want to construct a hypothesis that relates (a) academic success to (b) participation in intramural sports, detecting the covariance of these two factors amounts to detecting the relative frequencies of four different cases: (1) students who do well academically and are active in sports (this is often called the ++ case, since it contains instances that are high on both factors); (2) students who do well academically but are not active in sports (the +− case); (3) students who do poorly academically but are active in sports (the −+ case); and (4) students who do poorly academically and are not active in sports (the− − case). Rough knowledge of the relative frequencies of these four cases amounts to rough knowledge of the correlation between the two factors.

Recently psychologists have begun to study in detail how well people can detect covariation (see Nisbett & Ross, 1980). The results indicate that by and large, people are not very good at detecting it, and for two reasons. First, people tend to focus on the ++ case and ignore the other three cases almost entirely. In terms of the above example, people will conclude that academic success and sports participation go together as long as there are numerous instances of academically successful students who are active in sports. They will do so even if there are as many instances of academically successful students who are not active in sports (Jennings, Amabile, & Ross, 1981). Second, even when people lack detailed hypotheses about the relation between particular factors, they have some general preconceptions that seem relevant and these preconceptions affect people's perception of the occurrences of the factors (Jennings et al., 1981; Nisbett & Ross, 1980). In what is perhaps the classic demonstration of this bias (Chapman & Chapman, 1969), subjects were shown photographs of psychiatric patients and told the diagnostic category of each. Most subjects ended up with the hypothesis that paranoids were more likely to have unusual (suspicious) eyes than were other kinds of patients. Objectively, however, there was no relation in the photographs between diagnostic category and type of eyes (not even when we consider only the ++ cells!). The relation, or covariation, that subjects "detected" must have been due to the general preconception that paranoid people are distrustful, and that distrust can be seen in one's eyes.

Shweder (1977) has gone so far as to argue that correlation is not an intuitively available concept to normal adults who have not had any explicit instruction with respect to it. Resemblance, on the other hand is a readily available intuitive concept, and it is used inappropriately, he suggests, in place of the concept of correlation. For reasons that are not well understood, people come to affiliate certain concepts, e.g., self esteem and leadership, and will use these affiliations as the basis for predicting co-occurrences in the world. They do this even when the predictions are inconsistent with what they know or believe about the frequencies of occurrence of predicted events.

Shweder gives an example of an individual making judgments of the relative frequency of tense and tolerant people. The individual judged that out of 100 people, 70 are tense and 75 tolerant, but then when asked to judge the co-occurrence, he estimated that of the people who are tense, 10% are tolerant. This is obviously contradictory. If only 7 of the 70 tense people are tolerant, then at most 37 people can be tolerant (7 of the tense people and all

30 of the people who are not tense), which is inconsistent with the estimate that 75 people out of 100 are tolerant.

In general, Shweder argues, people ignore what they know or believe about relative frequencies of occurrences when they judge the relative frequencies of co-occurrences. The latter judgments are heavily and inappropriately influenced by conceptual associations, which do not necessarily bear any resemblance to the way things are correlated in the world.

> Normal adults seem disinclined to reason correlationally when they make claims about what predicts what in experience. They seem to lack a concept of correlation. Correlation relevant information is hard to think about. The concept of correlation is not intuitively available to the everyday mind. (p. 460)

Confusing Co-occurrence and Causality. In those cases in which people do manage to get some idea of the covariation or correlation between two factors, they may mistakenly hypothesize that the factors are causally related when in fact they are only correlated. To return to a previous example, if we have detected a covariation between academic success and participation in sports, we might try and link them causally (e.g., "Sports participation relaxes you, so you can go back to your studies refreshed"), when in fact there may be no causal relation at all between them.

The tendency to turn correlation into causation is particularly strong when the factors involved are temporally ordered. If A and B are not only correlated, but in addition B invariably follows A, it seems natural for us to assume that B is caused by A. But consistent temporal succession is not a reliable indication of a cause-effect relationship, a point readily demonstrated by counterexamples. Night invariably follows day; however, we would not say that day causes night. If we were to equate cause with invariable temporal succession, then we would have to say that day causes night; but for the sake of consistency we would also be obliged, of course, to say that night causes day, inasmuch as the temporal succession applies in this case as well.

Summary

Our review of errors and biases in inductive reasoning has yielded a number of major observations, which we now summarize. With regard to sampling information, the evidence suggests that we sample too little and in a biased way. One major source of bias is the availability heuristic, which is a reasonable procedure in many circumstances, but, like virtually any heuristic it leads us astray in certain cases. The other major source of bias appears to be our tendency to try to confirm rather than disconfirm the hypothesis we are currently entertaining. While we might be tempted to justify this bias on the grounds that the time pressures of everyday life motivate us to confirm hypotheses as quickly as possible, this will not do. Ironically, the ways in which the confirmation bias is expressed give an illusion of efficiency, but in fact they impede the effective evaluation of hypotheses; they often lead to the acceptance of false hypotheses, and they do not produce compelling evidence of the truth of hypotheses that happen to be true.

On the matter of relating sample information to a hypothesis, perhaps our biggest problems again stem from overuse of a heuristic and our tendency to cling to a hypothesis once it has been formed. In this case, the heuristic of interest is representativeness, which focuses on similarity and ignores abstract, statistical information. The heuristic probably works well in many situations, but there are cases in which it leads to erroneous conclusions. As for clinging to a hypothesis, we are concerned with the failure to discard a hypothesis after disconfirming evidence has accumulated; while this bias is conceptually distinct from the confirmation bias in sampling, both biases seem to be part of an overall disposition to determine the current state of affairs as quickly as possible, and to fit all subsequent information into that interpretation.

Finally, there are biases relating to the forming of new hypotheses. Here one major problem is that we are not very objective about establishing covariance: either we focus only on that case in which all factors occur when we should be considering all the data, or we allow our preconceptions to overwhelm the data. The other major problem at this level is that we are too quick to read causation into what may be correlation at best.

Perkins, Allen, and Hafner (in press) summarize the characteristics of such lapses in reasoning by suggesting that many people reason as though they were trying to minimize cognitive load, rather than to make sound inferences. Perkins, et al. speak of the careless reasoner as a "makes sense" epistemologist, whose tacit ground for belief is whether an account of a situation "makes superficial sense" relative to his world knowledge. Such a reasoner will casually elevate correlation to causation, affirm the consequent, perseverate with hypotheses, and do whatever else keeps cognitive load low, so long as the conclusion does not conflict with his intuitions. In contrast, an ideal "critical epistemologist" recognizes that intuitive fit is a weak test of truth and expends more effort to exercise stringent standards and cross-check claims in a variety of ways.

3. REASONING ERRORS DUE TO SOCIAL FACTORS

Thus far we have implicitly assumed that when people are engaged in a reasoning task, their only motivation is to be correct; therefore any error they make must have a strictly cognitive origin. While this view seems valid for many situations, clearly there are cases in which people's social motivations and social relations may lie behind reasoning errors. We turn now to a consideration of such factors.

While there may be many different ways in which social factors can bias reasoning, only two kinds of biases have received much attention, and only these concern us here. One kind of bias seems to stem from a desire to enhance our self esteem: we tend to evaluate hypotheses that we have formulated or adopted more favorably than those that we view as belonging to other people. The second kind of social bias of interest involves a sort of *argumentum ad hominem*: in evaluating a hypothesis we sometimes evaluate the people who hold the hypothesis rather than the hypothesis itself.

Favoritism in Evaluating Hypotheses in which One has a Vested Interest

Failure to View One's Own Opinions Objectively. Frequently, we fail to view our own opinions as objectively as we view those of others. Objectivity and openmindedness are everywhere recognized as requirements for logical thinking, but the ability to treat the opinion of another person as favorably as one treats one's own does not appear to be a common ability. Schopenhauer (undated) came close to claiming that it is non-existent:

> For human nature is such that if A and B are engaged in thinking in common, and are communicating their opinions to one another on any subject, so long as it is not a mere fact of history, and A perceives that B's thoughts on one and the same subject are not the same as his own, he does not begin by revising his own process of thinking, so as to discover any mistake which he may have made, but he assumes that the mistake has occurred in B's. (p. 3)

While we view this preferential treatment of one's own beliefs as evidence of lack of objectivity, we should point out that there may also be some rational reasons for defending our opinions and deductions with such tenacity. For one thing, the fact that we cannot immediately refute an argument against a position does not mean that a compelling refutation does not exist. Opinions, especially those that are important to an individual, often are formed over long periods of time, and the various kinds of evidence that contributed to the strength of an opinion may not be recallable on a moment's notice. If we were to let our opinions depend only on arguments that we could articulate on demand we would undoubtedly be less stable and predictable creatures than we are. This is not to suggest that the favored treatment of personal beliefs is always justified and that the problem is one of appearance only. Certainly we are often blind to the flaws in our own beliefs.

The notion that we fail to view our own opinions objectively is a rather general idea. It seems worthwhile to try to decompose this failure into several components. One component is our limited access to our own thought processes: while we may think we have access to all the mental processes that went into our deductions and inductions, often we have no more privileged access to these processes than does an outside observer. There are many experimental demonstrations of cases in which subjects were confident they knew their reasons for doing something, when in fact their behavior was being "controlled" by factors of which they had no awareness (Nisbett & Wilson, 1977). Thus we hold onto our own hypotheses so fervently, in part, because we think we used only rational processes in their construction, when in fact often we do not really know what went into the construction of these hypotheses.

Another component in our failure to be objective about our hypotheses stems, perhaps, from our need to maintain self esteem. Given our vested interests in our own hypotheses, we tend to confuse the strength of an opinion with validity or truth. In commenting on this phenomenon, Bartlett (1958) had this to say:

> It is not in the nature of the assertion, but in the manner of assertiveness that everyday thinking seeks to attain necessity. Its commonest introductory phrases, when it is expressed in words, are "of course," "beyond a doubt," and—especially perhaps in political circles—"I am (or "we are") confident that." The source of the compulsion being now within the thinker, and particularly in his social group, it is possible, and indeed common, for completely contradictory issues to claim the same necessity. Then the only way either side has of enforcing its claim is yet more violent assertiveness. It is partly on account of this that many people have said that everyday thinking is largely emotional thinking. (p. 181)

Still a third component in our failure to be objective about our own views is our tendency to overestimate our knowledge about various topics. There is ample experimental evidence that people fairly consistently overestimate their knowledge of matters about which they, in fact, know very little or nothing at all (Bradley, 1981; Einhorn & Hogarth, 1978; Fischhoff, 1980; Slovic, Fischhoff, & Lichtenstein, 1977; Slovic & Lichtenstein, 1971).

In one experiment, Bradley (1981) had subjects rate their level of expertise in each of 61 areas in which they attempted also to answer a variety of true-false questions. Among the questions were some whose truth or falsity was virtually impossible to determine. Upon giving subjects also the option of responding "Don't Know," as well as "True" or "False," Bradley found that the higher the subject's own rating of his expertise for a given area, the less likely he was to use the "Don't Know" option for an impossible question in that area. In the same study Bradley also found that the greater the level of self-judged expertise in an area, the greater the likelihood that a subject would express a high level of confidence in answers that were incorrect. Bradley interpreted these results as evidence of a reluctance to admit ignorance when one should, especially with respect to an area in which one considers oneself to be well informed.

Partiality in the Assessment and Use of Evidence. This is something of a special case (or component) of our general failure to be objective about our hypotheses. We treat the partiality issue separately here because much of the relevant work focuses on the specifics of interpreting sample data and because this partiality seems to occur with any favored hypothesis, not just one of our own construction.

Bartlett (1958) expressed the problem this way: "The truth is that in everyday thinking any person enters the circumstances which set his mind to work already predisposed in favor of certain argument sequences and against others" (p. 174). In short, people have vested interests in certain arguments and (whether or not they are of their own making), and such vested interests can affect an individual's ability to weigh evidence or sample data objectively and fairly. Most systems of jurisprudence acknowledge this problem in requiring that jurors have no vested interest in the outcome of cases on which they serve.

There are some experimental data that tend to support the notion that partiality and vested interests can affect the way evidence and data are assessed and used. In the context of Bayesian decision tasks, several investigators have found that evidence that tends to confirm a favored hypothesis may be given greater weight than evidence that tends to disconfirm it (Brody, 1965; Geller & Pitz, 1968; Pitz, Downing, & Reinhold, 1967; Slovic, 1966). At least one study has even shown that evidence that tends to disconfirm a favored hypothesis may be misinterpreted as supportive of it (Grabitz & Jochem, 1972). Apparently even scientists and journal manuscript reviewers have been known to be less than objective in their uses of evidence on occasion (Mahoney, 1977; Mahoney & DeMonbreun, 1977). It has also been shown that people are more inclined to seek confirmatory evidence if they have espoused the hypothesis publicly than if they have not (Geller & Pitz, 1968; Gibson & Nichol, 1964; Pruitt, 1961).

Bartlett (1958), citing experiments in which people were asked to project the outcome of certain situations involving the interaction of rival social groups, noted that people often effect and justify decisions by considering the available evidence selectivity. He concluded, moreover, that decisions often are not reached as a result of consideration of the evidence at hand, but rather evidence is selectively appropriated so as to support a decision that has already been made.

Francis Bacon clearly understood this problem of partiality in interpreting evidence (and that of the confirmation bias more generally). His incisive observation on the subject is worth quoting at length:

> The human understanding when it has once adopted an opinion (either as being the received opinion or as being agreeable to itself) draws all things else to support and agree with it. And though there be a greater number and weight of instances to be found on the other side, yet these it either neglects and despises, or else by some distinction sets aside and rejects; in order that by this great and pernicious predetermination the authority of its former conclusions may remain inviolate. And therefore it was a good answer that was made by one who when they showed him hanging in a temple a picture of those who had paid their vows as having escaped shipwreck, and would have him say whether he did not now acknowledge the power of the gods,—"Aye," asked he again, "but where are they painted that were drowned, after their vows?" And such is the way of all superstition, whether in astrology, dreams, omens, divine judgments, or the like; wherein men, having a delight in such vanities, mark the events where they are fulfilled, but where they fail, though this happen much oftener, neglect and pass them by. But with far more subtlety does this mischief insinuate itself into philosophy and the sciences; in which the first conclusion colours and brings into conformity with itself all that come after, though far sounder and better. Besides, independently of that delight and vanity which I have described, it is the peculiar and perpetual error of human intellect to be more moved and excited by affirmatives than by negatives; whereas it ought properly to hold itself indifferently disposed towards both alike. Indeed in the establishment of any true axiom, the negative instance is the more forcible of the two (Bacon 1620/1939 p. 36).

Evaluating People Rather than Hypotheses

We are very social beings, and often it is difficult for us to separate a hypothesis or argument from the person who holds it. In such instances we end up evaluating the person rather than the merits of the case and we engage in *argumentum ad hominem*. The fact that this particular fallacy has a Latin name suggests that it has been recognized for a very long time and is acknowledged to be exceptionally prevalent. It means arguing "to the man" instead of to the point of the argument.

When, for example, one is judging the merits of a position and instead of considering the pros and cons of that position, one attacks the credibility of people who hold it, one is arguing *ad hominem*. Not all ad hominem arguments are used to attack a position; such arguments can also be used to maintain a position. Sometimes one may refuse to acknowledge the weight of counterarguments against a position simply because that position is identified with an individual to whom one has a strong sense of loyalty. A child, for example, might refuse to consider the possibility that some strongly held belief of his parents is wrong. Demagogues and charismatic leaders often seem to have so much influence over their followers that whatever they assert is accepted uncritically and appropriated even in the face of compelling evidence that the assertion is false.

However, an important qualification needs to be made. Sometimes one cannot speak so casually of "evaluating the person rather than the merits of the case," because the person presents the assertion as partly grounded in his own authority. For instance, his stated or unstated justification may be, "I was there and saw it ," or "I've studied this area for years," or even simply, "I've thought about this carefully before." All of these are claims of being in a special position to know—claims of expertise in a broad sense. In such cases, an ad hominem complaint may quite appropriately reduce one's certainty in a claim, either by casting doubt on the supposed expertise, or by imputing bias to the person, who may be misrepresenting the situation consciously or even unconsciously. Thus, our legal system allows lawyers to go to some lengths to establish or discredit the credibility of witnesses in court proceedings. Also, when one needs to decide whether to believe some claim, and one has virtually no objective evidence on which to base the decision, one might well consider the credibility of the source.

Summary

Reasoning biases that are due to social factors are at least as important to recognize as the other biases we have considered. First there are the errors that result from favoring our own hypotheses, both those we have generated ourselves and those we have adopted. Such favoritism seems to be due, in part, to: our mistaken belief we have direct access to all our own mental processes, our confusion of strength of opinion with validity or truth, our general tendency to overestimate our knowledge, and our partiality in the assessment of evidence. These errors are added to the other errors we make in sampling data and evaluating hypotheses. Partiality in the assessment of evidence, for example, augments the usual confirmation bias, culminating in what can be very biased sampling indeed.

In addition, errors can result from evaluating the people behind hypotheses and claims rather than the hypotheses and claims themselves. Ad hominem arguments, appeals to authority, and appeals to numbers sometimes seem to be devoid of logical content. On the other hand, even these errors sometimes have heuristic value. An ad hominem criticism may be appropriate, for example, if the maker of a claim justifies it in whole or part by some special authority or expertise he allegedly has.

4. FAILURES TO ELABORATE A MODEL OF A SITUATION

Recently, Perkins, Allen, and Hafner (1983) completed an extensive investigation of informal reasoning. We describe the results here in some detail because they shed some light on a type of reasoning that has not been studied much in the laboratory, but that is especially important in everyday life. This is the reasoning involved in constructing and evaluating informal arguments.

Samples of reasoning were gathered from over 300 subjects, ranging from 10th graders to 4th year doctoral degree candidates. The subjects were asked to reason about issues like, "Would a law requiring a five cent deposit on bottles and cans reduce litter?" or "Would a military draft increase the influence of the U.S. on world events?" Each subject considered two issues, and the investigators tape-recorded their positions and arguments. In addition, after each issue, the investigators administered a follow-up interview that probed the reasoning of the subjects further.

Two motives prompted the inquiry. First, the improvement of informal reasoning is a commonly mentioned objective of education. The investigators sought to determine whether general education had any measurable impact. Second, "natural" samples of informal reasoning have rarely been gathered and analyzed with statistical methods. Accordingly, a sample of informal reasoning on everyday issues might reveal problems of reasoning neglected by the normal treatments of both deductive and inductive reasoning discussed above.

Measuring the Quality of Informal Reasoning

To provide measures of the quality of the arguments produced, two of the investigators listened to all the arguments and rated them on various scales. The ratings were checked for consistency between the judges and consistency across the two available samples of each subject's reasoning. Only those scales that proved significant in both respects were analyzed further. Also, some scales were eliminated because of considerable redundancy with others.

In the end, six scales were kept. Three reflected the complexity of the arguments subjects produced: the number of sentences, the number of "scripts," which meant the number of distinct lines of argument a subject developed on a particular issue, and the number of objections to his basic position a subject mentioned. Three other measures reflected other matters: the number of times a subject needed to be prompted to stick to the topic, a rating of the subjects' explanation of the connection between a reason he mentioned and his conclusion (this explanation was elicited during the follow-up interview), and a global rating of the quality of the argument.

These variables all showed a consistent pattern of slow gains. In high school, for example, the sentence count started at about 11 and went up by 1.19 sentences per year; the number of scripts started at 1.79 and increased by .13 scripts per year; the number of objections began at .63 with an increment of .06 per year; and the overall rating on a 5 point scale began at 1. 65 and increased by .17 per year. The rates of gain for college and graduate school were of the same order.

Although each of the six variables only addresses one aspect of informal arguments, taken together they provide a multifaceted, albeit perhaps still partial, picture of the development of ability to construct such arguments throughout the high school and college years. Note that the figures are upper estimates of the effect of schooling, since the gains noted might be attributed in part to other factors—for instance, general maturation.

One is struck by the modest size of the gains, even if schooling is responsible for the total gain on each measure. Surely a year of schooling that had any appreciable connection with informal reasoning skills should do more for students than add one sentence to their arguments, lead them to consider about a tenth of a line of argument more, or alert them to one twentieth of an objection to their position. Accordingly, these data can be taken as at least suggestive evidence that conventional schooling does not have nearly the impact on informal reasoning skills that one might hope.

Common Errors in Informal Reasoning

Two of the investigators independently listened to the subjects' arguments on the second issue they considered and generated spontaneous criticisms. At the same time, the investigators developed a classification system for objections to informal arguments, working from a small subsample of the data. Then the investigators classified all the objections they had generated, using this system. An adequate level of interjudge agreement on the classifications was achieved.

Consequently, the investigators could determine which types of objections were most frequent, that is to say, which sorts of lapses occurred most often in this sample of informal arguments. Since the relative frequency of objections did not vary much from issue to issue, or across subject groups, it seems reasonable to suppose that the lapses identified as most frequent in this sample are of high frequency in informal arguments in general.

There follows a brief review of the most frequent types of objections.

Contrary consequent (15%). Objections that fall into this category start with the same premise as the original argument, but reason to a conclusion contrary to the original conclusion, a "contrary consequent." For example, many subjects argued roughly as follows on the draft issue: "A draft would increase our military power, and other countries, more impressed by our power, would be more subject to our influence." However, the following objection inferred a contrary consequent: "If there is a draft, this would lead to widespread internal protest and dissension, and that, in turn, would weaken our image in the eyes of the world and reduce our influence."

Disconnection (13%). This category accommodates objections to the effect that there is a logical gap in the argument; the premises do not, in principle, bear on the conclusion. For example, one person argued, "The U.S. cannot have more influence; the U.S. already has a lot." A natural objection to this is, "Having a lot of something does not, in principle, mean that you cannot have more of it."

Counterexample (11%). Objections that gave counterexamples were common. For example, someone might say, "A large army means an effective army." Someone might object, "Against a well-entrenched guerilla force, a large army may be ineffectual."

External factor (8%). This category refers to cases in which a generalization would normally apply, but not in the case in question because of special circumstances. For instance, someone might assert as above that "A large army means an effective army." The objection might be, "That used to be so. But nowadays it is number of missiles and technical knowhow that count."

Contradiction (7%). Here the objection is that the original argument contradicts itself, at least implicitly, for instance by mentioning counterexamples that are never explained away or by using double standards.

Neglected critical distinction (6%). This refers to cases in which a sweeping generalization neglects a crucial subcase that runs contrary to the generalization. For example, recall the generalization that "People will return the bottles and cans for the five cents." An objection to this might be, "People usually may, but it is people in parks and on picnics that litter, and they will not bother for the five cents."

Contrary antecedent (5%). Such objections point to alternatives to the antecedent identified by the original argument. For instance, the original argument may attribute an effect to a particular cause, while the objection points out a possible alternative cause.

Taken together, these categories accommodated 65% of the objections generated. Another 11 categories, all with frequencies of 3% or 2%, brought the total to 90%. The remaining 10% was spread thinly throughout the remaining categories in the classification system, with no one type occurring frequently enough to be worth mentioning.

Failures of Elaboration

Clearly, such information about the relative frequencies of objections might have educational significance. It could be a guide to the sorts of lapses that education for better reasoning should directly or indirectly address.

But do the problems identified here differ at all from those discussed earlier?

Certain of the categories just discussed correspond roughly to what might be considered formal errors in reasoning. Disconnection signifies a logical gap in an argument, while contradiction indicates an inconsistency. The former would include certain formal errors treated earlier, while the latter does not seem to be much discussed in the literature on deduction, perhaps because it is so blatant a violation.

Another category corresponds to what might be considered an inductive lapse: counterexample. Here the reasoner is accused of maintaining a generalization subject to ready refutation by counter instances. However, such an oversight is not generally much discussed in the research literature on inductive inference. There are perhaps two reasons for that. Many experimental investigations provide the subject with the data to reason from in a very clear way, so that simple oversight is an unlikely explanation for failure to take something into account. Others address the weight of the evidence, as in studies of the "availability" heuristic, so cases in which one telling counterexample tells the story are not so much at issue.

So these lapses, although of a deductive or inductive character, do not seem to be well represented in the research literature on those themes. Moreover, the other categories fit the molds neither of deductive nor inductive reasoning as ordinarily conceived. For example, the most frequent category, contrary consequent, identifies cases in which the reasoner failed to think of an alternative line of argument leading to a contrary conclusion. Similarly, in "external factor," the reasoner overlooks a factor that qualifies an otherwise valid rule. In "neglected critical distinction," the reasoner overlooks a critical subcase. In "contrary antecedent" the reasoner overlooks an alternative cause or other antecedent. All of these errors of neglect point to a general failure in human reasoning that might roughly be called a failure of elaboration, or a failure to construct a more elaborate model of the situation under scrutiny. With reference to Johnson-Laird's (1983) theory of mental models, a reasoner should search for mental models of a situation that accommodate the premises but allow different conclusions. Reasoners commonly fall short in their effort to do this.

Although regrettable, this is certainly understandable. Besides problems such as cognitive load that can occur in any sort of reasoning, informal reasoning makes special demands on memory retrieval. Whereas in a typical formal problem a high percentage of the information is supplied either in the problem statement or in a very limited and well-defined system, in a typical problem of informal reasoning, a person might have to call upon all sorts of widely scattered experiences to construct arguments or judge the plausibility of those he encounters.

In their concept of availability, Tversky and Kahneman have recognized that probing one's knowledge base for data is a process that can be subject to some misleading biases. But the present analysis underscores a difficulty that may be even more widespread and pernicious: outright omission of whole lines of argument based on stored data. Such lapses of reasoning seem rather failures in creativity: the reasoner has failed to discern an alternative or qualifying account of the situation.

Accordingly, the elaboration of models becomes an objective for instruction in better reasoning alongside the improvement of practices in deductive and inductive reasoning, and the avoidance of social influences on reasoning.

5. SUMMARY

We have considered a number of the ways in which human reasoning is known to be less than optimal. The reasoning errors and biases we have discussed are not the only ones that occur; however, they are representative of those that do.

We have noted that some of the errors we have considered are errors only in a strict logical sense. In some contexts these "erroneous" modes of reasoning work reasonably well; in other contexts, however, they are certain to produce undesirable results.

A knowledge of reasoning deficiencies is relevant to the problem of teaching thinking in several ways. First, one reasonable objective of an effort to teach thinking would be to eliminate or mitigate some of these deficiencies. Simply increasing people's awareness of specific reasoning errors and biases could conceivably have a beneficial effect. When the problems appear not to be susceptible to training there may be other things that can be done to mitigate their effects. One way to deal with the confirmation bias in its many guises, for example, is simply to recognize it and to maintain a healthy skepticism regarding conclusions that one is particularly desirous of drawing.

It is important for teachers to be aware of common reasoning deficiencies, not only in order to be able to correct them by training, if possible, but, equally importantly, to avoid reinforcing these modes of thought. While teachers are probably neither more nor less susceptible to reasoning deficiencies than are other people, they have much greater opportunity than most people to pass them on. It is especially important, therefore, that teachers be aware of them.

6. SUMMARY OF PART I

In the preceding chapters we have considered, in an informal way, several topics that relate directly to the problem of teaching thinking. We try now to summarize what conclusions we can draw from these considerations that will help put the programs that are reviewed in subsequent chapters in perspective.

The history of the concept of intelligence, or intellectual competence, provides little guidance on the question of how to teach thinking skills or whether they can be taught. Although there seems to be increasing support for the idea that intelligence has many dimensions, or facets, there is still considerable controversy regarding precisely what it is, what its components are, or how it is best measured.

Nothing we know about intelligence rules out the possibility of teaching thinking skills. There is the possibility that effective instruction to this end would improve intellectual performance in ways that would increase scores on some standard intelligence tests. Even if this proved not to be the case, however, it would not follow that efforts to improve thinking skills through training are futile. If intelligence is not modifiable, there is still the possibility that training could be effective in increasing the quality of performance on intellectually demanding tasks by helping people to use more effectively whatever intelligence they have.

Questions relating to intelligence—what it is, whether it is modifiable by training—are clearly of secondary interest. The primary practical issue is whether people can learn to think more critically and creatively: whether they can become more effective problem solvers, decision makers, conceptualizers, planners, inventors, and so on. These are empirical questions and answerable in principle by research. There is not sufficient evidence at the present to support a confident negative answer to any of these questions. That being the case, efforts to develop methods to improve thinking skills are fully justified. Indeed failure of a society to make such an effort would, in our view, be irresponsible.

Thinking of thinking as a form of skilled behavior provides, we believe, a useful perspective from which to attempt to improve intellectual performance. It invites comparisons with the teaching of motor skills that can be used to advantage, and it encourages attention both to the component skills and to the question of how to coordinate them so as to produce a balanced competency and smooth execution. Especially important, in our view, is a keen sensitivity to the interdependency of thinking skills and knowledge; neither can be developed satisfactorily independently of the other.

Research on problem solving by humans and efforts to develop problem-solving programs for computers have revealed a number of heuristic procedures that are applicable in a variety of problem domains. Expert problem solvers use such procedures to advantage, and researchers in artificial intelligence have had some success in incorporating them in computer programs that can perform what are usually thought of as intellectually demanding tasks. Problem-solving heuristics are natural candidates for training objectives for efforts to enhance thinking skills.

Some readers may find it difficult to think of creativity as a type of skill, and as something that can be improved by training. The concept tends to be associated in our thinking with genius and intellectual prodigiousness, something to admire but not to understand. We have noted, however, that studies of creativity have identified some of the factors that contribute to it and have produced reasons to believe that some aspects of it can be taught. Certain cognitive styles and attitudes are primary candidates for instruction; and certain teachable strategies for breaking out of patterns of thought and for generating new ideas, are worthy of further research.

Metacognitive skills, which involve the managing of one's own cognitive resources and the monitoring of one's own cognitive performance, would also seem to be natural candidates for training objectives for efforts to enhance thinking. The relevance of such skills to the performance of intellectually demanding tasks seems obvious. Whether they can, in fact, be taught is an empirical question, and the available evidence is encouraging in this regard.

That people often reason suboptimally is very well documented. Common reasoning deficiencies, once identified as such, pose quite explicit challenges for efforts to enhance thinking through training. The elimination or amelioration of a specific deficiency is a precise and objective goal. A program that succeeded in correcting several of them would have an effect of some practical significance on one's general level of intellectual functioning.

On balance, the results of research most directly related to thinking, as we are using the term in this book, are supportive of the view that the teaching of thinking is a legitimate and reasonable educational objective. The literature does not provide clear and incontrovertible prescriptions regarding how the teaching should be done. On the other hand, research in areas such as problem solving, creativity, metacognition, and reasoning are yielding useful information about thinking, and about cognition more generally. Nothing that this research is revealing constitutes a compelling argument against the possibility of teaching thinking, and many of the results that are being obtained provide some guidance regarding specific aspects of thinking that might be taught.

II APPROACHES TO TEACHING THINKING

Numerous efforts have been made during the last few years to develop programs to enhance thinking skills through classroom instruction. Some of these efforts have certain features in common with others; however, the differences among the approaches are at least as apparent as the commonalities. There is, as yet, no obvious convergence to *an* approach that would gain wide acceptance as *the* appropriate, or even the most promising, one.

Some of the programs that have been developed are strongly influenced by theories of cognitive development, and some are not. Some place much emphasis on teacher training; others rely heavily on the adequacy of materials and predesigned student exercises that are intended to require little or no special teacher training. Some programs have been developed by consortia of researchers and/or educators; others are products of largely individual efforts. Programs differ considerably with respect to scope, age level of targeted student population, type and duration of instruction, theoretical orientation, and in numerous other ways.

Discussion of the individual programs that have been developed would be facilitated by some scheme for classifying them into a few distinctive categories. Unfortunately no organizational scheme that we have been able to devise is totally adequate for the task. The problem is that the programs differ on numerous dimensions; and any sorting of them into a few categories has some degree of arbitrariness about it and require s some force fitting.

Nonetheless, on the assumption that even a rough organization is better than none, we have elected to partition the programs discussed into the following five broad categories: (1) those that focus on the teaching of certain basic cognitive processes or skills that are assumed to be essential to, or components of, intellectual competence; (2) those that emphasize certain explicit methods (e.g., problem-solving heuristics) that are presumably applicable to a variety of cognitive tasks, and that teach these methods outside conventional subject-matter courses; (3) those for which the objective is to promote formal operational thinking within the context of specific conventional subject matter courses, (4) those that emphasize symbol manipulation skills, and (5) those that focus on thinking as subject matter. These categories are referred to, respectively, as (1) cognitive operations approaches, (2) heuristics oriented approaches, (3) formal thinking approaches (4) symbolic facility approaches, and (5) thinking-about-thinking approaches. We wish to stress that while this partitioning reflects real differences in *emphasis*, the distinctions between categories are fuzzy, and the differences among programs that we have placed in a given category are, in some cases, very substantial.

Inasmuch as we make no claim for comprehensiveness, there is the question of selection: Why do we review the particular programs discussed in the following and not some others? We believe the programs reviewed here are broadly representative of the efforts to teach thinking that are currently being made. Of course, we have made an effort to include a large percentage of those programs that are widely known. But we have also discussed many that have drawn little attention, in the interest of rounding out our sample, and on the assumption that visibility is not always the best indicator of potential. We have tried for variety, but we have described rather similar programs when that seemed informative. We have included programs for which some empirical evidence of effectiveness has been obtained, but also programs that appear to have failed such tests, and—the majority by far—programs for which we could find no evaluation studies. Certainly inclusion of a program in this review is not, itself, a recommendation of its use; equally certainly, exclusion is not a recommendation against it. One practical constraint was the unavailability of sufficiently detailed information about some programs to provide a basis for inclusion. And, of course, there is undoubtedly much ongoing work that our search failed to uncover. We hope that the sample of programs we discuss captures something of the variety and richness in this rapidly developing field, and provides the reader with leads to further information that may be of special interest.

One area that we do not highlight in this book that is at least indirectly relevant to the teaching of thinking is that that deals with the teaching of learning strategies or learning skills. Much of the work in this area has been directed at determining the relative effectiveness of the various methods that students use, or could use, to improve their assimilation and retention of information. For a review of some research in this area, see Nickerson, Salter, Shepard, & Herrnstein (1984).

6 Cognitive Operations Approaches

Some instructional efforts analyze the difficulties of thinking as lack of facility with various constituent cognitive processes such as comparing, classifying, inferring, and so on. These processes are taken to be primitive operations in some sense. They are seen as the "atoms" out of which all more complex cognitive activities are built. Moreover, like the atom as originally conceived, they are often treated as indivisible, at least for the purpose of instructional design. That is, the instruction tends not to break down such activities as comparing or classifying into constituent steps. Rather, they are treated as wholes that need to be strengthened by general advice and extensive practice. We comment further on the general characteristics of the cognitive operations approach at the end of the chapter.

1. THE INSTRUMENTAL ENRICHMENT PROGRAM

Among the best documented and most widely known approaches to the enhancement of cognitive performance is the Instrumental Enrichment program of Reuven Feuerstein. The program is based on a conception of intelligence that emphasizes processes as opposed to factors or products and grows out of a dissatisfaction with conventional methods of intelligence testing. It has been used fairly extensively in Israel for several years. It is described in numerous reports—and in a book (Feuerstein, Rand, Hoffman, & Miller, 1980)—and is one of the few programs for which a serious attempt at evaluation has been made. Most of the descriptive material presented here is from the book. Other sources include Feuerstein (1970);

Feuerstein & Rand (1974); Feuerstein, Rand, Hoffman, Hoffman, & Miller (1979); Feuerstein, Miller, Hoffman, Rand, Mintzker, & Jensen (1981).

Feuerstein's Concept of Intelligence and its Assessment

The view of intelligence underlying the Instrumental Enrichment program rejects the notion of immutable inborn abilities as the primary determinants of intellectual performance. Feuerstein contrasts his "open-system" view of the human organism with what he characterizes as "closed-system" views, which treat intelligence as a characteristic of the individual that is fixed and constant over his life span. According to the "open-system" view, the outstanding property of human beings is their receptivity to change and modification; in particular, "intelligence is considered a dynamic self-regulating process that is responsive to external environmental intervention" (Feuerstein, Rand, Hoffman, & Miller, 1980, p. 2).

Feuerstein's dissatisfaction with conventional methods of intelligence testing stemmed from efforts to use such tests in the planning of educational programs for young immigrants to Israel in the early 1950's. The test results had limited utility, in his judgment, because they revealed what an individual had or had not learned, but not what he was capable of learning. In particular, Feuerstein believes that IQ is of limited usefulness to educators who are interested in producing cognitive change because it gives no clue to the processes that determine the level of an individual's performance relative to that of other individuals within a normally distributed population. What is needed is an indication of the individual's potential for learning.

The evaluation instrument that Feuerstein and his colleagues developed—the Learning Potential Assessment Device (LPAD)—is intended to provide such an indication. The LPAD is designed to assess learning potential by producing cognitive changes during the testing process. The idea is to assess the individual's ability to learn by observing his learning performance in a controlled situation (Feuerstein, Rand, & Hoffman, 1979).

The fundamental notion underlying Feuerstein's approach to assessment is that what one wants to measure is not so much the current level of the individual's intellectual development but his susceptibility to change. The goal should not be to predict future performance by measuring one's stable characteristics but to determine the degree to which those characteristics can be modified. Inasmuch as the central purpose of education is change, what the educator wants to know about a given individual is the extent to which desirable change is possible.

An important objective of assessment in Feuerstein's view should be diagnosis. That is to say, the assessment instrument should do more than indicate the individual's level of performance. It should reveal *why* the individual performs at a particular level. It should provide some specific information about the cognitive processes involved and some guidance regarding the kinds of instruction that would be most likely to increase that level. This presupposes the existence of a theory that identifies the processes involved in cognitive performance. The LPAD approach is based on a model of cognition that Feuerstein refers to as the "cognitive map." This model is really a taxonomy of concepts ("parameters") that characterize seven aspects ("dimensions") in terms of which a mental act may be described. We consider this model in more detail later.

Feuerstein, Miller, and Jensen (1980) present the results of several studies that they believe demonstrate that conventional test measures may be not only misleading but educationally counterproductive. In particular, they conclude from their results that low performance levels on such tests often reflect cultural differences and not differences in the ability to learn. They argue that when decisions regarding placement in educational programs are made on the basis of the results of conventional tests, the test scores can become self-fulfilling prophecies. When a low performance score leads one to believe that a child lacks the ability to learn, and this belief leads in turn to a decision to place the child among a group of slow learners, he may in fact learn slowly. However, *any* child labeled a slow learner and placed in a class designed for slow learners may learn slowly, so the fact that a particular child does so, they argue, is not very convincing evidence of the predictive power of the test.

Feuerstein, Miller, and Jensen (1980) state their case against conventional standardized psychometric testing procedures quite strongly.

> There is a very real sense in which attempts to produce cognitive change while adhering to a psychometric conception of intelligence is an irrational endeavor. To ask how meaningful cognitive changes may be produced is tantamount to psychometric heresy because it is this question that undermines the entire statistical apparatus and conceptual foundation upon which the tests are based. It is difficult to conceive of an instrument that would satisfy the measurement requirements of predictability and modifiability. (p. 20)

Cognitive Modifiability and the Importance of Mediated Learning

A key concept underlying the Instrumental Enrichment program is that of "cognitive modifiability." The approach of the program is directed "not merely at the remediation of specific behaviors and skills but at changes of a structural nature that alter the course and direction of cognitive development" (Feuerstein, Rand, Hoffman, & Miller, 1980, p. 9). Structural changes are contrasted with changes that occur as a result of maturation or the learning of specific skills; they are viewed as changes in the individual's characteristic ways of dealing with information. "When we use the term 'cognitive modifiability,' we refer to structural changes, or to the changes in the state of the organism, brought about by a deliberate program of intervention that will facilitate the generation of continuous growth by rendering the organism receptive and sensitive to internal and external sources of stimulation" (p. 9). The assumption is that if a structural change can be realized, it will affect the future course of the individual's development.

The low achiever, in Feuerstein's view, is one whose degree of modifiability is low. He does not readily learn as a result of direct exposure to stimuli. Low modifiability manifests itself in a variety of symptomatic ways, many of which are reasonably well characterized as evidence of failure to process incoming stimuli effectively. A key assumption of Feuerstein's approach is that low modifiability is itself modifiable; it can be remediated by appropriate training.

Feuerstein distinguishes two forms of interaction between an individual and his environment that contribute to the development of cognitive structure: direct exposure to stimuli from the environment, and learning experiences mediated by an agent. Although both types of interactions are considered to be essential, differences among levels of cognitive development are attributed largely to differences in mediated learning experiences. Direct exposure to stimuli is insufficient, Feuerstein argues, to explain differential cognitive development even when constitutional differences among individuals are taken into account, nor can it explain why so many people fail to attain the level of formal operations in the Piagetian sense.

Furthermore, without appropriate mediated learning experiences the individual is less able than he could be to learn from his direct exposure to environmental stimuli. Adequate mediated learning experiences are essential to provide a child with the strategies and sets that will permit him to get the greatest benefit from exposure to such stimuli. Consequently, early deprivation of mediated learning experiences can impede the cognitive development of the individual in spite of rich stimulation from the environment. In particular such deprivation leaves the individual ill equipped to relate and organize events in his environment in such a way as to learn effectively from them.

The mediating agent in a mediated learning experience, often a parent or teacher, is one who

> mediates the world to the child by transforming the stimuli—selecting stimuli; scheduling them; framing and locating them in time and space; grouping certain stimuli or segregating others; providing certain stimuli with specific

> meanings as compared with others; providing opportunities for recurrent appearances; bringing together objects and events that are separate and discrete in terms of temporal and spatial dimensions; reevoking events and reinforcing the appearance of some stimuli; rejecting or deferring the appearance of others; and through this, providing the organism with modalities of selecting, focusing,and grouping objects and events. What is even more important, the mediating individual enables the child to extend his activities over dimensions of reality that are not in his immediate reach either temporally or spatially.... MLE [mediated learning experience] is considered in this framework to be the determinant of the proper use of direct exposure to stimuli. The more an organism has been subjected to adequate levels of mediation, the greater is its capacity to learn, i.e., to become modified, through direct exposure to stimuli. (Feuerstein, Rand, & Hoffman, 1979, pp. 365 366)

Mediated learning experiences are of two types: (1) Those that involve the transmission of information, values, and attitudes (information that represents the accumulated knowledge of the species and that could not be obtained except from other human beings); and (2) experiences that are aimed at making the individual better able to learn from the direct exposure to stimuli. The mediator in the latter case plays the role of one who manipulates stimuli in such a way that the child will learn things about them that will transcend his immediate needs and generalize to other contexts.

Arbitman-Smith, Haywood, and Bransford (1984) point out that Feuerstein's emphasis on mediated learning as a key contributor to cognitive development represents a major difference between his ideas and those of Piaget. Piaget, they note, gives little recognition to the role of parents, grandparents, and teachers as child-rearing agents, whereas Feuerstein makes the role that such people play both central and critical. Normal human cognitive development cannot, in Feuerstein's view, occur in the absence of the type of learning that such agents mediate.

Cognitive Structure, Deficient Cognitive Functions and Cognitive Maps

Feuerstein, Rand, and Hoffman (1979) take the position that although lack of mediated learning experiences can, and does, have detrimental effects on the cognitive development of the organism, these effects are reversible. The Instrumental Enrichment program represents an attempt to define procedures that may remediate the detrimental effects of lack of mediated learning experiences. The use of such procedures, Feuerstein contends, can change cognitive structure and increase an individual's capacity to learn.

The program was developed initially for the benefit of young people who had been diagnosed as retarded, and was motivated by the assumption "that manifest low cognitive performance need not be regarded as a stable characteristic of an individual and that systematic intervention, directed at the correction of deficient functions, will render the condition reversible by producing a change in the cognitive structure of the individual" (Feuerstein, Rand, Hoffman, & Miller, 1980, p. 1). "The goal is to change the cognitive structure of the retarded performer and to transform him into an autonomous independent thinker, capable of initiating and elaborating ideas" (ibid, p. 70).

The deficient functions—more specifically, deficient cognitive functions—that Feuerstein refers to are discussed in his book in some detail. Some twenty-eight such deficiencies are identified and grouped within three categories that reflect Feuerstein's conceptualization of "the three phases of the mental act": impairments in cognition at the *input phase*, impairments in cognition at the *elaboration phase*, and impairments in cognition at the *output phase*. A fourth category of deficient functions is also identified—affective-motivational factors—but no examples are given.

The list of impairments presented is considered representative, but not exhaustive. Under impairments at the input phase the list includes such deficiencies as: blurred and sweeping perception; unplanned, impulsive, and unsystematic exploratory behavior; lack of, or impaired, temporal orientation. Impairments at the elaboration phase include: inadequacy in experiencing the existence of an actual problem and subsequently defining it; inability to select relevant, as opposed to irrelevant, cues in defining a problem; and lack of, or impaired, strategies for hypothesis testing. Examples of impairments at the output stage: egocentric communication modalities, trial-and-error responses; and lack of, or impaired, need for precision and accuracy in communicating one's response. What is meant by these brief descriptors is more apparent in some cases than in others. The reader is referred to Feuerstein's books for details. A brief description of each of the twenty-eight deficits can also be found in Sternberg (in press).

Another central concept in Feuerstein's approach is that of a "cognitive map," a set of parameters in terms of which to analyze, categorize and order mental acts. Seven parameters comprise the cognitive map: content (subject matter of a mental act); operations (a set of actions by which information is elaborated upon); modality (language—figurative, pictorial, verbal—in terms of which a mental act is expressed); phase (input, elaboration, or output); level of complexity (quantity and quality of units of information necessary to produce a given mental act); level of abstraction (the "distance" between a mental act or operation and the objects or events to which it is applied); and level of efficiency (relating to effort involved in a mental act and the rapidity and precision with which it is produced).

Specifics of the Program

Inasmuch as Feuerstein believes that deficient intellectual performance typically results from a paucity of mediated learning experiences, which are essential if the child is to be able to benefit from exposure to environmental stimuli, it is not surprising that his program is intended to provide the learner with a phase-specific form of mediated learning experience designed to make up that deficit. The general goal is "to sensitize the individual so that he will be able to register, elaborate, and become modified by direct exposure to life events and experiences in such a way that learning and the efficient handling and use of incoming stimuli are increasingly facilitated" (ibid, p. 384).

Six specific subgoals of the program are identified: (1) correction of the deficient functions that characterize the cognitive structure of a particular individual; (2) acquisition of certain basic concepts, labels, vocabulary, operations, and relationships that are necessary for the performance of cognitive tasks such as those encountered in the program; (3) production of intrinsic motivation through habit formation (Feuerstein stresses the importance of establishing intrinsic motivation as the way to ensure transfer of what is learned to non-school situations); (4) production of reflective, insightful thinking by the student regarding his successes and failures with program tasks; (5) creation of task-intrinsic motivation (promotion of enjoyment of tasks for their own sakes); and (6) instillation in the learner of a perception of himself as an active generator of knowledge and information rather than as a passive recipient and reproducer of same. Feuerstein characterizes the last subgoal as "probably one of the most vital aspects of the program" and notes that

> the passivity of the culturally deprived retarded performer toward incoming stimuli and himself is also responsible for a host of other attitudinal, motivational, and emotional determinants of his behavior. (ibid, p. 118).

Feuerstein attaches considerable importance to the relatively "content-free" nature of the materials used in his program. The intent in the design of these materials was to make them as free of curricular content as possible. The rationale for this approach alludes to several "resistances" to the use of content material, resistances arising from the learner, the teacher, the material itself, and the student's history of failure with such material. Moreover, the use of content-free material is assumed to help keep the student's attention focused on the objective of correcting specific deficient functions rather than on the content itself, a focus that is presumed to facilitate realization of the program's general goal.

Rand, Tannenbaum, and Feuerstein (1979) make a distinction between what they refer to as "General Enrichment" and the "Instrumental

Enrichment" approach. By General Enrichment they refer to programs that provide direct help in standard school subjects, e.g., tutorial instruction in language and mathematics. The purpose for such direct assistance in conventional courses often is to help students who have fallen behind to catch up with their peers. In contrast, the Instrumental Enrichment approach emphasizes basic cognitive processes. Products in this program are means to ends; the real interest is in the processes by which those products are produced and in improvements in the student's mastery and understanding of those processes.

> The exercises are aimed at nurturing proper learning sets and systematic data gathering behavior at the input level, inducing skills in comparative analysis to improve the child's relational insights, and removing attitudinal inhibitions that often operate in low functioning adolescents. (Rand, Tannenbaum, & Feuerstein, 1979, p. 752).

Emphasis is placed on "metalearning habits" and the problem of learning how to learn.

The Instrumental Enrichment program is divided into 15 "instruments," each of which consists of a set of paper-and-pencil exercises focused on a particular deficient cognitive function. An instrument is defined simply as a means to an end, something by means of which something else is effected. Fourteen of the instruments, which are used in classroom implementations of the program, provide enough material for 3 to 5 1-hour lessons per week for 2 to 3 years. The instruments are also intended for individual use by students with particular needs.

The instruments are organized in three clusters: those that require little or no reading ability (Organization of Dots, Analytical Perception, Illustrations); those that require some reading ability, or teacher assistance in reading directions (Orientation in Space I, II, and III, Comparisons, Family Relations, Numerical Progressions, Syllogisms); and those that require independent reading and comprehension skills (Categorization, Instructions, Temporal Relations, Transitive Relations, Representational Stencil Design).

For detailed descriptions of these instruments the reader is referred to Feuerstein, Rand, Hoffman, and Miller (1980) in which they are discussed in terms of both Feuerstein's cognitive map and the subgoals of the Instrumental Enrichment program. Brief descriptions of several of the instruments may also be found in Arbitman-Smith, Haywood, and Bransford (1984) and in Feuerstein et al. (1981).

It is important to note that simply doing the exercises is not expected to produce the structural changes that the program is intended to effect. The instruments are viewed as tools that can facilitate the role of the teacher as a mediator of the kinds of learning experiences that can effect such changes. Lessons typically have four phases: (a) introduction, (b) individual paper-and-paper pencil work on the exercises, (c) class discussion, and (d) summary of the concepts and strategies employed. Mediation is expected to occur in each of these phases. A detailed description of how such mediation may be accomplished with specific lesson materials is given by Arbitman-Smith, Haywood, and Bransford (1984). Often it is by means of calling students' attention to the cognitive processes they are using, or have used, in working exercises, which is to say by getting them to think about their own thinking. Thus the program has a distinctly metacognitive flavor in some respects.

Evaluation of the Program

The Instrumental Enrichment Program has been available for a longer time and used more extensively than most of the programs reviewed in this book. Several of the users, including Feuerstein and his colleagues have collected data in an attempt to evaluate its effectiveness. The results that have been reported to date are well worth our attention, not only because of the evidence they provide regarding this program, but because of what they reveal regarding the difficulty of obtaining unambiguous indications of what is really being accomplished by educational innovations of this sort.

Rand, Tannenbaum, and Feuerstein (1979; see also Feuerstein, Miller, Hoffman, Rand, Mintzker, & Jensen, 1981) report an effort to evaluate the Instrumental Enrichment program with two groups (total sample size: 128) of low functioning, low socio-economic status Israeli adolescents, 12 to 15 years of age "who could be characterized as disadvantaged, socially backward, and culturally different and as members of minority groups." The general level of scholastic achievement of these students was 3 to 4 years behind that of their peers. One group lived in a residential facility "where the children received total care away from family influences and where the environment was far less crisis-ridden than in their homes." The second group attended a day-care center for after-school social and educational activities. On intelligence tests they scored at levels characteristic of educable mentally retarded persons. The Instrumental Enrichment program that was used was designed to meet the needs revealed by clinical assessments of the individuals' cognitive deficits. There were four subject groups defined by the four possible combinations of two training programs (Instrumental Enrichment and General Enrichment) and two settings (residential facility and day-care facility). The Instrumental Enrichment program involved 400 pencil and paper cognitive exercises, took between 200 and 300 hours to complete, and continued over a period of two years.

The investigators hypothesized that the children in both settings would show greater gains on both intellective and nonintellective measures after participating in the Instrumental Enrichment program than after exposure to a General Enrichment program. They also hypothesized that both Instrumental and General Enrichment programs would be more effective in the context of total care residential settings than in that of day centers where contact with the children was more limited. Finally, they hypothesized an interaction between type of enrichment program and setting, predicting that Instrumental Enrichment and residential facility would mutually reinforce each other.

Performance was compared by means of an aptitude test (The Thurstone Primary Mental Abilities Test), a specially prepared achievement test (The Project Achievement Battery) and two non-intellectual tests (the Classroom Participation Scale and the Levidal Self-concept Scale). Matched pairs were used and data were subjected to analyses of covariance. The results of the analyses tended to confirm the first two hypotheses but provided little support for the third.

The students exposed to the Instrumental Enrichment program made greater gains than those exposed to General Enrichment with respect to some of the scores on the non-intellectual tests, and in particular on tests designed to measure interpersonal conduct, self-sufficiency, and adaptiveness to work demands. The investigators report also that subsequent tests performed when students were later inducted into military service showed that the gains of the experimental subjects over the controls had persisted. Specifically, about two years following the completion of the program, 86 of the students who had participated in the Instrumental Enrichment program and 78 of those who had served as controls in the General Enrichment program were inducted into the Israeli Army. The mean scores of the two groups on the Army intelligence test (DAPAR, which yields stanine scores from 10 to 90) were 52.52 and 45.28 respectively. Analysis of covariance using preintervention Primary Mental Abilities test scores as the covariate showed this difference to be statistically significant. This is a particularly important result inasmuch as long-term effects, which are really what one wants to obtain, typically have not been demonstrated, or even, in fact assessed. More detailed analyses of the relationship between the pretreatment PMA scores and the DAPAR IQ's indicated that the individuals whose initial PMA scores were relatively low benefited more from the Instrumental Enrichment experience than did those whose initial PMA scores were relatively high.

As we have already noted, a key idea underlying the Instrumental Enrichment program is that appropriate mediated learning experiences can produce structural changes that will enable individuals to learn more effectively as a result of direct exposure to the environment—which is to say, to learn on their own. Realization of structural change should lead to increased improvement in cognitive performance over time. In keeping with these ideas, Feuerstein and his colleagues stated a hypothesis that they referred to as the "hypothesis of divergent effects," whereby individuals who have undergone such structural change should show a cumulative gain over time relative to those who have not. To test this hypothesis with the performance data obtained from the Israeli Army subjects, the investigators converted the PMA and DAPAR scores of each participant into standard scores and computed differences between the two scores of experimental (IE) and control (GE) groups for each of several times: before intervention, about one year into the program, immediately after finishing the program, and two years after finishing the program. (PMA scores were used at the first three times, and DAPAR at the last.) The fact that the difference scores increased nearly linearly as a function of time over this period (total of 3.2 years) was taken as strong support for the divergent effect hypothesis and therefore for the conclusion that the Instrumental Enrichment experience had, in fact, effected the desired structural change (Feuerstein, Miller, Hoffman, Rand, Mintzker, & Jensen, 1981).

Rand, Tannenbaum, and Feuerstein took their results as evidence that training such as that provided by the Instrumental Enrichment program can have a favorable effect on the cognitive development of retarded individuals even after they have reached adolescence, and that academic performance can be improved as a result of training with exercises that do not make use of the content of curriculum courses, provided they focus on appropriate underlying mental operations. Indeed they perceive the content-free nature of the material to be a particularly important feature. "The advantages demonstrated by Instrumental Enrichment may in part be due to its content being unrelated to that of the school subjects since it forces both teacher and student to concentrate on problem-solving strategies without being distracted by the curriculum material at hand and the need to commit so much of it to memory" (p. 761).

The basic problem one has in interpreting the results of this study is insufficient knowledge of the differences in the treatments between the Instrumental Enrichment and General Enrichment groups. Were they taught by the same teachers? Were they given equal amounts of instruction and attention? That is to say, was the general quality of teaching equally good in both cases? (Quality of teaching and teacher motivation are unknown variables in many, if not most, efforts to evaluate educational innovation.)

Other efforts to evaluate the effectiveness of the Instrumental Enrichment program are currently under way. In addition to Israel, the materials, which are commercially available, are currently being used in the United States, Canada, and Venezuela. Although the program was initially designed for adolescents, some attempts have been made to use it, or parts of it, with post-adolescents as well. Haywood and Arbitman-Smith (1981) describe an ongoing evaluation project in North America involving the use of Instrumental Enrichment material in five cities: Nashville, Louisville, New York, Toronto, and Phoenix. The activities at the various sites are coordinated by a traveling supervisor to assure certain common practices and features. All of these programs focus on children with special needs: categories of exceptionality include educable mentally retarded, learning disabled, behavior disordered, culturally and linguistically different, and slow learners. Instrumental Enrichment is taught four hours per week in experimental classes; control groups spend the same amount of time in the regular academic curriculum. Participating students are achieving from two to seven years below expectation for their chronological ages (11 to 18 years). Heavy emphasis is put on the training and supervising of participating teachers.

The primary method of evaluation has involved the giving of objective tests before and after participation in the program. Tests have been administered in the areas of intellectual functioning, school achievement, and personality and motivation. Tests representing the first area are the nonverbal portions of the Lorge-Thorndike (1954) Intelligence Tests, Raven's (1960) Standard Progressive Matrices, and some subtests of Thurstone's (1965) Primary Mental Abilities Test. Tests used to measure school achievement are the Peabody Individual Achievement Test (Dunn & Markwardt, 1970), the KeyMath Diagnostic Arithmetic Test (Connolly, Nachtnam, & Pritchett, 1971), and the Wide-Range Achievement Test (Jastak & Jastak, 1978). Personality and motivation tests are the Rosenberg (1965) Self-Esteem Scale, the Piers-Harris (1969) Children's Self-Concept Scale, the Picture Motivation Scale (Haywood, 1971), and the Nowicki-Strickland (1973) Locus of Control Scale.

Haywood and Arbitman-Smith note that immediate changes are most likely to be seen in the area of intellectual functioning. Changes in school achievement they view as a second-order effect that would occur as the consequence of changes in patterns of thought and problem solving that would require some time, perhaps one or two years following the intervention. Changes in personality and motivation they hypothesize might occur in the intermediate range and mediate effects on school achievement.

Haywood and Arbitman-smith present one set of data obtained during the project's pilot year (1977—1978), and another for the first year (1978—1979) of a two-year program. Data obtained during the pilot year showed increases in mean nonverbal IQ scores ranging from about 5 to 9 points for the various categories of students. Control subjects showed an increase of about 2 ½ points on the same measures. The difference between experimental and controls was significant. Data obtained from the first year of the two-year program did not show significant improvement in IQ scores for most of the experimental groups. Significant improvements were obtained on some subtest scores (e.g., 10.4 points improvement for the experimental group on the spatial relations subtest of Thurstone's Primary Mental Abilities Test as opposed to a mean decline of 1.2 points in the control group on the same test). Students in the experimental groups, as a whole, increased from a grade level of 4.9 to one of 5.6 on the general information subtest of the Peabody Individual Achievement Test, while the control groups increased from 4.7 to 5.0. The experimental subjects in the Phoenix group showed an increase in their Lorge-Thorndike nonverbal IQ scores of about 8.9 points and an increase in their raw scores on Raven's Progressive Matrices of about 33% (as compared with corresponding increases of control subjects of about 2.7 IQ points and 1%, respectively).

A shortcoming of the Haywood and Arbitman-Smith study is its selective reporting of results. Only a few of the apparently large number of measurements that were made are reported. One is left wondering how representative of the complete set of results these are, and, in particular, whether there were any cases in which experimental subjects did significantly more poorly on posttreatment tests than on pretreatment tests, or showed significantly less improvement than did controls.

While we see the selective reporting of results as a weakness in this study, the authors are careful to point out the inadequacy of the evidence (which was obtained halfway through the two-year program) for drawing definitive conclusions, and they state their own conclusions quite conservatively. "It appears that it is possible to bring about some increases, modest in some cases and less modest in others, in the processes of thought and problem solving in adolescents who are having difficulty in learning" (p. 138). They note, too, that the effects seem to be greater the greater the resemblance between the experimental subjects and the Israeli adolescents for whom the Instrumental Enrichment procedures were developed and on whom they were initially tested. They suggest that changes in thought processes of mentally retarded adolescents and adolescents with exceptionalities matching those of their experimental students may require a longer time and more intensive investment, and possibly materials altered so as to slow the pace of the program.

Additional evaluative data have been reported by Arbitman-Smith, Haywood, and Bransford (1984). This report also contains a thoughtful discussion of some of the problematic issues associated with evaluating innovative educational programs. The authors note that the relatively small (5-to-10 point) gains in IQ scores that have typically been found when standardized intelligence tests have been administered to Instrumental Enrichment students before and after participation seem inconsistent with the conviction that many teachers and students have that the program has had a significant impact on students' lives. They point out the possibility that positive changes may be occurring that are not measured adequately by standardized intelligence tests.

With this possibility in mind, Arbitman-Smith, Haywood, and Bransford designed a number of tests to attempt to answer three types of questions: (1) Does the program help the students learn to solve the specific types of problems that are encountered in the program (for example, does a program that teaches syllogistic reasoning improve the students' ability to solve syllogistic reasoning problems?); (2) Do the effects of training transfer to problems that have the same format and require the same processes for solution as do those encountered in the program? (Does domain-specific transfer occur?); (3) Do the effects transfer to dissimilar problems? (Does domain-independent transfer occur?) Evidence is presented that the answer to all three of these questions is "yes." Perhaps more importantly, the effects in some cases were relatively large.

In discussing their results, and the issue of evaluation more generally, Arbitman-Smith, Haywood, and Bransford make the very important point that training in cognitive processes cannot be expected to make one immune to the need for the knowledge that is necessary to do effective problem solving in a particular area. No amount of such training will equip one to solve problems in physics, chemistry, or economics in the absence of a knowledge of the fundamentals of these subjects. One of the reasons, they suggest, why gains shown on standardized tests have not been more impressive may be that such tests are not as content free as they are sometimes assumed to be. In general, there is always the possibility, as they put it, that the format of tests may prevent students from showing what they know. Any test that presupposes content knowledge students do not have may mask gains they have made and lead to an underestimation of a program's real effectiveness.

Conclusive answers as to the effectiveness of Instrumental Enrichment—whether it is more or less effective than alternative programs, whether it is sufficiently effective to justify the investment of student time that it requires—are likely to be difficult to obtain. But a similar comment could be made about any program of comparable scope. Indeed many of the problems relating to the evaluation of Instrumental Enrichment are general problems that are likely to arise in any evaluation effort, independently of the program involved. We return to a consideration of these in Chapter 11. Controlled experiments involving programs that require two or three years to administer are difficult to run, and tend to yield data that can be interpreted in various ways. It should be possible to manage studies addressed to questions about specific aspects of the program, however, and one can hope that such studies will be helpful in identifying some of its specific strengths and weaknesses. The results that have already been obtained include data that can be useful to this end.

Independently of data regarding effectiveness, several aspects of the Instrumental Enrichment program seem impressive. One need not agree with the theoretical view of intellectual competence on which the program is based to recognize that the fact that there is a unifying view that gives the program some cohesiveness. The program has been fairly widely used; and many of its users and evaluators, have been enthusiastic about it and about the effects that they believe they can see but cannot necessarily measure. The materials are quite thoroughly documented and accessible. We suspect that skilled teachers may be able to use them to considerable advantage.

2. THE STRUCTURE OF INTELLECT PROGRAM

The SOI Institute, a non-profit educational research corporation located in El Segundo, California, has developed an approach to the teaching of thinking and learning skills based on J. P. Guilford's "Structure Of Intellect" model of intelligence. The institute offers various tests for administration to students, diagnostic services for evaluating the test results, prescription of exercises to remedy weaknesses identified by the tests, and exercise materials to carry out the recommendations.

The Theoretical Basis for the Program

The basis of the SOI program is a theory of intelligence developed by J. P. Guilford and colleagues (Guilford, 1967; Guilford & Hoepfner, 1971). Whereas most psychometric theories of intelligence measure intelligence by one or a few factors, Guilford's Structure of Intellect model posits three dimensions with multiple categories associated with each dimension. The three dimensions are called "operations," "contents," and "products." "Operations" refers to different kinds of mental acts a person might perform, for instance, recognizing, remembering, or judging. "Contents" classifies different kinds of symbols or media with which the person might work, for example numbers, words, or pictures. "Products" addresses the varyingly complex things the person might produce or otherwise deal with using the operations, among them units, relations, and systems. The categories in the structure of intellect are summarized in Table 6.1. compiled from Guilford and Hoepfner.

According to Guilford's theory, any complex task involves one or more component processes representable by one category from each of the three dimensions. For example, remembering mathematical relationships presumably draws at least upon the Memory factor under Operations, the Symbolic factor under Contents, and the Relations factor under Products. The three taken together are represented as MSR. As this example

TABLE 6.1
Categories in Guilford's Structure of Intellect Model

Category	*Code*	*Characterization*
OPERATIONS		
Cognition	C	Ability to recognize, comprehend.
Memory	M	Ability to remember.
Evaluation	E	Ability to make judgments.
Convergent production	N	Ability to solve one-answer problems.
Divergent production	D	Ability to be creative.
CONTENTS		
Behavioral	B	Nonverbal nonfigural human interactions.
Figural	F	Pictorial and spatial matters.
Symbolic	S	Numbers and notations.
Semantic	M	Words and ideas.
PRODUCTS		
Units	U	Circumscribed chunks of information.
Classes	C	Classes defined by common properties.
Relations	R	Well-defined relations between things.
Systems	S	Organized or structured aggregates.
Transformations	T	Redefinitions, shifts, modifications.
Implications	I	Extrapolation, consequences, inference.

suggests, the Guilford model allows for 120 different combinations in all. Guilford views these as first-order factors in a factor analysis of the elements of intelligence, considering each of the 120 factors to represent a distinct mental ability related to intelligence.

Guilford's Structure of Intellect model is controversial. Guilford has claimed support for the 120 components through factor analysis, but some psychometricians have criticized his statistical techniques. For example, Horn and Knapp (1973) claimed that the factor analytic technique used by Guilford provided no more support for his theory than it would for a randomly chosen theory. Although Guilford (1974) argued that Horn and Knapp had overstated their case, such challenges naturally raise some doubts about the adequacy of Guilford's factor-analytic techniques. Sternberg (1977) reviewed a variety of difficulties with factor analysis as a means for analyzing the nature of int elligence; he argued that factor analysis was not able to isolate adequately the components underlying intelligence, because it failed to allow for comparison of theories and failed to explicate process, among other things.

The Structure of Intellect model was constructed through a process of administering, sorting, revising, and screening a great variety of tests. Taken as a whole, these tests resemble about every kind of instrument that has been used to measure mental abilities. On the other hand, all the instruments pose tasks of relatively short duration and, typically, little real ecological significance in themselves. It may be that the factors in the model, while adequately representing the range of test-like tasks that psychologist have employed, do not adequately represent the universe of humanly significant tasks.

For example, in the Guilford model, creativity is associated most of all with divergent production operations and transformation products (Guilford & Hoepfner, 1971, Chapter 6). However, as we have noted elsewhere in this book, divergent production abilities appear to bear little relation to demonstrated creativity in real-world situations (Chapter 4). For another example, in recent years psychologists have become increasingly aware that memory has many facets. One important aspect of memory that has received considerable attention from researchers in recent years is "episodic memory," memory for events or episodes in one's life (Tulving, 1972). This sort of memory seems to exhibit distinct properties and obviously plays a very important role in our daily lives. But it does not have an obvious place in Guilford's model. In general, we are wary of the notion that the Structure of Intellect model captures the abilities underlying the full range and variety of human intellectual performances, in spite of the large number of factors it assumes.

But such reservations notwithstanding, Guilford's theory still provides an interesting foundation for efforts to teach skills of thinking and learning. Even if the factors only sample, rather than exhaust, the space of intellectual performance, and even if there is some redundancy in the sampling, it might be that the sampling is good enough to provide useful diagnoses of students' difficulties. Training on the factors might transfer enough to related tasks to improve specific aspects of students' intellectual competence. Moreover, given the tenuous status of all theories of intellect, the question of the effectiveness of a program to teach thinking must be considered independently of the question of the soundness of the theory (if any) on which the program is based. We turn now to a consideration of the SOI program itself.

Content of the Program

Meeker, the head of the SOI institute, laid the foundation for this work in a book exploring the educational applications of the Structure of Intellect model (Meeker, 1969). She proposed that one could apply instruments to determine students' strengths and weaknesses on various factors of the model, and then provide instruction to improve performance on selected factors. A large part of the book is given to discussion of particular tests to measure factors. In addition, Meeker presents a scheme for extracting information about Guilford's factors from the Stanford-Binet, WISC, and WPPSI tests by isolating items on the tests that correspond to specific factors. Finally, Meeker suggests activities to exercise each factor for the purpose of improving performance on it. In effect, the mind is treated as a composite of "mental muscles"—the composite can be strengthened by toning up the individual muscles with focused exercises.

It would be a formidable task for educators to follow on their own the plan outlined by Meeker (1969), assembling tests, designing lessons, and so on. During the years since the publication of Meeker's book, the SOI Institute has addressed this problem by making appropriate materials available. The development of the SOI materials has involved some renaming: often in these materials, cognition is called comprehending, evaluation is called judgment or judging, planning and decision making, convergent production is called problem solving, and divergent production is called creativity. The renaming no doubt helps to communicate the assumed significance of the categories to lay users, but it also may overgeneralize that significance. For instance, according to Guilford and Hoepfner (1971, Chapter 6), creativity is most associated with divergent production *and* transformations. The idea of transformations gets left out of the picture when divergent production alone is called creativity. Also, the original label, divergent production, more modestly identifies the kind of test employed. Whether this corresponds to creativity is arguable. Similar questions might arise for the other renamings.

The SOI materials omit the behavioral category under contents altogether, a category that does not address academic matters. This leaves 90 combinations of Operations, Contents, and Products, and the SOI Institute addresses 27 of these, selected as most relevant to mathematics, writing, and creativity. The basis for this selection is not discussed in the materials to which we had access. No tests with transformation products are included in the cluster of factors for creativity, despite Guilford and Hoepfner's (1971, Chapter 6) assertion of their relevance. It is the case, however, that among the 27 all categories under Operations, Contents, and Products are somewhere represented.

Use of the SOI materials is straight forward. First one obtains a battery of diagnostic tests from SOI. Although the institute produces more than one battery for various purposes, here we concentrate on the instrument named SOI–LA, a learning abilities test that appears to be the mainstay of the program. The battery, which includes tests for 27 combinations as noted above, is administered to students. The materials can be returned to the SOI Institute for grading and production by computer of an analysis and prescription.

The analysis is neat, clear, and thorough. Samples are available from the SOI Institute. The analysis consists of seven parts. First is "test results," listing the raw score and percent correct for the 27 tests. Part 2 is a graphical presentation of a "grade placement interpretation," indicating the student's performance on each test on a scale that runs from 2 to 6, with two additional levels: intermediate and adult. The scale is continuous, with positions part way between the labels shown. Part 3 gives a percentile interpretation of the student's results in graphic form relative to other persons of the same sex and grade level, treating the "intermediate" and "adult" categories as grade levels.

Part 4 sorts the tests to provide an assessment of the student's abilities with reference to four key areas: reading, arithmetic, writing, and creativity. For instance, foundational reading abilities are represented by the six subtests: visual closure (CFU), visual conceptualization (CFC), visual discrimination (EFU), judging similarity of concepts (EFC), visual attending and concentration (MSU), and visual sequencing (MSS). Opposite each test, the form presents a verbal interpretation of the student's performance; "disabling," "expected level," and "superior level" are three of the terms used. Part 5 gives an evaluation of general intellectual abilities. Scores from the subtests are averaged to yield estimates for each of the 14 categories: five for operations, three for content, and six for products.

Part 6, an unusual element in a computerized scoring system, presents a clinical analysis in prose of the student's strengths and weaknesses. The analysis is organized according to the Operations dimension—comprehension abilities; memory abilities; judgment, planning and decision making abilities; problem solving abilities where answers are known; and creativity abilities. For instance, a sample analysis of comprehension abilities begins as follows: "CFU is a test of visual closure. Visual closure is a physiological development. CFU tests a cognitive presentation of the physiological process. You should be concerned abut JOHN's vision. Being low in CFU, he may not see the complete word from first to last letter with ease. Observe whether JOHN inclines his head when reading or writing, favoring one eye. A developmental visual examination needs to be made and repeated yearly until puberty." As this example suggests, the clinical analysis includes advice on the handling of the particular case.

The final section of the report specifies exercises selected to remediate the student's weaknesses. The exercises are chosen from "Sourcebooks" available from the SOI Institute. Each exercise addresses one or more particular factors, that is, particular combinations of categories from the three dimensions. Some, although not all, of the exercises are selected by an interesting strategy: if the student is weak in a certain category, the analysis recommends exercises addressing that category and categories under the other dimensions on which the student scored well, at least relative to his general performance. For example, if the student fared poorly with divergent tasks in general, but well with figural performances and classes, the analysis would recommend DFC exercises—exercise with divergent thinking on figural content involving classes.

Evaluation

Summaries of a number of studies of the effectiveness of the SOI program are available from the SOI Institute, which, according to its literature, acts as a clearinghouse for such investigations. We do not know whether all studies referred to them are included or what the selection criteria might be. An information sheet heading the study summaries notes that the institute "does not direct studies (other than norming studies), so the research reported herein was not sponsored or controlled by the Institute." The studies themselves are represented by one or sometimes two page summaries giving information about measures, treatments, levels of statistical significance, and so forth. Generally this information is less complete than one would like. For instance, rarely is there any information about the magnitudes of effects beyond significance levels, and sometimes significance levels are not given. Very few of the studies have been published in standard professional journals.

The studies are organized into three levels. Level I includes investigations on the reliability and validity of SOI assessment instruments. Here are found results of SOI tests applied to special populations, an inquiry into relations between memory scores and achievement, an effort to use SOI instruments to identify gifted students, and other investigations. In general, results at a modest level of statistical significance appear. One should not construe such results as representing strong support for the SOI approach specifically, as opposed to other psychometric models of intelligence: most IQ-like instruments will disclose correlations between test scores and academic achievement of various sorts.

Perhaps of greatest interest among the Level I studies are several relating reading ability and SOI measures, since the SOI Institute diagnostic report includes an assessment of factors relevant to reading. In one study, lacking statistical analysis, poor readers were found to have a common weakness on CFC, MFU, and NST. Another study of reading abilities compared first graders skilled in reading with others who were non-readers. The skilled readers were found to score higher than the non-readers on subtests DMU, CMU, NST, CFS, and CFT at the .02 level of significance (Kend, no date). Yet another study examined an SOI reading readiness test, and the usual SOI–LA test, as predictors of reading achievement (Crosslin, 1978). The significance level was an unacceptable .1, although CMS and CMR seemed positively related to reading achievement, with CMU positively related only on the SOI-LA test and MFU inconsistent.

These results are not in strong agreement, inasmuch as they identify different factors as important. One can also compare these results with the factors advanced as important for reading in the computer grading of the SOI–LA instrument. Foundational reading abilities are said to be CFU,

CFC, EFU, EFC, MSU, MSS. "Enhancing abilities" are CMU, CMR, CMS, MFU, MMI, and NST. Four of the measures identified by one of the foregoing studies as important do not appear on either of these lists: DMU, CMU, CFS, and CFT. Most of the others appear in the list of enhancing abilities. The lists include a number of subtests that did not disclose significant differences in any of the studies. In light of all this, one has to wonder about the basis for the constellation of subtests singled out as relevant to reading.

Level II studies address whether SOI training produces intellectual growth, primarily as measured by SOI instruments. Without going into details, it appears that for the most part gains were indeed found. Of course, it is not surprising that SOI instruction should yield gains on SOI subtests—the instruction was designed for that purpose and presumably "teaches to the test." However, such results should not be passed off lightly. They are a necessary condition, although not a sufficient one, for the soundness of the approach. If a program does not teach its specific targets, how can it be expected to produce more general results? The program of the SOI Institute seems to pass this criterion.

Level III studies concern the impact of SOI instruction beyond its own tests: is there a positive impact on school performance and work generally? Only two studies are included here. One concerns the impact of SOI training focused on abilities relevant to mathematics. Training was conducted over a four year period for second, third, fourth, and fifth grade Mexican-American students. The result was a significant gain in SAT assessments of arithmetic relative to a control group. There were no concomitant gains in reading ability, suggesting that the selected training indeed improved arithmetic skills specifically.

Another study applied the entire SOI approach for one year, with 40 students in the first through the eighth grades. Although not entirely clear from the description of the study, it appears that the students received about one period of exercises per week. On the SOI instruments themselves, significant gains occurred in 18 of 26 factors addressed. Also, scores on the subtests were found to be significantly correlated with school achievement as measured by the California Achievement Test. However, there was no control group. As is pointed out in the abstract, the results are consistent with an impact of SOI Institute instruction, but do not demonstrate it unequivocally. That is, even if the instruction improves scores on SOI subtests, and the subtests are correlated with achievement, this does not mean that the instruction yields greater achievement.

In summary, relative to many programs to enhance thinking skills, the program of the SOI Institute is theory based to an unusual extent. This should not be taken as a validation of the approach, inasmuch as the theory itself is controversial. Moreover, there are some questions about the theory as used in the program of the SOI Institute: why are transformations not included as part of creativity, why do not the results on reading reported above relate better to the factors singled out as relevant to reading, and so on? However, the highly developed theory behind the SOI program does give it a great deal of organization and coherence.

The studies obtained from the SOI Institute show that the SOI materials train abilities as measured by the SOI instruments. Therefore, if one accepts Guilford's Structure of Intellect theory of intelligence, or even if one views it as capturing a fair portion of intelligence, this is evidence that the SOI program improves intelligence. If one is not ready to accept that theory, studies demonstrating an impact on something other than the Structure of Intellect tests themselves become desirable. There are only two such studies in the materials we have, both addressing school achievement. The most clear-cut shows improvement in mathematics ability due to SOI training. Another shows improved performance on a number of Structure of Intellect factors that, in turn, correlate with school achievement in the same population. While this does not demonstrate a direct impact on achievement, the finding is consistent with that interpretation. Taken together, the various evaluations offer some amount of evidence favoring the effectiveness of the SOI approach. However, for full confidence in the viability of the approach, we would like to see more studies demonstrating a direct impact on achievement in school and in other contexts.

Perhaps our strongest reservation stems from the fact that training a skill correlated with another skill does not necessarily improve the second skill. This is the classic problem of "teaching to the test." For example, suppose we find that there is some correlation between scores on spelling and arithmetic tests. If we then subject the students to intensive training in spelling, we would not necessarily expect them to get better at arithmetic as a result. The same might happen with training SOI factors that correlate with certain academic achievements. Students might become better performers on the SOI tests without getting much better in school.

This is more a caveat than a criticism of the SOI approach. One *must* have direct measures of impact on school performance or on other intellectual activities to gauge the effectiveness of any approach. We have not seen enough data of the right sort to pass judgment on this point for ths SOI approach, nor, indeed, for most of the program reviewed in this book.

3. SCIENCE...A PROCESS APPROACH

The Science...A Process Approach (SAPA) program was developed over a period of six years by the Commission on Science Education of the American Association for the Advancement of Science with funding from the National Science Foundation. Initial plans for the program were formulated during two conferences held in the summer of 1962 and attended by both scientists and educators. The process by which the materials and methods were developed and refined involved the following annual cycle of activities: "(1) planning for development, during winter and spring; (2) a 'summer writing conference' of scientists and teachers; (3) a fall period of revision, editing, and publication of experimental materials; (4) a simultaneous activity, beginning in the fall and extending to the next summer, of trying out the newly developed materials in a group of participating schools in various parts of the country" (Gagne, 1967). A revision of the program, which eventuated in SAPA–II was undertaken under the terms of an agreement between the AAAS and Ginn and Company, the publisher of the instructional materials.

Specifics of the Program

As the title suggests, the program emphasizes the learning of processes involved in scientific work, as distinguished from learning about scientific facts and phenomena. A hands-on approach to learning is taken, in which the students work with materials, making observations and measurements, and performing experiments. Instruction focuses on eight "basic processes of science": (a) observing; (b) using space/time relationships; (c) using numbers; (d) measuring; (e) classifying; (f) communicating; (g) predicting; and (h) inferring.

Gagne (1967) distinguishes three meanings of "process" as the concept is used in the SAPA program: (1) Process as distinguished from content (while content is, of necessity, involved in the SAPA program—the students explore and manipulate real objects—the main purpose is not to have them learn facts about those objects or the phenomena they observe, but rather to have them learn *how* to observe, to manipulate purposefully, to classify, and so on); (2) process as a scientific activity, an activity in which a scientist normally engages; and (3) process as an intellectual skill, and in particular the kind of skill involved in "processing information."

The program is made up of 105 modules. The modules are organized in terms of a "behavioral hierarchy" that distinguishes five stages within each of seven grade levels (K through 6). Each module contains an instruction booklet for the teacher and the materials needed to conduct one class. The teacher's instruction booklet for each module includes a statement of one or a few explicit objectives, a rationale for inclusion within the program, the specification of an instructional procedure and a method of determining whether the learning objective has been obtained. The instructional procedures provide the teacher with considerable flexibility by offering optional exercises. Some explicit attention is given to the problem of transfer: each module includes "generalizing experiences" in which students are asked to relate what they have learned in that module to other contexts.

Modules are intended to be self contained and can be used individually to supplement other programs. They also can be grouped in either of two ways: in grade level sets or in "learning chains." A grade-level set is a set of 15 modules appropriate to students at a specific level from K to 6. In keeping with Piagetian notions about development, the grade level sets proceed from the more specific and concrete to the more general and abstract. A learning chain is a sequence of modules addressing a specific topic or skill. Learning chain topics include such things as the Metric System, Reading Readiness, and Special Education.

Supplementary materials that may be obtained in addition to the modules include Competency Tracking Cards (one per student, to record progress and report to parents), Program Guide (description of strategies for teaching of processes, etc.), and Commentary for Teachers (self-instructional units on the processes of science for use by teachers).

Although the program as a whole is focused on the teaching of skills and processes that would be useful in the further study (and doing) of science, some modules also provide instruction in mathematics and language skills. Moreover, the developers clearly expect the effects to generalize to other domains: "The goals to be achieved by any single exercise are modest. In a longer-term sense, substantial and general intellectual development is expected to result from the cumulative effects of an orderly progression of learning activities" (Gagne, 1967, p. 5). Promotional material claims the program has been shown to contribute to intellectual growth in areas other than basic science: math, reading readiness, logical reasoning, and basic communication.

Klausmeier's Work with SAPA Material

Some information about the effectiveness of the lessons and how they might be made more effective appears in Klausmeier (1980), who presents a theory and associated experiments on concept attainment. In applying his theory to improving learning in the SAPA program, Klausmeier defines four stages of concept mastery. In the first stage, a person simply apprehends as independent individual objects those objects that, later in development, will be classified as instances of the concept. Two intermediate stages lead to the final "formal" stage, which requires that the person be able to give a verbal definition of the concept, discriminate and name critical attributes, and evaluate how given nonmembers of the class differ from members in terms of the critical attributes.

Klausmeier argues that, according to contemporary research evidence, broad stage theories of cognitive development such as Piaget's are mistaken. Piaget's developmental stages can be found in the development of individual concepts, passed through anew each time a person adds a concept to his repertoire. Klausmeier also notes that, while the literature on concept attainment has stressed classification of instances and noninstances, his studies have concerned "process concepts," where the learner can learn to perform the operation the concept names. Klausmeier suggests that mastering a process concept at the formal level enhances performing the associated operation.

Klausmeier (1980) reports an elaborate series of experiments to test this proposal, using the SAPA materials and such process concepts as *observing*, *inferring*, and *predicting*. The basic design for the series of experiments was as follows. Control students, fourth and fifth graders, studied units from the 1967 version of SAPA (a revision was published in 1975), following the material as designed except that there was no further instruction for a student on a given lesson if he did not achieve mastery in the allotted time. This was the normal practice in the participating school systems, which were using SAPA already when the study began. Treatment students from the same grades studied the SAPA materials in exactly the same way, but, prior to commencing SAPA exercises on a given operation such as *inferring*, they received process concept instruction that ideally would yield a formal grasp of the process concept.

The results were reported both in terms of mean performance measures on post-tests of SAPA learning developed by the author and in terms of percentage of students achieving mastery, meaning performance of 80% or better on the post-tests. For instance, with SAPA instruction on inferring, the author found that various control groups achieved 17%, 24%, 10%, and 4% mastery. Corresponding treatment groups achieved 44%, 37%, 18% and 32% mastery. The first and last percentages were statistically significantly greater than the corresponding control group figures. In general, the author was able to show that often, although not always, the process concept instruction improved performance on the SAPA post-tests. For the most part, the percentages of mastery achieved even with the process concept instruction were not impressive, but it should be recalled here that the SAPA materials were being taught without the recommended effort to provide further instruction for students not mastering them initially.

Klausmeier also investigated the effects of additional SAPA instruction without process concept instruction, using the SAPA exercises on *inferring*.

Here, the control group received the usual SAPA instruction. After SAPA instruction and an initial posttest, the treatment group was divided into groups of varying performance, each of which received additional instruction tailored to their level of understanding. The treatment groups achieved 61% and 47% mastery in contrast with 17% and 9% in the control groups. In a further experiment, Klausmeier investigated the effects of process concept instruction plus additional SAPA instruction, achieving 71% and 64% mastery on *controlling variables* in the treatment groups, in contrast with 43% and 23% for control groups who received no process concept instruction and no extra SAPA instruction.

Taken together, the results suggest that process concept instruction can improve performance even when extra SAPA instruction is not provided, although extra SAPA instruction alone, targeted on the particular problems students have, yields greater gains than process concept instruction alone. It should also be noted that additional SAPA instruction plus the process concept instruction took nearly twice as much time as the control SAPA instruction alone, an important consideration in educational planning. Also, the tests of SAPA learning used were tied closely to the content of the lessons, so it is not clear to what extent the learning would generalize to other, somewhat different, content areas.

What can be said in summary about the effectiveness of SAPA? As is the case all too often throughout these reviews, we wish that we had been able to find more relevant studies. Although the SAPA materials themselves claim considerable success, supporting details are not offered. Klausmeier's work suggests that the SAPA modules can function quite effectively *providing* students' gains are measured and further instruction is undertaken to amplify those gains. Without such additional instruction, however, the gains appear much less impressive. It seems reasonable to conclude that the SAPA materials probably can be used to good effect, at least when student progress is monitored and time invested in further instruction to secure the benefits.

4. THINKABOUT

"ThinkAbout" is a series of sixty 15-minute video programs designed to give fifth and sixth grade students reasoning skills essential to learning and problem solving. It is a product of the Skills Essential to Learning Project, which involves a consortium of over 40 American and Canadian state and provincial agencies and is being managed by the Agency for Instructional Television (AIT). The design of the "ThinkAbout" series began in the summer of 1976 following several regional meetings and planning activities that occurred over the preceding three years. Experimental production of the series began in 1977 and regular production in 1978.

Content of the Program

ThinkAbout is organized around the following thirteen basic reasoning skills; a cluster of from two to six programs focuses on each one:

- finding alternatives
- estimating and approximating
- giving and getting meaning
- collecting information
- classifying
- finding patterns
- generalizing
- sequencing and scheduling
- using criteria
- reshaping information
- judging information
- communicating effectively
- solving problems

In addition to these thirteen reasoning skills, ThinkAbout identifies a larger number (about 65) of specific skills in mathematics, language arts, and study, which the curriculum material is intended to reinforce. These skills are organized under nine headings: reading; writing; listening; speaking/-discussing/presenting; viewing and observing; graphs, maps and scale drawings; measurement; computation; and study skills.

Sandwiched between program clusters are two special kinds of programs: *tips* and *challenges*. The tips focus on such topics as improving memory, setting goals, and handling anxiety, and are intended also to reinforce mathematics, language and study skills. The challenges are problems that the students are encouraged to try to solve after completing the program. They are also intended to provide teachers a chance to assess informally the degree to which the students have acquired the target skills.

The ultimate goal of the effort is to help the students become "independent learners and problem solvers." It is assumed that an effective way of doing that is to illustrate how other people solve problems, to stimulate discussion about problem solving and the application of the skills on which the material focuses, and to motivate the students to engage in problem solving activities.

Each cluster in the Teacher's Guide begins with a listing of the titles of the programs that comprise that cluster, a description of the goal for that cluster, and an explanation of why the reasoning skill addressed by the cluster is an important one to have. Following this introductory material, each of the programs within the cluster is described in turn.

The material for each program is organized under four topics: "Teaching Points," "Before the Program," "Program Summary," and "After the Program." Under "Teaching Points" is a list of the main points that the program is intended to convey. "Before the Program" gives the teacher suggestions regarding what to tell the students about the program they are about to see, or about a discussion they might have in preparation for seeing it. The "Program Summary" is a brief narrative description of the video program. "After the Program" provides a list of topics for discussion, and activities in which the students can practice the skills on which the program focuses. A more detailed description of the content of one cluster may be useful.

A Program Cluster

The first cluster, which is called "Finding Alternatives," contains three programs; "Why Bother?," "Brainstorming," and "Blockbusting." The goal of the cluster is to help students find alternatives when solving problems and to understand why it is important to be able to do so. The explanation of why the skill is important points out the role of alternatives in problem solving, decision making, invention, discovery and artistic creativity.

The teaching points included under "Why Bother?" are as follows:

- It is important to have alternatives.
- Alternative sources of information are found in a library.
- One alternative to reading an entire book is to use the table of contents, index, and bibliography to locate information.

"Before the Program" instructs the teacher to explain the subject of the program, and to ask the students to notice how the chief character discovers the importance of having many alternatives.

The program characterizes the experiences of a student faced with the problem of writing a three-page biographical report on George Washington Carver and not knowing how to proceed. There is an attempt to make the story interesting: the student falls asleep while working, not very effectively, in the library and dreams of meeting Carver, who gives her the idea of considering several alternative sources of information she had not thought to use.

The "After the Program" section contains several suggested topics for discussion, e.g., "Dr. Carver's advice on the importance of having alternatives," and "How to quickly locate information in a book without reading all of it." It also suggests some activities relating to the use of information sources.

The teaching points of the second program in the "Finding Alternative's" cluster, which is called "Brainstorming," are the following:

- Individuals or groups can use brainstorming to find alternative solutions to a problem
- Brainstorming requires (1) listing many ideas, (2) withholding comments, (3) building on ideas, and later (4) choosing the best ideas.
- Paraphrasing is useful for listing ideas during Brainstorming

For "Blockbusting," the third program of the cluster, the teaching points are:

- Blockbusting helps find alternatives when you are stuck on a problem
- Checking ideas, picturing a problem, and pretending are ways to blockbust a problem
- One way to picture a problem is by making a scale drawing

"Brainstorming" and "Blockbusting" follow the same format as "Why Bother?" and in each case the "After the Program" section contains both suggested topics for discussion and suggested activities for practicing what has been learned.

Evaluation

An investigation of the use of the ThinkAbout series in the classroom and its impact was undertaken during the 1979-80 academic year, its first year of use as an entire series. This investigation made use of surveys, case studies and objective tests. The tests, which were administered in 241 classrooms included problem solving exercises developed by Covington and the following subtests from the Comprehensive Test of Basic Skills: reading comprehension, language expression, mathematics concepts, mathematics applications, reference skills, science, and social studies. The results of the impact assessment have been published in a Technical Report and, in abbreviated form, in an Executive Summary (Sanders & Sonnad, 1982). The reports of the case studies have been published in three separate volumes, all of which are listed in the Executive Summary.

The results, as reported in the Executive Summary, were mixed. The way in which *ThinkAbout* was used in the classroom—how it was related to the rest of the curriculum, how the teachers prepared for it—differed greatly from one situation to another. Several barriers to the fullest use of the series were noted, among them other curricular priorities and inadequate teacher preparation. The use of television in the classroom was sometimes perceived by the students as a break from work. In some cases, the goals of the series became obscured as the school year went on: "the programs became isolated events, independent of the series as a whole" (p. 10)

Sanders and Sonnad noted that both teachers and students found the programs appealing. Survey data indicated that 93% of the responding teachers considered ThinkAbout to be high in educational effectiveness; about 50% reported some ("high or very high") degree of success in strengthening students' abilities in problem solving, systematic reasoning, flexible thinking, effective expression, independent learning, and management of one's own learning. Scores on the standardized tests that were administered, however, showed no systematic differences between the performance of students who participated in the ThinkAbout program and those who did not.

5. BASICS

BASICS is an acronym for Building and Applying Strategies for Intellectual Competencies in Students. The program was developed by the Institute for Curriculum and Instruction (ICI), which is located in Coral Gables, Florida. Its purpose is to provide training for teachers in certain thinking/learning strategies. The program includes a course that is offered to teachers in how to train other teachers in the use of the BASICS material. Such teachers are referred to as BASICS TRAINERS.

Content of the Program

The program identifies 18 thinking/learning strategies and organizes them in two sub-programs, the first of which (Program A) emphasizes data gathering and retrieval strategies and conceptualizing strategies, and the second of which (Program B) focuses on interpretation strategies, attitude-development strategies and skill-development strategies. Although the Manuals for these programs contain model lessons, teachers are encouraged to work the thinking/learning strategies of the program into subject matter courses.

The strategy for implementation of BASICS is for the ICI staff to train BASICS TRAINERS (teachers of teachers); the BASICS TRAINERS then are to train classroom teachers and the classroom teachers to teach students. Each program to train BASICS TRAINERS runs for 10 eight-hour days and it appears from the descriptive material that we have reviewed that participation as a trainee requires a commitment for the full 20 days required for the two programs. Upon completion of each 10-day course, a BASICS TRAINER is expected to conduct a minimum 30 hour BASICS (A or B) program for one or more groups of teachers. Following completion of both courses and the 60-hour practicum, BASICS TRAINERS are considered to be qualified to teach teachers on their own.

The strategies and skills addressed by the two programs are listed in Tables 6.2 and 6.3, which are taken from the Institute's promotional material. The strategies are described in detail in three participants manuals. Manual A addresses strategies of data gathering, observation, classification, and concept formation, as in the contents of Table 6.2. The introduction to Manual B characterizes the manual as concerning more

TABLE 6.2
Thinking/Learning Strategies for BASICS (Ehrenberg & Sydelle, 1980)

Program A—Data-Gathering/Retrieval Strategies and Conceptualizing Strategies	
Observing (Perceiving)	Noting a variety of physical characteristics, e.g., indicating the size, color, texture of a rock; the smell, taste, size, other features of a fruit; kind and number of letters in a word; characteristics of a painting, etc.
Recalling (Retrieval)	Remembering what is known or has been experienced, e.g., what was observed on a field trip; how certain tools are used; details of a story; what certain words mean; events of a period; findings of an experiment; etc.
Noting Differences	Identifying observed and recalled differences, e.g., differences in certain occupations; differences in word meanings and spellings; differences in types of governments; etc.
Noting Similarities	Identifying observed and recalled commonalities, e.g. what is alike about a group of insects; two or more communities; the characters in certain stories; etc.
Concept Formation	Processing data about the characteristics of selected examples and non-examples of a class, ultimately identifying the characteristics which distinguish a particular class from any other.
Classifying	Determining which items are additional members of a given class and identifying the attributes which make them so, e.g., explaining that a spider is not an example of an insect because it has eight rather than six legs; etc.
Concept Differentiation	Processing data about the characteriestics of examples of two similar classes, ultimately identifying the characteristics which distinguish one class from the other.
Grouping	Putting items together and identifying a common characteristic or other relationship among them, e.g. explaining that "hat," "ran," and "cab" belong together because the "a" is pronounced short; grouping meat and eggs together because they are rich in protein; etc.
Concept Extension	Processing data about the characteristics of a collection of items all of which are members of a broad class, ultimately identifying subclasses.

TABLE 6.3
Thinking/Learning Strategies for BASICS (Ehrenberg & Sydelle, 1980)

Program B—Interpretation Strategies, Attitude-Development Strategies	
Inferring Attributes	Attributing to a given item characteristics which cannot be directly discerned via observation and citing knowledge about the item to support the idea that it may have those characteristics, e.g. saying one thinks a particular person is honest and citing knowledge about the person that would support the idea that he (she) is honest.
Inferring Meaning	Identifying what one thinks may be the intended meaning of a given message (verbal and/or non-verbal) and citing information and reasoning which supports that interpretation, e.g. saying what one thinks is the meaning of a given passage in a reading and citing word and context meanings which support that interpretation of the passage.
Inferring Causes	Making inferences as to the causes for observed or recalled events and giving reasons for thinking they are causes, e.g. explaining reasons for thinking the method of production affected the price of the product, etc.
Inferring Effects	Making inferences as to the effects of observed or recalled events and giving reasons for thinking they are effects, e.g. explaining reasons for thinking that the change in location of the plant changed its growth pattern, etc.
Generalizing	Processing data about cause-effect relationships in sample situations, ultimately arriving at an idea of the general cause-effect relationship in any such situations.
Anticipating	Predicting the needed steps in a new procedure or the possible solutions to an analyzed problem, giving reasons for suggested steps or solutions and the conditions needed for each to occur, e.g. predicting the steps one would take in planning an interview and identifying the resources one would need to undertake each step—predicting possible consequences of new or changed situations, giving reasons for expecting predicted events and conditions under which they would occur, e.g. predicting that if given seeds were planted they would grow into plants like they came from and explaining the conditions needed for them to grow into healthy plants; etc.
Making Choices	Deciding which of a number of alternatives would be best in a given situation and explaining why, e.g. explaining reasons for thinking a biography would be a better source of information about a person than an encyclopedia; etc.
Attitude Formation/Change	Processing data concerning new opportunities to take action in given situations, ultimately developing or changing attitude toward situations calling for such behavior.
Skill Development/Refinement	Processing data concerning one's own proficiency level in the performance of a task as compared with a model performance, ultimately developing a higher level of proficiency in performing such tasks.

interpretive strategies by which students can arrive at individual ideas based on data, while C declares a special emphasis on practical applications, the strategies bearing such labels as "anticipating" and "making choices." Manuals B and C together are covered in Table 6.3, except that the last two entries, attitude formation/change and skill development/refinement, are not treated. However, Manual B does include a "Mini-Learning Sequence for Problem Solving." In both cases, the manual states that a more elaborate program is available from BASICS, but claims that the "mini" version will find many uses.

The following excerpt from Manual A, which describes a thinking strategy for classifying, conveys the format and flavor of the material:

Situation

When a person confronts the need to identify (or create) one or more examples of a particular concept.

Thinking Strategy

1. Retrieve the critical characteristics of any and all examples of the concept (the concept characteristics).
2. Determine and verify the specific characteristics of the item(s) to be identified (or created).
3. Identify the *similarities* and *differences* between the characteristics of the item(s) and the concept characteristics.
4. Decide whether or not the item(s) has enough of the concept characteristics to be considered an example and, if not, what characteristics are missing or different.
5. Verify the decision made in Step 4 by checking the accuracy of the identified similarities and differences.
6. Decide how to communicate and/or record (a) the decision as made in Step 4 and (b) the information on which the decision was based.

The entire BASICS sequence is constructed out of strategies presented in this and similar outline forms, along with explanations and elaborations. It is important to note that the outlines and text are for the teachers, not the students they will later teach. The teachers use the material to construct lessons embodying the strategies, and guide the students through the steps of the strategies. We cannot tell from the manual whether the students ever see the strategies stated in their abstract general form.

Evaluation

Unfortunately, we have not been able to find any empirical data on the effectiveness of the BASICS program. Our own assessment of it is, of necessity, very superficial because it is based solely on a perusal of the promotional material described above.

On the positive side, the manuals appear to be quite thorough. Not only are strategies outlined as above, but their importance is explained, they are redescribed in other ways, and the teaching of them is discussed extensively. The recommended teaching style is highly Socratic. Detailed sample lessons demonstrate how the strategies can be applied to specific content. For instance, one sample lesson for classifying asks the students to classify as a postage stamp/not a postage stamp such things as a gummed label from a postage meter, a specified foreign stamp, a Christmas Seal, an envelope with postage imprinted on it, and a once-cent stamp. Often the authors show how the strategies can be used to address standard curricular concerns such as reading comprehension or arithmetic.

The strategies themselves are organized so that later ones build on earlier ones. For example, the classification strategy depends on all those taught before it: observation, retrieval, identifying similarities, identifying differences, and concept formation. Also, all the strategies repeat certain characteristics that seem designed to foster a sound cognitive style. There is emphasis throughout on systematicity, thoroughness, checking judgments, storing or communicating results, justifying conclusions, and producing overt "thought products."

Besides these good features, there are some characteristics about which we have reservations. The strategies sometimes do not cut very deeply, and they fail to address explicitly characteristic pitfalls. For instance, in the strategy from Manual B for inferring the causes of events, there is no explicit mention of such common lapses of reasoning as failing to consider alternative causes, or elevating correlations into claims of causation. However, the sample lesson materials do suggest that the teacher maintain, and help the students to maintain, a critical posture toward such pitfalls.

Another potential difficulty is that the view of concepts and classification presupposed by BASICS sometimes seems outmoded. The strategy of concept formation is supposed to identify the critical characteristics that distinguish one particular class from another, but a good deal of recent work in cognitive psychology indicates that many concepts lack such critical characteristics (e.g., Smith & Medin, 1981). For example, the characteristics that people typically use to identify instances of concepts such as *bird* and *fruit* are not necessarily true of all instances. Thus the strategies being taught in BASIC may not work in all cases.

In short, although we have reservations about some aspects of the material, BASICS appears to be the result of a thoughtful effort to provide students with a fairly extensive variety of organized thinking experiences of the kind that are often represented in tests of intelligence. However, whether the program is effective in building intellectual competence, as it is intended to do, must remain an open question until the necessary evaluation studies are undertaken.

6. PROJECT INTELLIGENCE

Discussion of this project could be included either in this chapter or the next; it does emphasize fundamental processes such as observing, comparing, classifying, inferring, and so on, but it also focuses on some specific heuristics or strategies for problem solving, reasoning, inventing, and decision making. We place it here as a matter of convenience.

Background

Recently, the Republic of Venezuela made a decision to act upon the assumption that more could be accomplished by way of developing human intellectual potential than is now being done, and created a cabinet level position to initiate the exploration of possibilities. Project Intelligence is one direct consequence of that action.

The project involved a collaboration among researchers at Harvard University, Bolt Beranek and Newman Inc., and the Venezuelan Ministry of Education in an effort to develop some methods and materials that could be used to teach thinking skills in the Venezuelan secondary school system. The initiative for the project came from Venezuelan leaders, and in particular from Luis Alberto Machado, Minister of State for the Development of Human Intelligence. The project got its name from the fact that it originated in that office. Project Intelligence is one of several initiatives that have been undertaken recently by the Venezuelan government to explore ways to increase the effectiveness of educational processes and to facilitate the development of intellectual potential.

Whether the methods that are being tried in Venezuela will prove to be effective remains to be seen. The fact that considerable effort is being made is itself noteworthy, however, and there is, we believe, much to be learned from these efforts, both from those aspects of them that may succeed and from those that may fail, that can be useful for future efforts to enhance thinking. Here we describe Project Intelligence in some detail.

The project began in December 1979. During the first six months members of the project group met with numerous people in Venezuela including government officials, educational administrators, university professors, professors in pedagogical institutes, researchers, primary and secondary school teachers, and students. Several schools were visited in Caracas, Ciudad Guayana, and San Cristobal. The purpose of these visits and discussions was to learn as much as possible in a short time about the

Venezuelan school system, to attempt to determine what would constitute an innovation that would be consistent with the government's goals and within the project's means to help to design, to answer questions regarding what might and might not be attempted, and to establish dialogues with Venezuelan colleagues with whom the project group might be working in subsequent phases of the project.

The Course

From this initial study came the idea to try to develop an experimental course that could be tried at the seventh grade level in a small number of Venezuelan classrooms. (Seventh grade was selected, in part, because other projects were focused on other age groups.) The overall goal of the course was to be to enhance the ability of students to perform effectively a wide variety of intellectually demanding tasks. Intellectually demanding tasks, in this context, refers to tasks that require careful observation, deductive or inductive reasoning, the precise use of language, the inferential use of information in memory, hypothesis generation and testing, problem solving, inventiveness, and decision making.

Both the content and structure of the course evolved considerably while the material was being prepared. Major influences on this evolution were numerous discussions among members of the project staff, ideas evoked by review of other efforts to teach thinking skills, and feedback from attempts to use pilot material in Venezuelan classrooms.

The Teacher's Manual

The basic instrument for implementation of the course is a Teacher's Manual that is organized as six Lesson Series, each of which addresses a topic that the project staff considered to be important to thinking. Each Lesson Series is divided into two or more Units that focus on specific aspects of the Series topic. Table 6.4 gives a complete list of the Series and the Units that comprise them. Each Unit is composed of a set of Lessons. A Lesson is a prescription for one 45-minute classroom session devoted to a specific set of instructional objectives.

The individual lessons, of which there are approximately 100, are the backbone of the course. Each was prepared with certain design goals in mind, and each is addressed to specific instructional objectives. They are presented in a common format, and in every case a detailed set of suggestions is given regarding how to proceed in the classroom.

Lesson Design Goals. The intent in developing the lessons was that the following assertions would be true of each of them:

TABLE 6.4
Organization of the Project Intelligence Teacher's Manual

LESSON SERIES I:	FOUNDATIONS OF REASONING
Unit 1:	Observation and Classification
Unit 2:	Ordering
Unit 3:	Hierarchical Classification
Unit 4:	Analogies: Discovering Relationships
Unit 5:	Spatial Reasoning and Strategies
LESSON SERIES II:	UNDERSTANDING LANGUAGE
Unit 1:	Word Relations
Unit 2:	The Structure of Language
Unit 3:	Reading for Meaning
LESSON SERIES III:	VERBAL REASONING
Unit 1:	Assertions
Unit 2:	Arguments
LESSON SERIES IV:	PROBLEM SOLVING
Unit 1:	Linear Representations
Unit 2:	Tabular Representations
Unit 3:	Representations by Simulation and Enactment
Unit 4:	Systematic Trial and Error
Unit 5:	Thinking Out the Implications
LESSON SERIES V:	DECISION MAKING
Unit 1:	Introduction to Decision Making
Unit 2:	Gathering and Evaluating Information to Reduce Uncertainty
Unit 3:	Analyzing Complex Decision Situations
LESSON SERIES VI:	INVENTIVE THINKING
Unit 1:	Design
Unit 2:	Procedures as Designs

- It has at least one clear objective.
- That objective, if realized, will further the over-all goal of enhancing thinking skills in a general way.
- That objective is considered worth attaining for its own sake, independently of the over-all course goal. That is, if successfully completed, the lesson will leave the students with ideas and/or skills that they can apply to advantage outside of class.
- The teaching method is a practical one, and implementable by a competent teacher without extensive special training.
- The materials are meaningful and intrinsically interesting to the students.
- The activities are intellectually stimulating.

- The lesson challenges the students to use what is being learned, and provides some guidance regarding how to do so.
- There is a practical way to determine whether (or the extent to which) the objective(s) of the unit have been attained.

Undoubtedly these objectives were more completely realized in some cases than in others.

Lesson Format. The description of each lesson follows the same format, which addresses the following topics:

Rationale: An explanation of why the lesson is included in the course.

Objectives: A specification of what the lesson is intended to accomplish. The following are examples of lesson objectives:

- To increase skills in spatial orientation.
- To make students aware of the power of a strategic approach to problem solving.
- To introduce the relationships of contradiction and implication.
- To teach the students rules of antonymy.
- To show the importance of both negative and positive instances in the testing of hypotheses.
- To introduce a systematic procedure for choosing among objects whose preferability differs along several dimensions.
- To teach a general strategy for analyzing any design.

Target Abilities: A list of things the student should be able to *do* after completing the lesson. The following are examples of Target Abilities:

- To use a diagram to help figure out the meaning of a statement.
- To interpret a story from the points of view of different characters.
- To identify pairs of assertions in which one assertion implies another.
- To test hypotheses about the essential characteristics of a class.
- To generate negative antonyms by adding or subtracting the appropriate prefix.
- To evaluate a procedure.
- To analyze a decision situation to determine what decision alternatives exist.

Products: Tangible things the students are required to produce.

Materials: Materials, other than paper and pencil, that are needed for the unit.

Classroom Procedure: Detailed instructions to the teacher regarding how to proceed.

Classroom Procedure. The material presented under *Classroom Procedure* is intended to provide the teacher with a detailed plan for conducting the class. The objective in specifying the Classroom Procedure in considerable detail was to make the material usable by a wide variety of teachers with a minimum of special training. It was also considered important, for purposes of evaluation, that the course be taught in as nearly as possible in the same way by each of the teachers who participated in the evaluation effort. Often the plans for conducting the class included suggestions of things the teacher and the students might say. These imaginary dialogs are referred to as "scripts." Scripts are easily identified by the way the lessons are formatted. These scripts are not intended to be read in class or memorized by the teacher, but simply to illustrate for the teacher how a dialogue *might* go; most importantly, they are meant to convey the idea that every lesson should involve an interaction between teacher and students, and that active student participation is to be encouraged and reinforced throughout the course.

The Manual was prepared in both English and Spanish, each Unit was authored and edited by a different subset of the project team.[1] The Manual preparation was coordinated by Adams and the Manual is cited in the reference list at the end of this book as Adams et al. (1982).

Evaluation

The course was implemented for purposes of "formative" evaluation during the academic year 1981/1982. A subset of the lessons was tried informally in several seventh grade classrooms by experienced Venezuelan teachers. The teachers were trained and supervised by several other Venezuelan teachers who had worked with the project staff during the preceding summer, becoming familiar with the material and helping to shape it to the Venezuelan context.

The purpose of this formative evaluation was to provide feedback while the course was still being developed regarding strengths and weaknesses of various aspects of it. Feedback was obtained both from the classroom

[1]The author-editor group was composed of M. Adams, J. Buscaglia, A. Collins, C. Feehrer, M. Grignetti, R. Herrnstein, S. Herrnstein, A. Huggins, C. Laserna, R. Nickerson, D. Perkins, M. de Sanchez, K. Spoehr, B. Starr, and J. Swets.

teachers who used the material and from observers from the project team. It was used to modify some of the existing lessons and to guide the development of others.

A formal "summative" evaluation was conducted during the academic year 1982/1983. Roughly one half of the lessons were taught in 12 seventh grade classes from three schools in Barquisimeto (four from each school). Twelve matched classes from three other Barquisimeto schools served as controls. All the participating schools were designated by Venezuelan authorities as "Barrio" schools indicating schools whose students come from families of low socioeconomic status and minimal parental education. Each class had approximately 30 to 40 students: the total number of students in the experimental and control classes respectively was 463 and 432. Experimental classes participated in the program for about 45 minutes a day three or four days a week for the entire school year. Control classes had their normal curriculum.

A variety of tests were administered to both experimental and control students before the beginning of the course, after its completion, and, in some cases, at various points during the year. These tests included several standard tests: the Otis Lennon School Ability Test, the Cattell Culture-Fair Test, and some General Abilities Tests drawn from several sources, including Guidance Testing Associates' Tests of General Ability and the Puerto Rican Department of Education's Test of General Ability. In addition, several Target Abilities Tests (TATs) were designed by Swets, Getty, and Spoehr of the project staff to test specifically for the target abilities that the lessons were intended to teach.

Detailed results appear in the project's Final Report (Harvard, 1983) and in Herrnstein, Nickerson, Sanchez, & Swets (in preparation). Briefly, both experimental students and controls showed some improvement on tests scores over the year of the experiment: posttest scores were generally higher than pretest scores for both groups. In the large majority of cases, the gains shown by students in the experimental group were greater than those shown by the controls. The differences were both statistically significant and substantial in size. Not surprisingly, differences were greater in the case of the Target Abilities Tests than in that of the more general standard tests. More specifically, on the Target Abilities Tests, the experimental subjects gained an average of 12.8 percentage points and the controls 5.9. For the Otis-Lennon test, the comparable numbers were 16.0 and 10.9, for the Cattell, 8.6 and 7.1, and for the General Abilities Tests combined, 10.4 and 6.2. All of these differences were statistically significant with the exception of the Cattell Test, which was marginally significant ($p < .025$).

There are several possible factors that could help explain why the scores of the control groups improved over the duration of the experiment. First, one would expect some improvement, especially on the standard tests, by virtue of the year of maturation and traditional schooling. Second, there is the possibility of a Hawthorne effect, inasmuch as even the control students received some special attention and knew they were participating in an educational experiment. Third, there is the possibility that the teachers of the control groups were especially motivated by their knowledge that the performance of their students would be compared, at year end, against that of the students in the experimental groups. Whatever the explanation for the gains by the controls, the fact that the performance of this group did improve points up the inadvisability of evaluating any program strictly on the basis of a before- and after-program comparison of the performance of the experimental group. Evaluation of the effectiveness of the Project Intelligence intervention stressed the differences between the gains made by subjects in the experimental groups and those made by the controls. The fact that these differences were consistently positive and in some cases of moderate size led the investigators to view the approach as a promising basis for further exploration and development.

7. THE COGNITIVE OPERATIONS APPROACH IN GENERAL

We have reviewed several programs that can be roughly classified as having adopted a cognitive operations approach to teaching thinking. All of these programs try to exercise extensively component cognitive operations or activities that might be thought of as the "atoms" out of which more complex activities are constructed. Some of them have strong links with theories of intelligence, and the component operations on which they focus are similar to what theories identify as constituents of intelligence. With the various programs reviewed in mind, what can be said about the pros and cons of the cognitive operations approach?

It is difficult to make general statements when the programs show such diversity as those reviewed. Nonetheless, we think the following are fair summary remarks. The theoretical foundations of the programs reviewed are problematic, for reasons to be noted later. Also, for the most part, these programs tend to neglect the most complex types of cognitive performance—for instance, writing or mathematical problem solving. On the plus side, they characteristically offer a great deal of practice with a diversity of cognitive tasks, and often take care to monitor student progress with testing. They may well help students in general, and may be especially useful for weak students who need to have basic skills bolstered before tackling more complex types of cognitive performance. Let us consider these generalizations one by one.

First, consider the theoretical bases of the various programs. In general, the teaching of component operations seems consistent with the widely accepted idea that intelligence has many components; and the components on which these programs focus are presumably those that the program developers consider fundamental to intellectual competence. However, reviewing the various programs discussed, we are impressed by how easy it is to make up a list of fundamental operations, and also by the fact that the lists produced by different programs differ considerably from one another. Each of these lists can be seen as a theory of the components of intelligence or at least of determinants of intellectual performance. And this is the problem. There are too many of these theories for comfort. To be sure, some themes recur frequently but the differences are substantial.

Another concern is the relatively wholistic treatment of these supposed atoms. The activity of "classifying" provides one example. Clearly there is something very fundamental about classification. It is so basic to our thinking that we cannot imagine what thought could be without it. Moreover, *everyone* classifies spontaneously, quite apart from any explicit training aimed at developing the ability. That is not to suggest that everyone is equally adept at classifying, or that the ability can not be improved by training. We suspect, however, that classification is a much more complex process than it appears to be. It is true that classifying is classifying whether the class to which one is assigning something is the class of chairs, cumulus clouds, Italian baroque music, or unsolvable problems. But it is not clear that the underlying process is exactly the same in each case. It seems somewhat implausible (although not impossible) that there is a unitary skill of classifying that can be strengthened effectively by practice with a few exercises.

Finally, it is not surprising that the cognitive operations approach tends to neglect very complex cognitive performances, such as writing or solving mathematical problems, inasmuch as the approach aims to address relatively primitive components of performance. However, if and when a student achieves mastery of these basic skills, there remains the problem of handling more complex tasks. This, in itself, is not an objection to the cognitive operations approach, but simply an observation that there are other things to be taught too. Cognitive operations approaches may be more appropriate for weaker students, who have not mastered basic skills, than for stronger students, who have done so to a greater extent.

The various programs discussed prompt concern on these three points to varying degrees. However, there are two counter-tendencies in the cognitive operations approach that favor it: a trend toward extensive practice with a diversity of tasks, and a trend toward frequent testing. Of course, these could be features of any approach—but typically they are not. For instance, the heuristics approach, which is discussed in the next chapter, often suffers from the optimism that the student who has learned a strategy can apply it effectively and will do so on appropriate occasions. Why does the cognitive operations approach tend to differ in this regard? Perhaps because it deals with operations that, from the first, are viewed as problematic. The students are expected to need substantial practice. It is recognized that the amount of practice required may be hard to estimate, so this encourages routinely monitoring the progress of students and supplying additional instruction as needed. Not all the approaches discussed do these things, but some of them do it with care.

Theoretically oriented readers may have difficulty with the suggestion that an approach to teaching thinking that has a weak or controversial theoretical base may be effective nevertheless. Our position is that the state of theory relating to intellectual competence is still too primitive, in general, to warrant giving great weight to the underlying theory in assessing programs. Moreover, even a theoretically questionable list of basic cognitive operations may include many of the sorts of activities students need to perform. And such a list can provide a heuristic guide to constructing lessons. The lessons, emphasizing practice and monitoring student progress as they generally do, can, we believe, promote the learning of a variety of useful skills. Indeed some of the skills the students acquire may be quite different from those the authors of the program imagined. For instance, the students may acquire cognitive style traits much more general than anything acknowledged in the curriculum materials. Programs based on a cognitive operations approach appear to foster such ancillary effects.

7 Heuristics Oriented Approaches

As was noted in Chapter 4, researchers have given a great deal of attention in recent years to the study and development of heuristics for representing problems and devising plans for their solutions. Some of this work has been motivated by the desire to understand better how the methods used by skilled problem solvers differ from those of people less skilled in this regard. And some of it has been motivated by the desire to develop computer programs that can solve intellectually demanding problems as well as, or better than, humans do. Whatever the reason, as we noted earlier, this work on problem solving has yielded information that should be useful in efforts to train people to be better problem solvers. Indeed, several programs have been developed that emphasize the teaching of specific heuristics, strategies, or problem-solving techniques like those that have been identified and studied by researchers in recent years.

This approach sees thinking skill as a matter, at least in part, of appropriate know-how, though the know-how invokes general-purpose heuristics rather than specific facts. What one needs in order to be an effective thinker, according to this view, is a repertoire of heuristics that are likely to be effective in a variety of problem situations, along with metaknowledge about situations in which specific heuristics are appropriate. The approach typically assumes the presence of the abilities that programs focused on cognitive operations are intended to develop. That is, if a heuristic requires the problem solver to classify something at some point, it is assumed that the ability to classify is a skill he already has. This aspect of the approach is not very surprising given that it is based on problem solving research that typically uses intellectually demanding problems.

There is some evidence that training based on the mimicry of an expert's performance in a problem situation may sometimes be an effective approach (Larkin, 1980). Brown, Bransford, and Chi (1978) note, however, that such training probably only works for individuals who are ready for it, that is to say, those who have the necessary cognitive foundation upon which to build.

1. PATTERNS OF PROBLEM-SOLVING

The Course

One well known effort to teach problem solving as a college course is the "Patterns of Problem Solving" course introduced at the University of California in Los Angeles by Rubenstein beginning with a class of 32 students in 1969. By 1976 the course was enrolling approximately 1200 students per year. It attracts students from a variety of major fields and all levels from freshman to graduate students. It is taught by faculty and teaching assistants from various disciplines, including not only engineering, mathematics and computer science, but psychology, law, business, and philosophy. (A history of the course is given in Rubenstein, 1980.)

The primary objectives of the course are summarized by Rubenstein (1980) as follows:

- To develop a general foundation of problem-solving approaches, and master some specific techniques.
- To provide a foundation for attitudes and skills productive in dealing with problems in the context of human values.
- To emphasize the thinking processes at all stages of the problem-solving activity.
- To identify individual problem-solving styles and learn to overcome conceptual blocks and self-imposed constraints.
- To expose students to both objective and subjective aspects of problem solving.
- To provide a framework for a better appreciation of the role of tools and concepts that the students may have acquired or will acquire.
- To bring together students from diverse backgrounds so that they can observe different attitudes and problem-solving styles and learn from each other. (p. 26)

The course emphasizes problem-solving processes and the importance of transferring what is learned to practical applications. To encourage transfer, a project is required in which students apply the problem solving tools they have learned to a problem of their choice.

While Rubenstein's course provides some latitude for instructors to follow their own interests, all instructors are expected to cover the following aspects of problem solving:

- tools for problem representation
- models as aids to thinking
- identifying personal problem-solving styles
- learning to overcome conceptual blocks dealing with uncertainty
- focusing on the process of problem solving
- decision making, individual and group
- the role of values in problem solving
- the holistic and interdisciplinary nature of human problem solving (p. 30)

In addition to course content, Rubenstein considers the teachers' attitudes and interactions with students to be very important. The following are a few of several guiding principles that Rubenstein lists as having been helpful to him in his efforts to bring about learning and growth:

- If you really want your students to learn a concept, give them an opportunity to teach you, the teacher.
- Concentrate on a small number of concepts, and dig deeply into their implications in as wide a field as possible.
- Make explicit the connection between knowledge and its application whenever possible.
- Encourage questions. Some questions are so outstanding that they should not be spoiled by an immediate answer; we should take time to ponder them. If this is the case, tell the students.
- *Do not* tell a class: "We are behind." Your plan might have been unrealistic. Each class is unique; adapt your plans to the class and you will always be "on schedule," whatever it may be.
- Do not express doubt about the learner's abilities to learn. (p. 37)

Rubenstein considers the course to have been successful, the reasons for the success being "the course content; the preparation and training of the teaching staff; the varied opportunities for learning; the availability and helpfulness of the staff; the learning laboratories; and the enthusiasm, dedication, and commitment of the instructors and peer teachers" (1980, p. 36). Objective evaluative data on the course apparently do not exist, and the failure to attempt to gather such data has been the basis for some criticism (Reif, 1980).

The Book

An outgrowth of Rubenstein's course was *Patterns of Problem Solving*, which was published in 1975. The explicit purpose of this book, as expressed by the author in the preface, was "to provide the reader with tools and concepts which are most productive in problem solving and are least likely to be eroded with the passage of time."

In the book, Rubenstein identifies two difficulties that impede effective problem solving: (1) the failure to use known information, and (2) the introduction of unnecessary constraints. The first difficulty he sees as a consequence of the way the brain works, and in particular, of the fact that although a great deal of information is stored in memory, only a small portion of it is accessible at any given time. He attributes the limited accessibility of information to the constraints of the "human processing unit." His answer to this difficulty is not to rely on memory and to use techniques that make such reliance unnecessary, e.g., writing the problem down in as simple a form as possible, using mathematical notation, diagrams, charts, and so on.

With respect to the second difficulty, Rubenstein suggests that people often search for a problem solution in too small space; that is, they assume that constraints exist that really do not. For example, in trying to solve a stick-arrangement problem they may behave as though they assume that the solution must be a two-dimensional one and fail to consider the possibility of using the third dimension.

To help with these difficulties and various others, Rubenstein offers the following (paraphrased) general guidelines to problem solving: (a) attempt to get a total picture of the problem before attempting to solve it; (b) avoid committing too early to a course of action; consider several approaches before choosing one; (c) try to represent the problem with a model (verbal, mathematical, pictorial); (d) having found a representation, look for ways of transforming it into other representations that may suggest other approaches; (e) attempt to restate the question that is being asked; a restatement may prompt a new perspective and new ideas about approaches; (f) be willing to challenge premises and assumptions relating to the problem.

Other suggestions that Rubenstein gives regarding ways to facilitate problem solving include: work backwards; generalize the problem or particularize it when that would be helpful; feel free to explore various approaches; learn how to use partial solutions effectively; use analogies and metaphors; follow hunches and pay attention to how you feel about your progress; talk about the problem with others, and listen to their ideas.

Much of the book presents content that Rubenstein considers foundational for problem solving. This includes discussions of language, symbolic logic, Boolean algebra, computers, probability theory (and especially Bayes' theorem), information theory, and the purpose and nature of models. The second half of the book gives detailed information on a variety of models and formal tools for problem solving. Included in this coverage are descriptions of probabilistic models and their application to statistical inference, decision making models, optimization models including linear programming and sequential decision making, dynamic systems models, and models that deal with the assessment and application of values. The emphasis on the role of models in problem solving is central. One whole chapter is devoted to the discussion of the purpose and nature of models and to an illustration of roles models have played in history, science, and engineering.

Since the publication of the book, the first (and least quantitative) half of it has been used by Rubenstein in his course on "Patterns of Problem Solving" at UCLA. The course has admitted students from a variety of fields and from all levels, from freshman to graduate students. Material in the second half of the book has been incorporated in a second course entitled, "Applied Patterns of Problem Solving" also offered at UCLA. This course is presumably restricted to students who have had the necessary mathematical foundation.

In our view it is a fine text and reference book providing a broad coverage of formal approaches to problem solving and at the same time covering several areas in considerable depth. It is strongly oriented toward mathematical approaches to problem solving, however, and is not suitable for use with grade school students or with people lacking necessary mathematical sophistication. Aimed, as it is, at the college level student it assumes more than high-school level mathematics in several sections.

Whether instruction in mathematically based subjects such as statistical decision theory, linear programming, and utility theory, makes people better problem solvers in everyday life is an open question. Certainly it seems that such training *should* have an effect. There clearly are many problems to which formal mathematical approaches can be directly applied. If one encounters such a problem, knows an applicable mathematical technique, and recognizes its appropriateness, one presumably should be able to solve the problem more readily than someone who lacks such knowledge.

But to what extent are formal mathematical approaches to problem solving and decision making applied in real life situations by people who understand them and recognize their applicability? Unfortunately, the answer to this question is not known. It would not surprise us to learn, if the data were available, that such application is the exception rather than the rule. Certainly the fact that people learn to apply procedures to problems that are presented in textbooks is not evidence that they apply those same procedures to the problems they encounter outside the academic context. There is at least one reason for suspecting that procedures that could be applied often are not: the problems that are encountered in real life typically are not sufficiently well structured to permit a straightforward text-book analysis. If one wishes to use such an analysis, the first difficulty is to represent the problem in a form that makes the analysis possible.

There is a second way in which formal training such as that provided by Rubenstein's course and book might improve everyday problem solving. The methodical approach to problems that such training fosters, and the use of certain broad strategies (e.g., the use of concrete representations) are certainly applicable in principle to many real world problems. Moreover, cognitive style traits and very broad strategic advice may transfer better than particular techniques. A person who has had such instruction might be more likely, for example, to try to consider many alternatives systematically, using a list or a diagram to keep track of them. Although there is no formal evidence one way or another, we would not be surprised to find gains of this sort resulting from instruction such as Rubenstein offers. This question deserves to be investigated.

2. SCHOENFELD'S HEURISTIC INSTRUCTION IN MATHEMATICAL PROBLEM SOLVING

Alan Schoenfeld, a mathematician interested in the nature of expert problem solving and how to teach it, has been working for some years to produce an effective demonstration of heuristic instruction. He notes that any argument for the practical value of heuristic instruction should address certain issues. Whether a heuristic actually helps in solving a problem is not the only question. Perhaps heuristics help but students already pick them up from normal instruction about as well as they can. Perhaps mathematicians use heuristics but novices lack the detailed technical knowledge to make them meaningful. Running as a thread through Schoenfeld's work, one can find the following many sided argument for the merits of heuristic instruction:

- Heuristics help students to solve problems when the students know and apply the heuristics.
- Students lack a good set of heuristics.
- Students do not reliably pick up heuristics spontaneously from examples; heuristics have to be taught explicitly.
- Students do not reliably apply heuristics they know about; some sort of guidance or prompting is necessary.
- A "managerial strategy" for approaching problems, taken together

with heuristics, can help students to apply heuristics and lead to substantially improved problem solving performance in mathematics.

Instruction in Heuristics

A small scale experiment involving only seven students addressed the first three of these points, yielding statistically significant results (Schoenfeld, 1979, 1980). The experiment included only a few subjects, in part because think-aloud protocols were gathered from all the subjects during the pretests and posttests. This allowed intensive analysis of the problem-solving processes of the participants, a very time consuming procedure.

The students were upper division science and mathematics majors at the University of California, Berkeley, who volunteered for the study. Four were assigned at random to a treatment condition and three to a control condition. A pretest of five problems was administered, and, after instruction, a posttest consisting of five more problems thought to be of comparable difficulty. The pretest and posttest problems lent themselves to solution by means of five heuristics: (1) draw a diagram if at all possible; (2) if there is an integer parameter, look for an inductive argument; (3) consider arguing by contradiction or contrapositive; (4) consider a similar problem with fewer variables; and (5) try to establish subgoals.
Students in both treatment and control groups received nearly the same instruction administered in five sessions over two weeks. The instruction consisted in trying to solve a problem and then reading and hearing a good solution process. Twenty problems were treated in all. The suggested solution processes, presented through written and tape-recorded materials, illustrated the five heuristics.

For the treatment group, the heuristics were identified explicitly at the beginning of the instruction and whenever they were applied during the instruction. For the control group, the heuristics were not mentioned at the outset, nor pointed out when they were used in the presented solution processes. Also, for the treatment group the demonstration problems lending themselves to solution by the same heuristic were grouped in a single session of instruction; for the control group, they were scattered throughout the instruction, as is the natural circumstance when students pick up something that is not explicitly taught. In short, the control group was exposed to the heuristics without them being identified explicitly or highlighted by grouping.

Every five minutes during both pretesting and posttesting the students received a reminder to review their progress and decide whether they wanted to continue the same approach. The treatment students were asked to review their progress and also to look through the heuristics. A list of the heuristics was in front of the treatment students as they took the posttest.

Taken together, the control students solved five problems on the pretest and five problems on the posttest, and nearly solved two more and three more respectively. "Nearly solved" meant that, in the judgment of the scorer, the student was on a correct solution path and would have resolved the problem in a few more minutes. This result both suggested that the pretests and posttests represented roughly the same level of difficulty and indicated that the control students had not gained at all by the instruction.

In contrast, the treatment students, taken together, solved four problems on the pretest and thirteen problems on the posttest; they nearly solved an additional problem on both pretest and posttest. The contrast between the control and treatment groups was statistically significant at the .05 level, despite the small number of participants. This suggested that the heuristic instruction plus the presence of the list and the reminder to review the strategies allowed the treatment students to perform better than the controls.

But did the better performance of the treatment students actually stem from the heuristics? This question was addressed by having students "think-aloud" while trying to solve the problems. The protocols revealed that, in general, when the treatment students solved problems, they did so through explicit application of the heuristics they had been taught. In contrast, for the most part, nothing like the heuristics appeared in the protocols of the control students.

In summary, then, the study suggests that these students—all of them fairly successful students in mathematics and physics—lacked familarity with the heuristics that were presented during the study. Those students explicitly exposed to the heuristics learned to use them to some extent; those exposed to implicit applications of the heuristics did not. Those who did apply the heuristics solved more problems than those who did not.

The Importance of a Managerial Strategy

Presumably, the treatment students in Schoenfeld's experiment benefited not only from explicit heuristic instruction but from reminders to apply the heuristics. Perhaps, in general, heuristic instruction is not enough; students need to be prompted, or need to learn to prompt themselves, to review likely heuristics, and to approach problems systematically. That question was not addressed by this study, since there was no condition for students with explicit heuristic training but without the list and prompts present during testing.

However, an earlier study (Schoenfeld, 1978) examined the issue in the context of teaching calculus. The students had learned to use the standard methods of integration, but Schoenfeld observed that the conventional instruction did not offer much guidance about when to apply the methods.

He conducted an experiment in which some students prepared for an exam by learning a managerial strategy that guided them systematically through the available methods, considering which might work in the case at hand. The students who studied in this manner performed better on the exam than those who studied normally, even though the latter students spent more time preparing for the exam according to their own estimates.

Through experience and experiments such as the foregoing, Schoenfeld has developed a general managerial strategy and series of heuristics for mathematical problem solving. He views the managerial strategy and heuristics as a partial model of expertise in the area. The heuristics are summarized in Table 7.1, reproduced from Schoenfeld (1980). The managerial strategy, described in the same source, has the following five phases:

Analysis. This phase is entered with a given problem or with a related problem generated in the course of solving the given problem. One aim is to understand the problem and get a "feel" for it by examining the givens, the unknowns, and so on. Another is to simplify the problem by reformulating it without loss of generality. Relevant heuristics appear in the first part of Table 7.1.

Design. From the analysis phase, the problem solver moves to the design phase. The aim here is to maintain an overview of the problem-solving process, develop a broad plan for how to proceed, and ensure that detailed calculations are not done prematurely. Little mathematics per se is accomplished in this phase, but the problem solver constantly loops back to it for checks on progress. In other words, the design phase is a periodic "top level monitor" for the entire process. No specific heuristics are suggested.

Exploration. From the design phase, the problem solver branches either to exploration or implementation. Exploration is the choice when the problem presents difficulties and no clear plan for directly producing a solution is at hand. Exploration follows three heuristic steps of increasing extremity summarized in the second part of Table 7.1. The result might be an approach to part of the problem or the formulation of a subproblem or a related problem. The problem solver may loop back to the design phase to consider what to do next, or even to the analysis phase to think over a newly formulated related problem or the old problem again.

Implementation. This phase is entered from the design phase, reflecting a decision that a plan is in hand that should lead to a solution if carried through. For instance, there might be a set of equations to be solved or a proof discovered during exploration that needs to be set down step by step.

TABLE 7.1
Frequently Used Heuristics Described by Schoenfeld, 1980

Analysis

1. Draw a diagram if at all possible.
2. Examine special cases:
    a. Choose special values to exemplify the problem and get a "feel" for it.
    b. Examine limiting cases to explore the range of possibilities.
    c. Set any integer parameters equal to 1, 2, 3, ..., in sequence, and look for an inductive pattern.
3. Try to simplify the problem by
    a. Exploiting symmetry, or
    b. "Without loss of generality" arguments (including scaling).

Exploration

1. Consider essentially equivalent problems.:
    a. Replace conditions by equivalent ones.
    b. Re-combine the elements of the problem in different ways.
    c. Introduce auxiliary elements.
    d. Re-formulate the problem by:
        i. changing perspective or notation
        ii. considering argument by contradiction or contrapositive.
        iii. assuming a solution and determining its properties.
2. Consider slightly modified problems:
    a. Choose subgoals (obtain partial fulfillment of the conditions).
    b. Relax a condition and then try to re-impose it.
    c. Decompose the domain of the problem and work on it case by case.
3. Consider broadly modified problems:
    a. Construct an analogous problem with fewer variables.
    b. Hold all but one variable fixed to determine that variable's impact.
    c. Try to exploit any related problems that have similar
        i. form
        ii. "givens"
        iii. conclusions

Remember: when dealing with easier related problems, you should try to exploit both the *result* and the *method of solution* on the given problem.

Verifying your solution

1. Does your solution pass these specific tests?
    a. Does it use all the pertinent data?
    b. Does it conform to reasonable estimates or predictions?
    c. Does it withstand tests of symmetry, dimension analysis, and scaling?
2. Does it pass these general tests?
    a. Can it be obtained differently?
    b. Can it be substantiated by special cases?
    c. Can it be reduced to known results?
    d. Can it be used to generate something you known?

The result of implementation is a tentative solution to the problem. No heuristics are suggested for implementation.

Verification. This phase follows implementation. The aim is to check the solution. Several heuristics for this purpose are suggested in Table 7.1.

A Further Evaluation Study

While the investigations discussed earlier support the idea that problem solving might be improved by teaching heuristics together with a managerial strategy, they do not constitute a direct demonstration. Such a demonstration was sought by Schoenfeld (1982; Schoenfeld & Herrmann, 1982) through the teaching of an intensive course in mathematical problem solving based on the managerial strategy and heuristics discussed above. The course involved eleven freshmen and sophomores in a small liberal arts college, and was offered during a period set aside for intensive study on one subject. The students met as a class for two and one half hours per day for eighteen days. In addition, they did an average of four to five hours of homework per day. Schoenfeld notes that essentially the same results were also obtained for a group of twenty students taking the same course the year before, although data for these students are not presented.

All the instruction concentrated on the process of problem solving. Problems were solved in a variety of ways in class, always with an emphasis on the heuristics that could be used. The importance of self-monitoring was stressed, in keeping with the design phase of the managerial strategy.

Eight students of comparable background taking an intensive course in structured programming served as a control group. These students took the same pretest and posttest. To be sure, the ideal control group would receive experience with mathematical problem solving but not heuristic instruction. However, that was not so important for this experiment because the research discussed earlier had demonstrated that the learning and application of heuristics was necessary for improvement in mathematical problem solving. Accordingly, the real issue became simply whether the pretests and posttests presented were of roughly equal difficulty. The control group permitted a check on this point. One pretest and posttest consisted of five problems chosen to provide an opportunity to apply heuristics. When the students took the tests, they were urged not only to write down answers, but also whatever approaches they tried and their reasons for trying them. The students took the exams using pens, and crossing out rather than erasing steps they later rejected. The scoring of the pretests and posttests employed this information as well as the student's final solution, if any.

Three advanced undergraduate assistants were trained to grade the performance of each student on each test problem, counting the number of "plausible approaches" the student had taken to the problem and rating each approach as to how far the student had taken it, from just a mention to a complete solution. The pretests and posttests were intermixed and the graders did not know which were which. The graders worked on the tests independently with very high interjudge agreement. The results for the control group revealed that the pre and posttests were of roughly equal difficulty and that taking the pretest did not prime the students for a better performance on the posttest. The results for the treatment group revealed substantial improvement as a result of the instruction. For example, one way of counting up the plausible approach scores yielded a score on a scale from 0 to 100, the latter corresponding to solving all the problems. For the treatment group, the average pretest score was 20.8 and the average posttest score 72.2.

A second pretest and posttest instrument involved self ratings: after each problem, the students were given four minutes to answer a series of general questions such as "Have you seen this problem before," "Did you plan your solution or 'plunge' into it," and "Rate the difficulty of the problem." This instrument yielded a picture consistent with the improved scores mentioned above. For example, the students in the experimental group thought that they had seen related problems much more often on the posttest than on the pretest, saw the posttest problems as easier, and, on the posttest, saw themselves as not "plunging in" and as proceeding in a more organized way.

Even given these results, one might still question whether the students had learned anything very general. The problems in the pretest and posttest were parallel to problems discussed during the period of instruction. Would the students be able to handle problems less immediately connected with the instruction?

Schoenfeld examined this possibility by administering another pretest and posttest. The test included nine problems in three groups of three. One of each group was closely related to a problem discussed during the instruction, another was only somewhat related, and a third bore hardly any relation. The students were asked not to solve these problems, but simply to plan solutions, writing down how the problems might be approached. The students only had six or seven minutes per problem to do this.

As it turned out, the treatment students on the posttest performed much better than was expected, not only sketching detailed solutions but actually solving a number of the problems. It was decided that the "plausible approach" scoring scheme developed for the first pretest and posttest could be applied to this test as well.

The control students showed no gains from pretest to posttest, but the students who took the special course showed considerable ability to transfer what they had learned. For instance, simply in terms of number of plausible approaches suggested, on the "closely related" problems the experimental group offered 12 in the pretest and 30 in the posttest; for the "somewhat related" problems, 15 on the pretest and 38 on the posttest; and for the "unrelated" problems, 13 on the pretest and 18 on the posttest. For another example, each student's work on each problem was evaluated on a rating scale for degree of solution, from just mentioning an approach to a complete solution. Even though the students had only been asked to plan solutions, many in fact tried to carry them through. None of the problems was rated "solved" or "almost solved" on the pretest; however, on the posttest for the treatment group there were 64 cases of "solved" or "almost solved" for the closely related problems, four for the somewhat related problems, and one for the unrelated problems.

A fourth pretest and posttest examined students' perceptions of problems. Experts in physics are known to perceive problems quite differently from novices: the latter see problems as similar because of surface features such as involving the same sort of diagram, while the former see problems as similar because they exhibit the same underlying principle and invite solution by means of the same solution schema (Chi, Feltovich, & Glaser, 1981). Accordingly, it was natural to ask whether this course altered students' perceptions of problems. The results were reported in Schoenfeld and Herrmann (1982).

The pretest and posttest consisted of a card sort of the same thirty-two problems. Both experimental and control groups did the sort. The students were asked to place in the same piles problems that they thought were "similar mathematically in that they would be solved the same way." The sort was also performed by nine professional mathematicians.

Schoenfeld, in consultation with another mathematician, assigned each problem a "deep structure," reflecting an appropriate solution approach (among the categories were: induction, linear diophantine equation, analytic geometry, contradiction) and a "surface structure" reflecting superficial features of the problems (among the categories were: prime numbers, triangles, functions, limit). The analysis compared this classification of the problems with the pretest and posttest sortings of the experimental and control groups, and with the sortings of the professional mathematicians.

The analysis revealed that the sorting of the experts reflected the assigned deep structure much more so than did the sorting of the students prior to instruction. After instruction, the treatment group sorted more in accordance with the deep structure, although not as much so as did the experts. A correlation between the sorting matrices of the experts and the treatment group was .540 before instruction and .723 after instruction, a difference significant at the .01 level. These results demonstrate that the instruction altered students' perceptions of problem similarity in the direction of solution schemas.

The four approaches to evaluation here represent an unusually thorough assessment of an effort to teach problem solving skills. We think that these results demonstrate that the course had a significant impact on the mathematical problem solving skills of the participants. We note that these results were obtained despite the relatively small sample size, and, in a sense, *because* of that small sample size. The manageable number of students permitted a very fine grained analysis of their performance from several perspectives. Schoenfeld's research presents a good model for the careful investigation of the impact of heuristic instruction.

3. A PRACTICUM IN THINKING

Members of the Psychology Department of the University of Cincinnati have developed a course for college students that they call "A Practicum in Thinking." The course is described and the experience gained in teaching it is reported in a booklet edited by Wheeler and Dember (1979). The idea for the course was conceived by a philanthropist, Albert Steiner, who proposed to the University of Cincinnati that it be offered and funded its initial development. Steiner's motivation for supporting the development of the course followed from the conviction that "in general, our educational system does not teach its students how to think, nor does it seek directly to do so" (Steiner, 1979, p. 3).

Contents of the Program

The course evolved over several years (Steiner, 1979). The class, the size of which is limited to about 25 students, meets for 2 two-hour sessions per week for 10 weeks. It is divided into four groups of roughly equal size that stay together throughout the 10-week period. Class sessions are usually devoted to exercises, each of which addresses a specific goal. Each group works on each exercise as a group. The instructors (two for the class) circulate among the groups and assist when necessary. Each exercise ends with a set of questions for discussion to help the students analyze what they have learned in doing it.

Emphasis is placed on self-awareness. Students are encouraged to introspect on how they are performing the tasks. Thus, one might say the approach has a distinctly metacognitive aspect. One objective is to make students realize that most problems can be approached in more than one way, and to make them conscious of the fact that they have some options in that regard.

The course is organized around a series of topics, each of which provides focus for two or three days of exercises. These topics include the following:

- *Working in groups*: The point of the exercise is to teach some basics about group dynamics in general and some specifics about how their group functions.
- *Listening*: The objective is to demonstrate that students frequently do not pay attention to what other people are saying and to get them to do so. Students are required to paraphrase points that others have made before they can state their own.
- *Words and meanings*: Emphasis is placed on the importance of being precise in the use of words. Exercises involve the writing of definitions and the guessing of words from definitions that are given.
- *Assumptions*: The intent is to make students aware of the importance of assumptions in communication and problem solving and to be able to make implicit assumptions explicit.
- *Study skills*: Each of four groups does library research on one of four topics: reading, writing, concentration, or organization of time, and presents findings in class.
- *Memory*: Mnemonic techniques.
- *Problem analysis*: Analysis of problems in terms of goal and solution hierarchies.
- *Logical inference*: Hypothesis testing exercises drawing upon the research of Wason and Johnson-Laird (1972). The importance of considering what would be true if the hypothesis under consideration were false is emphasized. (Material on traditional logic emphasizing syllogistic reasoning and logical fallacies initially included in the course has been dropped.)
- *Problem solving*: Two phases of problem solving are distinguished: An idea generation phase and a phase during which a solution is worked out from the ideas that have been generated. Brainstorming is associated with the first phase and logical inference with the second.
- *Decision making*: A balance-sheet approach is used for weighing the pros and cons of a potential action.
- *Creative problem solving*: The Synectics analogical reasoning approach (Gordon, 1961) is applied to specific problems.

In a final class lecture the point is made that the approach to thinking taught in the course—an approach that emphasizes goal setting and methodical working toward goals—is not the only possible approach, and that it may not always be the most appropriate one.

Students are also required to work on a problem of their own choosing as a special course project. The aim seems to be to have them select a personally meaningful problem, one that they would really like to be able to solve; e.g., "finding a job, solving a conflict with a roommate, losing weight, deciding about graduate school." The purposes of the project are three: (1) to get the students to learn something about themselves by paying attention to how they go about solving the problem; (2) to make them aware of the element of choice in strategizing for problem solving; and (3) to teach them the value of approaching a problem systematically.

Evaluation Studies

Attempts to evaluate the effectiveness of the course have included self-evaluations by the students with respect to certain specific skills, before and after the course, and the administration of pretests and posttests of several types. In the self-evaluation, students rated themselves on a 5 point scale with respect to 15 specific skills. Table 7.2, which is reproduced from

TABLE 7.2
Mean Differences in Ratings on Self Evaluation Scale (Table 2 from Wheeler, 1979, p. 16.)

Item	*Posttest-Pretest Differences*
Working with Others	.58
Memory	.58
Generating new Ideas	.50
Making Decisions	.46
Concentrating	.42
Being Creative	.42
Using Words Precisely	.38
Using Intuitions	.38
Note Taking	.38
Test Taking	.33
Listening Accurately	.29
Reacting Accurately	.29
Observing Accurately	.25
Recognizing Assumptions	.17

Wheeler (1979), shows the mean difference in the ratings the students gave themselves before and after taking the course. Positive numbers indicate perceived improvement. Wheeler cautions that changes in such rating scores do not provide strong evidence that the skills have actually improved. The results do suggest, however, that the students considered themselves to be more adept with respect to these skills after the course than they considered themselves to be before the course. Even if there were no real gains in skill, this enhanced self-perception could have a positive effect on the students' handling of problems.

The pretests and posttests of specific skills included listening tests from the Effective Listening Program (Xerox Corp., 1964), tests of the ability to give word definitions, and tests of the ability to identify the assumptions in a passage of text. Significant improvements were found on the listening tests but not on the definitions and assumptions tests. Wheeler concluded that the course had worked well, that it had been valued by the students, and that similar courses should be introduced elsewhere. We would be more encouraged, however, by more decisive gains on pretests and posttests. We note that the authors used only three instruments and suggest that the results of the course should be evaluated employing a larger battery, as well as tracking the later academic performances of students who have received the course versus control groups.

4. THE COGNITIVE STUDIES PROJECT

The *Cognitive Studies Project* was being conducted at Manhattan Community College, a unit of the City University of New York. The program provides high-school level courses in reading, mathematics, science, social science, English, and problem solving to military veterans returning to school either for high-school equivalency instruction or for preparation for college.

The stated objectives of the one semester problem-solving course are as follows:

1. To assist the student to become aware and to intervene in his own thinking processes.
2. To assist the student to become more active in his learning experience.
3. To familiarize the student with systematic and deliberate methods of thought that would enhance his problem solving and thinking abilities. (Hutchinson, 1980, p. 9).

The course draws methods and materials primarily from Whimbey and Lochhead (1979) and secondarily from the Instrumental Enrichment Program of Feuerstein. (The Feuerstein program has been described in Chapter 6.) Before continuing the account of the Cognitive Studies Project, we digress to describe briefly the Whimbey-Lochhead approach and the material as presented in their book *Problem Solving and Comprehension*.

The Whimbey and Lochhead Approach

Whimbey and Lochhead identify and describe methods that good problem solvers use and provide the reader with a collection of problems on which these methods can be tried. While the authors expect that working through the book should produce a steady improvement in one's analytical thinking skills, they caution the reader not to expect to become an expert thinker immediately as a consequence. They note that expertise comes only as a result of regular and extensive practice. The intent of the book is to give the reader a start in the acquisition of *generally useful* skills; skills that should be helpful in the taking of tests, in academic courses and "in any occupations which involve analyzing, untangling, or comprehending knotty ideas" (p. 3). The types of problems that are used throughout the book are similar to those found in intelligence tests.

Whimbey and Lochhead identify four ways in which problem analyses and reasoning processes break down: (1) failure to observe and use all relevant facts; (2) failure to approach the problem in a systematic step-by-step manner; (3) failure to spell out relationships fully; and (4) sloppiness and inaccuracy in collecting information and in carrying out mental activities. The book places heavy emphasis on lack of accuracy and thoroughness in thinking as primary causes for errors on the types of questions that are commonly found in tests of reasoning ability. Accuracy and thoroughness, the authors suggest, are mental habits that can be improved through training and practice.

Whimbey and Lochhead advocate working in pairs or groups and "thinking aloud" while trying to solve problems, for two reasons: (1) by listening to other people solving problems, one may learn something about the techniques that work and those that do not; and (2) by exposing one's own thought processes verbally both to others and to oneself, one makes it possible for one's approach to be analyzed and criticized.

The authors also identify five characteristics of good problem solvers: (a) positive attitude (confidence that reasoning problems will yield to careful persistent analysis); (b) concern for accuracy (carefulness in making sure the problem is completely understood and rechecking the accuracy of one's own work); (c) breaking the problem into parts (decomposition of complex problems into small manageable steps); (d) avoiding guessing (working the problem through without resorting to hasty guessing or jumping to conclusions); (e) activeness in problem solving (good problem solvers engage in a variety of overt activities to facilitate the problem solving process, e.g., talking to oneself, writing on the problem, making diagrams).

Observations about the Project

The Whimbey-Lochhead problem-solving materials were used in the Cognitive Studies Project, as was their method of dividing the class into pairs, and having one member of each pair think aloud while the other member played the role of listener/inquirer. Feuerstein's methods and, in particular, the approach to the diagnosis and treatment of deficient cognitive functions were used when it appeared that the Whimbey-Lochhead approach required thinking skills on the part of the students that were not yet adequately developed. Hutchinson notes also that the Whimbey-Lochhead material had to be simplified somewhat for the student population in this particular program.

While Hutchinson reports that most students developed positive attitudes towards the materials after halting starts, some continued to believe that they could not manage the required activities. Hutchinson's description of these students' attitudes is quite thought provoking: "these few students' profound disbelief in their own mental ability, buttressed by a history of academic failure, greatly militated against their willingness to give themselves a chance. They seemed to believe firmly that they were born with just so much mental ability and that they were not going to develop any more" (p. 15). If such attitudes are at least as much a cause of poor performance as an effect, they represent a major challenge to anyone who would aspire to teach thinking skills, especially as part of a remedial program for adults with a history of academic failure.

Two particularly problematical behaviors were encountered in the cognitive studies project course. One arose from the inability of some students to treat their roles as problem solver and listener objectively. As a consequence, exchanges within pairs often became argumentative. Recognition of this problem led the course administrators to change the format so the listener and problem-solver roles were recast as those of discussants. Hutchinson reports that this change ameliorated but did not completely solve the problem in all cases.

In the context of discussing this type of problem, Hutchinson calls attention to the importance of recognizing the affective, as well as the cognitive, demands that are placed on students by learning tasks. He points out that a student with a history of academic failures may find himself and his self-view seriously threatened by a situation in which his academic inadequacies are exposed to others. And, consequently, the real problem that he faces in such situations (from his own point of view) may be that of protecting himself from further humiliation, rather than that of acquiring the skills and knowledge the course is intended to teach.

In an effort to address this difficulty, Hutchinson attempted to make the classroom a safe place in which to make a mistake. To do this, he encouraged the class to discuss and analyze mistakes that he himself had made either in class or while preparing the lesson in his office. Students were also explicitly encouraged to be accepting not only of their own mistakes but of those made by their classmates.

A second aspect of the course that proved problematical with this group of students was the demands the Whimbey-Lochhead approach makes on language and communication skills. Hutchinson notes that these students had a considerable difficulty in this regard. It is important, he points out, that the instructor be able to distinguish between when a student is having difficulty processing a problem and when he is having difficulty expressing what he is processing. Those difficulties may be quite different and require different types of remediation.

Formal evaluation of the Cognitive Studies problem solving course has not been attempted. Hutchinson's (1980) own subjective assessment is that the course has been moderately successful in achieving its objectives of assisting students to intervene in their own thinking processes, to become more active in their learning experience, and to become familiar with methods for improving their thinking abilities. This conclusion was based on the reports from the students that they were beginning to use the problem-solving skills effectively in other courses and from teachers' reports of improved classroom performance by the students who had taken the course.

5. THE PRODUCTIVE THINKING PROGRAM

The programs discussed in the remainder of this chapter differ somewhat from those that have been considered so far in that they focus more (although not exclusively) on inventive, creative, or divergent thinking. They are appropriately placed within a chapter on heuristic-oriented approaches because they involve the teaching of specific strategies, some of which are intended to enhance creativity or inventiveness.

One such program is the Productive Thinking Program of Covington, Crutchfield, Davies, and Olton (1974). This is a self-instructional program for fifth and sixth graders, organized in the form of fifteen booklets. It includes tasks that require divergent thinking, but many of the tasks involve problems with unique answers and also emphasize skills of analysis and inference. The materials—a kit including five copies of each of 15 short workbooks, a teacher's manual, wall charts, and a bookcase to house the workbooks—are available from the Charles E. Merrill company of Columbus, Ohio.[2]

The Productive Thinking Program deserves appraisal in any effort to consider how thinking skills might be taught, for several reasons. The program underwent an extended period of development, has been used in a wide variety of settings, and according to Mansfield, Busse, and Krepelka (1978) is the most tested of several programs designed to teach inventive thinking during the 60's and early 70's.

The Program

The Productive Thinking Program carries the subtitle "A course in learning to think." What this means becomes apparent through the philosophy

---

[2]We are grateful to the Charles E. Merrill Co. for the loan of a set of materials for this review.

expressed in the workbooks and teacher's guide. The program sets out to persuade the student that thinking can be an enjoyable and engaging activity. The course is structured around two easy-to-identify-with characters, a boy and a girl, who engage in solving a series of mysteries. These characters start off unsure of their mental resources and rather ineffective, and gradually become both more sophisticated and more enthusiastic over the course of the 15 lessons. Besides enthusiasm, the course aims to foster a high degree of persistence. Again and again, in both statement and dramatization, the point is emphasized that solutions to significant problems do not come easily, that many false leads will appear only to prove fruitless, and that dogged pursuit of a problem is a must.

These ideas, as well as the "thinking" content of the program, are presented through the cartooned adventures of the two principal characters. Students advance through each booklet at their own pace, attempting various exercises that occur in the booklet, integrated into the plot. In effect, the students are invited to participate in solving the same mystery the characters address. (There are further problems at the end of each unit for the students to do alone, plus a problem to be done in class.) The lessons both dramatize and state a number of principles for effective problem solving. Among these principles are the following:

- generate many ideas
- try to think of unusual ideas
- your idea does not have to be the same as the other person's—there are many ways to solve problems
- be planful—address a problem systematically
- when stuck, don't give up—think of a new approach
- make a branching tree, mapping the various possibilities in a problem situation
- think of general ideas and then particular variants
- assemble facts
- get the problem clearly in mind
- start with an unlikely idea and figure out how it could be true

Basically, the program aims to equip the students with good metacognitive habits of deploying their mental resources. It does not set out to improve the basic processing mechanisms at one's disposal, by, for instance, increasing one's fundamental ideational fluency. Rather, it provides heuristics for generating and evaluating ideas and for embedding them in an overall organized approach. It is important to note that the program concerns itself not only with producing ideas but with assessing them as well.

Most of the problems are "convergent" rather than "divergent." For example, there is one particular solution to the mystery being addressed, a solution that may require imagination and the conception of many alternatives, but that can only be reached by editing out and narrowing down, as well as by challenging early assumptions.

The program is thoughtfully conceived and carefully designed. This does not mean, however, that it achieves what it aims to—enhancement of the productive thinking of the participating students. What it accomplishes is a vexed question, as will become apparent in what follows.

Formal Tests

As mentioned already, Mansfield, Busse, and Krepelka (1978) report the Productive Thinking Program to be the most tested of the several programs that attempt to teach creative thinking. These authors review a number of efforts to measure gains, and reach a rather discouraging conclusion. The findings were mixed: sometimes the program produced significant gains on a range of posttests and sometimes it did not. Mansfield et al. note that the greatest successes seem to have been achieved under the least well controlled conditions; they suggest that the Productive Thinking Program may be effective when applied in small groups by enthusiastic teachers. The posttest instruments have included attitude inventories, ideational fluency tests, and problem-solving tests of sorts not specified in Mansfield et al.'s condensed review of this and several other programs. The following paragraphs draw on the original sources mentioned in the Mansfield et al. review.

Three studies included in their posttest problems some that were similar to those addressed in The Productive Thinking Program itself (Olton & Crutchfield, 1969; Treffinger, 1971; Treffinger, Speedie, & Bruner, 1974, the latter two reporting the same study; Wardrop, Olton, Goodwin, Covington, Klausmeier, Crutchfield, & Ronda, 1969). These problems were complex multifaceted ones not requiring any specialized knowledge but benefiting from exploring multiple possibilities, sifting evidence, eliminating hypotheses, and settling on a solution that best accommodated the facts. Indeed, the problems referred to have been incorporated as exercises in The Productive Thinking Program in its published form.

Administering these problems often involved not simply posing them, but leading subjects through them by presenting initial data, indicating a question to address at a given point, and providing further information, until a solution was reached. The problems were described by Wardrop et al. (1979) as "complex extended problems." However, it is not clear whether in all three of the studies mentioned, the problems were administered in this fashion. In any case, such a manner of administering the problems would parallel the way the mysteries making up the bulk of The Productive Thinking Program workbooks were treated. Performance on a problem typically was measured in several ways: ultimate success or failure, fluency in generating options, quality of ideas, noticing anomalies in the data that might point to a solution.

Concerning the influence of The Productive Thinking Program on students' ability to deal with these problems, a clear answer emerges. Findings in all three experiments significantly favored the treatment group over the control group, although on individual items sometimes the advantage might go with one measure of performance and sometimes with another. Often, the treatment group exhibited more fluency or quality of ideas or sensitivity to anomalies without solving the problem more frequently.

In addition to these measures, tests of divergent thinking often figured in the evaluations conducted in the above-mentioned and other studies of The Productive Thinking Program (Dacey, 1971; Moreno & Hogan, 1976; Ripple & Dacey, 1967; Schuler, 1974; Treffinger, 1971; Treffinger & Ripple, 1969, 1971; Treffinger, Speedie, & Bruner, 1974; Wardrop et al., 1969). In general, the various ideational fluency instruments used in these evaluations did not show gains of the treatment groups relative to the control groups. The only exception was the study of Moreno and Hogan (1976), in which the treatment group proved superior. The complex extended problems mentioned above typically required generating multiple perspectives, and often students who had experienced The Productive Thinking Program generated more ideas while addressing these problems. It appears from these results that The Productive Thinking Program enhances fluency in the context of problems that resemble its contents, but not particularly otherwise.

Several of the evaluations included additional problems and tasks—an imaginative story writing test (Ripple & Dacey, 1967; Dacey, 1971) along with the Maier two-string problem, arithmetic problems, and some general unspecified problems said to be quite unlike those in the course (Treffinger & Ripple, 1969, 1971), brief convergent and divergent thinking problems rather than extended ones (Wardrop et al., 1969) and anagrams and practical problems such as what to do about fighting on the playground (Treffinger, 1971; Treffinger, Speedie, & Bruner, 1974). Although there were occasional exceptions on individual items, in general no significant differences between treatment and control groups appeared in the performance of these tasks.

In short, the Productive Thinking Program apparently does enhance performance somewhat on certain types of problems, which the student may be led through to some extent and for which the measures include not only success in solving the problem but also "process" measures of number of ideas, quality of ideas, and sensitivity to anomalies. For problems and tasks of a markedly different character, there is no compelling evidence that The Productive Thinking Program helps. How well the Program might prepare students to deal with complex extended problems on their own is uncertain, inasmuch as the evaluations reviewed have not tested this.

Why the Productive Thinking Program does not yield more transfer is an interesting question. One factor may be the relatively short duration of the program. It consists of only fifteen lessons, quite a small number compared to some of the other programs reviewed in this book. In general, we have the impression that intellectual skills are not so easily taught, even though, in some cases, they may be succinctly described. Accordingly, short programs seem less likely than longer ones, other things being equal, to yield substantial gains.

Another relevant factor may be a certain lack of generality in the problems and pedagogical approach employed. Consider, for instance, the match between the program and real world creative activities. Many creative products in the real world—a poem, a scientific theory, an innovative business—are extended products, involving many parts and aspects. Also, as discussed in Chapter 4, defining the problem initially is an important part of the effort, and problem finding abilities seem to bear a close relation to creativity. Notable creative efforts appear to involve an element of abstraction: one constructs a product based on general and far-reaching considerations. And, of course, there is no guarantee of a satisfactory solution when one addresses a real world problem. Finally, most often there is no guide through the complexities of a realistic creative challenge. One is on one's own, or working with a group equally in the dark.

In all these respects, the problems emphasized in the Productive Thinking Program have quite a different character. The answers to the "whodunit" problems are short—the identity of the culprit and a brief explanation—rather than complex products. The problems are given rather than found by the problem solver. The problems are very concrete. The program guarantees that a solution exists. And, finally, the program leads the students through the entire process of thought to the solution. Of course, one should not make too much of such differences. It is certainly true that some real world creative problems, and parts of many others, involve short answers, little problem finding, and minimal abstraction. Practice with the Productive Thinking Program could help students to deal with such cases. Still, it seems that the Productive Thinking Program does not provide direct practice on many of the aspects most important to creative thinking as it occurs in realistic situations.

In summary, the Productive Thinking Program is a serious and thoughtful effort to teach certain skills of thinking and associated attitudes and beliefs. It addresses a variety of thinking skills and it touches upon most of the aspects of creativity identified in Chapter 4. The program also exemplifies a number of pedagogical tactics that would seem to be advantageous. The advice is dramatized as well as stated. The principal characters provide role models for the students. The cartoon format and the use of mysteries to be solved are engaging. The stories lead the student through the ins and outs of the mystery with the protagonists, so that the student participates at crucial junctures as do they. The most important principles are treated over and over, a facet that ought to facilitate overlearning and transfer, and the problem sets in the backs of the booklets specifically encourage transfer.

Nonetheless, some definite reservations have to be stated. The Productive Thinking Program may suffer somewhat from leading students too much and not giving them sufficient chance to coordinate complex problem-solving activities on their own. In addition, the program has a limited scope, reflecting more the patterns of thought appropriate for certain subproblems that arise in the course of inventive thought and action than inventive thought and action as a whole. Any extended effort to foster inventive thinking would want more breadth, although admittedly the Productive Thinking Program perhaps attempts quite enough for 15 lessons. Productive thinking as expressed in the program would be most useful if the student learned to detect such problems as fit its approach in the context of more complex activities. It seems plausible that the approach would help the student with solving such problems. However, the formal evaluations as summarized in Mansfield, Busse, and Krepelka (1978) leave ambiguous whether students gain or not.

6. LATERAL THINKING AND THE CoRT PROGRAM

De Bono (1968, 1970) distinguishes between what he calls vertical thinking and lateral thinking. Vertical thinking is, in his terms, logical thinking. It is sequential, predictable, conventional. In contrast, lateral thinking is not necessarily sequential, it is unpredictable, and it is not constrained by convention. Vertical thinking might be characterized as thinking *within* a structure or frame of reference; whereas lateral thinking tends to restructure the problem space. The necessity to be right at every stage of the thought process and the necessity of having everything rigidly defined are two of the major limitations of vertical thinking. Premature formalization and expression of an idea may inhibit its natural development.

In de Bono's (1968) words, "lateral thinking generates the ideas and vertical thinking develops them" (p. 6). Here again is the distinction between hypothesis generation and hypothesis testing. "Lateral thinking has to do with new ways of looking at things" (p. 14); "vertical thinking is digging the same hole deeper; lateral thinking is trying again elsewhere" (p. 26). De Bono suggests that skill in lateral thinking can be acquired and that there are specific techniques that can facilitate its acquisition. He cautions, however, that lateral thinking is "more a habit of mind than knowledge of some technique" (p. 147).

With respect to the question of relaxing of the "rigid control of vertical thinking," de Bono suggests that the purpose of logic should be less that of finding a conclusion than that of demonstrating the soundness of the conclusion once it has been found. This is reminiscent of Polya's point that, in mathematical reasoning, the thought process that initially leads to a theorem often is anything but rigorous. Having arrived at a theorem by a route that may involve numerous cul de sacs and redirections, intuitions and hunches, the mathematician then sets out to demonstrate the validity of the conclusion with as precise and rigorous an argument as he can construct.

Overview of the CoRT Program

De Bono is perhaps best known for his notion of lateral thinking, but he has presented a number of ideas about the teaching of thinking more generally in various books and articles (e.g. de Bono, 1967, 1968, 1970, 1975, 1983). The most extensive effort to apply them to the teaching of thinking skills in the classroom is seen in the CoRT Program, which was published in England around 1973. CoRT stands for the "Cognitive Research Trust," a British organization founded and directed by de Bono. The instructional program consists of six units each comprising 63 lessons. Each lesson is designed to take about 35 minutes, although de Bono notes that fitting a lesson into this span often can be difficult, and that additional time is welcome. The course plan is to offer one lesson per week, with the entire course spanning three years. The program has been administered to students from ages 8 to 22, and from slow to very bright groups. The Teachers' Notes indicate that the program has been widely used, although figures are not given.

Taken together, the units cover a considerable range of matters relevant to thinking. An outline of the six CoRT units can be found in de Bono (1983). CoRT 1, entitled, *Breadth*, emphasizes thinking about a situation in many different ways that a person might ordinarily neglect. For example, the student is urged to consider all factors involved in the situation, short- and long-term consequences, and objectives. CoRT 2, entitled *Organization*, offers ten lessons designed to help the student direct attention effectively and systematically to a situation, without loss of focus. CoRT 3, *Interaction*, is concerned with matters of adequate evidence and argument.

CoRT 4, *Creativity*, offers a number of strategies for generating ideas one might otherwise not think of; it also devotes some attention to the editing and evaluation of ideas. CoRT 5, *Information and Feeling*, is concerned with a variety of matters; some involve affective factors that impinge on thinking, while others rehearse themes taken up in the earlier units. CoRT 6, *Action*, presents a general framework for attacking problems. It can be used to knit the strategies introduced in the previous lessons together; alternatively, it can be used on its own. De Bono observes that, in general, CoRT 1 should be taught first. But the other units need not all be used in numerical order; each unit stands on its own and contributes something different.

The CoRT program rests throughout on what de Bono terms "operations." Basically, these are questions one can ask oneself, such as: what are the aims, goals, and objectives in a situation, what might others' points of view be, what is the present concern, what is the dominant idea here, how can I escape from it? CoRT provides students with a mental hook or mnemonic for each of these operations in the form of initials. For instance, CAF stands for "consider all factors." "Doing a CAF" means contemplating a situation and trying to list all factors that might influence it. "PNI" stands for "positive, negative, and interesting" points. "Doing a PNI" means trying to list all positive, negative, and interesting points about a situation.

De Bono emphasizes that CoRT operations are easy to apply. He acknowledges that they are fairly prosaic, the sorts of advice that might evoke the response, "But I already do that." He suggests, however, that most people do not spontaneously take such steps appropriately and consistently. The aim of the CoRT program is to make a range of such operations part of the learner's active behavioral repertoire.

Most of the CoRT lessons are organized around one, or sometimes two, related operations, with an occasional lesson for integration and review. The presentation is straightforward. The matter of concern and the operation are described. Examples are presented. Practice examples are executed by the group of students in dialogue with the teacher. There are some variations in format from unit to unit. For example, toward the end of each lesson in CoRT 1 and 2 (but not in 4), there is a discussion of general questions concerning the topic, such as " Is it necessary to plan one's thinking on tiny problems?" (CoRT 2, 7th lesson). CoRT 1 lessons include a statement of several general principles regarding the rationale and application of each operation, and CoRT 4 lessons include a single concise statement of motivation. CoRT 2 lacks these features.

The students receive notes with each lesson. The notes for a lesson comprise 2 or 3 pages of text plus a title page and cover all the content mentioned above. The notes adopt a number of presentational devices for underscoring the content—for example, large typography or boxing for important points, graphic symbols or cartoons on the cover to convey in another medium the core concept of the lesson. The teacher works from lengthy manuals for each of the CoRT units, manuals which, besides giving a general overview and some evidence for the effectiveness of the program, relate particulars about the conduct of each lesson and provide several possible answers to the exercises.

In general, de Bono holds that the lessons should be taught in isolation from other subject matter, with the compressed five-minute exercises that accompany them. He believes that attempts to fuse the lessons with other subject matters dilute the clarity of their principles, at least for younger students. CoRT principles should be acquired first in the context provided by the lessons as designed; then, transfer to other domains is expected to occur spontaneously. De Bono also notes, however, that for older students, the CoRT lessons could draw on problems related to conventional content areas under study and be administered more in the context of particular content areas.

As to the gains to be expected, de Bono's general position is that thinking is a skill, and a skill that can be enhanced by attention to the various operations set forth in the CoRT program. Intelligent people are not necessarily skillful thinkers, although they have more raw power with which to work. However intelligent, a person can improve substantially his intellectual reach by properly directing his thoughts. A somewhat less intelligent individual who has good thinking skills may well out think a more intelligent person who lacks them.

Evidence for the Effectiveness of CoRT

The CoRT 2 Teachers' Manual summarizes briefly three studies bearing on the effectiveness of some or all of the CoRT 4 sequences. In the first two studies, several groups of CoRT students, along with several control groups, were asked to discuss a complex question. For example, in the second study the question was "Should children be allowed to leave school as soon as they have learned to read and write?" The groups were scored for the number of relevant points they each generated; in both cases, the CoRT groups devised about twice as many points, reflecting a greater range of concerns as emphasized in CoRT 1. The third study required a number of treatment and control subjects to respond to a series of such questions individually. Here, the CoRT subjects, as a group, conceived nearly half again as many relevant points as the control subjects.

De Bono (1976, pp. 217-229) reports several experiments involving idea counts contrasting students who had received CoRT instruction with control groups. CoRT students always produced considerably more ideas. Some of the results also argue that CoRT instruction leads to a more balanced and less egocentric view of problems. In particular, CoRT students tend to give more attention to the side of a case opposed to their own, and to consider general and not just personal consequences.

Edwards and Baldauf (1983) report an instructional experiment using CoRT 1. The study was conducted as part of a science class in a large independent school for boys in Australia, yielding data for 72 grade-10 students. The boys in five different sections of the science class were rotated through five-week sequences of instruction in five different subjects, four science subjects and CoRT 1. Thus the students in the different sections received CoRT 1 instruction at different times over the school year. The CoRT 1 instruction consisted of about 20 fifty-minute sessions, covering an introduction, a pretest, the ten CoRT 1 lessons proper covered during 15 sessions, a posttest, and discussion of applications to science.

For part of the evaluation, Edwards and Baldauf used the students' responses to two questions, "Should pupils have a say in making school rules?" and "A man is found to have stolen a huge pile of left shoes. What do you think he is up to?" Based on ratings of the students' responses to these same questions before and after receiving CoRT 1 instruction, the authors found that for the School Rules problem, Mean Number of Ideas increased from 6.97 to 11.11, Quality Rating from 3.06 to 3.85, and Structure Rating from 2.07 to 2.50. For Left Shoes, which was scored somewhat differently, number of ideas went from 4. 65 to 9.63 and Novelty Rating from 1.26 to 1.61. All increases were statistically significant.

One might hope that the students who had received CoRT earlier in the term would become better students of science. However, the authors found no significant difference in final science exam scores among the groups of students. The authors also did an analysis of covariance controlling for IQ. They found a statistically significant relationship between CoRT gain scores and science exam scores. This says that those who learned CoRT better also learned science better, discounting IQ, suggesting that CoRT addresses some aspect of ability in science other than IQ. The finding does not, of course, demonstrate that learning CoRT caused better science learning; the finding could as well reflect a common factor as a causal influence. Unfortunately, the study lacked a control group that received no CoRT instruction at all.

CoRT 4 includes in the Teachers' Notes four examples of a simple experiment bearing on the first CoRT 4 lesson. That lesson invites students to use the invented word "po," which contrasts with the other possible responses to a proposition: "yes," "no," and "don't know." Po means "Let's suspend judgment and explore this idea." The four experiments compare subjects' classifications of lists of propositions, such as the one about children leaving school, given choices of yes and no, versus choices of yes, no, and po.

The results demonstrate that when po is available as a category, it is very often selected. Presented with that option, students did often recognize such propositions as matters that deserve further thoughtful exploration, whatever the initial reaction to them might have been. De Bono acknowledges that those who identify a proposition as a po probably would revert to their initial choices given a yes or no option again. However, he takes these studies as a demonstration that, when po is available as a classification, people will take advantage of it. The point of the first CoRT 4 lesson, in part, and the rest of the CoRT 4 sequence, is to make the equivalent of po available as part of the students' active repertoire. These experiments give some reason to believe that the use of po could alter habits of thinking, but provide no information about the success of the CoRT lessons in imbuing students with the habit of using po or equivalents of it. The lessons may succeed in this, but direct evidence is lacking.

Finally, we mention some results from an adaptation of CoRT employed in Venezuela under the name "Aprender a Pensar," or "Learning to Think." The results should be considered separately, inasmuch as the material has been substantially revised and extended by Margarita de Sanchez of the Venezuelan Ministry of Education and her colleagues. In particular, each original CoRT lesson has been expanded to about four lessons, to provide much more practice, with a gradation from relatively concrete to more abstract problems and from group to individual work.

Recently, deSanchez and Astorga (1983) reported a study of the impact of the Venezuelan program. The sample for a one-year study included 322 Venezuelan school children in the treatment group and 275 in a control group, mainly lower class children about 10-11 years old who received "Learning to Think" instruction twice a week throughout the academic year for one class period. A subsample of 63 treatment students received "Learning to Think" instruction for two more years. The instructional materials, extended as mentioned above, were drawn primarily from CoRT 1 in the first year, CoRT 3 and 4 in the second, and CoRT 2 and 5 in the third. The third year also included lessons combining strategies taught earlier.

A pretest was administered to the "Learning to Think" students and matched control students, and similar tests were administered at the end of the first, second, and third years of instruction. Each test consisted of a different set of three open-ended problems. These problems were the same type as those used in the instruction. For example, a typical problem was: Establish a series of rules for parents to follow in the daily care of their children. Another was: What would happen if the supply of water were interrupted for a month in a major city?

The students' answers were scored by judges who did not know whether a particular answer sheet represented the control or treatment groups, and who had practiced to achieve an adequate degree of interjudge agreement. Four measures were used: number of ideas, number of relevant ideas, level of abstraction, and level of elaboration. Level of abstraction referred to distance from daily experience estimated on a four point scale. Level of elaboration referred to syntactic complexity, vocabulary, and some other factors, also estimated on a four point scale.

The experimental group pretest scores were about 2.6 ideas per question, 2.3 pertinent ideas, 1.2 level of abstraction, and 1.4 level of elaboration. The control group scores were similar. After the first year of instruction, the control group showed no gains. The treatment group showed gains of .8 ideas and 1 pertinent idea per question, but no gains on levels of abstraction and elaboration. However, gains on the latter two variables did appear in the subsequent two years, with the group that received three years of instruction. These students in the course of the three years improved 2.8 ideas per question, 3.2 pertinent ideas (presumably there was a greater gain in pertinent ideas than ideas because initial pertinent ideas scores were very low), .8 on the abstraction scale, and .5 on the elaboration scale.

On balance the findings are favorable for the CoRT program, as far as they go. They demonstrate transfer of the performances explicitly trained in CoRT to tasks similar to those used during the training. Moreover, the numbers indicate that the CoRT students generate substantially more ideas, not just a few more with some progress on such matters as level of abstraction and a balanced view of problems. However, the data fall short of making a complete case for the general effectiveness of CoRT. Whether the CoRT training would help students solve problems that are different in character from those on which they were trained is unclear. Whether CoRT has enhanced the thinking of the students in other subject areas or in out-of-school situations also remains to be studied, although anecdotal reports to this effect have been made.

One can say something about the scope of CoRT simply by examining its operations. The "what to do and how to do it" advice of the CoRT operations is very simple and not closely adapted to the special needs of a number of important complex performances, such as mathematical problem solving as handled by Schoenfeld, or writing, as discussed in Chapter 9. In general, the CoRT operations seem more suitable for contexts of decision making and informal reasoning in humanistic, social, and design contexts. They have a straightforward and immediate application to the sorts of problems that arise in everyday life. The CoRT operations can be seen as simple practical tactics that may help individuals to think sensibly about non-technical things and, also, help them to come to perceive themselves as thinkers. Within its scope, it seems to us that CoRT is likely to have beneficial effects.

7. PROBLEM-BASED SELF INSTRUCTION IN MEDICAL PROBLEM SOLVING

For the most part we have shied away from discussion of programs for training specific professions. That is because our interest is in the teaching of the kinds of thinking skills that should have broad applicability in a wide variety of specific domains. In this section, however, we consider an approach that has been advocated for the training of medical professionals. We do that because the approach, which grew out of a concern about lack of transfer with more traditional methods, has much in common with several of the other approaches we have considered. In particular, it emphasizes the importance of student participation, inquiry, the acquisition of reasoning skills and problem solving, and self monitoring. Unlike most of the other approaches, however, it advocates starting with the problem, rather than with problem solving tools. While it does not fit neatly into any of our four categories of approaches it is more nearly like the heuristics-oriented approaches than any of the others, so we discuss it here.

Barrows and Tamblyn (1980) distinguish between the roles of content knowledge and professional skill in medicine and suggest that traditional approaches to medical education put too little emphasis on the latter. They see this as a weakness in traditional approaches and argue that whereas content knowledge is obviously essential, the emphasis in medical education should be on the application of that knowledge. The result of an adequate medical education, they suggest, should be describable in terms of what a physician is able to *do*. In particular, they suggest that:

1. The physician should be able to evaluate and manage patients with medical problems effectively, efficiently, and humanely (clinical reasoning).
2. The physician should be able to continually define and satisfy his particular educational needs in order to keep his skills and information contemporary with his chosen field and to care properly for the problems he encounters (self-evaluation and study). (p. 7)

Barrows and Tamblyn argue strongly for a problem-based learning approach to medical education, by which they mean an approach in which medical problems are taken as stimuli for learning. This approach differs from more traditional approaches in which students are given a great deal of factual knowledge before being presented with problems. In the problem-based approach, students are given a problem first and then must develop the knowledge to solve that problem.

Problem-based learning is defined as

> the learning that results from the process of working toward the understanding or resolution of a problem. The problem is encountered first in the learning process and serves as a focus or stimulus for the application of problem-solving or reasoning skills, as well as for the search for or study of information or knowledge needed to understand the mechanisms responsible for the problem and how it might be resolved. The problem is not offered as an example of the relevance of prior learning or as an exercise for applying information already learned in a subject-based approach. A problem in this

> context refers to an unsettled, puzzling, unsolved issue that needs to be resolved. It is a situation that is unacceptable and needs to be corrected. (p. 18)

Simply finding the answer to a question or applying a known principle to explain an observation is not problem-based learning; the learning required of the student in the problem-based approach is active, not passive.

> The student does not listen, observe, write, and memorize; instead, he is asked to perform, think, get involved, commit himself, and learn by trial and error. He is asked to learn both cognitive reasoning skills and psychomotor skills of interview and examination, and to identify learning needs made apparent by his work with a problem. (p. 83).

The teacher's role in this process is not that of a dispenser of information or knowledge but that of a guide or facilitator. His function is to stimulate the students to think for themselves and to "help them help themselves in the educational process."

Successful filling of the role of guide and learning facilitator requires an individual who understands the process of clinical reasoning and knows how to stimulate students to think productively for themselves. Barrows and Tamblyn suggest that the teacher should serve as an information source by responding to direct questions from the students only after he is convinced that "they have exhausted their own logic or information base and feels that the information provided will facilitate further work with the problem at the time, without sacrificing the value of self-study" (p. 108). The role of guide and learning facilitator involves, among other things, the ability to ask the right questions at the right times.

In defense of the problem-based approach, Barrows and Tamblyn claim that medical students often complete training by passing all the knowledge-oriented exams, but still do not know how to practice medicine effectively. In support of the view that knowledge that is not used is not well retained, they cite Miller's (1962) finding that before they graduate, medical students typically forget most of what they learned in their first-year anatomy and biochemistry courses.

On the basis of studies of physician's performance in diagnostic situations, Barrows and Tamblyn divide the clinical reasoning process into five behaviors:

- Information perception and interpretation: Cues are picked up from observations of the patient's appearance, age, behavior, comments, etc. that give the physician an "initial concept" of the problem.
- Hypothesis generation: Physicians tend to generate from two to five hypotheses regarding the possible explanation of the patient's problem based on the initial concept.

- Inquiry strategy and clinical skills: The physician asks two kinds of questions: search questions designed to provide information that can be used to evaluate the hypotheses and scan questions designed to provide new cues regarding the adequacy of the hypothesis set. Scan questions tend to be asked when search questions lead to blind alleys.

- Problem formulation: On the basis of the data obtained, a single hypothesis begins to emerge as the favored one and a conceptualization of the patient's problems is formulated.
- Diagnostic and/or therapeutic decisions: This involves a decision that sufficient time has been spent (at least for the present) on the diagnosis and a decision regarding treatment, management or further information gathering.

Problem formulation is seen as a particularly difficult and important stage of the process and Barrows and Tamblyn list several techniques (strategies?) that might be helpful in resolving difficult formulation problems: (a) simplify the problem (get rid of irrelevancies, divide into subproblems, etc.); (b) take a break from the problem (let the problem incubate); (c) force divergent thinking (broaden the set of hypotheses, brainstorm); (d) alter the manner in which the data are represented (use diagrams or other representations); (e) talk the problem out with someone else or present it formally to a group of peers (forces one to clarify one's own thinking and also evokes suggestions from others); (f) find data that can be eliminated; (g) try the shortest and most obvious path with the problem; (h) rethink the elements of the problem (checking for biases, errors or unwarranted tacit assumptions).

Several formats for presenting patient problems to medical students have been developed. All of them involve exposing students to simulated problems, permitting them to select alternative courses of action, and giving them feedback regarding the consequences of their choices. They differ in the degree to which they provide feedback regarding the choices of experienced physicians at various stages of the diagnostic reasoning process and the extent to which they permit students to pursue appropriate courses of action.

One of the more recently developed formats, the Portable Patient Problem Pack (P4), was designed to overcome some of the ways in which other earlier formats were considered to be deficient. P4 consists of a deck of several hundred cards. The cards are divided into several subsets, each of which represents a different type of action the student can take with respect to the patient: e.g., obtain information on medical history, request laboratory tests, get information of the sort obtained on a medical exam. The cards of each subset are different colors to facilitate identification. The intent is that as a group the cards represent all the possible courses of action that a student might wish to take with respect to any patient problem. Only a small percentage would actually be used in a particular case.

The student begins an exercise by reading a "situation card" that introduces a specific patient problem. The student then can select action cards one at a time. On one side of each card, below the title indicating the nature of the action, is a series of questions that is intended to stimulate the student to think more deeply about the problem and his approach to solving it. These questions might ask, for example, how the student has formulated the problem thus far or what hypothesis he is currently considering. On the other side of the card is information of a kind that would have been obtained had the action indicated by that card actually been taken.

> This format allows the student to take any action possible with the real patient, in any sequence he feels appropriate. As in the real clinical situation, the student is able to see the result of each action before deciding on the next and is challenged to evaluate and manage the patient's problem appropriately. He is as free to make mistakes, perform unnecessary tests, or order incorrect treatments as he is to manage the problem effectively. (p. 67)

P4 illustrates an approach to the teaching of problem solving that has been used in areas other than medical diagnosis, such as law and business administration, namely that of having students work with simulations of the actual problems that they will eventually have to face. The attempt in this approach is to make the simulated problems as realistic as possible. The objective is not so much to have the student acquire general problem-solving techniques but to acquire familiarity with the details of the problems he is likely to encounter in professional life and to learn by practice how to approach those specific problems.

Tamblyn, Barrows, and Gliva (1980) report a study in which performance of several medical students and nursing students with the P4 technique was compared with performance of students working on similar problems with simulated patients (people trained to answer questions as though they had the illness). No differences were found in the performance scores with the two techniques. The investigators interpreted this result, along with user opinions, as evidence that the approach is a feasible one and can be useful for medical education.

A problem that arises in the design of a problem-based learning course is that of selecting the problems on which the students are to work. One approach that was followed by Barrows and Mitchell (1975) for the development of a neurosciences course was to make a master list of all of the important concepts taught in a variety of such courses. They then selected some well-documented neurological patient problems from clinical records and for each problem checked off from the master list the information that a self-directed study of that problem should cover. In this case they found that

22 problems were sufficient to cover all the items on the list (of course some items were covered by more than one problem). Other methods for selecting problems are less comprehensive in their coverage of conventionally-taught concepts and focus on problems satisfying specified criteria, e.g., those that have greatest frequency in usual practice settings, those that represent life-threatening situations, and so on.

8. THE HEURISTICS APPROACH IN GENERAL

Just as the cognitive operations approach related closely to the various theories of intelligence reviewed in Chapter 2, so the heuristics approach to teaching thinking reflects contemporary investigations of human problem solving, creativity and metacognition treated in Chapter 4. We note also a connection between the heuristics approach and computer programming, and especially the kind of programming required in work on artificial intelligence. If the task to be performed by the program is intellectually difficult, the programmer typically will not be able to write an algorithm that is guaranteed to work; the program must include heuristic strategies, strategies that may not always yield the desired answer but are "good bets."

In spirit, the heuristics approach to instruction is very much the same. The aim is to break tasks into steps that the learner can perform readily. The instructor attempts to teach the learner what steps to take and when to take them. As in the case of programming complex tasks on computers, often the steps must be heuristic in nature, not guaranteeing a solution but being good bets. With this general perspective on the heuristic approach and the foregoing reviews in mind, what can be said about its prospects?

We think that the heuristics approach promises effective instruction. But such results depend on sound strategies, reflecting an insightful analysis of the performances to be taught, and also on instruction that pays heed to the problems of thorough learning and transfer. These conditions are not so readily met, a fact that may make the development of truly powerful heuristic approaches a gradual process.

In particular, the heuristics approach depends on an analysis of the task in question into manageable subtasks. This demand for a good analysis is a potential weakness of the approach. For example, as discussed in Chapter 4, certain heuristic strategies like brainstorming seem, upon investigation, to be of uncertain effectiveness. Moreover, heuristic advice often may be difficult to apply in a particular context, especially an unfamiliar one. Finally, the problem solver may forget to try to apply it. The heuristic approach tends to suffer from the illusions that a plausible-sounding task analysis is really effective and that once a person can recite a strategy, he can and will apply it appropriately in various situations. Identifying really effective strategies and getting people to use them in situations other than the instructional context seem to be the two main challenges in constructing such programs.

While a good heuristic analysis of a task may require considerable effort and insight, we also think that striving after such an analysis often yields an advantage over the cognitive operations approach discussed in the previous chapter. In the heuristics approach, one tries to improve performance on a task by training the subset of cognitive operations thought to be relevant to it and, of course, providing practice on the task itself. A cognitive operations approach does not normally break down a task into an organized series of subtasks, nor develop heuristic moves specific to the task. We think that, for many tasks, a plan of attack and heuristics specific to the task are helpful. This is particularly so for manifestly complex tasks that have a lot of structure inviting a heuristic analysis.

8 Formal Thinking Approaches

Numerous writers have claimed that a distressingly large percentage of students entering college—and especially those entering community colleges—are ill equipped to meet the kinds of intellectual challenges that their college experience will, or should, present to them. More particularly, it is claimed that many students who have completed secondary school are unable to engage in abstract or, in Piagetian terms, formal operational thinking (Carpenter, 1980; Chiapetta, 1976; Karplus, 1974; Kolodiy, 1975; Lawson & Renner, 1974; McKinnon, 1971; McKinnon & Renner, 1971; Renner & Lawson, 1983; Tomlinson-Keasey, 1972; Towler & Wheatley, 1971). These students appear to be stuck at the concrete-operations stage of cognitive development.

Concern about this problem has motivated the development of several programs designed to teach formal operational thinking to entering college students who appear to need such training. Many of these programs have a strong Piagetian orientation and make use of the "Learning Cycle" approach to instruction developed by Karplus (1974; also Campbell, Fuller, Thornton, Petr, Peterson, Carpenter, & Narveson, 1980; Fuller, 1980).

The "Learning Cycle" distinguishes three phases of learning process: (1) a relatively unguided *exploration* phase, (2) an *invention* phase, and (3) an *application* phase. The Piagetian flavor of the approach is seen in the care that is taken to introduce students to concrete concepts before confronting them with abstract relationships. During the exploration phase of the learning cycle, students engage in exploratory activities involving concrete experiences in a fairly open-ended and non-directed way. During the invention phase, they are encouraged to generalize concrete experiences to discover relationships and principles of a general or abstract nature. The instructor's role in this phase may be more active and somewhat more directive than in the exploration phase. During the application phase, emphasis is on the use of concepts or skills that were acquired during the invention phase of the cycle. In this case, the students' activities may be directed more explicitly than in either of the other two phases. The learning cycle approach places great emphasis on student-initiated activity. Perhaps this is most apparent during the exploration phase of the cycle; but even during the application phase, when the role of the instructor becomes most directive, instructors are cautioned against overplaying their director and facilitator roles (Fuller, 1980).

The programs discussed in this chapter emphasize not the strengthening of fundamental processes or the teaching of specific heuristics, but rather the conceptual schemes that Piaget has claimed characterize formal operational thinking. Also, unlike the programs reviewed earlier, in these the teaching of thinking is integrated with the teaching of conventional course content. Indeed, one way of characterizing the approach is to say that it is an effort to teach conventional subject matter in unconventional ways. In particular, memorization and rote knowledge acquisition are deemphasized, whereas exploration, experimentation, discovery, inquiry, and the forming of one's own ideas are stressed.

It is of at least passing interest that much of the initiative for the development of the Piagetian-oriented programs such as those described in what follows has come from physicists. This may simply be happenstance. On the other hand, if a large percentage of students arriving at college really are poorly prepared to engage in abstract thinking, it is perhaps to be expected that teachers of physics would be among the first to notice the problem. Many of the concepts that physicists use are indeed abstract. Moreover, there is increasing evidence that students can often get passing grades in physics courses without acquiring a very deep understanding of some of the concepts and relationships that are fundamental to the discipline. This is not to suggest that similar problems are not found in other disciplines—they are—but they seem to be better documented for physics and perhaps mathematics than for others (Nickerson, in press).

Whatever the reason, physicists or teachers of physics have been prominent among the developers and users of programs intended to enhance the ability of students to engage in abstract, or formal operational, thinking. Arons (1976) promotes a number of strategies or principles of teaching derived from experience in teaching an introductory physical science course to preservice and inservice elementary teachers, preservice nonscience secondary teachers and other nonscience majors. A goal of the program was to "lead as many students as possible to attainment of formal operations" in the Piagetian sense. Among the principles Arons studied, the following ones capture well some of the assumptions underlying the approaches described in this chapter:

- "Exploratory activity and question asking prior to concept formation and model building." Students should be given the opportunity to observe phenomena and to describe and ask questions about them in their own words before being introduced to technical terminology.
- "Idea first and name afterwards." Students should be introduced to concepts via observation and examination of objects, situations, phenomena to which the concepts apply before they are given the "names" of those concepts. The point is to impress upon the students the fact that words acquire meaning through shared experience and to dispel the idea "that knowledge and understanding reside directly in the technical terms they have learned."
- "How do we know ...? Why do we believe ...? What is the evidence for ...?" A goal should be is to promote within the students an awareness that one can and should have reasons for believing what one believes, and to discourage the willingness to accept all scientific explanations without evidence and without understanding simply because they have come from authoritative sources.
- "Inferences drawn from models." Students should be asked to answer "what if" questions by drawing inferences from their models of the physical systems involved. Arons stresses the importance of having the students think out their inferences and express them in their own words, and the futility—in terms of long-term effects—of giving them the answers rather than helping them find them themselves.

Before proceeding to a consideration of programs based on the Learning Cycle notion, it is appropriate to mention the Inquiry Training program of Suchman (1962). Suchman's approach is not as explicitly Piagetian based as are the other programs discussed in this chapter, nor does it make use of the Learning Cycle idea. In fact it predates the development of that by over a decade. It anticipates central aspects of the Learning Cycle approach with its strong emphasis on the importance of students arriving at their own ideas about natural phenomena, as opposed to being given those ideas in predigested form. It stresses student participation and, in particular, hypothesis formation and testing through questioning; and it deemphasizes lecturing. Suchman's work may well have influenced the form that the subsequently developed programs took. In any case, it is quite compatible in many ways with the other programs discussed in this section. Suchman's work was done with students much younger than college age and, from a Piagetian perspective, it could be viewed as an attempt to facilitate transition from concrete to formal operational thinking at about the time in a child's life when that transition is normally expected to occur.

The instructional approach of Inquiry Training is as follows. First, the students, a group of about 10 or 20 sixth grade children, watch a film demonstrating some physical phenomenon. One of the films, for example, shows a bimetallic strip bend in heat and then revert to its straight configuration. The children know nothing of bimetallic strips nor the differential effect of heat on the expansion of different metals. Then there follows something like a game of twenty questions. The students are charged to explain the phenomenon they have observed. They may ask the teacher any yes or no questions they wish, the teacher becoming a surrogate for lengthy processes of laboratory observation and experiment. Thus, Suchman suggests, the students are relieved of the cognitive load of actual observation and experimentation and freed to concentrate on the core of inquiry itself, the questions that need to be asked. In addition to many such group sessions, the students also receive guidance in the kinds of questions to be asked and the general course of inquiry, both in terms of general advice and critical examination of actual questioning sessions.

The effectiveness of the program was tested in five schools, each with a treatment and a control class of about 30 students. The 24 week program met for one to two hours per week, depending on the school. The control class saw the same films as the treatment class, but received conventional lessons about the phenomena displayed in the films. On a posttest of content concerning the phenomena examined during the course, differences slightly favoring the experimental group appeared even though this group never received any explicit instruction on any of the phenomena. They benefited only from the instructors' answers to their yes-or-no questions and their own efforts to generate explanations.

Another set of measures, which related to the questioning process, required the individual student to go through a miniature version of the inquiry process. The treatment subjects asked considerably more questions during the posttest than did the control subjects, and the treatment subjects' questions were more analytical in character and otherwise more to the point. A third set of measures concerned whether the treatment subjects explained the phenomena used in the posttest any better than did the control subjects. Here, no significant differences were found.

Thus, the inquiry training program did not demonstrate gains in the most obvious measure of success—more effective analysis of phenomena. Suchman speculated that this may have been due in part to the heavy role of prior knowledge in the subjects' abilities to make sense of the phenomena, knowledge that differed substantially from subject to subject. At least, the program provided knowledge of content as well as or better than the control treatment and, in the context of the course, reoriented the students' patterns of questioning in ways that could reasonably be expected to facilitate inquiry. Whether this effect would survive the course is an open question. Suchman emphasizes the importance of continued inquiry training in diverse subject areas.

1. ADAPT (ACCENT ON THE DEVELOPMENT OF ABSTRACT PROCESSES OF THOUGHT)

The ADAPT program was developed at the University of Nebraska, Lincoln, by a group of professors who wished to integrate the teaching of thinking skills into conventional content courses. The orientation was strongly Piagctian, and thc goal was to come up with an approach that would help students develop the reasoning abilities required by college courses as well as master the content of those courses. The Learning-Cycle model was taken as the point of departure.

Description

As initially implemented, ADAPT was a full freshman program and included courses in anthropology, economics, English, history, mathematics, and physics. Students who enrolled in the program were required to take all of the ADAPT courses. ADAPT students were apparently self-selected: enrollment was voluntary and there appear to have been no special admissions requirements. Although ADAPT was not designed specifically for special students, Moshman, Johnston, and Tomlinson-Keasey, Williams, & Eisert, (1980) report that ADAPT students have tended to be below average in cognitive development and in preparation for college work. Apparently the program has become increasingly perceived as a remedial one designed for students who anticipate difficulties in college.

The design of each content course was the responsibility of the professor for that course. However, considerable emphasis was placed on the coordination of activities across courses so as to encourage the development of the same reasoning skills in each of the disciplines being taught. A sample of ADAPT units in physics, mathematics, economics, anthropology, logic, and English is described by Campbell, Fuller, Thornton, Petr, Peterson, Carpenter, and Narveson (1980).

A narrative account of a teacher's experience in using the ADAPT approach to teach college level economics is given by Petr (1980). According to this account, if one accepts the Piagetian view of developmental stages and accepts the evidence that many college students do not have the ability to think effectively at the level of formal operations, one has two choices. One possibility is to "ignore the theory and the data and continue to teach, presumably at the formal level, with continued mixed results." The other is to "attempt to revise our pedagogy to make it accessible to the concrete as well as the formal student" (ibid, p. 53). The ADAPT approach represents one result of opting for the latter possibility.

The motivation for revising content to make it more accessible to concrete thinkers extends beyond that of simply accommodating to the students' limitations. It involves also

> the speculation that experience and self-regulation are two of the agents which foster progress from one stage to the next. The idea of restructuring higher education to make it accessible to pre-formal thinkers is attractive to me only as a development-stimulating process. *If* we can provide the environment and experience necessary for self-regulation to occur, and hence to assist the transition from concrete to formal, the potential worth of such pedagogical modification is immense. (ibid, p. 54)

The hope is that by carefully designing the curriculum so as to make key concepts meaningful to pre-formal students the developmental process might be stimulated in such a way as to move these students to the level of formal thinking. The notion is to meet students where they are and to bring them to where, according to the theory, they should be.

It is instructive to note the distinction between the concepts assumed by Petr to be accessible to a person in the concrete operational stage of development and those assumed to be accessible only to a person who has advanced to the formal operational stage. Concepts in the former category are claimed to possess some of the following characteristics:

1. drawn directly from personal experience;
2. involve elementary classification and generalization concerning tangibe objects;
3. utilize direct cause and effect relationships in a simple two-variable situation;
4. can be taught or understood by analogy, or algorithm or "recipe";
5. are "closed," not demanding exploration of possibilities outside the stated data. (ibid, p. 54)

Concepts that are accessible to formal operational thinkers are assumed to have some of the following characteristics:

1. may be hypothetical, imagined, contrary-to-fact;
2. may be "open-ended," demanding speculation about possibilities not spelled out;
3. may require deductive reasoning from unverified hypotheses;

4. may require definition by means of other concepts of abstractions, with no obvious correlation to tangible reality;
5. may require intermediate steps or concepts not established in original data. (ibid, pp. 54–55)

As an example of the application of the learning cycle approach in economics, Petr describes an attempt by one class to develop a College Student Price Index. The class began by surveying the students to determine what they bought and how much they spent for it. In the process of developing the index the class discovered the necessity of classifying purchases, of weighting them in terms of the extent to which they represented changes in purchasing power, the need to develop standards for product specification, the need for replicability, the effects of seasonal changes, and so on. This approach, which paved the way for introduction of the more abstract Consumer Price Index, is contrasted with the more conventional one of lecturing about the latter concept straightaway. Petr notes that introducing concepts in this discovery fashion is relatively time consuming and that, as a consequence, fewer economic concepts were presented during the academic year than would have been covered by a more conventional approach. He concludes, however, that those concepts that were introduced were more firmly grasped by the students than they otherwise would have been.

Evaluation

Several evaluations of varying degrees of objectivity have been performed on ADAPT programs (Johnston & Moshman, 1980; Sheldon, 1978; Tomlinson-Keasey & Eisert, 1978). Among the instruments that have been used in these evaluations are the following:

- A test of formal operational reasoning developed by Tomlinson-Keasey and Campbell (Arnold, Lonky, Kans & Eckstein, 1980).
- The Omnibus Personality Inventory (Sanford, 1956)
- The Conceptual Complexity Assessment (Harvey, Hunt, & Schroder, 1961)
- The College Student Questionnaire Part II (Educational Testing Service)
- The Watson-Glaser Critical Thinking Appraisal (Watson & Glaser, 1964)
- Loevinger's Measure of Ego Development (Loevinger, 1976)

The results of several evaluations have been summarized by Moshman, Johnston, Tomlinson-Keasey, Williams, and Eisert (1980). Evidences of positive effects include the finding that ADAPT students consistently showed significantly greater gains in formal operational reasoning than did several control groups. They also showed greater gains in conceptual complexity and in critical thinking. There was little evidence to show that the ADAPT program had negative effects on participants; however, there were several findings of no difference between ADAPT students and controls. No effects either positive or negative were found on grades in the year following the ADAPT program.

Moshman et al.'s interpretation of the available evidence as a whole is

> that it is sufficiently positive to suggest continuation and expansion of Piagetian programs at the college level, but not so positive that we can afford to be complacent. An important area for future analysis might be the degree to which ADAPT is beneficial to particular sorts of students and whether some screening in the selection of students might be advisable. (p. 119)

2. DOORS (DEVELOPMENT OF OPERATIONAL REASONING SKILLS)

Description

The DOORS project is located at the Illinois Central College, a community college in East Peoria, Illinois. Like ADAPT, after which it was patterned, Project DOORS was motivated by the belief that many incoming college students have not progressed beyond the Piagetian concrete operational stage of thinking. The goal of the program is to facilitate the movement of entering college students into the formal-reasoning stage. It too uses the Piagetian-based Learning-Cycle paradigm.

DOORS staff members were introduced to the learning cycle approach at University of Nebraska ADAPT workshops in 1976. Although the DOORS program was patterned after ADAPT, it was modified to be more responsive to the needs of a community college. The particular students for which DOORS was targeted were:

1. Beginning students with undefined career goals,
2. Beginning students with average to just-below-average high school academic records/classwork,
3. Older, returning students who were beginning their college careers. (Schermerhorn, Williams, & Dickison, 1982, p. 10)

The designers of this program intended to integrate the teaching of reasoning skills with conventional subject matter; thus DOORS courses were offered in English, mathematics, economics, sociology, history, and physics. Incoming students who were accepted in the program were required to enroll in DOORS English and DOORS mathematics courses (each one semester) and at least two additional DOORS courses elected from the remaining possibilities. Enrollment was voluntary, so the program was self selective to a degree. According to pre-training test scores, students who were attracted to the DOORS program tended to be less likely than other students to have attained the stage of formal reasoning ability.

DOORS was offered for the first time in the spring semester of 1977. During the summer of 1977, the curriculum was modified on the basis of experience gained in the spring semester as follows: The DOORS staff (subject-matter teachers for the various disciplines covered by DOORS) attempted to identify several major thinking skills basic to the six disciplines and then to design the DOORS classes so that each of them would be emphasizing the same skill at the same time in the semester. The skills identified for this purpose are shown in Table 8.1. The courses were offered in the fall semester of 1977 and thereafter according to this format. Thirty-two students were enrolled in the program in the fall semester.

Evaluation

In order to test the effectiveness of the program, the DOORS staff used an

TABLE 8.1
Reasoning Skill Identification for the DOORS program (Schermerhorn et al., 1982)

Week	*English, History, Sociology*	*Math, Economics, Physics*
1.	Observation (Identification of Variables)	Observation (Identification of Variables)
2.	Description (Describing Variables)	Description (Describing Variables)
3.	Comparing or Relating (Comparison and Contrast)	Comparing or Relating (Graphing)
4.	Comparing or Relating (Comparison and Contrast)	Inferring (Graphing)
5.	Classification	Classification
6.	Classification	Separation and Control of Variables
7.	Summary	Hypothesis Statement
8.	Cause and Effect	Separation and Control of Variables
9–15.	More Advanced use of Skills	More Advanced use of Skills

evaluation instrument that is apparently being collaboratively developed by several colleges involved in programs for enhancing cognitive abilities. (See following section.) The test addresses the following reasoning areas:

- proportional reasoning
- combinatorial logic
- hypothesis formation
- spatial relations
- correlation
- exclusion of irrelevant variables
- probabilistic reasoning

Both DOORS students and controls showed significant gains in thinking skills during the semester (as indicated by pretest and posttest results with the cognitive assessment instrument); however, control students showed greater gains than did students in the DOORS program. The evaluators attributed this to the greater preparedness of the control students than of the DOORS students upon entering college. This points out a difficulty in assessing the effectiveness of this kind of program; inasmuch as the DOORS students are self selected and tend to be more in need of remedial training than other students, it is not clear what constitutes an appropriate control group against which to compare their progress.

The students in the DOORS program had a lower drop-out or attrition rate than did those in the control group (18.5% vs. 29.5%). The control group attrition rate was comparable to that of the school as a whole. These data pertained to the fall semester of 1977. Subsequent data (collected in the fall of 1978) suggest that the attrition rate for the DOORS students decreased still further. This result also must be interpreted in the light of the self-selected nature of the experimental group. The fact that students had voluntarily enrolled in a program of this type might be taken as evidence of not only an awareness of their need but of determination to do something about it. If the enrollment procedure had the effect of channeling the more motivated students, at a given ability level, into the DOORS program, it would not be surprising to find a lower attrition rate among those students than among their classmates.

The results of questionnaires administered to students and students' open-ended evaluations of the course indicated that students considered their participation in the DOORS program to be a positive and beneficial experience. The participatory nature of the classes was a feature that they seemed especially to appreciate.

Schermerhorn, Williams, and Dickison (1982) admit to some disappointment over the failure of the DOORS program to produce evidence of effectiveness in enhancing beginning college students' formal thinking processes. Whether this failure should be attributed to ineffective evaluation efforts, the short duration of the intervention period or to some other variable is not clear. The positive effects of the program are summarized this way:

> the results do seem to suggest that DOORS students, even though they are as a group much less academically prepared, make as much intellectual growth as a typical group of community college students and do so with a significantly lower attrition frequency. This conclusion is even more significant in the light of longitudinal evidence showing that the DOORS students are continuing in their pursuit of academic courses with nearly the same frequency as typical students. (p. 16)

An important aspect of the DOORS program is the fact that it was initiated, designed and administered by faculty. The people responsible for teaching the conventional course material (e.g., English, mathematics, history) were the people who concerned themselves with the problem of teaching reasoning abilities. One description of the DOORS program notes "a deep running thread of basic conviction by the faculty that most traditional education stagnates the cultivation of students' thinking abilities." This comment prompts two thoughts. First, one must wonder to what extent it is representative of the attitude of college faculty in general, and second, one might assume that a program initiated by faculty in response to what they see as shortcomings of traditional methods might stand a much greater chance of success than one that is imported from elsewhere or imposed from the top. At least it should derive whatever benefits are to be gained from commitment of the faculty to its implementation.

As one evidence of success of the DOORS program, Schermerhorn et al. mention the continuing dedication of the participating six faculty members and the enthusiasm of the students. Faculty participants in this program claimed that their experience was a beneficial one to them and enhanced their teaching methods even in courses not associated with the program.

3. COMPAS (CONSORTIUM FOR OPERATING AND MANAGING PROGRAMS FOR THE ADVANCEMENT OF SKILLS)

Description

COMPAS (Schermerhorn, Williams, & Dickison, 1982) was a direct outgrowth of the DOORS project. It involved seven community colleges (six in addition to Illinois Central College) engaged in a collaborative effort to develop programs patterned after DOORS but tailored to the needs of the individual schools. The plan was to engage this consortium in preparatory activities during the fall of 1979 and spring of 1980 and then to offer the programs at the seven community colleges in the fall of 1981. The seven programs were indeed offered in the fall of 1981 with the participation of 235 students and 40 faculty. The seven schools, comprising the COMPAS consortium, and the program acronym for each school were as follows:

ALLEGHENY COMMUNITY COLLEGE - LIFT Program
HARPER COLLEGE - PATH Program
ILLINOIS CENTRAL COLLEGE - DOORS Program
JOLIET JUNIOR COLLEGE - STEPPE Program
PRAIRIE STATE COLLEGE - RISE Program
SEMINOLE COMMUNITY COLLEGE - STARS Program
CURRY COMMUNITY COLLEGE - CREATE Program

Preparation for the individual programs began with a two-and-one-half day workshop for project personnel, conducted by DOORS faculty at Illinois Central College in December, 1979. Participating faculty developed their own material at their respective colleges, with some help and consultation from DOORS participants, during the spring of 1980, and the courses were offered in the fall semester of 1981. The individual programs differed in many particulars, but they had in common the Piagetian orientation and the use of the Learning Cycle approach.

Evaluation

A summary of an attempt to evaluate the effectiveness of the project is reported in Schermerhorn, Williams, and Dickison (1982). Evaluation data consisted of the results of interviews, classroom observations, and objective testing. Tests included a revised version of Furth's (1970) Inventory of Piaget's Developmental Tasks and some problems developed by Tomlinson-Keasey and Campbell (1974). The report notes considerable variability in faculty assessment of cognitive development both within and across project sites, and acknowledges that COMPAS participants had both positive and negative assessments of how successful the project was in preparing students for college work.

The objective tests that were administered, pretreatment and posttreatment, to both experimental and control students measured conservation of quantity, conservation of weight, conservation of perspective (abilities that are assumed to characterize the concrete operational stage of development), conservation of volume, ability to use propositional logic, and ability to reason inductively (abilities that are assumed to characterize the formal operational stage). At the beginning of the study 31% of the students did not give evidence on these tests of being able to engage in formal operational thinking, which adds credence to the claim that many students entering college have this problem. Unfortunately, while the report presents data that indicate significant improvement in posttest scores over pretest scores in four of the seven participating schools, and in the combined sample, no comparisons are reported between the performance of students in the experimental and control groups. Hence one is left unsure as to whether the program was more or less effective than conventional instruction in effecting these changes.

The Schermerhorn, Williams, and Dickison report contains a number of "reflections" written by faculty participants in the various COMPAS programs. In general they indicate quite positive reactions to the experience, while acknowledging that much remains to be learned about how to improve upon more traditional methods of instruction. Many of the participating faculty mentioned specifically the benefits they derived, as teachers, from the opportunity that the project gave them to exchange ideas frequently with other teachers who were attempting to enhance the same reasoning abilities in other course contexts. An observation that serves as a caveat is that the approach necessitated the sacrificing of some content; because "students needed time to grope through the specifics and arrive at their own conclusions, some content had to be left out" (p. 6). Whether the cost of the omitted content is offset by an increased capacity to learn on one's own, and better retention of what is learned, is a question deserving of further research.

4. SOAR (STRESS ON ANALYTICAL REASONING)

Description

Project SOAR was developed by the Departments of Biology, Chemistry, Computer Science, Mathematics, and Physics at Xavier University of Louisiana. The goal of the project was to improve performance in science and mathematics courses. The main vehicle of the project is a summer course offered to incoming college freshman. The design of this course also was motivated by Piagetian notions about stages of intellectual development, and also takes as its point of departure the claim that many college freshmen in the U.S. cannot function at a formal reasoning level.

The course was built around a set of concrete problems, and was intended to be given daily for five weeks. It has two components: (1) three-hours of laboratory exercises in the morning, and (2) instruction in problem solving/comprehension and vocabulary building for two hours in the afternoon. The first component uses the Learning Cycle approach, as do the other programs that have been discussed in this section. During the first three and one-half weeks the second component employs Whimbey and Lochhead's *Problem Solving and Comprehension* and their thinking-aloud approach to cognitive process instruction. The thinking-aloud approach is continued through the last one and one-half weeks when texts and problem sources other than that of Whimbey and Lochhead are used. One half hour per day is devoted to vocabulary study using Levine's (1965) *Vocabulary for the College-Bound Student*. The afternoon session is described by Carmichael, Hassell, Hunter, Jones, Ryan, and Vincent (1980) as "designed to improve vocabulary, note-taking ability, and ability to visualize in three-dimensions."

Each week the laboratory exercises focus on a different one of five topics or "components of problem solving": control of variables, proportional reasoning, combinatorial reasoning, probability, and recognizing correlations. On each day of the week the problem material represents a different one of the five participating disciplines. Thus over the five week period every problem-solving component is encountered in the context of each of the disciplines.

An interesting feature of the SOAR program is its reserving of Friday afternoon each week for competitive exercises among the five groups into which the class has been organized for the entire week. The course developers report that these competitions produce enthusiasm and group cohesiveness and motivate out-of-class study and within-team support and reinforcement.

The program was originally intended for students who were unsure of their career goals, those with average to just below average high school performance, and older students who did not go to college directly after high school graduation. A low student-faculty ratio is maintained (about 7 to 1) thus permitting a considerable amount of individual attention. Fifty-seven students participated in the project in 1977, 109 in 1978, and 113 in 1979.

Evaluation

The effectiveness of the course given in 1977 and 1978 was measured by administration, before and after training, of a test of formal reasoning developed by Lawson (1978). About three-fourths of the students in both groups got higher scores on the test administered following training. The greatest gains were obtained by students who had been classified as being in a concrete or transitional stage of development. However, the relatively smaller improvements obtained with students who could reason formally may have been a consequence of ceiling effects on the test scores for the latter group. (To rule out the possibility that the improvements they obtained were due to the fact that the same test was given both before and after training, the investigators administered the same test twice to several freshman who did not take the SOARS course, and their improvements in the second taking of the test were very small—less than half a point out of 15 points on the average—relative to the improvements obtained in the experimental group.) From these results the investigators (Carmichael, Hassell, Hunter, Jones, Ryan, & Vincent, 1980) concluded that it is possible to improve intellectual development with such learning-cycle techniques, at least as intellectual development is measured by Lawson's test.

Tests other than the Lawson test have been used to evaluate the course, including the Nelson-Denny Reading Test and the PSAT. Whimbey, Carmichael, Jones, Hunter, and Vincent (1980) have reported the results of some of these tests for the students who took the course in the summer of 1979. Gains on the comprehension part of the Nelson-Denny Reading Test (Form C for the pretest; Form D for the posttest) range from 1.4 grade levels for participants who scored at or below 12th grade level on the pretest to 2.3 grade levels for those who initially scored at or below the 10th grade level. These gains were statistically significant. On the vocabulary portion of the Nelson-Denny test, the average increase in performance ranged from 1.8 grade levels for students at or below 12th grade on the pretest to 2.2 grade levels for those initially below the 10th grade level. These gains also were statistically significant. Increases in the PSAT score averaged 11.4 points for students who initially scored less than 70 on this instrument and 7.3 points for the entire group. These gains are substantial, but one would be more comfortable with them if they were accompanied by comparisons with corresponding scores from matched control groups. In the absence of such comparisons one is left wondering to what extent the greater gains by the poorer students represent a simple regression on the mean.

5. DORIS (DEVELOPMENT OF REASONING IN SCIENCE)

Description

Project DORIS is yet another example of an effort to facilitate the transition from concrete to formal thinking in college freshman. The heart of the project is a course, developed over a period of about two years at California State University at Fullerton. The course, which follows the Learning Cycle approach, is offered to (primarily freshman) college science majors. It is designed around five components of formal thinking: combinatorial logic, correlational reasoning, isolation and control of variables, and proportional reasoning (which are referred to as abstract-thinking abilities) and hypothetico-deductive reasoning, or hypothesis testing (which is referred to as a problem solving strategy). Each lesson focuses on one of these components and presents it in the context of the subject matter of one of four disciplines: chemistry, physics, earth science, or mathematics.

As of November 1980, over 80 lessons had been developed and tested in a classroom setting. Thirty-nine of these lessons survived the initial testing and were selected for further use. Although the documentation is not clear on this point, one gets the impression that a lesson is what is covered in one class session. The developers' hope for the course was that the participating students would improve their reasoning abilities, become more independent as thinkers and more effective at problem solving (Collea & Nummedal, 1980).

The initial version of the course (then called CAUSE for Comprehensive Assistance to Undergraduate Science Education) was tried out with 13 science majors in the fall of 1978. The duration of the course was 15 weeks, 4 weeks each on chemistry, physics and mathematics, and 3 on earth science. It was taught by its developers, who were faculty members in these disciplines.

A course book for the DORIS program has been published (Carlson, Clapp, Crowley, Hiegel, Kilpatrick, & Pagni, 1980). It contains a series of individual lessons organized in five main sections corresponding to the five components of formal thinking mentioned above; within each major section, the lessons are organized in terms of the disciplines covered. Individual lessons are described in accordance with a fixed format that prescribes identification of the reasoning skill, the problem content, the objectives of the lesson (in terms of what the student should be able to do after having completed the lesson), prerequisites, and equipment or supplies required. Two types of objectives are given for most lessons, a reasoning skill objective and a content objective, but the distinction between them is not always clear. The instructional content of the lesson is divided into three types of activities: exploration, invention and discovery. The basis for this distinction also is not always clear. An abbreviated list of the reasoning skills addressed by the DORIS course book is given in Table 8.2.

Evaluation

Effectiveness was evaluated with a battery of five puzzles designed by Campbell (1977) to measure the ability to carry out the five target formal operations, and with a self-descriptive "Learning Style Inventory" designed by Kolb (1977) to measure a student's preferred mode of learning. Differences between before- and after-treatment performance on the formal operations puzzles were not significant. Results on the Learning

TABLE 8.2
Examples of Reasoning Skills Addressed by DORIS Course Book

- Hypothetico-Deduction

  Deduce from experimental evidence the relative reactivity of a series of metals and their ions.

  Deduce a basis for deriving molecular structure from atomic structure.

  Use the truth table to examine and solve problems requiring simple deductive reasoning (including the conditional).

  Use hypothetico-deductive logic to find solutions to cryptarithmetic problems. To do this the student will use conclusions from *contradictions* and *if, then* arguments.

- Isolation and Cosntrol of Variables

  Develop a method for isolating and controlling or varying one variable at a time.

  Isolate and control the variables of surface area, normal force, and surface texture, and examine their effect on the force due to kinetic friction between two surfaces.

  Develop relationship between independent variables and dependent variables (area) of a polygon.

  Isolate one dimension at a time in order to graph in the other two dimensions before making a composite graph.

- Reasoning Ability: Combinatorial Logic

  Express combinations and permutations of a group of chemicals

  List the possible outcomes of an experiment with an ordered sequence of sub-outcomes.

  Determine combinations in a variety of electric circuits.

- Reasoning Ability: Proportional Reasoning

  Develop the proportional relationship between weight and volume.

  Transfer proportional reasoning from two dimensions to three dimensions.

  Use proportional reasoning to estimate the size of an unknown population.

  Use proportional reasoning to calculate the center of mass for the earth and moon system.

- Reasoning Ability: Correlational Reasoning

  Develop the relationship or correlation between molecular structure and physical properties.

  Develop a relationship or correlation between reactant structure and product composition.

  Use correlational reasoning to interpret graphical data.

Style Inventory indicated that after the course students were more likely to state a preference for abstract conceptualization over concrete experience than they were before. They also became more likely to state a preference for active experimentation over reflective observation.

For the spring semester of 1979, the course was reorganized around the thinking skills mentioned above. Lessons were chosen on the basis of their merits vis-a-vis the teaching of these skills without regard for the discipline involved. Sixteen students took the spring semester course. Effectiveness was evaluated by the puzzles designed to measure formal operational thinking and by the Watson-Glaser Critical Thinking Appraisal (Watson & Glaser, 1964). The Learning Style Inventory was dropped because of questions of validity and reliability. The Watson-Glaser test is intended to assess one's ability to: (1) make inferences, (2) recognize assumptions, (3) make deductions, (4) make interpretations, and (5) evaluate arguments.

On some of the puzzle problems performance improved slightly; on some of the others it got slightly worse. The change was statistically significant in only one case: students did significantly better after the course on the puzzle designed to require combinatorial reasoning. Performance on the Watson-Glaser test improved significantly; the average percentile rank moved from 43.5 on the pretest to 60 on the posttest.

Control groups were not used in either the fall or spring 1979 evaluations. However, Collea and Nummedal (1979, 1980) report evaluations for fall 1979 and spring 1980 in which control groups were matched with the groups receiving DORIS. The matching was based on scores on the Watson-Glaser Critical Thinking Appraisal and other variables such as academic major.

The fall course was completed by 12 students. Ten puzzles designed to assess formal operational thinking in four of the five components of formal thinking (omitting correlational reasoning) and the Watson-Glaser instrument were used as pretest and posttest. The same puzzles were used for both, while different forms of the Watson-Glaser instrument were used for the pretests and posttests. Analysis of performance on the puzzles revealed that both groups gained significantly on proportional reasoning, the control group alone gained significantly on combinatorial reasoning, and the DORIS group alone did so on hypothetico-deductive reasoning and control of variables. For the total test, the DORIS group gained significantly more than did the control group. Only the DORIS group showed a significant improvement on the Watson-Glaser Critical Thinking Appraisal.

Although these findings argue for the effectiveness of DORIS, the findings from the spring 1980 evaluation were less favorable. Twenty-six students participated along with matched controls. Two of four puzzles addressing isolation and control of variables were replaced by two addressing correlational reasoning, so that the modified puzzle test covered all five of the target abilities. Two lessons on correlational reasoning were added to the course. The puzzles were administered only as a posttest, to guard against the possibility that gains from the previous evaluation simply reflected taking the same test twice. The comparison of puzzle scores from the DORIS and control groups disclosed significantly better performance by the DORIS group only on combinatorial reasoning. On the Watson-Glaser instrument, the groups did not differ significantly on pretest or posttest, and neither group improved significantly.

6. FORMAL-THINKING PROGRAMS IN GENERAL

Are these Piagetian-based programs effective on the whole? It is difficult to say. The quantitative data that exist, which are relatively sparse, are not very compelling. The qualitative data, of which there are considerably more, are very difficult to fit together into a single coherent picture, but are generally positive. On balance, participants who have gone on record appear to be enthusiastic about the approach. Undoubtedly, one major plus has been the stimulus it has provided for teachers to think hard about their teaching goals and methods, and another is the framework it has given them for exploring alternatives with colleagues from other disciplines. It is clear that these programs have grown out of dissatisfaction with more conventional methods of teaching and the conviction that those methods were not producing acceptable results. But qualitative reactions usually carry less weight than do reliable quantitative data. Probably the best one can say is that the effectiveness of these programs appears to have varied considerably from situation to situation; the approach seems to have worked well in some cases and less well in others.

One would like to be able to say with confidence that at least they have done no harm. Unfortunately, even that conclusion requires one to go beyond the evidence. The courses reviewed in this chapter are (at least in most cases) taught in lieu of traditional content courses on the same subjects. Therefore, in evaluating their effectiveness, one must ask how the students fared in their mastery of the subject matter relative to students in the more conventional courses. The observation that the teaching methods required the sacrificing of some content highlights this potential problem. Of course the question of the cost of missed opportunities is one that might be raised with respect to any educational innovation that consumes time that could be spent in other ways.

These reservations notwithstanding, at least two positive points can be made about the efforts reviewed in this chapter. First, a few of the efforts fared fairly well in formal tests of effectiveness. This, of course, raises important issues for further inquiry. Why did *these* programs do well, and not others, especially since they all had more or less the same theoretical base? Second, if these experimental programs taken as a whole have failed to produce incontrovertible evidence of immediate success, that probably should be neither greatly surprising nor demotivating. Finding better ways to teach conceptually difficult material is unlikely to be trivially easy; if it were, the old techniques probably would not have survived so long. The important thing is that the effort is being made. In time either this effort will yield better approaches or it will give way to other efforts that do. Or, if existing approaches cannot be improved, then at least efforts to improve them should restore some confidence in the older techniques.

A particularly noteworthy aspect of the programs reviewed in this chapter is the fact that they were developed, for the most part, from within the educational establishment. The motivation and the material came from professors with years of experience in teaching basic courses—physics, mathematics, English, biology—in standard ways. This fact speaks clearly to the need for new approaches as perceived within the teaching profession.

Finally, we should comment briefly on the paradoxical relation between the programs reviewed here and the developmental psychology of Jean Piaget. In recent years, Piaget's notion that abstract thinking depends on a small unitary set of structures has increasingly come under attack. Piaget (1972) himself acknowledged that a person may attain formal operations in personally important and familiar domains while failing to do so in others. Not finding this concession enough, numerous investigators have presented arguments and evidence that intellectual development has a much more piecemeal character than supposed by Piaget (e.g., Brainerd, 1978a, b; Fischer, 1980). One does not acquire formal operations in all contexts at the same time, nor even very close to the same time. This, of course, brings into question whether people ever really have anything like "formal operations" in Piaget's sense.

We do not want to enter this debate, but only to make two points about it. First, granted that the status of Piaget's theory is controversial, the general richness of the phenomena he discovered and concepts he evolved cannot be denied. Second, uncertainty regarding the reality of cognitive "stages" notwithstanding, it seems to us that an understanding of such things as proportionality, control of variables, and the hypothetico-deductive method are manifestly important to the development of a logical scientific understanding of the world. Whether or not they are seen as aspects of a unified construct called formal operations, Piaget's theorizing has done a valuable service in dissecting various aspects of scientific thinking. Moreover, building a pedagogy on bridges from concrete experience to abstract thinking seems sound regardless of whether such a philosophy is couched in the language of concrete versus formal operations. For all these reasons, the question of the merits of the programs reviewed here seems somewhat independent of the eventual status of Piaget's position, although of course, they are not immune to criticism on other grounds.

The suggestion that programs based on questionable theories may be effective nevertheless perhaps itself deserves comment. We have made the suggestion before. In discussing programs based on cognitive operations, we noted that a questionable analysis of "atomic" cognitive operations might still lead to an effective instructional program. The point is much the same here: an underlying rationale often gives a program coherence and leads to the teaching and exercising of important abilities somewhat independently of the scientific adequacy of the rationale. It may be useful to think of the relation between theory and practice as heuristic: to have a theory guiding practice is a good strategy, so good a strategy that it may help even if the theory is questionable.

9 Thinking Through Language and Symbol Manipulation

The relationship between language and thinking has been a topic of debate for a very long time. It would not be useful to enter that debate here. However, nearly every program we have considered acknowledges the importance of language facility to effective thinking in one way or another. Some approaches focus on language, or symbol manipulation more generally, as the central theme. We turn now to a few examples of these. The distinguishing feature of these approaches is the idea that effective thinking requires "skill in a symbolic medium" (Olson, 1976). One must become an adroit manipulator of language, logical forms, computer programs, or other symbol systems that, in effect, can serve as vehicles for thought.

1. LANGUAGE IN THOUGHT AND ACTION

Recent years have seen some intensive work on writing, the mental processes it involves, and the mental processes it might develop. Before examining such efforts, there is some value in touching on a much earlier and less formal source, Hayakawa's (1964) *Language in Thought and Action*. This is book offers both an eloquent plea for the importance of language in guiding thought, and advice on how to improve one's abilities in that regard.

Interestingly, Hayakawa argues that language is as much the source as the solution of difficulties in reasoning. His message is that we live inside language. Our world of knowledge and our world of interactions with others both are in large part linguistic constructs, and, to deal soundly with life, we need to avoid the traps as well as tap the resources of language. To this end, the book offers a program for improving one's understanding of language and the way it influences thinking. The perspective derives from many sources, most notably, the "General Semantics" of Alfred Korzybski.

Hayakawa sees language and life as constructs of symbols, sometimes used for purposes fundamentally different from that of asserting and testing propositions. Many difficulties in reasoning come from confusions about language and its purposes. For instance, what appear to be empirical claims sometimes are mere expressions in disguise, Hayakawa suggests. "She's the sweetest person in the world," is not really a claim, but "purr words." There are many sorts of "purr words" and "snarl words" which amount to purrs and snarls with little denotative content. As this example may suggest, metaphor makes up one of the important instructional devices of the book.

Language in Thought and Action sets out to reform ineffective thinking, providing the student both with a conceptual framework and numerous exercises. Broadly speaking, Hayakawa's concern is with reasoning and the grounds for belief, but he offers a somewhat different view of the nature of ineffectual reasoning than that adopted in many programs to foster reasoning skills. Such programs often take what might be called a "rules of inference" approach: the emphasis falls on the rules of making sound inferences from given knowledge. The instruction tries to fashion students into effective syllogistic reasoners, reasoners cautious of generalizing from small sample sizes, alert to various formal or informal fallacies, and so on. Guidance is taken from the pitfalls of inference recognized by philosophy or identified by the psychological research reviewed in Chapter 5.

In contrast, Hayakawa sees weak reasoning more as a matter of poor navigating among the various levels of "reality" we construct with words and other symbols. One distinction central to this point involves "intensional" versus "extensional" meaning. Intensional meaning concerns what our terms mean relative to one another in the semantic network we carry around in our minds. Extensional meaning, in contrast, refers to the extensions of terms—the real-world objects and events to which the terms refer. According to Hayakawa, the source of ineffective thinking, in the broadest sense, is an "intensional orientation." The thinker with such an orientation travels in verbal circles at some level of abstraction, never testing matters against real world experience or data, or sometimes not even testing at lower levels of abstraction, in terms of knowledge of the particulars the abstractions concern. As remediation, Hayakawa recommends an "extensional orientation," an orientation that constantly checks higher levels of abstraction against lower ones and data.

This general caution sometimes is expressed through the familiar map-territory distinction: Verbal descriptive systems are like a map of territory, which should not be confused with the territory itself. Some other cautions offered by *Language in Thought and Action* include:

- The meanings of words are not in the words, but in us. Therefore, we should not presume those meanings to package an immutable reality.
- Contexts determine meaning. A term never means *exactly* the same thing in different uses, and many problems of thinking arise from slippage of meaning during a course of thought or conversation.
- "True," in particular, means several different things, sometimes referring to verifiable reports, sometimes to directives that we believe should be obeyed, and sometimes to formal truths or theorems.
- Definitions are suspect because they are words about words and risk the pitfalls of an intensional orientation; so one should deal with examples as much as possible.

Although these precepts sound somewhat abstract as listed here, Hayakawa dramatizes them effectively in the book by setting them in a context of points and anecdotes on such matters as advertising, poetry, prejudice, ethics, and medicine.

How should we understand the contrast between Hayakawa's approach and the "rules of inference" approach? One way to put the contrast in context is to recall the last section of Chapter 5. Research on informal reasoning reviewed there suggests that people sometimes drastically underutilize their own knowledge in constructing models of situations about which they are reasoning. This is not just a failure to make sound inferences from knowledge explicitly at hand, but rather a failure to bring to bear knowledge available in one's memory. Such a lapse corresponds roughly to Hayakawa's concern about an intensional orientation, an orientation out of contact with the concrete information to which one has access.

For a second point, Nisbett and Ross (1980) emphasize that many of the lapses in reasoning can be ascribed to the human tendency to assimilate information to existing schemata. In consequence, we often "read in" when more caution would be warranted. Nisbett and Ross note that this is not simply an unfortunate lapse in human information processing. Assimilation to a schema lies at the foundation of mental efficiency. Occasional problems with "reading in" are an inevitable consequence.

Hayakawa does not discuss such research—indeed, for the most part his book predates it—but the general orientation is the same. Hayakawa avers that the abstractive, world-building powers of language are the fundamental resources of humanity. At the same time, however, these conceptual devices lead us into the intensional orientation, in which the map may lose touch with, or be mistaken for, the actual territory.

Language in Thought and Action should not be considered a very precise book. It would be easy to criticize certain of the author's concepts as too broad and sweeping, for instance. Nor, we think, should its general viewpoint be considered a substitute for the "rules of inference" approach. On the other hand, neither does the latter approach address very emphatically or vividly the dual opportunity-trap character of our language and, more generally, our conceptual systems. It is this dual character that makes effective reasoning more than a technical challenge of avoiding certain slips, exactly because those slips are not isolated blunders like typographical errors. Rather, they often follow what might be called the natural momentum of the mind, while the right moves run counter to it.

2. WRITING AS AN OCCASION FOR THINKING

"Frozen speech" is a natural metaphor for writing. The phrase is apt, in one sense, in that it captures one of the most fundamental contributions of writing to civilization: the permanent record. The preservation of each generation's increased knowledge for use by the next is crucial to the intellectual and technological development of the species. Although knowledge can be transmitted orally, writing allows it to be passed on without personal contact. This is a great plus, because it facilitates the accumulation of knowledge in a way and at a rate that would not be possible otherwise.

However, the activity of writing outdoes the "frozen speech" metaphor in at least two ways. First, writing demands much more of the writer than the transcription of spoken words, an activity that is limited to a few special situations such as court stenography. Second, writing often becomes not merely a way of representing thoughts for purposes of transmission, but a means of thinking itself. Accordingly, writing is relevant to teaching thinking both because (1) writing demands thinking, and (2) writing is a vehicle for thinking. We expand on both of these themes in what follows.

The Demands of Writing

That writing is a demanding activity is apparent to anyone who spends much time putting words to paper. The popular belief that truly gifted writers produce fluently, while only amateurs and hacks plod along, is contradicted by evidence showing that even the gifted, for the most part, work and rework to achieve their products (Perkins, 1981, Chapter 6). The writer who can produce "final copy" easily and on the first pass appears to be a rarity, even among professionals.

So writing demands much of the writer, or at least of most writers, but what of that? The point is that writing is a particularly characteristic reflection of thought. There are many difficult tasks that we would not necessarily take as prototypical of thinking. Playing chess or bridge and designing electronic circuits pose formidable intellectual challenges, but we do not usually treat skill in any one of these activities as a certain indication of thinking ability more generally. Even the ability to do well on tasks such as those found on aptitude and IQ tests may leave a lingering doubt as to whether such tasks capture the essence of thinking, especially thinking that is required outside school settings. Writing seems to be different. If a person writes well of substantive matters, one tends to believe that that person has the ability to think effectively in a fairly general sense, which is to suggest that the ability to write well depends strongly on the intellectual maturity of the writer (Kitzhaber, 1968).

This line of reasoning suggests that if one would understand what is involved in improving thinking, one might do worse than study writing, and the approaches that people have taken in trying to improve it. It also suggests that instruction in writing might be a good context in which to exercise thinking skills.

Scardamalia and Bereiter (1985) argue that expository writing is paradigmatic for many intellectual tasks that occur in everyday life and in particular of tasks for which the goal is at least partly emergent, with many potential routes to its attainment. By a partly emergent goal, they mean a goal that becomes clear, and perhaps is modified, as a consequence of one's own goal-seeking activity. Scardamalia and Bereiter call such tasks "compositional" to convey the notion that written composition is a subclass of the more general task type. Another characteristic of compositional tasks is that one typically brings to them a great deal of knowledge that is potentially applicable to their performance. One of the problems is to access the relevant knowledge that one has.

What makes writing difficult? The short answer is that writing is like juggling: Many things have to happen at once, and to keep them all "in the air" poses a challenge the novice cannot readily meet. Flower and Hayes (1980) express this view, arguing that skilled writing cannot be understood simply as an extended process, in which the writer deals with one thing at a time. On the contrary, they claim, writing requires that several processes operate in flexible interaction with one another. They offer a process model of writing, which features planning activities, generating activities, and organizing activities. The details of the model, which is based on protocol analysis, need not concern us here. Suffice to say that, in their view, the popular pedagogical concept represented by the adage "prewrite-write-rewrite" does not face up to the intrinsically interactive nature of planning, word-generating, and organizing activities.

Bereiter (1980), commenting on stages of development in writing skill, also sees the essential difficulty as one of managing multiple constraints. The novice writer's first efforts fall naturally into a minimally demanding pattern that Bereiter calls "associative writing." The writer puts on paper whatever comes to mind, reaches for another thought, transcribes that, and so on. The result may be a repetitious meander around the main theme.

Bereiter and Scardamalia (1981) see in such writing a more general cognitive strategy they term "knowledge telling." Not only in essay writing, but in other contexts, students respond by telling what they know in the simplest possible way—retrieving a piece of knowledge, writing it, and recycling until they fail to think of anything else. Of course, telling what one knows often does not address the real question. Moreover, two psychological problems compound the weaknesses of the knowledge-telling strategy: Bereiter and Scardamalia note that students recall only a fraction of what they actually know about a topic, perhaps because of ineffective retrieval strategies. Also, students have a poor sense of what topics they know more and less about.

Furthermore, the authors note that many educational practices reinforce a knowledge-telling strategy, which is often an adequate response to the school situation. The authors see all this as one instance of a more general problem they call the problem of "inert knowledge." Writing is just one among many areas of cognitive performance in which knowledge available in principle may remain inert. The finding reported in Chapter 5 about people not utilizing their available knowledge in constructing arguments provides another example of inert knowledge.

Bereiter (1980) characterizes additional stages in the development of skilled writing as follows: "performative writing"—similar to associative writing, but with good control of grammar, spelling, and other aspects of mechanics; "communicative writing"—writing shaped to the audience, taking account of its strengths and weaknesses in knowledge and in other respects; "unified writing"—writing in which the writer uses himself as a critical reader or model of the audience; and, finally, "epistemic writing"—writing that functions as a means of questing for knowledge. Bereiter maintains that writing skills typically develop in something like this order, an order in many ways "natural." For instance, communicative writing depends on the development of social perceptivity and the decline of egocentricity, gains in sophistication more general than writing but which nonetheless have implications for it. Thus, one would not expect a child to begin writing at the communicative stage, even if there were not problems of cognitive load. However, Bereiter also warns against considering the order of his stages inevitable. Natural though they may be, given the typical instructional context, a different instructional approach might revise the order, perhaps in fruitful ways.

This brings us to what may be one of the fundamental problems in conventional writing instruction: the insistence on starting with mechanics.

Generations of English teachers have stressed grammar, punctuation, and spelling as steps on the way to more meaningful writing activities. Obviously, matters of mechanics should not be neglected. However, it is hardly surprising that many students find writing a meaningless chore when instruction concentrates mostly on commas and "i before e," without venturing as far as possible into the aspects of writing that motivate the activity and demonstrate its usefulness.

We note in passing that considerable work is being done at the present time on the objective of applying computer technology to the problem of helping children acquire effective writing skills. Tools similar to those used in "electronic offices"—text editors, electronic mail—customized for use by young children, are being used to facilitate the acquisition of the more cognitive aspects of writing—planning, composing, editing—independently of lower-order aspects such as penmanship and spelling (Bruce, Rubin, & Loucks, 1983; Rubin & Bruce, 1983).

In summary, the problems of writing and writing instruction, to a first approximation, appear to amount to these: (1) the management of multiple constraints, including audience needs, the demands of epistemic content, and thorough retrieval from one's own knowledge base; (2) the problem of managing them "at the same time" at least in part; and (3) the problem of making writing as meaningful as possible for the student. What can instruction do about all this?

The Pedagogy of Writing

In this overview of efforts to teach thinking skills, the pedagogy of writing deserves a glance exactly because, as we argued earlier, writing is so paradigmatic a case of thinking. Therefore, on the one hand, to teach people to write better *is* to teach them to think better in an important sense. Second, whatever instructional tactics serve well in improving writing might also contribute to other sorts of thinking.

However, the pedagogy of writing is vast. Here we can do no more than mention a couple of sources that seem particularly relevant to our conception of writing as a manifestation of thinking. One interesting approach is described in a two-volume text on writing entitled *Confront, Construct, Complete* (Easterling & Pasanen, 1979) directed at secondary school students. Initially, the students are asked to concentrate on the "starter sentence" of a paragraph—essentially the topic sentence—and the relationship it bears to the rest of the text. A good paragraph, the book claims, elaborates the starter sentence, selecting specific observations that illustrate and substantiate its assertion. For several brief chapters, exercises in paragraph writing occupy the student, who must relate observations made of photographs, poems, or other materials to starter sentences and attempt to construct pointed paragraphs.

This represents the "confront" phase of the treatment of paragraphs. "Construct" follows, with attention to some finer points of building an effective paragraph. Adding, deleting, and reordering are the principal concerns. Finally, in the "complete" phase, finer points yet become the young writer's focus. Here is the place to worry about sentence fragments, various difficulties with punctuation, overuse of declarative sentences, and other subtle matters along the way to a polished product.

In Part II of the first volume, the concern broadens for another cycle of "confront, construct, complete." "Confront" here introduces the concept of the dialogue as something from which to write. While the first part of the book focuses on writing about the thing or situation singled out, the second part emphasizes the interplay between two persons or points of view. The student writes paragraphs highlighting such relationships and interactions. "Construct" moves on to the problem of joining paragraphs when a situation allows more than one dialogue and yields more than one paragraph. At this point, the emphasis on the "starter sentence" is decreased. Paragraphs can often do perfectly well without them, and, indeed, "starter sentences" may sometimes be overbearing and artificial, the student is warned.

Broadly speaking, the authors of *Confront, Construct, Complete* take what might be called a schematic approach to the teaching of writing, providing the students with schemata that can guide their novice efforts and that presumably also guide, if covertly, the more facile work of experienced writers. This is one approach to meeting the cognitive load problem mentioned earlier. The schematic basis of human performance has been persuasively argued by numerous people (e.g., Bartlett, 1932; Bregman, 1977; Minsky, 1975; Neisser, 1976; Schank & Abelson, 1977). Schemata, which appear to be a natural solution to the problem of cognitive load, suggest an equally natural instructional approach: If schemata are what people need, perhaps instruction should be designed to provide those schemata directly.

It is worth noting that Easterling and Pasamen urge flexibility in the use of the formulas they provide, and in doing so address a standard problem in schema-based instruction (Perkins, 1979, 1981). The reservations introduced in the second part of Volume One regarding "starter sentences" illustrate the concern; the authors note that elements useful in getting the student started may later become optional and sometimes perhaps even undesirable. A related point has been made by Resnick (1976b) in the context of mathematics instruction. Resnick argues that instruction need not, and perhaps should not, provide students with the elaborated plans that guide expert performance. Instruction could better supply simplified versions that make the basic idea apparent and leave the streamlining to the student.

The "mechanics-first" orientation of much writing instruction is not adopted by the *Confront, Construct, Complete* program. Mechanics do not come first. On the other hand, neither does "epistemic writing," Bereiter's last stage. The program proceeds from what might be called the "middle out" rather than from either the "top down" or the "bottom up." That is, the program neither starts with extremely small units such as sentences nor with very broad matters such as the structure of narrative or the problem of finding something worthwhile to say. The initial entry point for the student is the paragraph, a unit perhaps large enough to be meaningful but small enough to be manageable.

On the whole, the *Confront, Construct, Complete* approach looks to us as though it ought to be effective; although so far as we can tell from examining the two textbooks, its impact has not been demonstrated formally. The approach incorporates design features addressing the several difficulties of instruction in writing identified earlier. Indeed, one question that arises is whether more responsibility for selecting topics of more scope and interest should be given to students sooner. Or would such a modification raise the cognitive load above an acceptable level? This is an empirical question and presumably could be settled by research.

Another interesting source of writing instruction is *The Little Red Writing Book* of Scardamalia, Bereiter, and Fillion (1979). Not a text, this book offers a collection of exercises that teachers might adapt to their efforts to enhance various writing skills. Many of the proposed activities have an inviting game-like quality. For example, "Direct a Robot" requires a student to write explicit instructions to direct another student around the room as though the other student were a robot. This is reminiscent of some of Wittgenstein's language games, which emphasize the difficulties of framing sufficiently explicit directions in a situation where, for real or contrived reasons, the usual metalinguistic and other contextual cues to meaning do not help. Another example posing difficulties of direction-giving asks some students to learn a trick and then to write directions permitting other students to perform the same trick.

Generally clever and engaging, the lessons of *The Little Red Writing Book* often incorporate a strategy that seems to us powerful and applicable in contexts other than that of a writing task. Recall that Bereiter (1980) identified "unified writing" as the achievement of using oneself as a surrogate audience and revising accordingly. How to teach people to assume that sort of objectivity poses a serious instructional problem. Consider this approach: In an exercise designed to promote objective evaluations, a critique of a piece of student writing is done by two people—the original writer and another student. The task of the original writer is to write the critique so objectively that the class cannot tell which critique was his, and which was that of the second student.

Here is another example: Students are challenged to write two versions of an exercise—a well-written version and a poorly written version—and to exemplify each so well that the rest of the class can tell which is supposed to be the good instance and which the bad one. These examples, as well as others in the book, share an interesting feature. The subtle and value-laden issues of the quality of writing and its fittingness for an audience are at least partly translated into a highly objective and motivating question: can the other students detect a specified difference? By this means, the teacher-as-critic is taken out of the process and the reaction of an audience substituted. In general, *The Little Red Writing Book* suggests the desirability of finding sources of feedback on student writing other than simply corrections from the teacher.

Bereiter and Scardamalia recently have described some further approaches to the problems of composition. Earlier, we mentioned their observation that young writers suffer from a problem of "inert knowledge," failing to access much of what they know about a topic. Bereiter and Scardamalia (1981) report that their colleague, Valerie Anderson, found an effective procedure for activating inert knowledge. Children were asked, prior to writing on a topic, to list words that they might use in the composition. After the children had practiced for several hours on various kinds of writing, this strategy was shown to double the length of compositions and to triple the number of uncommon words used. Of course, longer compositions may simply reflect more thorough "knowledge-telling," with no greater depth or coherence. But at least the strategy appears to help students to gain better access to their knowledge-base.

One might think that other, more conventional, preparatory techniques would have similar effects—for instance listing the key ideas to be expressed. However, the research also disclosed that children bogged down with this strategy as with writing prose: they failed to access much of the knowledge they in fact had. Bereiter and Scardamalia suggest that restricting children to listing vocabulary rather than ideas forces them to activate high level nodes in their mnemonic representations.

Scardamalia and Bereiter (1981) discuss another approach to writing instruction they call "procedural facilitation." This means adding a self-regulatory mechanism to the learner's normal procedures, but one carefully designed and supported by external cues so as to minimize added cognitive load. The authors discuss an example where fourth, sixth, and eighth graders wrote with the help of a procedural facilitation for revision, involving steps of comparing, diagnosing, choosing a revision tactic, and generating alternatives. Each student worked with cards that stated alternative points to evaluate, such as interestingness, clarity, and convincingness, and also stated revision tactics such as: leave unchanged, delete, change wording, replace whole sentence. An investigator monitored their diagnosing by asking for reasons for each evaluation. The students executed the revision cycle after every sentence, some working on original compositions and some editing. The investigators found more revisions than otherwise would be expected and revisions that improved the products. The children followed the procedure without difficulty and most claimed that it made the writing easier, some explicitly appreciating that the procedure would be a good one to follow without the help of the cards.

These several examples suggest that efforts to devise better means of teaching writing skills may contain some useful lessons for those concerned with teaching thinking skills more generally. Clearly, the problems that make writing difficult are not unique to writing. Problems of cognitive load, of taking into account others' needs and perspectives, of using oneself as a model of one's audience, and so on, arise in many contexts. Accordingly, such instructional strategies as teaching schemata (and their flexible use), organizing instruction from "the middle out" rather than from the bottom up or even from the top down, and "operationalizing" subtle standards into public tests seem likely to be good tactics to keep in mind wherever the goal is improvement in the performance of a significant intellectual task.

3. WRITING AS A MEANS OF THINKING

We turn now to the notion that writing is not just an occasion for thought, but a means of thinking. That is, writing may not only follow upon and express already fully developed thoughts; sometimes it may provide a medium through which those thoughts can be worked out in the first place.

It is not hard to see how writing might fulfill such a function. Anyone who writes a lot need only imagine what it would be like to treat the same topics without writing. Suppose, for example, that one had to dictate all that one wrote to a secretary who never read it back. There would be no chance to make a chapter outline, no chance to reshuffle the order of points or sections on scratch paper, no chance to list point-by-point the key arguments on both sides of the case in question. One could, of course, try to handle these tasks mentally, but clearly that would pose serious problems of memory.

Here emerges one of the primary contributions of writing to thinking: writing functions as an adjunct to short term and long term memory, relieving the thinker of the need to keep everything in his or her head. Because of this, the writer can develop lines of thought that would be too complex to keep track of without writing.

Olson (1976) states an extreme form of this proposition in his claim that the very character of contemporary Western civilization derives from the written word. Only in writing, Olson suggests, can the complex logical arguments that provide the foundation for contemporary science be framed. Verbal communication is too ephemeral. Only when thoughts can be made to stay still for a while can they be criticized, revised, and elaborated into sophisticated logical structures.

It might even be the case that thinking by means of writing improves one's thinking when one is not writing. This would be in keeping with Vygotsky's (1962, 1978) model of development, according to which thinking develops, in part, as an internalization of speech. To oversimplify a bit, the youngster learns to talk to himself from talking with others. By the same token, one might learn from overt writing to "write to oneself." For instance, one might learn from overt writing to think in the topic-sentence-plus-elaboration structure of paragraphs, or of the point, counterpoint, counter-counterpoint structure of many written arguments.

If one accepts this perspective, it urges the importance of what Bereiter (1980) calls "epistemic writing"—writing as a quest for knowledge. What would instruction in such writing be like? One suggestion comes from a text by Young, Becker, and Pike (1970) called *Rhetoric: Discovery and Change*. Designed for college students, the book sets out to revive the Greek tradition of rhetoric in the word's best sense. The term rhetoric, the authors point out, has ranged in meaning from a method of inquiry to a means of persuasion. It is the first sense that the authors intend.

In *Rhetoric: Discovery and Change*, Young, Becker, and Pike offer the reader a number of tools to facilitate writing as a process of inquiry. For example, they suggest a general approach to analyzing something, whatever the something is. First, the thinker must pay heed to "contrastive features"—features that define how the thing of concern differs from other things. Second, there must be attention to "range of variation"—how something can differ and still remain a thing of that kind. Finally, attention must be given to "distribution," meaning the occurrence of the something in context: when, where, how, why, and in what role?

Among other things, these analytical tools are meant to help the writer with the context-bound character of knowledge. What is apparent or important for one person may not be so for another. The tools encourage a broad even-handed treatment more likely to make contact with the perceptions of others. In short, they foster what Bereiter (1980) calls "communicative writing," writing in a manner suitable for the intended audience.

For another sample of Young, Becker, and Pike's approach, in later chapters the authors address the writing of arguments. In Chapter 11, they outline a fairly conventional view of argument, providing information about the types of formal and informal fallacies that often plague effective justification. In the subsequent Chapter 12, the authors turn to what they call "Rogerian argument." This is a strategy to undercut the contentious aspects of argument that interfere with communication. The authors propose three general goals for the writer presenting an argument about an issue: (1) to show the reader that the reader's position is understood and empathized with; (2) to define the points of agreement between the writer's and reader's position, thus putting disagreements in context; and (3) to show the reader that the writer is a person of honor and good will, sharing with the reader the objective of resolving the issue at hand.

Perhaps this is enough of a sample to convey the approach of *Rhetoric: Discovery and Change*. The text requires considerable writing by the reader, and incorporates advice on matters such as joining sentences with operational connectives such as "because." However, the approach is emphatically top-down. The book starts with epistemology and only toward the end approaches the more mechanical aspects of writing. As with the previous examples of writing instruction, this source offers no data on its effectiveness. However, it is interesting to find an effort to teach writing that has more than pragmatic advice to offer. *Rhetoric: Discovery and Change* makes an effort to dissolve the distinction between writing on the one hand, and thinking on the other, and to present the two as one integrated human endeavor.

Despite our positive view of writing as a means of thinking, one general concern should be mentioned. It should not be assumed that the conventional forms of written expression—discursive essays for example—are the only, or even necessarily the best, forms for thinking by writing. Many forms of writing activities that never make it as far as a final draft may be more suited to the questing side of writing. We refer here not so much to conventional outlining as to strategic note taking, informal diagram making, listing problems and checking them off as solved, trying to write out the central proposition one seeks to deal with, and so on.

We can imagine instruction, under the rubric of "thinking on paper," that would not deal with conventional literary products. Instead, it would emphasize heuristics of using writing (as well as diagramming and symbol manipulation more generally) for oneself as means of thinking through a problem or issue. We suspect that instruction of this sort, carefully worked out and coordinated with more conventional instruction in writing, would do more for both writing and thinking than conventional writing instruction alone.

4. UNIVERSE OF DISCOURSE

Rarely has a general theoretical perspective been applied to the conventional subject matters of primary and secondary school. James Moffett's approach to teaching the language arts is an interesting exception. In a book of essays entitled *Teaching the Universe of Discourse* (Moffett, 1968) and in other writings, Moffett sets out to reform education, with a more skilled and flexible listener, speaker, reader, and writer as the goal. Moffett's recipe for reform is relevant here because of his view about the key role of language in thought and the importance of general thinking skills in schooling.

Discourse is a key term in Moffett's pedagogy. He defines it to encompass listening, speaking, reading, and writing, pleading the need for a term that recognizes a fundamental unity in the four activities. Moffett criticizes conventional education for fostering artificial and unproductive divisions among this quartet of related performances. For instance, he maintains that reading would benefit from closer links to writing instruction. We understand and learn in large part by transforming, and writing is one available means for transforming what one reads—writing summaries, abstracts, scripts from stories, stories from plays, and so on. Speaking also provides a powerful means of transformation, as texts are discussed, read aloud, or performed dramatically.

Decentration is another key concept is Moffett's approach. He (1968, pp. 57–59) cites both Piaget and Bernstein, relating the former's concept of decentration to Bernstein's (1973) notion of restricted versus elaborated codes. Moffett proposes several dimensions of decentration along which discourse advances, as follows:

1. From the implicit, embodied idea to the explicitly formulated idea.
2. From addressing the small, known audience like oneself to addressing a distant, unknown, and different audience.
3. From talking about present objects and actions to talking about things past and potential.
4. From projecting emotion into the there-then to focusing it in the here-now.
5. From stereotyping to originality, from groupism to individuality. (p. 57)

This general framework provides a guide to which sorts of discourse learners would best approach first, and which sorts later. Moffett offers, with a grain of salt, the following sequence (p. 47): Interior dialogue (egocentric speech), vocal dialogue (socialized speech), correspondence, personal journal, autobiography, memoir, biography, chronicle, history, science, metaphysics. As to the grain of salt, Moffett warns that he does not expect this scheme to be more than a rough guide, both because prior life and schooling have prepared children in various ways for further work with discourse and because of preferences children bring to discourse, somewhat apart from their abilities.

Instructional Approach

In *Student-Centered Language Arts and Reading, K-12*, Moffett and Wagner (1976) describe a general plan for teaching discourse skills that puts the foregoing philosophy into practice. Not a lesson-by-lesson recipe, the plan is a fairly specific outline for a learning environment in the style of an open classroom. The authors recommend a classroom laid out for simultaneous group and individual activities, including a game area, art and science areas, a listening area, a reading area, and a drama area. The students should be organized into small groups, the teacher rarely addressing the whole class at once. Five is a good group size for general discussion, large enough to provide for a variety of stimulating input, but small enough to keep all the students participating. For writing workshop groups, three may be better, considering the time the group has to give to the products of each of its members.

There is no set curriculum. Individuals and groups choose what activities to undertake. These are suggested on activity cards that describe how to proceed, and through other self-directing materials. The authors maintain that many routes to discourse skills are suitable, and that children spontaneously avoid activities they have already thoroughly mastered as well as ones beyond them, so personal choice is both apt and highly motivating. Students need to learn to choose wisely, but this itself is a skill to be fostered. The students keep logs of the activities they undertake and the people with whom they work. Periodically, the teacher meets with individual students to review what they have done and to make suggestions, but always in a spirit of mutual planning.

In a series of chapters, Moffett and Wagner discuss the kinds of activities appropriate for such instruction. Talking and listening are key elements of the curriculum. The authors recommend extensive small group discussion on themes appropriate to the level of the students. "Level" does not mean age, since the authors have observed dramatically different skills in children of the same age with different social and educational backgrounds. The teacher is warned against directing the group discussions, a practice that leads to dominating the group and destroying its interactive character. The teacher may work with individual groups but must troubleshoot while not becoming the center of attention.

Another oral activity is dramatic inventing. The authors discuss a variety of dramatic activities—group pantomime exercises, miming familiar stories, acting out responses to given provocative situations. Performing texts is another suggested activity: students may simply read aloud, in unison or individually, act out a story while it is being read aloud, or sit and read aloud the parts of plays.

As this suggests, reading is emphasized, and an individual reading in a corner is considered quite appropriate. However, the basic approach to reading is to yoke it to activities such as those mentioned above, that require the reader to transform what he has read. Reading provides an occasion for writing as well as drama, as students transform a story into a play, a film script, a series of letters. But not all writing need start with other writing. The authors recommend activities such as writing sensory impressions—what the student sees, hears, or feels at the time—writing observations, for instance of animals kept in the classroom, with the activities gradually advancing toward more complex forms such as the essay. (We note that the authors also provide an approach to teaching decoding in reading, a matter outside our present concerns.)

The authors devote a number of chapters to discussing the genres to which these activities could be applied. Attention directed to labels and captions, charts, graphs, maps, newspaper headlines, actual and invented dialogue as in script writing or speech transcription, invented or true stories exploring such sources and styles as letters and personal journals, instructions, informative discourse about what experiments show or what the student observes, and explorations of ideas through such forms as definitions, dialogues spoken and written, and essays.

Evaluation

As has been the case with many other programs or approaches discussed in this book, we have not found empirical studies comparing Moffett's approach with control approaches to teaching the language arts. Indeed, Moffett's recommendations pose an awkward problem for anyone wishing to attempt such a study, since, while providing a generative scheme, he offers no standard version. Rather, the individual teacher composes a personal version to suit the circumstances. Nonetheless, we can comment on theoretical grounds, and certain empirical studies do bear on major elements of Moffett's approach. We turn to several reservations, followed by a survey of what appears to us to be the special strengths of the program.

The scope of Moffett's program leaves little room for any one activity to be taken up in great detail. Perhaps partly because of this, the program does not reflect contemporary analyses of some of the intellectual performances it addresses. For example, we have discussed elsewhere (Chapter 5) the difficulties in everyday reasoning identified by researchers over the last decade (e.g., Nisbett & Ross, 1980; Tversky & Kahneman, 1971, 1973, 1974). A more conspicuous omission concerns contemporary theories of the writing process, reviewed in preceding sections of this book. For instance, it is generally agreed that the sheer cognitive load of writing is one of the main impediments, but Moffett's program includes no specific strategies for dealing with the problem. In fairness, some of this research is very recent. Moreover, Moffett might care little for it, invoking the dangers of an atomistic approach and maintaining that the most important thing is to keep the students writing a lot on matters of increasing complexity that engage them.

Moffett advocates what might be called a "by-your-bootstraps" model of learning discourse skills. Although the teacher provides some criticism and strategies, the principal source of instruction is the students' interactions with one another. Skill develops as they present products, receive criticism from their peers, or simply observe what works and what does not, and revise. The teacher's role is more one of facilitating than informing or even Socratically guiding.

McQuillan (1979), in a generally useful critique of Moffett's theory of composition, questions whether the "by-your-bootstraps" approach is sound. He points out that many theorists of language learning see linguistic sophistication as the product of interaction with adults, not with peers. McQuillan cites a cautionary, though very small-scale, study by Searle (1975), who gathered information on group discussion in the presence and absence of the teacher. Searle found that, without the teacher, the discourse remained at a low level of abstraction. Perhaps the catalyst of the teacher is needed to create some pressure toward more sophisticated discourse. The Socratic model of instruction investigated by Collins and Stevens (1980) stands in contrast to the facilitative model of Moffett as an approach to the development of discourse skills.

Another fundamental premise of Moffett's approach is that verbal discourse skills transfer readily to writing. Composition is composition, according to Moffett. This can be challenged on both theoretical and empirical grounds. Olson (1976) has argued that writing makes possible the logical complexity of contemporary thought by freeing discourse somewhat from the constraints of memory and allowing for revision. On this view, oral discourse lacks one of the most important aspects of written discourse for the development of thinking skills.

A review article by Groff (1978) gives empirical reason for doubt. Groff reports that the balance of the research on the comparative complexity and error rate of oral and written discourse shows written discourse on a par with, or superior to, oral discourse after the middle years of elementary school. Groff also considers several efforts to improve writing skills through some sort of oral training, finding that, for the most part, they yielded no significant differences. Accordingly, oral discourse cannot unreservedly be accepted as a model for written discourse. McQuillan (1979), doubting the potency of oral practice, cites an especially discouraging finding: Harpin (1976) investigated the effects of oral preparation for writing and found them to be negative. Oral preparation tended to lower various measures of complexity, and, although one might think that simpler is better, impressionistic readings also suggested that the orally prepared pieces were not generally better than the pieces written from scratch.

The foregoing reservations give considerable reason to doubt that Moffett's approach to teaching skills of discourse is optimal. Nonetheless, the program illustrates several instructional tactics that seem important to teaching thinking and that rarely appear in other programs. We conjecture that efforts to teach thinking would benefit from much more attention to the following features of Moffett's program:

- *Complex products.* Much thinking addressed to the real needs of life or scholarship involves complex products of some kind—a functioning business, the layout of one's living room, career plans essays, symphonies (Perkins, 1985). However, most instruction in thinking skills is atomistic, emphasizing test-like or at least very short-term tasks. The realities of thinking are better modeled by Moffett's approach.
- *Time on task.* Considerable research suggests that even finely calculated heuristic guidance will not yield skilled performance quickly. Growth of skills requires a great deal of practice, a feature provided by Moffett's multi-subject multi-year program.
- *Transfer.* The problem of transfer is a recurrent one in the teaching of thinking skills. Moffett's emphasis on applying discourse skills across content areas such as history, science, and the social studies should foster transfer.
- *Transformation.* Transforming activities lead to "deeper" processing of information, with benefits to the student's understanding and retention (Craik & Lockhart 1972; Craik, 1973). In Moffett's program, such transforming tasks as reading aloud, dramatizing what is read, rewriting something in a different genre, or discussing something put this principle to work.

5. MODELING INNER SPEECH AND SELF INSTRUCTION AS A MEANS OF TEACHING THINKING

In his *Cognitive Behavior Modification*, Meichenbaum (1977) reviews a number of recent innovations in therapy that focus on the patient's inner speech and seek to resolve the patient's problems and enhance effectiveness by remaking patterns of inner dialogue. Meichenbaum's work is of interest here both because many of the cases he discusses can be viewed as cases of deficiency in cognitive skills, and because the method seems applicable to teaching cognitive skills in general.

Meichenbaum analyzes a person's activity into three elements: overt behavior, inner speech (including not only language but images) and cognitive structures, reflecting the individual's belief system, covert skills, and so on. The least familiar of the three, inner speech, refers to the ongoing stream of consciousness by which we represent our actions and intentions to ourselves. Meichenbaum's argument is that inner speech plays a pivotal role in one's control of one's own behavior. Roughly speaking, one's covert directions to oneself function in much the same way as do instructions to another, inducing mind-sets, focusing action, criticizing and repatterning prior modes of behavior, and so on. Moreover, often one's inner speech to oneself is the vehicle of cognition, not only reflecting but coming close to constituting one's understanding of the matter at hand. To describe something differently to oneself is to understand it differently.

Therapies that address inner speech seek to alter the ongoing process of the patient's internal dialogue. If the inner speech can be modified, both overt behavior and internal cognitive structures are likely to follow suit.

In practice, the training Meichenbaum advocates involves roughly the following. The therapist or instructor works with individuals or small groups, seeking initially to understand the existing patterns of internal speech and to define directions for revision. For example, impulsive, hyperactive children have been found to lack patterns of inner speech that would focus their attention on the matter at hand and effect a careful deliberate approach. Also, such children may respond more to the rhythm of their inner speech than to its content, thereby limiting its effectiveness (Meichenbaum, 1977, Chapter 1).

For another example, instruction concerned with creative thinking has sometimes proceeded from the observation that many people define themselves as uncreative, tell themselves they are being uninventive while performing creative tasks, and in general talk themselves out of their own potential (Goor & Sommerfeld, 1975; Henshaw, 1977). As the instructor or therapist defines the problem, he begins to model for the learner more effective patterns of internal dialogue, thinking aloud as he himself addresses some task. For example, an instructor might say "Now, I have this problem to solve. I don't want to give up too easily. I'm going to have to be really inventive. That means I'm going to think of lots of ideas. Here's one possibility (the instructor names it). Okay, now another. Yes, and another. I'm just going to let ideas suggest themselves as I look over the problem. Yes, there's another." And so on. Such performances provide patterns of inner-speech behavior that a learner can emulate. This gradual process may involve the learner also thinking aloud as he addresses a task. It may involve Socratic dialogues between instructor and learner. It may involve immediate silent inner speech by the learner, revised according to the instructor's example. In any case, as instruction continues, tasks become progressively more difficult while the attention to inner speech becomes progressively less overt. As the instructor ceases modeling, the learner ceases thinking aloud, dialogue falls off, and the learner, hopefully, develops a silent pattern of coping with the problem at hand.

Meichenbaum reviews considerable evidence for the effectiveness of this general instructional and therapeutic method. To mention one example, treatment of impulsive, hyperactive children has resulted in calmer, more orderly behavior generally and enhanced performance on formal tests of general aptitude and achievement. Furthermore, such gains have proved stable upon retesting after one to three months (Meichenbaum, 1977, p. 31–44). For another example, an effort to teach more inventive patterns of thinking yielded performance superior to that of control groups on standard tests of divergent thinking, preference for complexity, human movement response to an inkblot test, and in self-concept (Meichenbaum, 1975). These measures may not be adequate individually, but taken together they are suggestive of genuine gains in creativity.

This does not imply that modeling inner speech always enhances performance; negative findings also appear in the literature. For example, attempts to improve writing skills (Robin, Armel, & O'Leary, 1975) and arithmetic performance (Burns, 1972) by self-instructional training yielded no gains. Meichenbaum interprets such findings in terms of the learner's readiness for such help. Promoting good problem-solving habits of a general sort will not aid the learner unless he already has at his disposal the basic skills to marshall for the required performance. When such general instruction fails, Meichenbaum suggests, it is because the learner requires better mastery of the component operations. In short, modeling as an instructional tactic can only contribute when it provides know-how the learner is in a position to use. An adequate task-analysis of the problem as the learner faces it is crucial.

The foregoing paragraphs might suggest that one standard format governs instruction by modeling inner speech. On the contrary, a number of variations are promising and have demonstrated advantages. An important option concerns modeling mastery versus modeling coping performance. On the one hand the instructor might "think aloud" in the manner of an expert, smoothly dealing with a situation. On the other hand, the instructor might model problems arising, control slipping, the struggle for direction, good tactics remembered, and so on. Various experimental findings suggest that the latter, staying closer as it does to the learner's actual circumstances, yields superior gains (Meichenbaum, 1977, pp. 120–129).

Another option is to combine a program of rewards with the remaking of patterns of inner speech. Meichenbaum reports that in some instances this double-barreled approach seems to have been especially effective. Often, such efforts have involved the gradual replacement of external rewards with internal rewards administered by inner speech itself, as the student learns to praise himself for following the recommended strategies and dealing effectively with the task.

Modeling can address directly the performance ultimately to be improved, of course. However, very often this seems to be too big a step to take at once. Especially in therapeutic circumstances, in which the learner may face emotional difficulties in connection, for example, with test-taking or social interaction, the new patterns of inner-speech are introduced in connection with imaginary situations of a somewhat different sort. Gradually, practice moves closer to the real problems of concern.

Within the general character of this instructional approach, many other opportunities arise. To mention one example, instruction in inner speech can also include metaphor and images. For example, one program of treatment for overly aggressive children taught them to "go turtle," in times of mounting excitement, emphasizing the turtle image of momentary withdrawal (Robin, Schneider, & Dolnick, 1976). Concerning the practice activities employed, Meichenbaum suggests that role-playing and imaginary scenarios may promote transfer to similar contexts outside the classroom, more so than the use of problems detached from everyday life.

It should not be thought that systematic answers will always be available to the question of which method is best. A case in point concerns the usefulness of learners thinking aloud in imitation of the instructor, rather than proceeding at once with covert speech. While Meichenbaum and Goodman (1971) as well as Palkes, Stewart, and Freedman (1972) found that overt rehearsal yielded greater gains, research in other circumstances disclosed no such effect (Denney, 1975), or an interaction effect with IQ; overt rehearsal benefiting low IQ subjects but perhaps even hindering high IQ subjects (Ridberg, Parke, & Hetherington, 1971). Meichenbaum notes that other choices also seem subject to aptitude-treatment interactions. Above all, Meichenbaum stresses the importance of tailoring the treatment to the situation and the individuals involved. Overriding recipes are less to the point than a sensitive appraisal of the learner's skills and their patterns of deployment under the guidance of inner speech, and an intervention tuned to yield the most gains for the particular circumstances.

In summary, Meichenbaum presents not a program of instruction but an instructional method, along with some evidence for its effectiveness. The method seems appropriate for teaching cognitive processes in general. Some programs discussed here have used it, for instance, the Cognitive Studies Project (Chapter 7), employing Whimbey and Lochhead's (1979) *Problem Solving and Comprehension*. Indeed, the method might be applied to teaching many matters discussed in this book—heuristics for mathematical problem solving, concepts like control of variables from programs based on Piaget, and writing techniques, to name a few. Whether the strategy would serve such diverse content better than other instructional approaches is an empirical question, and one worth exploring in light of the intimate link between inner speech and thought.

6. LOGO AND PROCEDURAL THINKING

The approaches to teaching thinking considered so far in this chapter all have focused on one or another type of language usage—reading, writing, discourse, inner speech. The approach that is considered in this section also focuses on language usage, but the language in this case is one used to communicate with a machine. With the explosive growth in computer technology and the rapidly increasing accessibility of computing resources to people of all ages, facility with one or more computer languages is becoming an increasingly valuable asset. Although many people probably think of computer programming as something that can be done only by specialists after fairly demanding technical training, there is growing evidence that primary school children are capable of writing programs of some complexity if provided with a suitably designed language. Moreover, programming is sometimes considered prototypical of many intellectually demanding tasks, inasmuch as it requires creativity, planning, problem decomposition, hypothesis generation and testing, attention to detail, and so on. Not surprisingly, there has been some speculation that programming could be an effective vehicle for the acquisition of generally useful thinking skills (Nickerson, 1983; Papert, 1972, 1980).

Perhaps the best known effort to use programming in this way is the work that has grown out of the development of the programming language LOGO and the early attempts to use this language for the teaching of what might be called procedural mathematics. Few students discover in mathematics the fulfilling quest that mathematicians do. One could hardly expect this with the mechanics of arithmetic, but one might hope for it with "real" mathematics, as in the axiomatic method of Euclidean geometry or the formalisms of algebra. Yet students often find these disciplines painfully obscure. An innovative approach to this problem involved the design of a new computer language and use of this language with school children of various ages (Feurzeig, Papert, Bloom, Grant, & Solomon, 1969)

The LOGO Language and Early Uses

Central to the approach is a computer language called LOGO, designed to be natural and accessible to beginners. A flexible and powerful programming language despite its simplicity, LOGO provides for subroutining and recursion. LOGO programming serves as a vehicle for exploring varied mathematical and logical concepts.

In the early 70's a number of lesson sequences were developed examining various topics, for instance syllogistic logic, number representations, functions and equations, and strategies in problem solving (Feurzeig, Lukas, Faflick, Grant, Lukas, Morgan, Weiner, & Wexelblat, 1971). In all cases, the students are guided through a series of programming problems in LOGO that help them to explore in detail a particular concept.

For example, the sequence on numbers begins with a number representation consisting simply of marks (xxxxx stands for 5) and LOGO programs to add such marks by concatenation. The sequence advances through various other representations, culminating with the normal Arabic system. The sequence is intended to convey an understanding of the design characteristics of the Arabic and simpler number systems to students who already can use the former, but probably have little understanding of its structure.

For another example, a lesson sequence on number series introduces various strategies of problem solving in the context of writing a LOGO program to solve number series puzzles such as appear on IQ tests: 1, 4, 7, 10, what is the next number? The students help to develop an increasingly complex program, that by the end uses some sophisticated strategies to solve a wide range of such puzzles.

The LOGO view of mathematics education contrasts with conventional approaches in several ways. For instance, the child is invited to use the actions of his own body to model the construction of geometric figures; a computer, not pencil and paper, is his principal tool; and computer programs, not equations solved or theorems proved, are his principal products. Concepts such as the differential are considered accessible to youngsters.

Within this general framework, there is room for more than one philosophy about LOGO-based instruction. One view, reflected in much of the early work at Bolt Beranek and Newman Inc. sees in LOGO a potent vehicle for the conventional contents of mathematics. Fractions, algebra, algebra word problems, trigonometry, and so on, are considered important subject matters to be learned directly. However, the content can be enlivened and made more meaningful and accessible through the LOGO language and LOGO projects, as discussed above. According to this view, LOGO is subversive enough, even in the context of conventional mathematical content. It will transform students' understanding of mathematics without any need to bypass the normal content.

Perhaps because LOGO has not been widely available to school children, it has not yet played an extensive role in mathematics instruction. However, the advent of relatively inexpensive microcomputers with LOGO on them could change that. Currently, there is a resurgence of interest in the use of LOGO as a vehicle for teaching certain aspects of mathematics. The next few years may see increased efforts to develop curriculum around this tool.

Another view about LOGO and mathematics considers the content of conventional mathematics instruction hopelessly moribund. Genuine mathematical thinking has little to do with the contents of conventional mathematics instruction, but a lot to do with the kinds of problem solving issues that arise when students attempt to develop projects in LOGO. Conventional mathematical content has a place in this conception, but a less central one. This view is best represented by the work of Papert and his colleagues in the Artificial Intelligence group of the Massachusetts Institute of Technology over the last decade. It's most familiar application is "turtle geometry."

Turtle Geometry

LOGO mathematics centers on programming activities designed to make things happen that will interest children. Computer generated music or sentences have been utilized, but most extensively developed is "turtle geometry." The "turtle," a triangle pointing in its direction of motion on a CRT screen, will obey simple instructions in LOGO such as "RIGHT 5" followed by "FORWARD 10," which directs the turtle to move five units in its current direction, rotate to its right five degrees, and go forward another ten units. The turtle leaves a trace, creating a line on the screen. The turtle also can be directed not to leave a trace, when this is desired.[3] Out of such commands, programs can be written to fashion geometric designs and pictures. For a simple example of turtle geometry, consider the following routine to draw a square:

```
TO SQUARE
REPEAT 4 [FORWARD 100 RIGHT 90]
END
```

Deceptively simple, this program embodies considerable geometric knowledge—for instance, that the corners of a square are 90 degrees, that the sides are equal, and that therefore the square can be generated by making precisely the same "moves" four times in a row. Students soon direct their activities not to elementary programs like these but to more complex projects.

Documentation of the LOGO project provides numerous examples of what students have done with the resources of LOGO. Here we summarize one presented by Papert (1980) to convey the flavor of a typical session. Two students decide to make a flower on the screen. How can they go about this? One remembers a program written last week to draw a quarter circle of arbitrary size. To make a petal, they try to put two quarter circles together. Their first effort yields a half circle instead of a petal shape. However, they quickly diagnose the problem: they need a turn at the end of the first quarter circle.

---

[3]The first turtles were mechanical, directed by remote control from the computer. Such a turtle can draw pictures on a sheet of paper by lowering and raising a pen as it moves about in response to programmed commands.

Prescribing a turn, they get two arcs one after the other. The turtle turned the wrong way. One student, though, notices that the figure looks like a bird flying. Perhaps this can be used later. The students try a turn in the other direction, and after some further thinking determine the correct angle to turn to get the figure to close. Making a subroutine called PETAL, they use it as a component in a higher-level subroutine called FLOWER. They soon discover how to make flowers of various sizes with varying numbers of petals, and move on to a program that makes fields of flowers on the screen.

Such activities certainly sound engaging, but can the student learn through them? Underlying the approach is the assumption that learning depends, more than anything else, on the learner relating new information to models he already has. In this spirit, the LOGO turtle is an entity the student can think of as a creature navigating in the real world. Students doing projects such as the one above are encouraged to tackle programming problems by "walking out" what they want the turtle to do, and then translating their own actions into a program for the turtle to follow. Papert (1980) writes of "ego-syntonic" mathematics, meaning mathematics chosen and presented so that the learner can map it into domains with which he is familiar, such as the actions of his own body.

Is there a risk of sacrificing mathematical content to method in LOGO based instruction? Papert argues that LOGO activities convey considerable content. By their nature, LOGO projects raise many mathematical problems that children thereby face and learn about in a realistic, well-motivated context. Problems of trigonometric relationships come up naturally, for instance, in the course of trying to write programs that construct various shapes. Nor are theorems left out of the picture. LOGO and turtle geometry provide a context in which theorems can be proved and applied—and sometimes the proof is clearer than in the conventional approach. For example, the classic theorem that the sum of the angles of a triangle equals 180 degrees takes on a simpler logic if one sees the triangle as the trace of a turtle drawing its perimeter. The turtle has to make three turns totaling 360 degrees on its path around the triangle (ending up pointing in its original direction), and the interior angles are simply the complements of the angles the turtle turns. The same proof generalizes immediately to polygons of any number of sides. Whereas the traditional proof has an ad hoc character, this one seems to reflect the real structure of the situation in the sense that Wertheimer (1959) espouses.

Papert (1980) proposes that LOGO also can be used to lead students toward an understanding of more advanced topics, such as Newton's laws of motion. Here, the students work with "dynaturtles," which behave like Newtonian particles. Instead of specifying the distance a turtle should travel, the student might specify the velocity or the acceleration operating on the turtle. Research has shown that the equations of the physics of motion lack concrete intuitive meaning for many students. Indeed, they predict interactions that most people find counterintuitive, although students who only manipulate equations may never realize this. LOGO and dynaturtles might provide experiences of Newtonian motion that would develop in the learner an intuitive model matching the formalisms of dynamics. It is even easy to introduce the concept of the differential, which takes on a natural meaning in the world of turtles as an incremental step in a specified direction. Papert (1980) acknowledges the natural objection that such playing around is not real physics as a student of physics would do it. But he argues the importance of transitional experiences in making physics meaningful.

Papert expects LOGO worlds like the world of the dynaturtle to provide models for much more than their immediate contents. So far, we have considered the LOGO approach principally as an innovative way of learning certain aspects of mathematics, an approach that is intended to engage children in something much more like mathematical thinking than conventional instruction usually does. But mathematics aside, Papert sees LOGO as a means of fostering thinking and learning skills in general. He argues that programming in LOGO provides students with practice in dealing with process descriptions and with powerful concepts such as "debugging." The activities of thinking and learning themselves are best viewed as processes, indeed processes subject to "programming" and "debugging." Accordingly, a student versed in LOGO might be expected to transfer his skills for dealing with procedures to other mechanisms that also use procedures—such as himself. One might wonder whether students would make such transfers spontaneously. Whether or not they would, it is not part of the LOGO philosophy to wait and see; students are explicitly encouraged to make such transfers in appropriate circumstances.

LOGO with Handicapped Persons

Another area of application for LOGO, as well as other computer systems, involves physically and mentally handicapped children and young people. Goldenberg (1978) discusses a number of cases in point. Jay, for example, was an 18 year old victim of cerebral palsy who was generally thought to be mildly retarded. Given access to LOGO and turtle geometry, Jay was able, by typing painstakingly on the keyboard of the computer with a headstick, to display a keen intelligence and rapid mastery of a number of computer skills. Goldenberg notes that the reactions of several handicapped children to the LOGO system challenge accepted theory about human development. In particular, these children showed much more ability than any theory that makes intellectual development strongly dependent on the development of motor skills would have predicted.

Goldenberg offers an interesting perspective on such interventions that has bearing on improving mental functioning in general: the computer as eyeglasses. Goldenberg notes that most interventions either provide exercise to impart skills, such as eye exercises for the weak-sighted, or provide a substitute, such as Braille. However, eyeglasses supply an interesting synthesis of the two: eyeglasses assist the eyes but, at the same time, maintain their use. Goldenberg suggests that computers might be used as eyeglasses—to give abilities an assist but, at the same time, to keep the person using those abilities. This same philosophy could apply to teaching thinking to able-bodied people. For instance, it is often suggested that word processing equipment can make writing a more manageable and engaging activity by making editing and the production of clean copy easier. Thus, the "eyeglasses" of a word processor might foster the development of thinking skills relevant to writing.

Besides physical impairments, Goldenberg (1979) also discusses autism. Joey, for example, was a 12-year-old autistic child who seemed deaf and reportedly never had spoken. Joey showed interest in driving a robot turtle around the floor by hand to draw on the paper there, but had difficulty with the pen coming out and being placed too high. After Joey, eventually with the help of Goldenberg, had resolved these problems, Goldenberg announced for the sake of a video camera that he was going to raise the pen using the computer, to see what Joey would do. In a few moments, Joey said, "Down!," and, upon Goldenberg complying, "Thank you." These were the first words Joey was known to have spoken.

Because of such experiences, Goldenberg urges the importance of computers not only as "eyeglasses" but as motivators. The engagement that computers can engender with both children and adults is a well-known phenomenon, and it applies to people who have handicaps as well as to those who do not. The point is particularly important because undermotivation is as much of a problem for people with physical or mental handicaps as for those without them. In particular, retardation may reflect two factors that compound one another: the faulty functioning of mental processes, and the lack of motivation, which means that the person does not strive to master tasks and skills, and hence does not accumulate an adequate repertoire of them.

Evaluation

The early work on LOGO received only limited evaluation on a very small scale. Applications of LOGO to handicapped children have not been subjected to formal evaluations. Consequently, we concentrate here on two recent efforts to evaluate the impact of LOGO, turtle geometry, and similar projects, on students.

An evaluation of the effectiveness of LOGO instruction appears in Papert, Watt, diSessa, and Weir (1979) and Watt (1979). These documents report detailed case studies and summary conclusions for a LOGO course involving 16 students, conducted in Brookline, Massachusetts during the 1977/1978 academic year. The participants were selected to span a wide range of academic abilities. Included were several with considerable learning difficulties, some mediocre students, and several good academic performers. The classes consisted of four students, each one having at his disposal a computer with keyboard, display, and disk memory. There was one teacher for the four students, plus frequent observers. (The authors maintain that one terminal per student is a necessity, but they suggest that a single teacher could handle many more than four students.) Each class met for about 25 sessions with a total exposure of from about 22 to about 35 hours.

The instruction was relatively non-directive. The teacher introduced the basics of LOGO, offered advice when asked, occasionally made suggestions when students encountered difficulty, recommended projects when students seemed at sea, and generally refrained from criticism and from resisting directions the children found attractive.

Assessment was based on a case study approach. The students' activities were closely analyzed by the teacher and observers, and their progress traced. The computers the students used kept complete records of their keystroke-by-keystroke actions, and these records were analyzed. The evaluation appears to us to have been reasonably conservative.

Papert et al. (1979) give special attention to reviewing the work of the exceptional students, those academically talented or disadvantaged. A student who had shown high academic skills in other contexts performed exceptionally well on the LOGO instruction too, understanding concepts quickly, undertaking complex projects, and working flexibly in a top-down or bottom-up manner. Of equal interest is the progress of those with minimal academic talent. One such student had been diagnosed as having severe learning disabilities. These indeed showed up in his LOGO work: he had trouble remembering how LOGO commands were spelled and what names he had given to programs he had written. He found typing a painful process, having to scan the keyboard for the next letter, not remembering where it was, and often passing over it several times before locating it. Yet he found the LOGO environment engaging enough that he pushed on despite these difficulties, carrying out projects of some sophistication.

Another interesting case involved an exceptionally poor academic performer whose scores on national achievement tests ranked in the second and third percentiles. In fact, this student never learned to use LOGO in the intended manner at all. However, she became engaged by the machine as a text editor. Painstakingly eliminating typographical errors and frequently asking the instructor for help with spelling and grammar, she wrote two short letters and several stories. These were only eight or ten lines in length, but they represented a substantial achievement for her since she had never written stories *at all* in her conventional classroom setting. In the LOGO setting, however, she not only did so but printed out multiple copies on the printer, distributing them to teachers, friends, and family.

Papert et al. (1979) mention several occasions in which students of doubtful ability did creditable work. They also note that the students' attitudes and performance in other classes seemed to improve, according to the students' teachers, although they have no formal measures of this. However, the LOGO program was not uniformly successful in engaging and stimulating the students. For instance, Watt (1979), writing detailed accounts of the experiences of each of the sixteen students, discusses one student classified as learning disabled who resisted learning LOGO in various ways until the last few sessions, and a couple of able students who competently dealt with LOGO projects but remained uncaptivated by LOGO, achieving less than they otherwise might have.

One of the objectives of the Brookline LOGO course was that the students learn the elements of the LOGO language. Papert et al. (1979) report that two of the students did not attain independent use of a set of LOGO skills considered basic. They had hoped that all students would do so. One of those who did not was the student who used the computer for writing instead; the other was the learning disabled student who resisted acquiring LOGO skills.

The authors break down gains in knowledge of turtle geometry into a number of aspects. For instance, some students initially have little sense of the magnitude of numbers, thinking that although FORWARD 10 makes a very short line, FORWARD 12 might make a much longer one. Students may not at first appreciate the complementarity of operations such as RIGHT 20 and LEFT 20, or that RIGHT 10 followed by RIGHT 10 has the same effect as RIGHT 20.

Earlier, we noted that certain theorems of geometry can be formulated and proved rigorously in LOGO. Some of the students discovered versions of these theorems, although typically just special cases of them. Proofs of the theorems were not explored. Sometimes the authors provide information about how many students achieved understanding of the elements of turtle geometry under discussion, but sometimes they do not. In general, it seems clear that the students mastered a number of aspects of turtle geometry that would be straightforward to a mathematically and geometrically sophisticated person, but are not obvious to youngsters. Turtle geometry seems likely to us to have fulfilled one of LOGO's aims: providing a model in terms of which abstractions such as angle and distance come to have concrete meanings.

Another objective of the LOGO instruction was developing problem-solving skills. Unfortunately, progress on this theme is not discussed as such by the authors. Throughout Papert et al. (1979) and Watt (1979), the treatment of individual episodes and commentary on such matters as cognitive style gives some sense of the students' progress with problem-solving skills helpful in the LOGO environment. Clearly, the students developed a number of skills specific to programming, but we are less certain that they developed powerful general skills. Rather, it often seems that the students discovered ways to work within the limitations of their own cognitive-stylistic predilections. We do not find bottom-up programmers becoming top-down programmers too, for example. However, it may be too much to expect LOGO instruction to induce such changes in a few hours.

Other somewhat more quantitative and critical evaluations of LOGO instruction have been conducted by the Center for Children and Technology of the Bank Street College of Education. One study focused on two classes of 25 children, the first composed of 8 to 9 year olds and the other of 11 to 12 year olds. The students in each class received about 25 hours of LOGO instruction during an academic year. The conduct of the class followed the generally non-directive style favored by Papert.

The evaluation examined the students' abilities to predict what would happen when various LOGO commands were executed, to write LOGO programs to draw shapes, with constraints as to the kind of program, and to debug some simple programs. In many respects, the results were disappointing. The mean score for commands understood was 34 out of 100 possible points, with a very large standard deviation of 25. As to programming, the children generally could write drawing programs consisting of a series of direct commands, but many could not use variables or a procedure with a conditional test. The students usually could locate syntactic bugs, but most of them missed bugs in the procedures (Pea, 1983).

Another study singled out seven children 11 to 12 years of age who averaged over 50 hours of LOGO programming experience and had used iteration and recursion in some contexts. The study probed the students' understanding of recursion by asking them to predict the behavior of a series of increasingly complex programs. The study confirmed a number of concerns about the students' level of understanding that had emerged from classroom observation. Most of the students did not understand how recursion works. They did not understand conditional test statements in reading a program, even though they had used such statements in writing programs. In general, the students often produced programs without really comprehending how the programs worked, by the rote use of "chunks" of programs from other students or the teacher (Kurland & Pea, 1983).

A third experiment examined whether LOGO instruction improved general planning skills. A number of students who had had considerable LOGO programming experience in the course of a year and a matched control group with no programming experience were given a planning task of scheduling classroom chores. The students had to devise and refine a plan for executing the chores. The measures addressed the efficiency of the plans, the quality of the revisions, and the types of decisions made during the planning process. No differences emerged between the LOGO group and the control group (Pea, 1983). This could be viewed as a failure of planning skills to transfer outside the LOGO context. However, the experimenters also observed that the students did not do that much planning in the LOGO context, typically developing programs at the keyboard by a serendipitous process rather than thinking them out in advance.

Taking these two sources of evaluative information together, we are inclined to the view that LOGO represents a potentially powerful instructional tool, but that, just how to use that tool best has not been adequately explored. Findings to date give little reason to believe that simply having students use LOGO in the classroom for a limited period dramatically transforms the minds of those students. Adequate mastery of the LOGO language to permit more sophisticated projects may call for much more direct instruction than anticipated by Papert. Development of thinking skills in a LOGO context and transfer to other contexts are again matters that may require direct instructional attention for good results. On the other hand, it is also possible that simply a substantially longer period of immersion in LOGO would yield stronger effects. In any case, the question of how best to tap the potential of LOGO clearly needs more investigation before firm conclusions can be drawn regarding the potential of this tool for developing or enhancing generally useful thinking skills.

7. THE LANGUAGE APPROACH IN GENERAL

In this chapter, we have reviewed several efforts to enhance thinking skills based on fostering language skills, and, in one case, skills with a computer language. What can be said about the prospects of this approach in general? As with the other major approaches reviewed here, one would like much more in the way of solid empirical evaluations. As with the other approaches, some encouraging data exist, but one would like more.

What distinctive features might the language perspective have to offer? We think that perhaps its single most advantageous feature is the emphasis on complex products—essays, stories, arguments, computer programs, and the like. In real world situations the products of intellectual activities range far from typical textbook problems. They characteristically have many parts and aspects, and require an extended process of construction and revision, as with, for example, a mathematical proof, an essay, a painting, a business operation. The language approach, in its attention to complex representation, mirrors this reality, at least to some degree.

In addition, we recall the generally acknowledged importance of representations to problem solving. Whether one is doing mathematics, designing an advertising campaign, or planning a picnic, such devices as diagrams, lists, and narrative descriptions can abet powerfully the systematicity and objectivity of thought. In some real-life situations, these representations can become quite complex. Furthermore, we should keep in mind the proposal of Vygotsky that thought is, in part, internalized speech. Therefore, if attention to overt representation allows us to handle matters in a more systematic and objective way, subsequent internalization might do the same for our silent thinking.

This is not to say the other approaches reviewed hold contrary positions on these points. Clearly, for example, a Piagetian approach might involve the design of whole experiments, and one certainly can use a heuristics approach to writing. But the fact is that nothing in the philosophy of these approaches pushes in such a direction and many programs based on these approaches do not pay much heed to the construction of complex representations. A language centered program tends to do so, an emphasis we take to be one aspect of instruction in how to think.

10 Thinking About Thinking

Some programs to teach thinking have taken the approach of focusing on thinking as subject matter. The assumption is that a better understanding of the nature of thought will improve one's own thinking ability. In some cases the material is structured so as to help the student discover principles; in other cases the principles are presented directly. What is taught about thinking draws from many areas—philosophy, logic, rhetoric, cognitive psychology, linguistics, decision theory—and addresses a variety of topics—human cognitive capabilities and limitations, common reasoning problems, effects of culture on thinking, and so on. Programs that fall in this category often also teach heuristics, but tend to emphasize the importance of not only knowing how to apply particular heuristics but understanding why they work.

1. THE PHILOSOPHY FOR CHILDREN PROGRAM

Like many of the other programs described in this book, the Philosophy for Children program, which was developed by Matthew Lipman, grew out of a conviction that traditional educational curricula were lacking something of fundamental importance.

> The intellectual possibilities of the American school child remain largely unrecognized and unexplored. We teach him to think *about* various subjects—English, history, social studies and so on. But we do not teach him to think about thinking, although he is capable of doing so and would be

interested in doing so. We do not sufficiently encourage him to think for himself, to form independent judgments, to be proud of his personal insights, to be proud of having a point of view he can call his own, to be pleased with his prowess in reasoning. (Lipman, 1976, 21–22)

Concerning whether children should be taught *about* the human mind, Lipman (1976) asks why not?

Certainly the physical environment is a fit subject for the child to study. The human body is a fit subject. The structure of society is a fit subject. Why then is the human mind not a fit subject? Children are as much aware of and as keenly interested in their thoughts as they are in their bodily functions, but nowhere is *mind* in the curriculum. (p. 23)

With respect to *why* this omission, Lipman makes the following somewhat cynical but thought-provoking suggestion: "Mindlessness does not seem to threaten the established order; thoughtfulness might. An irrational social order is threatened far more by rationality than by irrationality" (1976, p. 23).

Children as Natural Philosophers

A basic assumption underlying the program is that children are philosophers by nature and that when philosophical issues are phrased in terminology that children understand, rather than in the formal jargon of the professional philosopher, children find them intrinsically interesting. Indeed, not only do children find philosophical, and especially epistemological, questions intrinsically interesting, they often reflect on them and discuss them in their own terms spontaneously.

Matthews (1976) notes many examples of what he calls "philosophical whimsey" in children's literature. By philosophical whimsey he means a style of writing in which questions of the kind that engross philosophers appear in the context of stories that are meaningful to the young reader. Matthews (1976) puts it this way. "What philosophers do (in rather disciplined and sustained ways) is much closer than is usually appreciated to what at least some children rather naturally do (albeit fitfully, and without the benefit of sophisticated techniques)" (p. 14 and 15). Matthews concludes from his examination of philosophical whimsey in children's literature that "the impulse to do philosophy comes very naturally to at least some members of the human race. To have philosophical thoughts is for them as natural as making music or playing games, and quite as much a part of being human" (p. 15).

The General Approach

Bynum (1976) describes the Philosophy for Children Program as being focused upon "the encouragement and development of philosophical reasoning skills and the application of such skills to questions of personal significance to the student" (p. 2). By way of contrasting the program's aims with that of indoctrination, he characterizes one of its chief goals as helping children to think for themselves—"to explore alternatives to their own point of view, to consider evidence more logically and objectively, and to search for presuppositions and reasons for their beliefs" (p. 2). Philosophy is emphasized not simply because it provides a way of teaching process (an argument that one might make in defense of a choice of puzzles as content); rather, the philosophical issues the children meet are considered important issues to confront. The hope is to reinforce an interest in philosophical questions that will persist long beyond the duration of the course, and an enrichment of the lives of the students not only in terms of their ability to think but in terms of what they think about.

Evans (1976) identifies three aspects of classroom sessions in the Philosophy for Children Program that he considers to be of philosophical importance and to justify calling such classes philosophical. The three aspects are: (1) philosophical commitments to impartiality and objectivity, to relevance, to consistency, to comprehensiveness, to nondiscrimination with respect to the source of information, and to the search for defensible reasons as the basis for decision making and behavior; (2) philosophical skills (the skills necessary for rational inquiry and critical analysis); and (3) the confrontation of genuine philosophical issues (even if on a rudimentary level).

The Philosophy for Children program places much stress on class discussions, an emphasis that is predicated on the assumption that discussion skills are the foundation of thinking skills. The sharing of ideas, the pooling of intellectual strengths, the process of reasoning collaboratively are promoted by the instructional approach, and the class is encouraged to perceive itself as a "community of inquiry." Although great care is taken to ensure that the subject matter of the class discussions is intrinsically interesting to the students, the fundamental purpose of the course is not so much the acquisition of knowledge, but the development and strengthening of basic reasoning skills.

> The skills involved include, for example, drawing perceptual, logical, and causal inferences; making associations and analogies; forming hypotheses; making significant distinctions; considering alternatives; and searching for reasons, explanations and assumptions. They presuppose, and therefore encourage, an objective and impartial attitude, a commitment to consistency, and a respect for other people as important sources of information, ideas, and attitudes. (Bynum, 1976, p. 4)

Lipman does not share the view that in order for a program to be effective in improving basic reasoning processes it must be devoid of meaningful content. On the contrary, he argues for enrichment of content across the board. He decries what he calls the "deplorable trivialization of content" of much of the material that grade school students encounter in their typical courses (Lipman, 1976). Moreover, he reacts strongly negatively to the approach that is sometimes taken of attempting to sensationalize the trivial "so as to compel the child's interest in what remains fundamentally inane."

The role of the teacher in the program, as characterized by Bynum (1976), is that of a "talented questioner" who guides but does not dominate discussions in which children are encouraged to share ideas and explore them as a group. The teacher is responsible for creating a classroom climate that facilitates the kinds of interactions among the students that will lead to discoveries about their own minds and thinking processes.

While the importance of discovery as a means of learning is emphasized throughout the program, Lipman takes care to point out that *what* is discovered is not incidental:

> Discovery as a method can be only as important as the product that is discovered. If discovery techniques were to be restricted to trivial or banal materials, the result would be to disenchant students as to the possibilities of a technique that turned out always to be so fruitless and unrewarding. (1976, p. 27)

It is important, in other words, to structure materials and situations so that the things the students discover, at least some significant portion of the time, are things that they find not only interesting but of some lasting value.

The Program

Curriculum materials are contained in a set of novels to be read by the students, and accompanying instruction manuals for use by the teachers. The basic novel, which is titled *Harry Stottlemeier's Discovery*, is intended for fifth and sixth graders. The goal is to provide the students with certain fundamental reasoning tools that can be applied in a variety of contexts. A central theme is "thinking about thinking." As the title of the book suggests, the possibility of discovering the principles of reasoning is emphasized, as opposed to learning them by consulting authoritative sources.

The book features Harry Stottlemeier and several of his friends and classmates, and describes in story form their interactions and conversations, many of which center on one or another aspect of thinking. Each of the 17 chapters in the book can be read in a few minutes (probably less than 10) by a moderately skilled reader. Each chapter introduces, in the context of the story, several "leading ideas." Among the leading ideas that occur in Stottlemeier are the following:

The process of inquiry
Discovery and invention
Figuring things out: inference
How thinking leads to understanding
Inductive reasoning
Styles of thinking
Considering consequences when deciding what to do
What is a generalization?
Contradiction
What is a possibility?
Causes and effects
Explanations and descriptions

No claim is made of dealing definitively with these topics. Sometimes they are introduced in the story only indirectly. However, the story does provide a context in terms of which such ideas can be discussed and it motivates discussion of them.

Accompanying *Harry Stottlemeier's Discovery* is an instructional manual, *Philosophical Inquiry*, that contains discussion plans, exercises and suggested activities designed to facilitate the assimilation and use of the leading ideas. The manual is organized to match the chapter organization of the novel. Each of its 17 sections begins with a listing of the leading ideas in its corresponding chapter. Each of these ideas is treated in the manual in turn. Discussion plans and exercises are provided for the teacher's use. The teacher is encouraged, however, not to use such materials to structure the class rigidly, but rather to facilitate the emergence of the key ideas from the students' discussion of the story and to reinforce those ideas when they appear.

Other texts or novels, which are intended to be sequels to "Stottlemeier," are somewhat more narrowly focused, and appropriate for higher grades. These include: *Tony: Reasoning in Science*, for grades 6 and 7, *Lisa: Reasoning in Ethics*, for grades 7 to 9; *Suki: Reasoning in Language Arts*, also for grades 7 to 9; and *Mark: Reasoning in Social Studies*, for grades 8 to 10. Each text has an accompanying instructional manual. The approach in each case is fundamentally the same. The characters in the novel find themselves confronted with an intellectual or philosophical question or challenge of one type or another—what constitutes a good scientific explanation; how does one determine the acceptability of a set of moral values; what is a society? These issues are then discussed in class, with the aid of the plans, exercises, and activities presented in the instructional manuals, and the hope is that both teachers and students will discover important principles not only about the issues raised but about reasoning and thought processes per se.

The Philosophy for Children materials are available from The Institute for the Advancement of Philosophy for Children (IAPC), which was established as a division of Montclair State College in Montclair, New Jersey in 1974. IAPC engages in curriculum development, educational research and teacher training. It publishes books for both children and teachers and the periodical, *Thinking*.

In addition to curriculum material, the Institute has produced some books that are intended to provide for teachers a rationale for the Philosophy for Children Program and general guidance regarding the teaching of philosophy to grade school students. It also has produced a set of filmstrips to illustrate for teachers some of the classroom methods that are used in the program. These materials are not promoted as sufficient, however, to equip a teacher to implement The Philosophy for Children Program or to use the curriculum materials effectively in the classroom. Considerable emphasis is placed on the importance of obtaining some formal training in the program's methodology before attempting to use the materials. Three ways of obtaining the necessary training are offered by the Institute: (1) year-long workshops (2–1/2 hours per week) conducted on site by IAPC-trained teachers, (2) two-week on-site workshops also conducted by IAPC-trained teachers, and (3) two-week residential workshops conducted during the summer at camp locations.

Material describing the program lists the following as the thinking skills that it attempts to teach:

Analyzing value statements
Constructing hypotheses
Defining terms
Developing concepts
Discovering alternatives
Drawing inferences from hypothetical syllogisms
Drawing inferences from single premises
Drawing inferences from double premises
Finding underlying assumptions
Formulating causal explanations
Formulating questions
Generalizing
Giving Reasons
Grasping part-whole and whole-part connections
Identifying and using criteria
Knowing how to deal with ambiguities

Knowing how to treat vagueness
Looking out for informal fallacies
Making connections
Making distinctions
Operationalizing concepts by citing effects
Providing instances and illustrations
Recognizing contextual aspects of truth and falsity
Recognizing differences of perspective
Recognizing interdependence of means and ends
Standardizing ordinary language sentences
Taking all considerations into account
Using ordinal or relational logic
Working with analogies
Working with consistency and contradiction

The purpose of the Institute's journal, *Thinking*, as expressed on the editorial page of the first issue (January 1979), is "to act as a clearinghouse of information, an arena for controversy, and a forum for philosophy and educational articles dealing with philosophy for children and related topics." The stated intent is to publish transcripts of classroom dialogue, reports of educational experiments, selected excerpts from published writing both traditional and contemporary, articles by philosophers of law on children's intellectual rights, and other things relevant to the teaching of thinking skills to children.

Evaluation

The first effort to apply the approach occurred in the school year of 1970–71 when a course was given at the Rand School in Montclair, New Jersey, by Lipman and two assistants. The student body of the school was described as being quite heterogeneous, and included children from lower-middle and middle-income families. The class, which contained 20 fifth grade students, met for 40 minutes twice a week for nine weeks.

Harry Stottlemeier's Discovery was used as the basis for discussion. A chapter was read either by the instructor or by the students at the beginning of a class session and then Stottlemeier's discoveries were discussed by the class. Lipman's notes written following the second class session expressed pleasant surprise at how readily the students appeared to grasp the ideas that the story was intended to convey.

A control group of 20 children received social science instruction instead of the Philosophy for Children course. Both groups (the experimental and the control) were given four parts of the California Test of Mental Maturity (1963 Revision Long Form) before participating in the courses and showed no difference in their scores. The four sub-tests that were used were "Inferences," "Opposites," "Analogies," and "Similarities." Immediately after the completion of the nine-week course, the students were retested on the same four tests excepting that the items were taken from the short form (1963 Revision), and the experimental group did significantly better than the control group (Lipman, 1976).

In 1973, Milton Bierman, who was Director of Pupil Services in the public schools of Montclair and the person responsible for the original design of the study, compared the two groups with respect to grade equivalency scores on the reading sub-test of the Iowa Test of Basic Skills (Form 6). The students were now 7th graders and two and one-half years had passed since their participation in the Philosophy for Children course. The comparison yielded a statistically significant difference in favor of the treatment group (Lipman, 1976). The magnitude of the difference is not given.

The Philosophy for Children material has now been used in several schools. Several testimonials as to the effectiveness of the program have appeared in *Thinking*. Some formal evaluations have also been done. One of these involved eight students (five experimentals and three controls) ranging in age from 11 to 16 who were enrolled at the Devereux Day School in Scottsdale, Arizona, a school for learning disabled and emotionally handicapped youth (Simon, 1979; also briefly reported in Lipman, Sharp, & Oscanyan, 1980, Appendix B.) All eight of the students had been referred to the program by teachers in response to a request to refer their "best thinkers." The partitioning into experimental and control groups was made on the basis of which of the students' schedules permitted attendance at a philosophy seminar that was to meet three times a week. It is interesting to note that the seminar was treated as a "gifted program," a point the investigator considered important for motivational purposes. The mean WISC IQ of the experimental group was 93 and that of the control group 102. The students in the experimental group attended approximately fifty 30-minute sessions with the Stottlemeier program over a period of about eight months. No information is given regarding the instructional procedures used with the control subjects.

Several additions and/or modifications were made to the Philosophy for Children program as presented in the manual accompanying *Harry Stottlemeier's Discovery* to meet the special needs of these students: (1) the novel was read aloud only by the most proficient readers and discussion of leading ideas and enrichment activities were inserted at appropriate times during the class; (2) each session began with a review of the major points covered in the preceding session (including pertinent vocabulary and concepts); also two sessions devoted entirely to review were inserted following every three or four chapters; (3) practical applications of the principles of logic that were being studied were emphasized, and practice was provided in analyzing logically such things as advertisements, letters to the editor, and political cartoons; (4) the Stottlemeier novel was edited in places to make the story move faster when this was necessary to hold the interest of this age group (Stottlemeier was written with 10-year-olds in mind); and (5) when it seemed appropriate, activities other than those prescribed in the course guide were added for remedial or enrichment purposes.

Performance was evaluated before and after the training period by means of four tests: Levels II and III Inference Subtests of the California Test of Mental Maturity (CTMM) and the Auditory and Visual Association Subtests of the Illinois Test of Psycholinguistic Abilities (ITPA). The Inference Subtests were given without the enforcement of the specified time limitations. For both groups performance on the second taking of the tests was better than on the first, but the magnitude of the improvement was generally greater for the experimental subjects than for the controls. The performance of the two groups did not differ significantly on the pretraining tests; however, the experimentals did significantly better than the controls on two of the tests administered after training (Level II Inference and Auditory Associations), and did marginally significantly better ($p = .07$) on a third (Level III Inference). The post-training between-group differences were greatest with respect to critical thinking skills as measured by Level II of the CTMM Inference Subtest (35% improvement by experimental group, 13% improvement by controls).

Simon offers a number of specific suggestions regarding how to make effective use of the Philosophy for Children program with learning-disabled or emotionally-handicapped students. Among other things, he advocates emphasis on quality of understanding rather than quantity of material covered, which seems like good advice for any educational endeavor. With respect to the effectiveness of the Philosophy for Children program, Simon concluded that "the data indicate the program is valid, and the degree of improvement in critical thinking skills merits the continuation of the philosophy seminar for Upper School students who are referred by their teachers as the 'best thinkers' in the classroom" (p. 33).

Lipman, Sharp, & Oscanyan (1980, Appendix B) summarize the results of four evaluative studies of implementations of the Philosophy for Children program, the two studies already mentioned (Lipman, 1976; Simon, 1979) and two others, one of which was conducted by Haas (1976) and one by the Educational Testing Service of Princeton, New Jersey. The Haas study is reported very sketchily. It involved two groups of 200 students each (5th and 6th grade) from four schools in the Newark, N.J. school system; the students from two schools served as the experimental groups and those from the other two as controls. Details regarding the teaching of either the experimental or control groups are not given. The investigator reported good results in reading improvement for the children who had had the Philosophy for Children instruction but not conclusive evidence of improvement in logical thinking. Noting the difference between her results and those reported by Lipman (1976), she concluded that they appear to be highly teacher dependent: "Teachers who stress reading can produce significant improvements in reading with it, while a teacher who stresses reasoning can produce significant improvement in reasoning using the materials" (Haas, 1976, quoted in Lipman, Sharp, & Oscanyan, 1980, p. 218).

Perhaps the most ambitious evaluation of the Philosophy for Children program was undertaken by the Educational Testing Service of Princeton, N.J. This involved a two-year experiment from September 1976 to June 1978. Subjects were children in grades 5 through 8 in school systems of Newark and Pompton Lakes, New Jersey. In each location there were about 200 students in the experimental group and 200 in the control group. Teachers were given training two hours per week for a year. Teacher training occurred in parallel with the classes for children. Students were exposed to the program for approximately 2–1/4 hours per week. The objective of the experiment was to determine whether such students would be able to attain:

1. Significant improvement in any or all of the three areas of reasoning treated in the philosophy for children program:
   a. drawing formal inferences and identifying fallacies
   b. discovering alternatives and possibilities
   c. providing reasons and explanations
2. Significant improvement in ideational fluency or productivity
3. Significant improvement in academic readiness as measured by teacher assessments
4. Significant improvement in basic skill (reading and mathematics) performance (p. 220).

To assess the effect of training, the Metropolitan Achievement Tests were used in Newark and the Comprehensive Test of Basic Skills was used in Pompton Lakes. The test results were generally supportive of the conclusion that the Philosophy for Children program was effective in improving the intellectual performance of the students. In particular, improvements (over and above those realized by the control groups) were noted in reading and mathematics and in various aspects of both creative and formal reasoning. Teachers' appraisals of the effect of the program were also reported to be highly favorable.

A problem in assessing these results is that no information is given regarding the treatment of the control subjects. Moreover, the magnitudes of the gains on individual tests that were used for assessment purposes are not given. The emphasis throughout the report is on statistical significance as opposed to degree of improvement.

Our own subjective assessment of the Philosophy for Children program is positive. The assumption that children are natural philosophers and capable of thinking deeply about matters of philosophical significance, especially if given some encouragement to do so, is an appealing one. In taking the students seriously as thinkers whose thoughts are worth sharing and understanding, we suspect the program has a positive effect on students' attitudes that may be difficult to measure. The materials that have been prepared for classroom use are rich in content and seem likely to engage the students in thoughtful discussion. We do suspect that results obtained in the classroom may depend rather strongly on the skillfulness of the teacher, but that is a comment that could be made of just about every program we have considered.

2. THE ANATOMY OF ARGUMENT

Teaching *about* can be a risky approach to teaching *how*: teaching anatomy to the athlete will not necessarily improve his athletic performance. However, a recent text by Toulmin, Rieke, and Janik (1979) may well impart reasoning skills by teaching about them. Entitled *An Introduction to Reasoning*, the text could be considered an anatomy of argument. A general structure for arguments is presented, along with examples from science, medicine, sports writing, ethics, and other fields. Thoughtful, systematic, and obviously pertinent to everyday reasoning, this text teaches a perspective on argument that could improve reasoning skills. Toulmin, Rieke, and Janik make no explicit claim that this will occur; nonetheless, the text seems to us better suited for the purpose than many others that specifically address it.

In general approach, *An Introduction to Reasoning* is an extension of Toulmin's (1958) *The Uses of Argument* in which the author presented a revisionary view of the nature of argument. Toulmin held that the conventional emphasis on syllogistic and other formal patterns of inference yielded a misleading view of argumentation. A more realistic model of argument can be found by examining examples from science or law. A basic premise of Toulmin's earlier work, and of the volume we are now considering, is that arguments in different fields differ in fundamental ways, and that the syllogistic approach fails to acknowledge this sufficiently. For instance, in science principles of inference attempt to capture the structure of nature, whereas in law principles of inference are matters of statute and precedent. Likewise, fields differ importantly in what is at stake: in science, the fate of a theory, which in any case would probably not be settled by any single episode, and in law, the fate of a person, who might be sent to prison. Again, manners of argumentation differ. Despite controversy, science is fundamentally a cooperative venture, the authors hold. Law, on the other hand, uses the adversarial format of the courtroom.

This plea to recognize important differences might suggest that the authors have no general view of argument. On the contrary, such a view is one of the strongest features of the book. The structure of argument that they suggest, which is inherited from Toulmin (1958), appears in Figure 10.1. The basic relationship is between the *grounds* and the *claim*, as represented by the leftmost and rightmost boxes. *Grounds* are the particulars of a situation that support the claim, for instance the behavior of the wind in the example. In many argumentative contexts, one never makes explicit just how the grounds support the claim. Whether explicit or not, this connection is provided by the *warrant*. A warrant is a general rule connecting particular grounds to their implications (in the illustration a general rule about local patterns of weather). The warrant itself also requires support. Such support is called *backing*. The appropriate backing for a warrant differs from field to field. For instance, the backing for a scientific principle is usually a previous history of confirmation; in law, a principle is backed by precedence or a law.

Two other elements complete the authors' anatomy of argument. *Modality* refers to qualifiers that may be present, such as "chances are" in the example. The final element is *rebuttal*. This refers not to the response of an adversary but to something the arguer may include and acknowledge: exceptional conditions under which the usually sound warrant does not hold.

Why would such an analysis help people to reason better? First, the distinctions of the model, the authors emphasize, amount to alternative ways to challenge an argument. Are the grounds really so? Does the backing for the warrant appear sound, or how can it be impugned? Is the argument appropriately qualified—the matter of modality? Concerning rebuttal, should the possibility of exceptional circumstances be taken seriously? In short, the structure of argument is a guide to testing and revising arguments, including arguments with oneself.

The schema also provides the reasoner with a plan for expanding elliptical arguments. Many arguments, Toulmin et al. note, do not present all of the elements that they could or should. Often, when only grounds and claim are mentioned, the effort to state an argument in full form provides instant criticism. For instance, stating explicitly a tacit warrant may make it obvious that it has no sure backing.

Toulmin et al. seek to build student awareness of such points by a methodical presentation with many exercises. Following an overview of

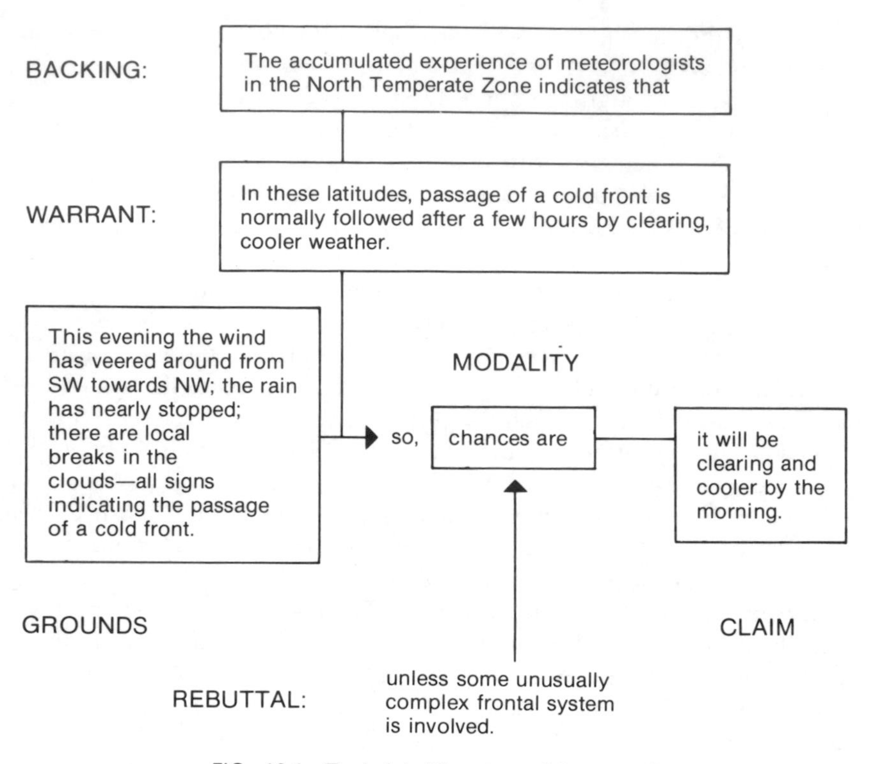

FIG. 10.1 Toulmin's "Structure of Argument"

the argument schema, the first several chapters discuss the various elements of the schema at length. There follows a section of the book devoted to general issues about argument, including a chapter on informal fallacies and a chapter on argument and communication. Here we learn that the authors have an essentially Vygotskian view of reasoning and argument (Vygotsky, 1962, 1978) although they do not cite Vygotsky, or scholars in any field for the most part. The authors hold that skilled reasoning about the soundness of propositions is learned from social interactions with others, beginning with arguments in child-rearing contexts. Argument is a kind of specialized discourse that people acquire as they do other patterns of discourse. Eventually, people use such discourse privately, even though it is learned through interactions with others. The last several chapters of the book focus on the special character of arguments in different disciplines or contexts, the chosen examples being law, science, the arts, management, and ethics.

We know of no data on the effectiveness of the material in *An Introduction to Reasoning* in improving thinking. For several reasons, however, we think the book should have a favorable influence. The students receive considerable practice in dealing with argument of diverse sorts. The emphasis on a common structure of argument provides a coherent, economical view of the nature of reasoning. The emphasis on the variations of arguments from field to field, despite the common structure, seems likely to foster transfer. We also suspect, however, that the book could be used more effectively for teaching reasoning skills if exercises were added in which students were required to construct their own arguments, rather than simply analyzing those of others.

A rather different reservation relates to the psychological factors that lead to faulty argumentation and private reasoning. Nisbett and Ross (1980), concluding their recent survey of problems of inference with a chapter on educational remedies, emphasize that these influences are both rarely recognized and remarkably powerful. Some anomalies in reasoning seem to have the persuasive force of perceptual illusions. Indeed, it often proves very difficult to convince people that the illusion *is* an illusion. We think that instruction in reasoning should take account of such research and alert students to the stubborn failings it has disclosed (see Chapter 5).

Thinking Straight (Beardsley, 1975) which is a college-level text designed to teach reasoning skills, is similar in some respects to *An Introduction to Reasoning*. Both Toulmin and Beardsley are philosophers, and both texts approach the difficulties of reasoning from philosophical foundations and with philosophical style and precision. Despite this commonality, however, there are some interesting contrasts. One of these is the abundance and contemporary character of the examples and exercises. Although *An Introduction to Reasoning* does well in this respect, *Thinking Straight* is exceptional.

Another special merit of *Thinking Straight* is its emphasis on reading and writing as vehicles of thought. Indeed, the book is subtitled "Principles of reasoning for readers and writers." As discussed in the preceding chapter, argumentation often is necessarily complex and the resource of the written word permits us to hold arguments in a way not permitted by the fleeting nature of speech. Along with this emphasis goes a somewhat broader range of topics than addressed in *An Introduction to Reasoning*. Formal deduction and syllogistic reasoning, bypassed in Toulmin, Rieke, and Janik, receive full attention in Beardsley's text. In part, this reflects differing doctrines. Toulmin (1958) has criticized deductive formalisms on principle, and the text of which he is senior author reflects this view. Beardsley, on the other hand, observes the traditional distinction between inductive and deductive reasoning, and exercises the reader in both. Beardsley makes deductive argument seem more relevant than it often does in such instruction by finding for many of his exercises and examples discourse that sounds quite natural.

Besides this attention to problems of deduction and induction, Beardsley addresses problems of argument arising out of the nature of language. Ambiguity, equivocation and vagueness are discussed in Chapter Four, connotation and metaphor, suggesting and slanting, and emotive language in Chapter Five. Chapter Six, the last, has the title "Definition and the control of meaning."

Although rather informally written, *Thinking Straight* is quite technical. There is considerable terminology to be learned, along with certain techniques such as the use of Venn diagrams. We conjecture that the students who would benefit most from *Thinking Straight* would already be fairly skilled in the uses of language.

Also, the model of argument propounded in *An Introduction to Reasoning* by Toulmin, Rieke, and Janik (1979) provides that text with a conceptual center *Thinking Straight* lacks. The cost to the former text is commitment to a doctrine that might well be challenged. However, the cost to the latter is greater cognitive load for the learner.

3. METACOGNITIVE SKILLS

If metacognition is defined as cognition focused on itself, or more simply, as knowledge about knowledge, many of the programs we have considered, especially those in this chapter, have metacognitive aspects. Here we review some work for which metacognition has been the explicit focus. For the most part, this work has not had the short-term objective of developing instructional programs, but has been more concerned with doing experimental research on specific questions relating to the teaching of metacognitive skills. However, some of the experimentation has involved trying instructional procedures in the classroom and the results are clearly germane to the general topic of teaching thinking.

There can be little doubt that metacognitive skills of the sort mentioned in Chapter 4 are valuable skills to possess. But are they teachable? And assuming they are, to what extent might an emphasis on self-management and monitoring, and on attention to one's own thought processes, be counterproductive with respect to the internalization and automatization of problem-solving abilities? Might it not be the case that attending to one's own behavior would interfere with attending to the structure and constraints of the problems one wants to solve and to the tools one can apply to solve them? A growing number of investigators believe that metacognitive skills are teachable and useful. Some of them have been attempting to develop methods for teaching such skills.

Flavell (1978) has suggested that general knowledge about human cognitive abilities and limitations may be useful in improving cognitive performance. It is especially important to be aware, he suggests, of the fact that our direct feelings about what we, as individuals, do or do not understand may often be wrong:

> We can fail to understand something in two ways: we can not achieve any coherent representation of it or we can understand it incorrectly, i.e., misunderstand it. Misunderstandings are especially pernicious because they usually produce the same satisfied feeling (or lack of feeling) as correct understandings do.... While present feelings concerning the comprehensibility and memorability of information can certainly be very useful, they can also deceive us. Things that feel well understood and readily recallable now may not prove to be so easily recomprehended or remembered later. Conversely, the click of comprehension or memory that eludes us now may yet happen later, even with no additional conscious effort. Just because the meaning of the concept being explained is crystal clear to me, it need not be to everyone else in the audience, or to my listener (if I am doing the explaining). The egocentrism-based feeling that it *must* be clear to others if it feels *this* clear to me probably cannot be extinguished, but it should not be allowed to engender egocentric judgments and actions. Thus, there are conceptual as well as perceptual illusions and ambiguities, and intuitions about their existence can be valuable components of a person's metacognitive knowledge. (p. 12, 13)

Brown and Campione (1978) suggest that problem-solving performance may be enhanced by teaching children an explicit set of metacognitive admonitions and questions to review before proceeding with the problem, e.g., A. Stop and think! B. Do I know what to do (i.e., understanding instructions both explicit and implicit)? C. Is there anything more I need to know before I can begin? and D. Is there anything I already know that will help me (i.e., is this problem in any way like one I have done before)? This suggestion is consistent with Flavell's (1978) recommendation to cultivate children's introspective abilities by engaging them in cognitive activities designed to evoke metacognitive ideas and feelings and turning their attention to those ideas and feelings.

Self Monitoring for Reading Comprehension

The importance of comprehending what one reads is apparent. But comprehension is a matter of degree. How is one to tell, in any particular case, whether one's comprehension is adequate. This question is complicated by Flavell's observation that the feeling that one understands something is not aways to be trusted.

Though not much is known about the effects of training of comprehension-monitoring skills, Markman (1979) has some suggestions about instruction. Children should be made aware, she suggests, of certain cues that can provide indications of how adequate one's comprehension is. One such cue might be considered an "inconsistency" cue, because it would reveal an inconsistency between a reader's expectations and information subsequently obtained from the text. But procedures are needed that induce children to check for such inconsistencies.

One way to sensitize children to inconsistencies is to require them to predict what is likely to happen next in a text or story. Disconfirmed predictions would indicate inconsistencies, which suggests that comprehension has been imperfect, whereas confirmed predictions would suggest that comprehension is accurate. Of course, text comprehension does not assure plausible inferences, inasmuch as the inferential processes themselves might be faulty; thus children also need to be taught how to evaluate the plausibility of their own inferences. This might seem like an impossible task, but it may be that the teaching of a few general evaluation principles (e.g., an inference is a good one to the extent it interconnects many of the statements) would improve performance significantly. Also, children may already have knowledge of some of these principles, but lack the skill to apply them effectively in all appropriate contexts (Collins & Smith, 1982).

More generally, training on comprehension-failure cues may be implemented by inserting cues in a simple text in such a way that one cue is inconsistent with another and asking children to find what is wrong with the text. Once children have learned to detect a certain cue, they can presumably be taught how to remedy the comprehension failure that has been signalled.

Metamemory

If we accept the view that the acquisition, retention, and use of knowledge should be considered metacognitive skills, or that they can be facilitated by such skills, the question arises as to the degree to which these skills can be taught. Several investigators have recently turned their attention to this question.

Campione and Brown (1978) point out that when faced with the problem of trying to commit some material to memory, mature memorizers use a variety of strategies to do so whereas immature memorizers do not. Citing as evidence experiments of Belmont and Butterfield (1977), Brown (1974) and Campione and Brown (1977), they note further that these strategies can be taught and the teaching of them results in improved memory performance. Brown and Barclay (1976) have shown that moderately retarded children improve their recall performance when instructed with an anticipation or rehearsal strategy as opposed to a simple labeling strategy. The benefit persisted for the older of two groups of subjects (9 years 67 months to 13 years 9 months) but was transitory for the younger group (7 years 2 months to 11 years 7 months). As Campione and Brown (1978) note, however, results have shown that often the trainees do not retain the learned strategies over a long period of time, nor do they spontaneously use them in situations other than those in which they were learned. That is to say, the effects of training often fail either to persist or to generalize.

There seems to be fairly general agreement among investigators that how much one retains of what one reads depends upon, among other things, how deeply one processes the material when one reads it. Depth of processing is a rather abstract—not to say vague—concept, but that is not to suggest that is a meaningless one, or that people who use it have no idea what they mean. The notion that one can process text to different depths, or to different degrees, is to some of us at least, intuitively compelling. It has to do with the amount of effort that we devote to comprehension, with relating what is being read to other things that we already know, and with working hard to be sure we *really understand* what the author is trying to say.

Translating these notions into overt activities that can be taught, and observed, and that will have the desired effect on retention is another matter. Several possibilities are fairly apparent, and some of them have been tried. Examples include underlining, paraphrasing, and summarizing.

Brown and Campione (1978) point out that an important prerequisite for the effective use of limited processing capacity and limited study time is the ability to identify the essential organizing features and crucial elements of texts, to be able, in other words, to distinguish between critical and incidental aspects of textual material. This is an ability that they assume increases with age during early developmental years.

These investigators had students of different ages (grade school, high school, college) study and attempt to recall two stories. Before recall, they were asked to select 12 out of approximately 24 idea units that they would like to have available as retrieval cues when attempting to recall the passage. The idea units were categorized in terms of four levels of importance. Before the initial recall trial, subjects in all groups selected as retrieval cues ideas from the highest importance level. Before subsequent efforts to recall the same material, the older subjects shifted their preference to cues from lower importance levels, whereas the younger subjects persisted in selecting the highest importance level items as cues.

Brown and Campione's interpretation of this result was that the older subjects were sufficiently insightful about their own performance (after the first recall trial) to realize that they would be likely to recall the highly important units without the aid of retrieval cues, and therefore selected cues that would be helpful on material that they would be less likely to recall spontaneously. The younger subjects did not have the same understanding of their own performance. The ability to select suitable retrieval cues,

Brown and Campione suggest, is one of several metacognitive abilities that develop relatively late.

Can knowledge *about* one's own memory improve one's ability to retrieve information from it? This question has recently attracted the attention of several investigators (Keniston & Flavell, 1980; others referenced in Keniston & Flavell, p. 3). Flavell (1980) has proposed three items of knowledge which, he suggests, should facilitate memory retrieval: (1) the knowledge that a systematic exhaustive search through memory, or a part thereof, is appropriate in some cases, and in particular when there exists a method for conducting the exhaustive search effectively; (2) the knowledge that sometimes it may be appropriate deliberately to retrieve non-target items, because their recall may trigger the recall of target items; and (3) the knowledge that more than one strategy may be applicable to a given retrieval problem.

In one experiment designed, in part, to demonstrate the effectiveness of an explicit memory retrieval strategy, Keniston and Flavell (1980) had subjects (including first graders, college students, and students in intermediate grades) write down each of several letters of the alphabet as an experimenter read them aloud in random order. Subjects were not informed that they would later be asked to recall what they had written; however, after a brief period during which the experimenter engaged the subjects in conversation, they were asked to do so. During the recall task, some subjects used the strategy of thinking of each letter of the alphabet in turn and attempting to remember whether it was one of the letters that had been written down, thus effectively transforming the recall task into a recognition task. Older subjects were more likely to use this strategy spontaneously than were younger subjects. But even the youngest (first graders) were capable of using it when instructed to do so. In general, all subjects who used this strategy, whether spontaneously or at the experimenter's behest, did better on the memory task than those who did not.

Keniston and Flavell speculated that the reason the younger subjects typically did not use this strategy spontaneously was because they simply failed to think of it. This possibility gets some support from the fact that the younger subjects were more likely to use the strategy spontaneously when given the task of reporting letters that they had *not* been asked to write down, a task which forced them to think of letters other than those that may have been fresh in memory as a result of the initial writing-down task.

Keniston and Flavell noticed that their older subjects often used a mixed strategy during recall. Initially they reported letters that seemed to be fresh in memory and that were accessible without any structured search. When they began to have difficulty recalling further items in this way, they resorted to the sequential alphabetic search strategy. A similar mixed strategy for recall has been observed in other contexts. When asked to generate a list of words of a specified type from long-term memory, subjects often report something of this sort. If asked to generate a list of vegetable names, for example, subjects may begin by producing names that just seem to "come to mind"; at some point, however, they discover that names are no longer suggesting themselves very rapidly and they resort to a more structured approach for finding them. They may, for example, visualize their garden, their dinner table, or the shelves of their pantry or of a familiar grocery store.

Keniston and Flavell suggest that the two-phase behavior of their older subjects in their experiment is prototypical of the behavior of adults in many everyday situations. "People often begin intentional retrieval ventures by simply letting the mnemonic system bring to mind whatever it will. If this passive, wait-and-hope method does not accomplish their retrieval objectives, they begin to take a more active and thoughtful part in the proceedings" (p. 32). This actively directed behavior includes the systematic searching of "memory spaces" such as events occurring during some particular time period, groups of people and things, spatial layouts and so on.

The important implication of such studies, for our purposes, is the suggestion that a memory search strategy that is observed to occur spontaneously among adults, and to be effective in facilitating access to stored information, may be taught to children before they have discovered it on their own. The strategy involves the use of information stored in memory in a highly structured and readily accessible form, and the use of it in such a way as to change a recall task into a recognition task. Keniston and Flavell's demonstration experiment made use of knowledge that children typically acquire at an early age knowledge of the letters of the alphabet and their order. However, the applicability of such knowledge to practical situations is doubtful. The question is whether one can find ways of applying the principle they have demonstrated in real-world situations that have some practical significance for the children involved. This is an empirical question worthy of further research.

Metacognition and Transfer of Training

The issue of transfer has always been a central one in training research. Until recently, however, transfer per se has not been an explicit focus of training procedures. In the traditional investigation of transfer, subjects were simply trained in one context and tested in another. Attempts to increase the probability of transfer typically keyed on maximizing the similarity between the training and testing contexts in certain critical respects.

The lack of correspondence between training situations and the context in which thinking skills must be used in real life has been the subject of some concern. Some investigators have criticized the use of puzzles and the kinds of contrived problems one finds in logic books to teach or investigate problem solving on the grounds that these problems lack some of the important ingredients of the types of problems that we encounter in our day-to-day lives. Bereiter and Scardamalia (1980), for example, distinguish between knowledge-restricted and knowledge-unrestricted problem environments and suggest that the kinds of problems that are typically used in experimental studies are of the former type whereas those that are more often encountered in real life are of the latter type. A restricted-knowledge problem domain is one in which the problem solver is not allowed to make unlimited use of his knowledge resources. In the familiar missionaries and cannibals problem, for example, the problem solver is not allowed to make use of any knowledge he may have of ways of crossing the river other than in a small boat. In contrast, when one is confronted with a problem in real life, one is free to make use of any information one has that is relevant to the solution of that problem.

Another characteristic distinction between problems used in laboratory studies of problem solving and those encountered in real life relates to the availability of information. In the former case the information that is needed to solve the problem typically is given, whereas in the latter case determining what information is relevant and how to access it may be the most difficult part of getting the problem solved. Most school tasks, Bereiter and Scardamalia suggest, differ from those encountered in everyday life with respect to their knowledge-access demands. An exception, in their view, is the task of expository writing. Here the knowledge access demands are not precisely bounded and therefore more representative of other tasks found outside of school.

Metacognition relates to the issue of transfer of training in at least two ways. First, there is some evidence that metacognitive skills are more likely to transfer spontaneously than are other types of skills. Second, there is the possibility of treating transfer itself as a metacognitive skill and attempting to train it directly.

With respect to the first point, Brown (1978) has suggested that effective transfer of specific skills requires a discrimination by an individual regarding those situations for which the skill is appropriate, whereas general metacognitive skills are by definition generally applicable. Some evidence supporting this view comes from an experiment reported by Campione and Brown (1978). Some mildly retarded children were taught anticipation and rehearsal strategies to apply to a task of studying a set of pictures until they were sure they could recall them perfectly and in order. Experimental subjects were taught either to attempt to anticipate the names of the pictures or to rehearse them explicitly. Control subjects were given no such instructions. The generalization experiment was performed 15 months later when some of the same subjects were asked to read each of a set of short stories until they could tell the story in their own words. Subjects who had had the earlier training in anticipation and rehearsal techniques recalled more of the story units in the generalization task than did matched subjects who had not had the prior training.

Campione and Brown attributed the positive results obtained in this experiment to the fact that their training efforts were focused on metacognitive skills. "Having failed to effect generalization when attempting to inculcate specific mnemonics we turned to a more general problem-solving routine involving self testing of the effects of these mnemonics" (p. 416). They concluded that at least the self-monitoring skill of estimating recall readiness is susceptible to training and does generalize across different tasks. The general conclusion these investigators draw from this and previous attempts to teach mentally retarded children to perform better on memorization tasks is that "the types of cognitive activities which are most suitable for intensive intervention should have certain properties, (a) they should have wide transsituational applicability, (b) they should readily be seen *by the child* to be reasonable activities *that work*, (c) they should have some counterpart in real-life experiences, and (d) their component processes should be well understood so that effective training techniques can be devised" (p. 416). Among the metacognitive activities that they see as satisfying these criteria are checking, monitoring, and reality testing.

With respect to the second way in which metacognition relates to transfer, one sees evidence in the literature of a growing interest in the possibility of teaching generalization and transfer directly. That is to say, rather than viewing generalization and transfer as hoped-for by-products of teaching that focuses on something else, educational researchers are beginning to take the position that if what one wants a child to learn is how to apply a principle or a skill in a variety of contexts, that is what one should explicitly try to teach him to do (Brown, 1975, 1978; Belmont, Butterfield, & Borkowski, 1978; Flavell & Wellman, 1977).

Two ways of facilitating transfer or generalization are especially worthy of attention, Brown (1978) suggests. One is to give training in several different settings. This should preclude the possibility of the skill being "welded" to the single situation in which it was acquired. The other is to make the individual aware of the importance of transfer by giving him explicit instructions with respect to it. As part of the training procedure, the trainee should be informed that the skill he is acquiring can be useful in a variety of contexts. He should be challenged to learn to recognize those situations for which it is appropriate. In other words, transfer itself should be taught as a metacognitive skill. Presumably the two methods complement each other, inasmuch as the ability to recognize situations for which a specific skill is appropriate should be enhanced by the practice of exposing one to a variety of tasks for which the skill is useful as well as some for which it is not.

Brown also points out the importance of accurately diagnosing the reason for failure of transfer. Failure due to the individual's lack of appreciation for the appropriateness of the skill would call for a different type of remediation than failure due to one's inability to perform some component of the transfer task.

Summary

Most of the work to date on teaching metacognitive skills is essentially an extension of the experimental research on the basic nature of such skills. The experimental work that has been done is encouraging in its pedagogical possibilities, and an emphasis on metacognitive skills may soon find its way into many instructional programs. In particular, the research on reading comprehension has enumerated a number of cues to monitor as indicators of breakdown in comprehension, and a sensitivity to these cues seems to be teachable. Similarly, the experimental work on memory has demonstrated that memory-search strategies observed with adults (e.g., converting a recall task into a recognition one by generating alternatives) can be taught to children before they themselves have discovered them. This is particularly important because some children may never develop highly effective strategies without being explicitly taught them.

4. THE COMPLETE PROBLEM SOLVER

The Complete Problem Solver by John Hayes (1981) is a textbook designed to teach thinking skills to college students and to inform them about the findings of contemporary research on thinking. Because of its emphasis on heuristics, it could appropriately have been discussed in Chapter 7. We have chosen to consider it here, however, inasmuch as it goes considerably beyond describing problem-solving techniques and does treat thinking as subject matter in a broader way. The book's organization reflects its aim to be "complete." In the introduction, Hayes gives examples of six important aspects of human problem solving—representation, invention, the search for solutions among many alternatives, decision making, memory, and knowledge—emphasizing that problems vary widely in the difficulties they pose.

To expand on the six topics a little, one problem may yield only if a certain way of representing it is found. Another may call for thinking of a creative solution one well might miss. A third may require finding a way to select among thousands or millions of options, too many to sift by trial and error.

As to knowledge, Hayes emphasizes that problem solving often depends crucially on specialized knowledge of the domain, a point that efforts to teach very general problem solving skills tend to slight. Finally, besides considering problems in general, Hayes singles out decision making and learning as two special but very important problematic situations that deserve special treatment. Of course, these six aspects of problem solving are not six kinds of problems: a problem may be problematic in several ways at once, requiring, for example, a fund of specialized knowledge, invention of an apt representation, and search through a sizable space of alternative courses of action.

With these general concerns in mind, Hayes organizes *The Complete Problem Solver* into four sections, suggesting that the first, "Problem Solving Theory and Practice," should be read at the outset for an overview, although other than that the sections can be taken in any order. The first section begins with a division of problem solving into six steps:

1. Finding the problem (recognizing and accepting it)
2. Representing the problem
3. Planning the solution
4. Carrying out the plan
5. Evaluating the solution
6. Consolidating gains (learning from the experience)

There follows a discussion of representing problems that offers two fundamental pieces of advice: when stuck, change representations; and, for difficult problems, use external representations such as written lists and charts. Through examples and descriptions of research, the student learns that finding solutions often depends on finding good representations, and that developing a representation is a highly active process with much sifting and supplementing of data and many individual differences in preferred kinds of representations.

Hayes defines four categories of search strategies—trial and error, proximity methods, fractionation methods, and knowledge-based methods. Systematic trial and error, in which one keeps track of trials to avoid repetition, has a factor of two advantage over blind trial and error. One proximity method is hill climbing, whereby a problem solver takes trial steps, judges whether they move toward the goal, and so advances toward a solution by increments. Another is means-ends analysis, in which the problem solver can associate various differences between the goal state and the present state of affairs with operations that are likely to reduce those differences, and so transform the present state gradually into the goal state. Fractionation methods involve generating subgoals to solve parts of the problem at hand or to solve related problems.

The second section, chapters 4–6, is a tutorial on how to learn more effectively. The student is warned of research findings showing that repetition in itself does virtually nothing for memory. Memorizing is better accomplished by elaborative encoding, including such tactics as adding mental imagery, reading to answer questions, noticing categories, attending to hierarchical structure, and finding examples to illustrate principles. Furthermore, the student will do well to spend more time practicing retrieval than going over material again and again. Hayes presents some old and new learning systems, including the well-known SQ3R method. He suggests that all such systems depend on seven basic learning strategies: (1) structuring—searching actively for relations; (2) context—relating material to what one already knows; (3) monitoring—testing oneself, noting progress, isolating troublesome parts for further work; (4) inference—making inferences, seeking counterexamples, taking the material further; (5) exemplifying—generating instances; (6) multiple coding—representing the material to be learned in more than one way, paraphrasing or adding images for instance; (7) attention management—concentrating, finding the time to study.

The section on decision making divides problems into four kinds: decisions under certainty, risk, uncertainty, and conflict.

Decisions under certainty arise when one knows all the options and their properties but may have difficulty sorting out the pros and cons. Hayes discusses various strategies. For instance, lexicographic ordering chooses the most important dimension of variation and counts differences on that first, then treats the next most important dimension and so on. Among the other approaches examined are weighted sums of attributes and "satisficing," in which the decision-maker examines options only until one is found that exceeds some threshold of adequacy. Decisions under risk arise when events transpire with a known or estimatable probability. Gambling of all sorts is an example. Hayes writes here about expectation values and their limitations. Decisions under uncertainty occur when there is no reliable means of estimating the probabilities involved, and decisions under conflict occur in competitive situations, such as games or wars. For both of the latter types of decisions, Hayes considers elaborations and variants of the mini-max strategy, which uses a matrix of the possible payoffs of all courses of action under all conditions to minimize the maximum loss. Bayes' theorem is presented, as well as the modifying of a pure mini-max strategy in competitive situations to a mixed strategy in which different approaches are taken with different probabilities. This optimizes payoffs according to game theory. Finally, Hayes discusses cost-benefit analysis, which requires determining all possible consequences of courses of action and figuring the costs and benefits. Consideration is given to the problem of discovering all the potential costs and benefits, and the "apples and oranges" problem of assigning commensurable values to such different factors as health and convenience.

Turning to creativity in its last section, *The Complete Problem Solver* first takes up the cognitive processes involved. Creative thinking is defined as thinking that yields original and valued outcomes. Recommended strategies for creative thinking include problem-finding to locate and accept problems that need solving, searching for counterexamples, seeking alternative interpretations of phenomena, generating ideas by brainstorming and finding analogies, and planning the conduct of an endeavor at the outset by considering many options carefully. The last chapter of the book deals with the social conditions that foster creativity, arguing that parental encouragement, available time, a tradition of scholarly pursuits, and other factors influence substantially the likelihood of creative achievement.

As its title suggests, *The Complete Problem Solver* is full of heuristic advice. However, the book also follows through on its promise to provide up-to-date information about the psychology of problem solving. Research citations are frequent and much of the heuristic advice is supported by findings either that skilled people behave in the recommended way whereas unskilled people do not, or that people adopting such strategies in fact perform better. For example, Hayes summarizes Getzels and Csikszentmihalyi's (1976) research on creativity in artists, which shows that more creative artists do more planning (as Hayes' puts it, although Getzels and Csikszentmihalyi call this problem finding.) Hayes presents biographical tabulations showing that even the gifted Mozart required many years of practice before his compositions achieved respectable quality. Findings on the difficulty people have estimating probabilities are presented in the section on decision making. Findings on conditions that foster memorization are cited in the learning section. Hayes commits Chapter 3 to a discussion of protocol analysis as conducted, for instance, by Newell and Simon (1972). In general, the book effectively reviews cognitive psychology's current understanding of thinking.

As tends to be the case with such books, no data are available on whether courses taught with *The Complete Problem Solver* indeed make students more able problem solvers. We can only offer a few conjectures. First, *The Complete Problem Solver* is a sophisticated work, apparently intended for college students, and perhaps best suited for fairly bright ones. It is problem solving for those who are already fairly good problem solvers. This is not so because of style, since the book is written in a lively anecdotal fashion. It is in part a reflection of content, such content as mini-max strategies and Bayes' theorem to mention two matters that are likely to cause many students trouble. It is also a reflection of density. There is a *lot* of content in the book's two hundred and fifty pages. Although no unified work could incorporate all the varied approaches that have been taken to teaching thinking skills, in our view *The Complete Problem Solver* encompasses a wide range of the best heuristic instruction that has been attempted.

In fact, it is probably fair to say that *The Complete Problem Solver* trades depth for breadth, not so much in settling for shallow presentations as in moving fast and offering little practice. One oddity of the book compared to others in its genre is that it rarely provides exercises for the students. Illustrative examples occur throughout, but only occasionally do problem sets appear, for instance in the chapters on mnemonics and on cost-benefit analysis. Although some sort of practice is no doubt intended, Hayes says nothing in the book about what sort, how much, nor other aspects of using the book in a course. At least so far as appearances go, *The Complete Problem Solver* contrasts with the approach of, for instance, Whimbey and Lochhead (Chapter 7), who cover far less ground but insist on and provide examples for extensive practice.

The pros and cons of the tradeoff between breadth of coverage and extensive practice within a narrower focus are hard to gauge. Throughout his book, Hayes stresses the importance of domain-specific experience and one would think that this principle ought to apply also to the use of general thinking strategies. On the other hand, brighter students are likely to need less practice. Also, they are most likely to benefit from the very broad perspective on thinking offered by *The Complete Problem Solver*. In the long run, the generally heightened awareness of one's own thought processes that might be imparted by the book could pay off better than would thoroughly practicing and mastering a few particular strategies.

Such judgments are, of course, easy to make but notoriously difficult to validate. We suggest that, when time is available, the best approach may be to supplement the text with exercises, including ones in which the students apply the strategies Hayes teaches to problems arising outside the course—in other courses, for instance. *The Complete Problem Solver* is unique in its breadth and its foundations in the psychological literature, and should we believe, be a valuable resource for programs designed to teach thinking skills.

5. THE "THINKING ABOUT THINKING" APPROACH IN GENERAL

We remarked earlier that teaching *about* something is not necessarily an effective way to teach someone how to do it. This applies to thinking as much as to ice skating. However, it is a problem that the programs reviewed here seem to have avoided. Broadly speaking, they have done so by making an alliance with the heuristic and language approaches, often emphasizing linguistic products like arguments and offering advice about how to proceed as well as practice in doing so. We confess to finding this alliance particularly attractive, because it supplements the straightforward teaching of heuristics and language skills with an understanding of their motivation in human psychology and in epistemology. However, the absence of evaluative data for most of the programs reviewed precludes any strong conclusions about the effectiveness of the approach.

Let us examine the general picture a little more. In fact, an alliance between the "thinking about thinking" approach and the heuristic and language approaches comes naturally, because there, if anywhere, one would expect the understanding to strengthen performance. In contrast, a cognitive operations approach to teaching thinking skills assumes that the learner needs to improve a variety of fundamental cognitive operations by exercise. There is no apparent reason why this sort of mental muscle building should benefit from the understanding of the learner, any more than the athlete gains strength by studying physiology.

As to the Piagetian perspective, the position of Piaget is that the basic structures underlying formal operations cannot be explained to a person that does not have them. Rather, they must be acquired by roundabout routes. Accordingly, if we accept Piaget's view, there is no point in explicating formal operations to people who do not already have them.

A characteristic of the "thinking about thinking" approach is its frequent recourse to philosophy. Most approaches to teaching thinking take psychology as the parent discipline, but in this section we have seen several that draw upon epistemology broadly speaking, that is, on a philosophical understanding of what constitutes adequate grounds for knowledge and belief. A bonus comes with this philosophical accent: such programs bring with them a cognitive style of critical thinking and care with language that, we think, cannot help but be fruitful. At the same time, a better synthesis of philosophical and psychological perspectives on reasoning would be useful. The philosophically based programs often fail to incorporate contemporary findings on the pitfalls of human reasoning (see Chapter 5) and the experimentally based theoretical ideas about human cognition.

The advantages of an approach that explains itself thoroughly and that has roots in philosophy as well as psychology notwithstanding, evaluative data would be useful, and these have proved hard to come by for most of the programs reviewed in this section. One reason for this may be just exactly the philosophical basis for several of the programs: one cannot expect philosophers instantly to start functioning like psychologists with their armamentarium of pretests and posttests. But belying that point somewhat is the fact that the Philosophy for Children program, explicitly philosophically based, has put considerable emphasis on evaluation, although the data are still somewhat sparse.

6. SUMMARY FOR PART II

The programs that we have considered share the assumption that thinking can be improved through training. They differ from each other, however, in many respects, including the following:

- Scope
- Specific skills addressed
- Ages and academic abilities of participating students
- Amount of class time devoted to the program and its distribution over calendar time
- Amount of special training given to teachers
- Amount and type of program material (instructions to teachers, student exercises or workbooks)
- Latitude given to teachers
- Completeness and availability of documentation
- Degree of integration with other courses
- Backing of administration and colleagues
- Amount of emphasis put on evaluation
- Evaluation instruments used
- Evidence of effectiveness

While the programs differ in many ways, we have noted that it is possible to cluster them on the basis of certain similarities. Although any classification scheme has some arbitrariness about it, this one does highlight certain major differences in philosophy and approach that are worth emphasis. *Cognitive-operations* programs focus on certain operations or processes such as comparing, classifying, and inferring that are considered to be fundamental to cognition. These programs aim to develop and strengthen these operations on the assumption that, as a consequence, thinking ability will be improved in general. *Heuristics-oriented* approaches emphasize the teaching of specific methods, techniques, or strategies for dealing with problems. The constituents in this case include planning, problem decomposition, representation, and solution checking or verification. Instruction is intended to provide one with a variety of problem-solving strategies that are applicable across many domains and an understanding of the specific conditions under which each is appropriate.

The programs we have classified as *formal-thinking* approaches tend to have a Piagetian orientation. They have been motivated by the assumption that a primary reason why many students entering college have difficulty with their studies is that they are stuck at a pre-formal stage of cognitive development. The intent of these programs is to provide students with the types of training and experiences that will move them into the formal-operations stage. These programs place considerable emphasis on exploration and learning by discovery. Typically, material progresses from the more concrete to the more abstract, in keeping with the Piagetian notion that the ability to deal with concrete ideas developmentally precedes the ability to deal with abstract ones. Another characteristic of these programs is that the teaching of thinking skills is merged with the teaching of conventional course content.

Programs that we have classified under *language and symbol manipulation* emphasize language and symbol systems as media, not only for expressing the results of thought but for thinking. These programs focus on such symbol manipulation activities as writing, analyzing or composing arguments, and computer programming. Probably more than the other programs we have considered, those in this category tend to emphasize complex products such as prose compositions and computer programs.

Programs that fall in the category we have labeled *thinking about thinking* tend to focus attention directly on thinking as subject matter. That is to say, students are encouraged to think about thinking, to learn something of the intellectual capabilities and limitations of people in general, and to become more directly aware of their own thought processes in particular. Included in this category are programs that emphasize the teaching of metacognitive skills involving conscious management of one's own intellectual resources.

Our review of specific programs has not left us with the strong conviction that any one of these approaches is manifestly superior, or inferior, to all the others. Testing has not been sufficiently extensive to permit a firm conclusion on that issue. Our view is that the variability with respect to quality is probably as great within categories as across categories and that one can find quite good programs as well as not so good programs of each type. Perhaps most importantly, the range of approaches that are being tried indicates the exploratory nature of this work. This is, we believe, inevitable in the absence of a widely accepted theory of cognition from which prescriptions for the enhancing of thinking skills could be derived.

III PROSPECTS FOR TEACHING THINKING

In the first two parts of this book we have discussed a number of topics that relate to thinking and have described several programs developed for the purpose of teaching thinking skills. The review of programs has not been comprehensive, but we believe it has been representative of the programs that exist. In this final part we consider what the evidence, on the whole, suggests regarding the teaching of thinking skills. Is the teaching of thinking a legitimate educational objective? Can thinking be taught? Do we know how to teach it? What determines whether a program is likely to be successful? How should a teacher who is interested in implementing a program choose from among the various possibilities?

We begin with a general discussion of the issue of evaluation. Then, in the concluding chapter, we turn to several specific questions such as those mentioned above. We have no aspirations to present "the final word" on any of the questions we address. This field is young and definitive answers may be a long time in coming. The answers we propose are opinions, but opinions that are informed, at least to some degree, by data or experience.

11 Evaluation

Evaluation is the watchword of educational research and development. And it is not surprising that this is so. What could be more obvious than the need to evaluate efforts to improve the educational process? And what could be more straightforward? One establishes a goal, works to attain it, and then determines how close one has come to doing so. Or so it might appear.

In fact, evaluation is an extremely complex enterprise, especially in educational contexts. There are many methodological traps, variables that are difficult if not impossible to control, and more than a few conventions, preconceived notions, and vested interests that can exert both subtle and not-so-subtle influences on the interpretation of results.

In this section, we discuss some of the issues relating to evaluation, especially as they pertain to the task of assessing efforts to enhance thinking skills. We make no pretense of prescribing *the* appropriate approach to evaluation. Many books have been written on this subject, and controversies regarding both philosophy and methodology persist. Our modest objective here is to note that the problem of evaluating efforts to teach thinking is both important and complex, and to illustrate some of its complexities.

1. PURPOSES OF EVALUATION

Educational evaluations are undertaken for several purposes. Sometimes the aim is to provide grounds for deciding whether to accept or reject a particular educational innovation teaching technique, curriculum modification, administrative policy—or for deciding whether an innovation that has been introduced should be continued or terminated. Sometimes the aim is to determine which of two or more competing possibilities should be adopted in a particular context. Another possible purpose is to try to identify the strengths and weaknesses of some innovation for the sake of guiding its further development. Yet another is that of studying alternative ways of applying an innovation in order to maximize its impact. Other purposes can undoubtedly be identified. The point is that evaluations come in many different guises, and in designing an evaluation effort it is important to be quite precise about what its purpose is.

One common distinction contrasts "formative" evaluation—the kind of evaluation that is conducted while a program is being developed, to provide results that can guide that development—and "summative" evaluation—which is typically done after a program has been completed, to assess the program's effectiveness in accomplishing its developers' objectives. Formative evaluation tends to be relatively informal, often largely qualitative, and usually focuses on specific aspects or components of a program rather than on the program as a whole. Summative evaluation is more formal, often involving the statistical comparison of pretest and posttest measures of the performance of experimental and control groups. Typically it is used to assess the merits of a program in its entirety; although, of course, it may also provide data regarding specific aspects as well.

Undoubtedly both of these broad categories of evaluation have their place in educational research and development. Formative evaluations that are designed to identify the strengths and weaknesses of innovations, so as to guide their further development and use, seem to be particularly important for most efforts to improve the educational process. Bruner (1966) makes essentially this point by arguing that evaluation after the fact is often of little use. Much to be preferred, he suggests, is an evaluative effort that occurs before and during curriculum construction, yielding the kind of information that can be fed back into the curriculum development process to help shape the design of materials and the refinement of methods.

We agree with this view, and believe that formative evaluation is not only desirable, but indispensable. We believe too that some efforts to develop programs to enhance thinking skills have suffered from a lack of emphasis on this kind of evaluation. However, formative evaluation is a tool for program development; the results it yields are of use primarily during the development process and of interest primarily to the people engaged in that process. Educators who are faced with the problem of deciding whether to implement a particular program need summative evaluation data if their decisions are to be firmly based. They need to know whether a program, if implemented, is likely to affect the ability of their students to think, and what the nature and magnitude of the effect(s) are likely to be. For this reason, we focus, in what follows, primarily on the problem of summative evaluation.

2. OBSTACLES TO EVALUATION

Solid evaluative data on the effectiveness of programs for teaching thinking are scarce. In many cases, little, if any, attempt at summative evaluation has been made. Some of the programs that have been discussed in this book are still being developed, so there has not yet been an opportunity for such data to be obtained. In some cases, program developers have shown little interest in evaluation, perhaps because they feel that demonstration of the effectiveness of their approach is not necessary or they consider it inappropriate for a program to be evaluated by its developers.

For a variety of reasons, summative evaluation data are not easy to collect. The obstacles to controlled scientific experimentation in educational contexts are formidable. They include the problem of controlling for the quality of teaching, the difficulty of defining appropriate control-group treatments, the problem of selecting appropriate performance measures, and many others. Moreover, ideally one wants data that demonstrate whether or not a program has had generalized and lasting effects. This requires that performance be assessed in situations different from the classroom contexts in which the teaching occurred, and at a succession of points over a substantial period of time. Such requirements are rarely easily met, because they involve the manipulation of variables over which the program developer or evaluator usually has very limited control.

Even when summative evaluation data are available, difficulties may be encountered when one tries to compare the findings for one program with those for another. Seldom is it possible to conclude, on the basis of two independent evaluations, that one program proved to be more effective than another. Comparisons across evaluations require at least as much care as does the interpretation of the results of a given evaluation effort. Difficulties arise from many sources: incomparability with respect to control groups or control group treatments, differences in the beginning ability of students or in the quality of teaching, differences in classroom situations and in the degree of control over extraneous variables, differences in the duration of the evaluation experiment, and so on.

A difficulty worth special mention is the problem of assuring equally competent and enthusiastic teaching by teachers of experimental groups and teachers of control groups. Often in these programs, the teachers who work with experimental groups have selected themselves by volunteering for the task. It seems reasonable to question whether teachers who volunteer to participate in innovative educational programs are representative of teachers in general; in particular one must wonder about the extent to which they correspond, in ability and motivation, to teachers who are sometimes appointed to serve as controls.

3. PERFORMANCE MEASURES AND TESTS

A major problem facing a designer of an evaluation effort is to select appropriate performance measures for determining whether thinking ability has been improved. Some evaluations have used standardized tests (e.g., IQ tests); some have used tests specially constructed for the purpose. Many have looked for evidence of effectiveness in responses of participating students and/or teachers to questionnaires, and in specially designed tests of the ability of students to do such things as generate ideas, ask insightful questions, tell when they are ready to take a test, retain information, write compositions, and so on.

We make no attempt here to list all the tests that have been used to try to evaluate programs to teach thinking. It may be helpful to mention some of them, however, to give an indication of their variety. Among the many tests that have been employed to evaluate the Instrumental Enrichment Program, in whole or in part, are the following: non verbal subtests of the Lorge-Thorndike (1954) Intelligence Tests, Raven's (1960) Standard Progressive Matrices, the Intellectual Achievement Responsibility Questionnaire (Crandall, Katkovsky, & Crandall, 1965), the Rosenberg (1965) Self-Esteem Scale, Thurstone's Primary Mental Abilities Test (Thurstone, 1965), the Piers-Harris (1969) Self-Concept Scale, the Peabody Individual Achievement Test (Dunn & Markwardt, 1970), the Key Math Diagnostic Arithmetic Test (Connolly, Nachtman, & Pritchett, 1971), the Picture Motivation Scale (Haywood 1971), the Nowicki-Strickland (1973) Locus of Control Scale, the Student's Environmental Preference Survey (Gordon, 1975), and Jastak and Jastak's (1978) Wide Range Achievement Test.

Several tests have been used to evaluate the Philosophy for Children program, among them some subtests (Inferences, Opposites, Analogies and Similarities) of the California Test of Mental Maturity (Lipman, 1976); the Auditory and Visual Association subtests of the Illinois Test of Psycholinguistic Abilities (Simon, 1976); and the Comprehensive Test of Basic Skills (Lipman, Sharp, & Oscanyan, 1980). A test of formal reasoning developed by Lawson (1978) has been used to evaluate Project SOAR (Carmichael, Hassell, Hunter, Jones, Ryan, & Vincent, 1980), as has the Nelson-Denny Reading Test and the PSAT (Whimbey, Carmichael, Jones, Hunter, & Vincent, 1980). The Watson-Glaser Critical Thinking Appraisal (Watson & Glaser, 1964) and the Campbell puzzles (Campbell, 1977) have both been used in connection with Project DORIS (Collea & Nummedal,

1979). The Watson-Glaser test is intended to assess one's ability to (1) make inferences, (2) recognize assumptions, (3) make deductions, (4) make interpretations, and (5) evaluate arguments. The Campbell puzzles were designed to measure the ability to engage in several aspects of formal thinking: (1) combinatorial logic, (2) correlational reasoning, (3) isolation and control of variables, (4) proportional reasoning, and (5) hypothesis testing. Project Intelligence has used the Otis Lennon School Ability Tests, the Cattell Culture Fair Test and General Abilities tests drawn from several sources (Herrnstein, Nickerson, Sanchez, & Swets, in press). The Practicum in Thinking program has made use of listening tests from the Xerox Corporation's Effective Listening Program (Xerox, 1964). Various attitude inventories, ideational fluency tests, and problem-solving tests have been used in several studies to evaluate the Productive Thinking Program (Mansfield, Busse, & Krepelka, 1978).

This sample of tests that have been used to evaluate programs to teach thinking prompts two observations. First, clearly there is a diversity of opinion regarding what constitutes an appropriate test. Perhaps this should not be surprising in view of the fact that thinking is generally considered to be multifaceted and different programs emphasize different aspects of it. Nevertheless, the variety of assessment instruments that have been used attests to the difficulty of making meaningful cross-program comparisons and does not promote optimism about the possibility of converging easily on a consensus as to how thinking ability should be measured, let alone taught.

Second, one must wonder about the extent to which attempts to teach thinking skills are constrained by the tests that happen to be available. For example, the ability to judge the merits of a plausible argument is a skill of considerable practical importance, but rules of inference appropriate to this task do not exist as they do in the case of deductive arguments, and therefore the development of objective tests to assess this skill is a difficult matter. Not only may available tests focus on certain aspects of thinking to the exclusion of others, but they may not always do an adequate job of measuring what they are intended to measure. Neisser (1979) has argued that IQ tests fail to measure some aspects of what intelligence is reasonably considered to be. De Bono (1970) has suggested, in particular, that intelligence tests are designed to give high marks for high-probability, sensible, conventional answers to questions and to penalize low-probability, unusually imaginative answers. And Costa (1981) has reminded us that an important aspect of evaluation is to determine "not what answers the student knows but how the student behaves when he or she doesn't know" (p. 31).

Bruner (1966) suggests several criteria in terms of which effects of any training program might be judged: "speed of learning; resistance to forgetting; transferability of what has been learned to new instances; form of representation in terms of which what has been learned is to be expressed;

economy of what has been learned in terms of cognitive strain imposed; effective power of what has been learned in terms of generativeness of new hypotheses and combinations" (p. 50). He notes, too, that these factors are not necessarily mutually reinforcing, indeed they might in some instances work in opposition to each other: "speed of learning, for example, is antithetical to transfer or to economy."

It is not difficult to think of other criteria that would make reasonable candidates for judging the effectiveness of a program to enhance thinking skills, or to improve intellectual performance in a general way: evidence of the development of thoughtful, careful work habits; ability to see things from another perspective or from another person's point of view; evidence of an effective balance between inventiveness and critical thinking, to name a few.

4. SOME NEGLECTED ISSUES

There are several issues that should be addressed explicitly in any effort to evaluate the effectiveness of an innovative educational program. Some of these, such as the importance of using valid and reliable test instruments, of adequately controlling variables, of selecting appropriate control groups and treatments, and of subjecting data to appropriate statistical analyses, are well covered in standard textbook treatments of evaluation. However, some issues have not, we believe, received the attention they deserve. In particular, we have in mind three neglected distinctions the overlooking of any of which is bound to make an evaluation incomplete. These are the distinctions between statistical and practical significance, between direct and indirect effects, and between short-term and long-term effects. In addition to these distinctions, there are three other issues that have not received much attention in the context of evaluation efforts, but that are relevant to the task of assessing the merits of programs. These involve the need to assess goals, the need to assess negative effects, and the risk of premature closure.

Statistical versus Practical Significance

The type of evidence of program effectiveness that is most commonly sought involves comparing the improvements in performance made by an experimental group (a group that has participated in the program of interest) with those made by a control group. Typically before-treatment and after-treatment test results are obtained in both cases, the comparison of interest being between the difference scores of the two groups.

This is, of course, an appropriate comparison to make. Unfortunately, sometimes attention is focused exclusively on whether the differences obtained are statistically significant. While the question of statistical significance is undeniably an important one, the magnitudes of those differences should not be ignored. Very small differences, whatever the degree of statistical reliability, may be of dubious practical significance; decisions about whether or not to implement a program should be made not only on the basis of whether the program has been shown to have *some* effect, but on whether the gains are sufficiently large to justify the cost of implementation.

Direct versus Indirect, or Primary versus Secondary, Effects

Efforts to evaluate programs usually try to ascertain whether the programs attain the objectives that the developers of those programs have set for them. Several investigators have noted, however, that programs have sometimes produced effects others than those that were anticipated. Such indirect, or secondary, effects include improved reading ability (in a program not focused on the improvement of reading skills), better communication among students (or among teachers, or between students and teachers) and other improvements in social behavior, greater participation in classroom activities, better work habits and attitudes, and so on. Negative secondary effects have also been noted on occasion.

We wish to stress the point that the possibility of indirect or secondary effects should never be overlooked. To be sure, a primary objective of an evaluation should be to determine whether a program accomplishes what it is intended to accomplish; however, evaluations that are narrowly and exclusively focused on explicit program objectives run the risk of overlooking effects (either positive or negative) that could, in a larger view, prove to be of equal or even greater importance.

Short-Term versus Long-Term Effects

A strikingly consistent limitation of most of the evaluations we have reviewed is their attention solely to short-term effects. Typically performance measures that are used for evaluation purposes are taken immediately before and immediately after participation in the program. Seldom have efforts been made to determine whether immediate improvements in performance persist over appreciable periods of time.

Clearly, the hope for any program designed to improve thinking skills is that any improvements achieved will endure, and, indeed, will provide a basis for further improvements into the indefinite future. Ideally, one wants to develop leverage skills—skills that are useful in a wide variety of contexts and skills that will facilitate the development of other skills.

One evidence that such a hope has been realized would be a divergence over time between the performance measures obtained from program participants and those obtained from controls, as suggested by Feuerstein (1980). In general, one would like to know the time course of any gains that are realized as a result of a program: how long do they persist, and do they increase or diminish over time? But to answer this question requires a prolonged evaluation effort of a kind that has seldom been made.

The Need to Assess Goals

Evaluation efforts have seldom focused on goals and objectives per se. Understandably, evaluations typically are undertaken to determine the extent to which programs have realized their objectives; the objectives themselves are seldom questioned, or even explicitly related to more comprehensive educational purposes. To be sure, the face validity of some program objectives is sufficiently great that challenging them seems unwarranted: who would question, for example, whether the ability to think more effectively is a desirable educational goal? But such a goal is probably too general and too abstract to be of practical value. Everyone will agree with it, but there is unlikely to be a consensus about what the ability to think more effectively means. To be of practical value such a high-level goal must be translated into a set of more specific objectives; and we can expect wide differences of opinion regarding the relative importance, or even appropriateness, of these lower-level objectives.

How much emphasis should a program to improve thinking put on reasoning? How useful in everyday life is some facility with formal logic? Should specific methods (e.g., problem solving heuristics) be taught? How much attention should be given to inventiveness or creativity? Should mnemonic techniques be included? To what extent should thinking be treated as a subject about which facts and theories are taught? How much emphasis should be placed on self knowledge, self monitoring, self management, and other aspects of metacognition?

These are important questions and they deserve to be addressed more explicitly than they have been in the past. That is not to suggest that answers to them are likely to be easy to obtain. Indeed, we suspect that such questions can be the basis for debates that may persist for a long time. Until such questions are addressed explicitly, and at least tentative answers are forthcoming, however, efforts to evaluate programs will necessarily produce, at best, limited and qualified results. One might hope to obtain evidence regarding the relative effectiveness of a given program in realizing one or more specified objectives, but in the absence of some evidence, or a consensus, that the realization of those objectives really enhances thinking, the evaluation must be considered incomplete. That is not to say, of course, that it would have no value, but only that something else of importance remains to be done.

The Need to Assess Negative Effects

Evaluations have seldom explicitly addressed whether a program has any negative effects. Some possible negative effects would be relatively easy to identify: if, for example, students did more poorly on criterion tasks after participating in a program than before, this would be apparent and would undoubtedly be interpreted as evidence that the program was not successful.

Secondary negative effects are difficult to measure; it is not difficult to imagine, however, that they occur. One such possibility results from "opportunity costs." Most programs to teach thinking require a considerable time commitment by both teachers and students. To the extent that a program fails to accomplish positive results, one might argue that it thereby, in effect, causes negative results, because it wastes time and resources that might have been used in more productive ways.

Other types of possible negative effects are more insidious because the decrement can be seen only from a broad perspective. For one instance, a short-term benefit may constitute a long-term loss. For example, imagine a program designed to improve the solving of word problems in mathematics by giving intensive training on several of the most important kinds of problems. Might such instruction, by focusing explicitly and narrowly on particular cases, deprive students of practice in figuring out how to handle different kinds of problems by themselves? Possibly it would be better to focus on strategies for *learning* how to solve problems, rather than on strategies for specific kinds of problems.

Another insidious factor concerns the balance between different sorts of thinking skills. For example, success in teaching a student to think expansively and creatively and to be able to generate many novel ideas would undoubtedly be considered a worthwhile accomplishment; however, if not balanced with the ability to think analytically and to evaluate critically the ideas that are generated, the accomplishment may be of dubious value.

The Possibility of Premature Closure

The null assumption is the default assumption that is usually made when one is attempting to determine whether an educational treatment has had an effect. That is to say, one hypothesizes no effect and looks for evidence that would permit the rejection of this hypothesis. This is a conservative approach, inasmuch as it minimizes the probability of concluding that there has been an effect when in fact there has been none. A good case can be made for this policy. It is consistent with the philosophy that an innovative educational program should be implemented (on other than an experimental basis) only if the evidence is compelling that it will produce some worthwhile results. Adopting the converse policy of assuming there is a positive effect unless convincing evidence to the contrary is obtained obviously would promote chaos.

It is well to recognize, however, that the conservative policy risks the premature dismissal of some promising programs. This is probably an acceptable risk, but a risk nonetheless. Moreover, the risk is compounded by the inherent difficulty of educational evaluations. It is important, we believe, to be especially sensitive to the possibility of dismissing a program on the basis of noisy data obtained from a poorly conceived or poorly executed test. There is no easy solution to this problem, but recognizing it points up the importance of designing evaluations to be as fair as they possibly can be and to give a program an opportunity to demonstrate what it can do.

In short, the fact that an evaluation effort fails to substantiate a difference between the performance of an experimental group and that of a control group does not demonstrate that a difference does not exist. Failure to find a difference *may* be due to the fact that no difference exists. It also may be due, however, to the noisiness of the data or the imprecision or inappropriateness of the measurement technique.

12 Prospects for Teaching Thinking

1. IS THE TEACHING OF THINKING A LEGITIMATE EDUCATIONAL OBJECTIVE?

We would argue that the teaching of thinking is not only a legitimate educational objective but an imperative one. Evidences of irrationality in the world abound in the behavior of individuals, groups, and nations. We are reminded constantly of the many serious threats that humankind faces—an exploding population, the amassing of enormous destructive power, international economic instability, environmental pollution, the depletion of natural resources. While we hesitate to claim that irrational human behavior is the fundamental cause of all of them, it is certainly a major contributing factor. It is difficult to imagine a more important educational objective than the teaching and learning of how to think more effectively than we typically do. Indeed, if we cannot learn to think more rationally and effectively, we are, as a species, in serious trouble.

We find it useful to distinguish four types of educational objectives: abilities, methods, knowledge, and attitudes (Nickerson, 1981). We believe the teaching of thinking should involve all four types: abilities that underlie thinking, methods that aid thinking, knowledge about thinking, and attitudes that are conducive to thinking. Abilities that underlie thinking include classification, analysis, hypothesis formation, and many of the other foci of the programs discussed in Chapters 6, 8 and 9. Methods that aid thinking include problem solving heuristics and self management strategies highlighted by programs discussed in Chapters 7 and 10. Knowledge about thinking includes knowledge not only about thought processes in general, and about the cognitive capabilities and limitations of human beings as a species, but about one's own idiosyncratic strengths and weaknesses in this regard. Knowledge about thinking is stressed by some of the programs discussed in Chapter 10. Among the attitudes that efforts to teach thinking should promote are a sense of curiosity and wonder, the thrill of discovery, and the excitement and deep satisfaction that come from productive intellectual activity. In general, attitudes have not, we believe, received the emphasis they deserve.

Sometimes the teaching of thinking is contrasted with the teaching of conventional subject matter; thinking ability and domain-specific knowledge are viewed as opposing educational goals. This is unfortunate. Thinking ability is not a substitute for knowledge; nor is knowledge a substitute for thinking ability. Both are essential. Knowledge and thinking ability are two sides of the same coin. They are the yin and yang of intellectual competence and rational behavior.

There is one major reservation to be considered about the objective of teaching thinking: namely, the possibility that it cannot be done. In an early chapter of this book, we responded to this possibility with a form of Pascal's wager. If it cannot be done, and we try to do it, we may waste some time and effort. If it can be done, and we fail to try, the inestimable cost will be generations of students whose ability to think effectively is less than it could have been. So we are better advised to adopt the attitude that thinking can be taught, try hard to teach it, and let experience prove us wrong if it must.

Now, however, we are at the end of this book, and have looked at the results of a number of programs designed to teach thinking in various ways. To be sure, these programs constitute but a fraction of the evidence that might ultimately emerge. Nonetheless, there is some evidence to consider. How does that evidence lean? What does it say about the teachability of thinking?

Can thinking be taught?

In a word, yes.

Despite the fact that the majority of programs we have discussed lack adequate empirical evaluations, enough evaluative data have been obtained and enough of these investigations have yielded positive results to conclude that instruction can enhance thinking skills. In the aggregate results of these efforts, we find many existence proofs of this fact.

It is important, though, to understand just what the collective results demonstrate and what they do not. First, they do not show that all sincere attempts to teach thinking skills will be successful. Serious efforts to teach thinking skills that have been evaluated with pretests and posttests sometimes have shown no significant gains. Improvements are not to be assumed.

Second, in most cases, gains demonstrated with objective testing have been modest in size. To be sure, teachers and students participating in programs often report their impressions of gains seemingly greater, or of a different kind, than those the objective tests indicate. We have had such experiences ourselves in connection with our own work in this area. We think that these impressions should not be ignored, but scientific caution dictates that the most objective data carry the most weight. It is appropriate to emphasize, therefore, that most measured gains have been modest, while acknowledging that a few instances of more dramatic gains have been reported and that the frequently observed positive impressions of teachers and students suggest that the evaluation instruments commonly used may not capture all of importance that is happening.

Finally, the collective results speak with more certainty about some populations and kinds of gains than others. Consider, for example, three dimensions: the initial ability of the population, the breadth of the gain—the variety of cognitive performances it encompasses—and whether the gain is lasting.

There exist some clear cases of broad and lasting gains with populations of low initial ability, populations at risk for what is sometimes called psychosocial retardation. See, for example, results from the Instrumental Enrichment program (Chapter 6) or the Milwaukee Project (Chapter 2). With average populations, there are cases of gains in some specific and useful performances, as in the Venezuela adaptation of de Bono's CoRT program (Chapter 7), and cases of gains along a broad front, as in the Philosophy for Children program (Chapter 10), and Project Intelligence (Chapter 6). However, we do not presently have good evidence of lasting gains in these cases because of lack of follow-up data. For more able students, there is clear evidence that performance on particular tasks can be improved from, for example, Schoenfeld's success in enhancing skills of mathematical problem solving (Chapter 7). Again, however, we know of no follow-up data that speak about lasting effects one way or the other.

To summarize, there is some fairly persuasive evidence of gains for less able, average and more able populations, broad gains for less able and average populations, and broad lasting gains for less able populations. The record does not reveal whether gains are lasting for average and more able populations. Nor does it say whether broad gains are possible for able populations.

Why the lack of evidence on these latter points? One explanation relates to some practical realities of investigations into the teaching of thinking skills. Programs addressing less able and average populations are more likely to receive support because of their wide applicability to social problems. As to documenting lasting gains, the cost and effort required to locate and re-test students one or more times years after they have received the instruction assure that long-term follow-up is rare.

Besides these practical realities, there are other factors to contend with as well. It may be easier to achieve broad gains with less able students than it is with more able students, because the latter have already acquired on their own many of the general skills of attention, self-monitoring, and so on that programs directed at the less able students foster. As to breadth of gains, it is probably easier to improve performance on a particular set of important tasks than to improve intellectual performance generally, because particular tasks tend to involve specific approaches that can be taught directly. Finally, it is certainly easier to document short-term gains than lasting gains, because, even if the gains persist, as time passes it becomes increasingly difficult to separate the effects of the initial experience from those of others that have occurred during the interval before testing.

We are optimistic about the prospects for overcoming these problems, even in the case of broad lasting gains for high ability populations. Given the progress that has been made to date, we view that challenge as one that quite likely will be met.

2. INGREDIENTS OF SUCCESS

It would be desirable to be able to end a book of this sort with a sure prescription for success: If you want your students to be better thinkers, do a, b, c.... We are not able to do that. Nor, in our view, is anyone else. However, examination of programs and reflection on what it means to be able to think well have left us with several impressions, which we describe in the following.

The Teacher

The results of any program will depend heavily on the quality of the teaching involved. An especially able teacher will often get good results even with mediocre material, while the best of material is unlikely to compensate for poor teaching. This is not to say that the content of a program is not important; we strongly suspect that the best results are obtained when highly skilled teachers have excellent materials with which to work.

As a corollary to teacher competency, an important ingredient of success, in our view, is the extent to which a program helps the teacher with the teaching, rather than just providing the content to be taught. Some programs offer much more guidance to teachers than do others on a lesson by lesson basis. At one extreme, some programs make heavy use of prepared materials and provide teacher's guides that detail how each lesson might be taught. The Instrumental Enrichment program (Chapter 6) and Project Intelligence (Chapter 6) are examples. This does not mean that the teacher has no discretion; but the teacher exercises discretion within a framework that anticipates some of the problems that may arise in teaching a particular lesson. Although we do not necessarily advocate thorough lesson by lesson guidance—perhaps that is not even possible for some kinds of programs—we do think that some programs leave the teacher at sea by not supplying enough guidance.

Help for the teacher takes another form as well, namely formal teacher training. Some programs offer explicit and even extensive training to teachers who will use the program; The Philosophy for Children program (Chapter 10) and Instrumental Enrichment (Chapter 6) are examples. For many programs, no such training is available. Although, for a variety of reasons formal training is not always possible, we think that in general it is a definite plus.

Most developers of programs to teach thinking agree that the role of the teacher in such programs should *not* be primarily that of a dispenser of knowledge. It rather should be that of a *facilitator* of learning, and perhaps more importantly, that of a collaborator in an exploratory process. The teacher's challenge is not that of giving students information, but that of getting them to think. It is not so much that of putting something into the students' heads as that of getting something out of them. Polya (1965) expressed the notion with the metaphor of helping students give birth to their own ideas: "What the teacher says in the classroom is not unimportant, but what the students think is a thousand times more important. The ideas should be born in the students' minds and the teacher should act only as midwife" (p. 104).

Most of the programs we have reviewed do stress the importance of student participation, exploration, and discovery, and deemphasize lecturing as a teaching method. However, most also recognize the need for *guided* exploration and discovery. The challenge is to provide the kind of guidance that will maximize the chances that specific target knowledge and skills are acquired, and, at the same time, foster curiosity, inquiry, inventiveness, and individuality. Enough structure is needed to keep the class focused on specific instructional objectives, but structure easily becomes rigidity, and rigidity is anathema to creative thinking. Achieving the right balance in this regard undoubtedly depends on sensitive skillful teaching more than on anything else.

Teacher Acceptance of the Program

Given the critical nature of the teachers' role, it is foolhardy to undertake a program that lacks the participating teachers' confidence and enthusiastic support. The point is illustrated in a case study reported by Ware (1980), who describes the efforts of one local school system to implement an instructional program in thinking skills, and contrasts the results of this effort with those of a similar one by the same system to improve writing skills. The thinking skills on which the program focused included the following, the last four of which were taken from Bloom, Engelhart, Furst, Hill, and Krathwohl (1956):

Inquiry
Application (of previously learned material in a new situation)
Analysis (or breaking something down into its parts in order to understand its structure)
Synthesis (or putting parts together to create a whole)
Evaluation (of something in terms of a set of standards)

The program was a requirement levied on the schools by the school board. Each school in the system was required to have an annual plan in which it described its instructional objectives, the strategies for accomplishing those objectives and assessment procedures for determining whether the objectives had been achieved. Teachers were expected to develop their own classroom materials and methods, but were provided with lists of verbs and phrases to guide their thinking. The list for use on the analysis objective within the context of teaching science included the following items:

Analyze
Classify and state the basis for the classification
Distinguish between cause and effect relationships
Distinguish between fact and hypothesis
Distinguish between relevant and irrelevant
Hypothesize
Infer
Recognize assumptions

Ware reports considerable resistance on the part of teachers to the program. There were doubts about the appropriateness of the specific thinking skills that had been selected as the course objectives. Teachers did not feel adequately trained to develop and use the necessary materials and methods for teaching and assessment. Some felt they were doing a good job of teaching thinking already.

Ware contrasts with this the reaction to the expository writing program. In this case a curriculum was developed and teachers were trained under a Title IV-C grant. The writing process was conceptualized as having five steps: prewriting (brainstorming), outlining, writing, proofreading, and rewriting. Objectives were related to these steps and methods of evaluation—an objective test and a procedure for scoring written paragraphs—were developed. Students were obliged to write a paragraph each week, which was scored in accordance with this procedure. The writing project was considered to be successful "because of the clarity of its objectives (both program and instructional), because of its replicability from school to school which facilitated staff development, and because of the expectations of practice and assessment" (p. 21).

By way of explaining why the program to teach writing was successful whereas the one for teaching thinking was not, Ware points out that there is an accepted, basic technology to the teaching of writing as well as accepted methods for assessing writing; also most professionals in education have had formal training in writing. None of these conditions holds in the case of thinking skills. There is, therefore, a need in the latter case to give special attention to issues of objective setting, assessment, and teacher preparation.

Objectives, Instructional Procedures, and Evaluation Procedures

In keeping with Ware's observations, we believe that three important ingredients of any program to teach thinking that is to have a reasonable chance of success are:

- Instructional objectives
- Instructional procedures
- Evaluation procedures

These ingredients are so closely interrelated that we find it convenient to discuss them as a group. The most basic of the three, however, must be the objectives. In the absence of objectives it is not clear what rationale one can use to derive the instructional methodology or the purpose for which one would attempt an evaluation.

Instructional Objectives. The ultimate instructional objective, of course, is significant enhancement of the ability to think effectively. Such an objective is not very helpful to the teacher, however, because it is too general and vague. What is needed are some more limited objectives that satisfy certain criteria, among which are the following:

Validity. Instructional objectives should be such that achieving them facilitates realization of the long-term goal of improving thinking ability generally. How one determines whether any particular objective is consistent with that long-term goal is not apparent in the absence of a better theory of thinking than any that now exists. The best we can do at this point is attempt to devise from the literature some consensus of what some of the major aspects or components of thinking ability are. Theoretically, this is not very satisfying, but for practical purposes it must suffice. In view of our inability to define to everyone's satisfaction what should be meant by thinking ability in a general sense, it seems a good idea to establish objectives that are also valued in their own right, independently of their relationship to the top-level goal.

Examples of objectives that satisfy this criterion, in our view, are the following:

- Understanding of the difference between empirical truth and logical validity
- Ability to design tests of hypotheses
- Ability to use effectively specific strategies or heuristic procedures for solving problems
- Ability to construct, evaluate, and modify plans
- Knowledge of what an analogy is an of how to use analogies effectively
- Awareness and avoidance of some of the more commonly made errors of reasoning

Feasibility. Instructional objectives should be realistic in the sense that there is a reasonable expectation of achieving them. This implies the need for graded objectives that are applicable at different stages of cognitive development or different levels of intellectual proficiency.

Feasible objectives also imply limited objectives. The teacher or school system that wishes to implement new programs to teach thinking skills would do well, we believe, to begin by targeting a few quite precise skills: how to analyze and evaluate arguments; how to apply some specific problem solving heuristics; how to plan; how to test hypotheses. What one selects as objectives will depend on several factors: the age and ability level of the students, the availability of material and resources, the interests and special abilities of the teachers, the academic context in which the innovation is to occur. Having limited objectives does not preclude one from going beyond them as opportunities to do so arise, but setting objectives that are unrealistically ambitious almost guarantees frustration and disappointment.

Assessability. Instructional objectives should be defined in such a way that one may determine whether or not they have been attained at any particular time. To the extent possible, they should be quantitative. Ideally, they should be expressed in terms of the properties and measurements that can be used as a diagnostic profile.

Some people concerned with teaching thinking doubt the relevance of quantitative measures on two grounds. They feel that the effects of the instruction should be plainly observable in the behavior of the students, so quantitative measures are not necessary. And they fear that many quantitative instruments miss the most important part of what the students are learning, so that a program may seem to fail on quantitative grounds while, in fact, succeeding.

We resonate to both these points. In our own work on developing Project Intelligence, we have felt that we could directly perceive some of the impacts of the instruction. We also believe that many quantitative measures sometimes used to assess instruction do miss some important aspects of what is being learned. But neither of these factors persuades us that quantitative measures can be safely neglected. It is a fact reaffirmed in numerous contexts that wishful thinking distorts casual observation. "Obvious improvements" may be illusory entirely, or, short of that, may indicate real and valuable changes in attitude but not in competence, or may reflect only a few individual students who were particularly affected by the instruction, and especially visible to the teacher or program developer. We do not say that informal observation is always wrong and should be ignored; but simply that the field cannot afford to operate on the assumption that it is generally accurate and can be accepted uncritically.

As to the risk of tests missing the point, we see this as a challenge to select or develop tests more finely tuned to the objectives of programs. There is no need, for example, to restrict assessment to IQ tests or to multiple-choice formats. One can collect and score essays, arguments, designs, and other wholistic products of thinking. Although such scoring often must be judgmental, interjudge agreement is not that difficult to obtain. It is simply not the case that contemporary strategies of testing are baffled by the sorts of objectives that programs designed to teach thinking want to achieve. What *is* so is that, for a sensible and sensitive evaluation, one often must search hard for appropriate instruments or construct them explicitly for the program in question.

Ideally, we would like programs that have been through some period of development to come with instruments appropriate for assessing student progress on the program's objectives. The local user of a program should not be burdened with problems of assessment technique that the original developers were in a much better position to solve. Unfortunately, most programs do not provide such instruments.

Instructional procedures. Knowing where one wants to go is a large step toward determining how to get there. A set of unambiguous instructional objectives that satisfy the criteria listed above should facilitate the design of procedures for realizing those objectives and the preparation of teachers to use the procedures. In our view, much of the difficulty associated with the development of instructional procedures is attributable to the vagueness of objectives. This is not to claim that the specification of instructional procedures is a trivial task once objectives have been specified, but to suggest that it may be an impossible task when they have not been.

As to the instructional procedures themselves, there is room for a wide variety of approaches. Nonetheless, we think that a number of factors are likely to foster the best results. As noted earlier, explicit and rather detailed guidance for the teacher seems to help, granted that the teacher will always need, and should always have, the freedom to decide how to handle particular situations.

Maintaining the active engagement of the students is an important aspect of such instruction. Several tactics can help with this. First, as mentioned earlier, it is generally agreed that instruction in the teaching of thinking skills should be highly interactive. Second, student engagement will be fostered by giving students choices as to which problems to pursue or projects to undertake, whenever this is consistent with the other goals of the lesson. Third, an effort should be made to present whatever skills are being taught through genuinely interesting contexts and problems. Since, usually, the objective of teaching thinking skills does not entail teaching a narrow body of content, the designer of the instructional procedures has an unusual opportunity to select areas of application that the students are likely to find intrinsically interesting.

Instructional procedures should avoid the mistake of giving too little practice and rushing too quickly from one skill to the next. Our impression is that students need to practice applying a skill a number of times before it becomes a stable part of their repertoire. Many programs move too quickly. We return to this point in the discussion of "time-on-task" below. Also treated below is the problem of transfer. A skill learned in one context often does not spontaneously transfer to others. Accordingly, the instructional procedure should include elements designed to stimulate such transfer.

It often seems beneficial for students to work in small groups, especially as a new topic is introduced. Extensive support from the teacher during this period is helpful as well. On the other hand, the treatment of any topic should eventually involve some problems that the students do alone. This not only provides the students with practice in "soloing," but gives the teacher important feedback about whether each student is learning the skills.

Evaluation procedures. The importance of evaluation is widely acknowledged. So too is the difficulty of doing it well. There are many problems associated with evaluation and we have discussed some of them in Chapter

11. For the present, we wish to emphasize that one of the main reasons for difficulties in conducting evaluations and getting interpretable results has unquestionably been the vagueness of the objectives of some programs.

Evaluations can be more or less comprehensive. Ultimately, of course, one would like to know of any program whether it has substantial and lasting effects on students' thinking in a general sense. This is very difficult to ascertain, and impossible over a short time. There are less ambitious types of evaluations, however, that are both doable and worth doing. A type of evaluation that need not be especially difficult is one that focuses on the short-term objectives of a program and examines whether the specific abilities, methods, knowledge, or attitudes that the program was intended to convey were actually acquired by the students. We argue that such an evaluation is the minimum that should be expected of any program; if a program fails to present evidence of its effectiveness in realizing its most immediate short-range objectives, there is little reason to take it seriously.

How easy it is to perform this type of evaluation will depend, in no small measure, on how carefully and precisely the program's objectives have been defined. It is desirable to specify them in sufficiently objective and quantitative terms that determining the extent to which they have been realized will be a relatively straightforward matter. The question of long-term general effects aside, an evaluation of immediate effects can produce highly useful results, especially if the short-range objectives are considered important in their own right. If, for example, one considers the ability to analyze or evaluate an informal argument to be an important ability in and of itself, and if the development of such an ability is a specified objective of a program, then evidence that that program enhances the development of that ability provides one bit of evidence of that program's success.

Time on Task

One of the most obvious possible reasons why many efforts to teach thinking skills have not demonstrated their effectiveness by pretest-posttest comparisons is insufficient time-on-task. Frequently, efforts to teach thinking skills have involved relatively brief periods of instruction. However, considerable educational research has demonstrated the importance of time-on-task in teaching conventional content and has emphasized the slow, accretive nature of most learning. Several studies have shown a strong connection, for example, between the amount of instructional time allocated to a subject and the level of student achievement in that subject (Karweit, 1976; Nieman & Gastright, 1975; Wiley, 1973). The correlation is even greater when time that is allocated for instruction but is spent inappropriately or ineffectively is discounted and attention is focused on time when the students are in fact engaged in appropriate learning tasks (Fredrick, 1977; Good & Beckerman, 1978; Stallings & Kaskowitz, 1974). ("Appropriate" includes the notion of level of difficulty that is neither so easy as to pose no challenge nor so difficult as to preclude successful performance.)

A recent and especially thorough study of time-on-task identified three distinct measures (Fisher, Berliner, Filby, Marliave, Cahen, & Dishaw, 1980). *Allocated time* is the most familiar and straightforward. This refers to the time allocated to instruction in a particular content area. *Engaged time* refers to the percentage of time within allocated time during which a student actually is engaged in learning activities. Engaged time often fell far short of 100% for many reasons such as daydreaming, play, some students finishing desk work before others, and time spent passing out papers or rearranging seats. *Success rate* refers to the percentage of engaged time students spend working with high success, medium success, or low success. In the language of the report, a high success rate meant that a student was making mostly careless errors, low success meant near random performance, and medium success meant something between these extremes.

The investigation found relationships between learning and all three measures. Although this research concerned teaching in conventional subject matters, we see no reason why it should not apply directly to the teaching of thinking skills as well. Accordingly, programs designed to teach thinking skills should seek high allocated time—time of the order given to any other subject matter such as English or arithmetic, rather than, say, one period per week. We recognize that such programs have to compete with other school content for time, but, as the potentials of teaching thinking are recognized, thinking instruction may be seen to merit serious time commitment. As to engaged time, the research recommends careful design of the instructional procedure to avoid slack time, which can easily become substantial. This makes as much sense for teaching thinking as for teaching anything else.

Concerning success rate, the study disclosed the most learning with what the investigators term "successful practice," that is, a very high success rate on exercises. This was especially true of weak to average students, while brighter students learned effectively with a somewhat higher failure rate on exercises. The findings do not mean, of course, that exercises should pose no challenge at all, but that the students should be able to do nearly all of them successfully. This is relevant to the design of programs to teach thinking skills, inasmuch as many of these programs, after teaching some heuristics, escalate rather quickly to fairly difficult problems. More extensive practice at a modest level of difficulty, leading on to harder problems as the student is able to handle them with a high success rate, seems to be a better formula.

Transfer

Transfer in some sense has to be the concern of any program designed to teach thinking skills. All such programs aim to equip students with skills that they later will apply in circumstances different from those of the instruction. For instance, it is hoped that skills of reasoning learned in a philosophical setting will later find use in writing an essay, deciding for whom to vote, or pondering where to live. Skills of inventive thinking learned in the context of writing stories or designing simple gadgets should be useful in planning a term project, devising a new business, or resolving a dispute in an unexpected way.

Transfer poses a special challenge to efforts to enhance thinking. Belmont and Butterfield (1977) reviewed a number of studies designed to teach cognitive skills, finding little signs of transfer. Even though a skill learned in one context may in principle apply to another, quite commonly a person who has mastered the skill in the first context does not think to apply it in the second. Moreover, many skills acquired in one context do not carry over straightforwardly to others, but require significant adjustment, another barrier in the way of smooth transfer.

Given these considerations, the most secure program is one that minimizes the transfer required by teaching as directly as possible to the target performances it hopes to improve. A number of situations that at first might seem adequate approximations to that ideal may well not be. For instance, instruction that highlights critical assessment of certain products will not necessarily improve the making of those products. For a particular example, heightening students' critical awareness of flaws in others' arguments may leave them no more careful in constructing arguments of their own. Another pitfall is practicing a strategy only in exercises in which the student knows the strategy is likely to apply. The student may flounder later when new occasions of application have to be discovered. For a particular example, it is commonplace in mathematics instruction that the student almost always knows what technique to use in a problem set—namely, the technique that was just introduced. In consequence, students get little experience in searching their full repertoires for appropriate techniques and may fare badly when facing problems outside the guiding context of the text. In summary, rough approximations to the target performance may not be enough; the safest match is a complete match.

We also need to acknowledge both that transfer does sometimes occur spontaneously and that, in many situations, it is impossible to provide direct practice in all the many tasks to which one would like a skill to transfer. In facing this problem, instructional programs do well to address the problem of transfer head-on by helping the learners to become explicitly aware of the importance of transfer and to achieve it rather than leaving it to fate.

It is reasonable to expect better transfer from programs that utilize some of the following tactics. The instruction can explicitly encourage students to carry over the skills to other contexts. Exercises can provide practice in making connections to remote contexts. The teacher can ensure that any principle being taught is repeatedly stated in a general, context-free form that facilitates transfer. The exercises can include problems of several very different kinds, so that students will encounter in their own experience the broad range of applicability of the skill in question. Belmont, Butterfield, and Ferretti (1982) argue that, in general, the key to transfer is self-management; students must learn not only the particular skills in question, but general skills of self-monitoring and strategy selection that help to mediate transfer. By such tactics as these, we think that the probability of transfer can be considerably increased.

Conducive Environments

The idea that some environments are more conducive to thinking than are others is intuitively compelling. But what constitutes a favorable thinking environment? Papert (1971) has argued that the best way to teach children to think is to put them in environments in which they will "become highly involved in experiences of a kind to provide rich soil for the growth of intuitions and concepts for dealing with thinking, learning, playing, and so on" (p. 4-1). As an example of such experiences, Papert points to the writing of simple computer programs that cause something interesting to happen immediately for the child to see. Such happenings include the computer-controlled movement of a mechanical creature, or the drawing of patterns on a computer-driven display. We agree with Papert that computer technology has much to offer to the problem of providing environments that are conducive to thinking; we believe also, however, that much can be done without computer involvement to provide such environments.

Maintaining an atmosphere in which ideas can be expressed freely without fear of ridicule is surely an important aspect of this issue, as is the consistent provision of reinforcement for efforts by students to think things through and to figure things out. A genuine and obvious interest on the part of the teacher in what students think will undoubtedly do much to increase their willingness to share their thoughts. Most programs designed to teach thinking, because of their general character, offer ample opportunity for establishing such an environment. But opportunity is not the same as specific guidelines. Many have not given the matter of how to make classroom environments conducive to thinking the attention that it deserves.

A significant body of research defines some helpful strategies. How a teacher responds to a specific effort by a given student can greatly influence the student's willingness to try again. Costa (1981) cites several studies as sources of evidence of specific teacher responses that appear to facilitate intellectual performance: "silence after a question or after a student responds" (Rowe, 1974); "accepting, building upon, integrating, and extending students' ideas" (Flanders, 1969); "clarifying" (Klevin, 1958); and "providing additional information" (Andre, 1979; Suchman, 1966). "Such behaviors," Costa suggests "seem to create a stress-free, cooperative classroom condition where experimental ideas can be risked, alternative hypotheses explored, and answers changed with additional data; where value is placed on creative problem-solving strategies rather than on conformity to 'right' answers" (p. 30).

For the most part, program developers have not given as much attention to the question of how to make classroom environments conducive to thinking as the question deserves. Hutchinson's (1980) report of experiences with the Cognitive Studies Project at Manhattan Community College makes it clear that the issue is an important one not only for children but for adults as well. His report also points out the importance of the role of the teacher in establishing and maintaining a non-threatening intellectual environment in which students feel free to express ideas and opinions and are confident that genuine efforts to think will be respected, whether or not they lead to correct answers and text-book solutions.

Certainly the intellectual atmosphere in the classroom is of paramount importance. We suspect, however, that the physical aspects of the classroom may have more of an influence on the intellectual atmosphere than has generally been acknowledged. This is not to suggest that better equipped classrooms are necessarily more conducive to thinking than are poorly equipped ones. But much can be done, at very little expense, to make a classroom an interesting and intellectually stimulating place to be. One key to this is variety: frequent changes in seating arrangements, in wall displays, in books, in objects of interest, in products that the class has produced. The posting of questions, challenges, analogies to be completed, problems to be solved, can add to the intellectual excitement of a space. Periodically challenging the students to specify how the room has been changed since their last class can be a method of encouraging careful observation and perceptivity. The possibilities are many. This aspect of a program—the physical setting in which it is carried out—is worth some attention, and it is an especially easy one to overlook.

Motivation

Learning theorists and educators are in general agreement on the point that motivated students learn more readily than unmotivated students. Ebel (1974) has expressed the centrality of the role of motivation well: "The essential condition for learning is the purposeful activity, the willingness to work hard to learn, of the individual learner. Learning is not a gift any school can give. It is a prize the learner himself must pursue. If a pupil is unwilling or unable to make the effort required, he will learn little in even the best school" (p. 11). This is not to say that teachers are powerless to influence the students' interest in learning and willingness to make the effort that learning requires. Very likely, a major difference between outstanding and mediocre teachers is the ability not so much to impart knowledge as to promote the desire of students to acquire it.

What is true of learning in this regard is undoubtedly true also of thinking and certainly of learning to think. Indeed, we believe that a very large fraction of the problem of learning to think—and of thinking—is a problem of motivation. Thinking can be hard work—diagnosing a faulty mechanism, analyzing a complex situation, evaluating a lengthy argument, developing an effective plan for solving a complicated organizational problem—and quite possibly the most pervasive reason why people do not do more of it is simply a disinclination to make the effort. Interestingly enough, it is also the case that some people find thinking pleasurable and rewarding in and of itself. Such people will devote considerable effort to the solving of problems for no reason other than the enjoyment of meeting the intellectual challenge the problems pose. But how to instill such motivation when it is not there to begin with?

We think there are at least two plausible answers to this question. The first is to try to select problems that are likely to be intrinsically interesting to the students. When a student shows no interest in thinking, one might do well to consider whether it is more likely that he has no interest in thinking per se, or rather has no interest in thinking about what he is being asked to think about. If the topic bears no relationship to the student's own world it should be less than surprising if he finds it uninteresting. Thurstone (1923) makes the point this way:

> If we assume that the child naturally seeks satisfactions that are typical for its age and maturity, we shall find interest to be merely the relevancy of the environment to the wants that originate in the child. A stimulus that does not serve as a tool for the child's satisfaction, as seen by the child, is simply not a stimulus. It is not attended to. The central problem of interest is, therefore, first of all, to list the desires of children and the numerous ways in which these desires may be satisfied. It is the teacher's task to use the innate desire of the child as the motive power for its own work, and to make available those stimuli which the child normally seeks and which also serve the instructional purposes. If a lesson is not so arranged that it serves as an avenue of natural self-expression for the child, there is no internal motive power to make the child think, and the teacher is thereby increasing her own labors. (p. 66)

We suspect that what is true of children in this regard is true of adults as well.

Second, programs designed to enhance thinking must respect the students' desire to know why they should be interested in learning what they are being asked to learn. Especially if the material presented is not intrinsically interesting to them, it is incumbent on the teacher to let them know why they should apply themselves to the task. Failure to do this can convey messages that demotivate thinking in subtle ways. Students can take it as evidence that the teacher believes they are incapable of understanding the usefulness of some particular information or skill, or as evidence that they should not be concerned about reasons but simply do as they are told. Neither effect is supportive of the goal of encouraging students to think.

Third, undoubtedly the causal linkage between motivation and performance is bidirectional. Success fosters success, because it motivates. One quickly loses interest in an activity if one persistently fails at it. Exercises intended to promote an interest in problem solving and the development of thinking skills should be calibrated to the students' abilities. It is important that students succeed and experience a sense of achievement. Only if they do so are they likely to maintain an interest to going on to more challenging problems.

In general, instruction should preserve and encourage intrinsic motivation, motivation to pursue the task for its own sake. For instance, teachers can make plain their own enthusiasm for the topic, thus becoming models for the students in this regard. Students can be given some individual choice about which problems to do, a strategy that both lets each select what is personally most interesting and helps them to maintain a sense of internal rather than external locus of control. Teachers can take pains to avoid creating the impression that the students are being constantly evaluated. According to the research summarized by Amabile (1983), intrinsic motivation is much more easily undermined than created. Instructional strategies like those mentioned above may foster the development of intrinsic motivation and at least avoid some of the practices that undermine it.

Attitudes

We have noted that attitudes have not received the emphasis they deserve in programs to teach thinking. And we have mentioned the importance of the teacher's role in conveying attitudes. At the risk of being redundant, we focus on the issue here because we believe it to be a critical one.

Among the attitudes that an effort to enhance thinking might attempt to foster are the following:

- A lively sense of curiosity and inquisitiveness.
- A willingness to modify one's views when evidence indicates that they should be modified.

- A commitment to figuring things out, to thinking things through, to evaluating claims in the light of relevant information, as opposed to accepting them uncritically.
- A respect for the opinions of others when they differ from one's own.
- Acceptance of the idea that winning arguments is less important than arriving at conclusions that are supported by facts.

It is appropriate in this context to note also the importance that investigators have given to cultivating habits of carefulness and thoughtfulness in intellectual work. It is one thing to acquire tools and to assimilate knowledge that can be useful on cognitively demanding tasks; it is quite another to develop the habit of making use of those tools and that knowledge. Familiarity with problem solving heuristics, for example, does not guarantee that those heuristics will be applied appropriately and effectively.

We suspect that attitudes are not easy to teach. Indeed, perhaps they cannot be taught at all. However they are, we believe, contagious. Perhaps in no other aspect of thinking is the example that is set by a teacher quite so important as it is in the case of attitudes. A teacher who shows no real enthusiasm for the subject is unlikely to inspire enthusiasm on the part of his students. On the other hand, students of a teacher who gets real satisfaction out of facing intellectual challenges and genuinely enjoys stretching his mind are very apt to show symptoms of the same disease.

3. SOME RECOMMENDATIONS

We have tried in this book to review quite broadly research relevant to the enhancement of thinking skills. The review has touched upon several major topics—intelligence, problem solving, creativity, metacognition—and has drawn upon numerous research efforts. The picture that emerges is a complex one: a collage of facts, theories, opinions, attitudes, and speculations regarding what thinking is all about and how it might be improved.

The question we now face is a practical one. What can we extract from all of this by way of specific recommendations that might help guide others who wish to enhance thinking skills through school programs? Given a specific individual or a group of individuals whose thinking skills one wants to improve, how does one determine where to begin and what to do? What first steps should one take toward establishing a program? How should one select the material to use? How should one adjust it for the circumstances? Should one continuously evaluate progress? And if one decides progress is not satisfactory, what can one do to increase the chances of getting better results?

Without any pretense of offering definitive answers, we have some recommendations to make based on opinions that have been shaped by our study of the programs we have described and the evidences of their effects. These recommendations fall into two categories: the first has to do with selecting existing programs for suitability in specific situations; the second concerns implementation of existing or newly designed programs. Our top-level recommendation is that the reader bear in mind that our specific recommendations are *only* that. We believe they are worth making, else we would not make them, but we offer them as suggestions deserving of some consideration, not as a recipe that will guarantee success.

On Selecting Programs

- Be clear about your objectives before you start. Make them few in number and quite specific. Do not try to accomplish too much. If you can succeed in realizing a few specific objectives, then you can set some additional ones and attempt to accomplish those also.
- Select specific short-range objectives that you consider to be supportive of important longer-range, more general objectives; but be sure that some of your short-range objectives are, in your view, worth while in their own right. In other words, target some skills that you would consider to be important in and of themselves, not only because they are essential to the development of higher-level skills. If you use an existing program or material without modification, be sure you agree with that program's objectives.
- Think about the way the program you are considering construes thinking skills. Is this thinking of the sort that you want to improve? For instance, if the program teaches strategies, are they directly and straightforwardly applicable to the performances you want to improve, or are you just hoping that "somehow they'll help?"
- Favor programs that teach directly the skills you want students to acquire. Do not expect a program that is intended to teach one set of skills to improve another. It may happen, but counting on it is risky.
- Be cautious about adopting a program that is close to what you want but does not quite address it. For instance, a program on reasoning may concentrate overwhelmingly on analysis of arguments, when, in fact, you want students to learn how to construct their own arguments. The one may help the other, but may not. There is the possibility, of course, of modifying a "close" program so that it more nearly matches what you want.
- Favor programs that provide a lot of practice, or add practice yourself. For instance, programs designed to teach problem-solving strategies often devote only a single class period of practice to the assimilation of two or three heuristic rules for improving some

performance. We think that for most heuristics several periods of practice are probably required.

- In general, beware of short programs. Ten lessons or so seems too short an intervention to have much of an impact.
- Select a program that has a theoretical perspective with which you agree. But recognize that a good theoretical base does not guarantee a good program and that a questionable one does not necessarily mean that the program will be ineffectual. Programs can be effective in spite of a weak theoretical base, or ineffective despite a strong theoretical base.
- Beware of programs that teach about something rather than teaching how to do it. They may improve performance in an area, but may well not.
- Pay careful attention to whatever evaluation data are available and review it critically so as to get a realistic model of what you can expect to accomplish. The absence of evaluation data, especially if the program was only recently developed, is not necessarily evidence that it will not work. But in the absence of some, you should be reasonably convinced of the potential of the program in your situation on other grounds.
- Be sure the program's documentation and provision for teacher training are adequate to your needs.
- Think through the problem of evaluating your own effort before beginning your program. Make a plan to determine, on a more-or-less continuing basis, whether the program is accomplishing what you want it to accomplish.

On Implementation of any Program

- To the degree possible use tasks that are intrinsically interesting, tasks that satisfy the students' natural curiosity and that relate in obvious ways to meaningful aspects of their lives. Teaching is likely to be most effective when the students are learning something they really want to know.
- If it is necessary sometimes to violate the preceding principle and have students perform tasks that are not intrinsically interesting, take care to inform the students, in terms they can understand, as to why the performance of those tasks is important.
- Calibrate the objectives to the students' current level of knowledge and abilities. Exercises should be designed and selected so that the students experience the right level of challenge, which means that a sincere effort should usually assure success and a sense of accomplishment.

- Promote the idea that learning—the acquisition of new information and skills—is not only useful for practical purposes, but, can be very gratifying and even great fun.
- In assessing performance on a cognitively demanding task, try not only to determine whether a student succeeds or fails at the task, but, if he fails, to determine why.
- Provide the students with feedback that does more than inform them how well they did on a task. It should let them know *what* they have done well, *what* they have done poorly, and *how* they can do better.
- Discourage the oversimplified view that performance on a task is always either correct or incorrect; promote the idea that performance may be "incorrect" for a variety of interesting reasons. Treat "failures" as opportunities to learn, to diagnose needs and to guide subsequent training goals and procedures; try not to permit them to demotivate or stigmatize.
- Never penalize students when inventive approaches to problems yield unorthodox or unanticipated results.
- If a given problem-solving strategy or heuristic is intended to be generally useful, be sure it is encountered and practiced in a variety of problem contexts. Draw the students' attention explicitly to the fact that the same approach is being used in the several situations and challenge them to think of other situations in which it would be applicable as well.
- Look constantly for ways to make connections between your efforts to teach thinking skills and what is being taught in other classes. Reinforce the idea at every opportunity that the thinking skills on which you are focusing are valuable precisely because they are applicable in many contexts. Perhaps the most convincing way to do this is to illustrate the fact by frequently showing how to apply them in different problem areas.
- Remember that attitudes are more effectively projected than taught. Nothing that you say in class is likely to have as lasting an impact on your students' attitudes toward thinking as will those that you consistently display.

4. RISKS

There are some risks associated with trying to teach thinking. We mention three: the risk of failure, the risk of indefinite results, and the risk of disappointment. A fourth risk we note is not a risk associated with trying to teach thinking but the risk that comes from failing to try.

The most obvious risk, of course, is the risk of failure. In the worst case, one might find students less able to perform intellectually demanding tasks after participating in a program to enhance thinking skills than before. This seems to us to be an unlikely result of careful implementations of any of the programs we have reviewed in this book, but it is not an impossible one.

A more likely outcome would be the failure to obtain any reliable effects, either negative or positive. This is the risk of indefinite results. A lack of demonstrable positive effects probably should be considered a negative outcome in view of the opportunity costs incurred by any program that makes use of time that could be devoted to other purposes. While we unreservedly subscribe to the goal of teaching thinking skills, and we believe that several of the programs we have reviewed are promising vehicles for pursuing this goal, we caution against the practice of offering courses to enhance thinking in lieu of courses in language, science, mathematics, and other standard core subjects.

A greater risk than that of failure to obtain positive results is the risk of disappointment because the positive results one does obtain are not commensurate with one's initial expectations. We are prone to want too much too quickly. But educational innovation takes time. The problems are complex and there are no quick fixes. Progress is bound to be slow and to involve many false starts. We believe it is extremely important when undertaking a program to enhance thinking to do so with objectives and expectations that are realistic.

A disconcerting aspect of some of the material we have reviewed is its promotional character. People who have developed a program undoubtedly find it easier to see the program's virtues than to see its faults or limitations. In describing one's own program one quite naturally focuses more on its strengths than on its weaknesses. Unfortunately we believe that some of the promotional material that has been prepared for programs to enhance thinking may, if taken literally, foster expectations on the part of potential users that are unlikely to be realized. When this is the case, even if the program produces positive effects, the outcome is likely to be perceived as a failure, or at least a disappointment; and this in turn may discourage the further efforts that would be required to extend or magnify the effects.

We believe that none of these risks associated with trying to teach thinking outweighs the risk of failing to try. All of them combined are not nearly as serious as this one. One might grant that we should attempt to teach thinking in schools but argue that we should wait until we know better how to do so. There is not general agreement, after all, on what constitutes thinking ability, or on what is expected of a thinking person. In a sense, all of the programs we have reviewed are surely wrong. All have limitations and inadequacies of one sort or another. In no case is there the kind of evidence of effectiveness that would convince the most skeptical educators that the program merits implementation without reservation. And, it could hardly be otherwise, given our very limited understanding of how human beings learn and think.

Should we not, therefore, wait until some fundamental issues are better understood before trying to develop thinking-enhancement programs? In our opinion we cannot afford to wait. We should, of course, attempt to resolve these issues, but it would be folly to put off trying to do anything else until answers are forthcoming that everyone will accept. We must try to find better ways to develop thinking ability. And, if we fail, we must learn from the failures and try again.

In the meantime, it is not necessary to have a perfect program in order to teach something of value. Most, perhaps all, of the programs we have reviewed are capable, in the hands of skilled teachers, of enhancing some aspects of thinking. That is not to suggest that there are no differences in quality or effectiveness among the programs we have reviewed. But perhaps (almost) any program is better than none, independently of the specific techniques that are used. Indeed it may be that among the things that any program might do, nothing is quite as important as simply getting teachers and students focused on thinking processes and genuinely interested in attempting to improve them.

In any case, it is less the business of science to be right than to be wrong in interesting and useful ways. One states hypotheses not necessarily because one believes them to be true, in any absolute sense, but because one believes that in testing them one will acquire information that will permit the development of theories of increasing scope and predictive power. What is being done now will provide a basis for more successful efforts to teach thinking in the future and those efforts, in turn, will themselves give way to more effective efforts still.

The question of how best to teach thinking is one that we should not expect ever to be answered in any final sense. No matter how well thinking is taught at any given time, there will—*should*—be a desire to teach it better. Thus, we are dealing with a quest that is, rightfully, always beginning.

References

Ackoff, R. L. Management misinformation systems. *Management Science*, 1967, *14*, 147–156.

Adams, J. L. *Conceptual blockbusting*: *A guide to better ideas*. San Francisco: W.H. Freeman, 1974.

Adams, M. J. Inductive deductions and deductive inductions. In R. S. Nickerson (Ed.), *Proceedings of the VIIIth International Symposium on Attention and Performance*. Hillsdale, NJ: Lawrence Erlbaum Associates, 1980.

Adams, M. J., et al. Teacher's Manual. Prepared for Project Intelligence: The Development of Procedures to Enhance Thinking Skills, submitted to the government of Venezuela 1982.

Amabile, T. M. *The social psychology of creativity*. New York: Springer-Verlag, 1983.

Anastasi, A. *Psychological Testing*. New York: Macmillan, 1954.

Andre, T. Does answering higher-level questions while reading facilitate productive learning? *Review of Educational Research*, Spring 1979, *49*, 280–318.

Arbitman-Smith, R., Haywood, W. C., & Bransford, J. D. Assessing cognitive change. In P. Brooks, R. Sperber, & C.M. McCauley (Eds.), *Learning and cognition in the mentally retarded*. Hillsdale, NJ: Lawrence Erlbaum Associates, 1984.

Armer, P. Attitudes toward intelligent machines. In E. A. Feigenbaum & J. Feldman (Eds.), *Computers and thought*. New York: McGraw-Hill, 1963.

Arons, A. B. Cultivating the capacity of formal reasoning: Objectives and procedures in an introductory physical science course. *American Journal of Physics*, 1976, *44*, 834–838.

Bacon, F. The new organon. In H. G. Dick & F. Bacon (Eds.), *Selected writings, modern library edition*. New York: Random House, 1955.

Bacon, F. *Novum organum*. (Originally Published, 1620) In E. Burtt (Ed.), *The English philosophers from Bacon to Mill*. New York: Random House, 1939.

Bailey, S. E., Perlmuter, L. C., Karsh, R., & Monty, R. A. Choice for others and the perception of control. *Motivation and Emotions*, 1978, *2*, 191–200.

Bar-Hillel, M. The base-rate fallacy in probability judgments. *Acta Psychologica*, 1980, *44*, 211–233.

Baron, J. What kinds of intelligence components are fundamental? In S. F. Chipman, J. W. Segal, & R. Glaser (Eds.), *Thinking and learning skills, Vol. 2: Research and open questions*. Hillsdale, NJ: Lawrence Erlbaum Associates, 1985.

Barron, F. *Creative person and creative process*. New York: Holt, Rinehart, & Winston, 1969.

Barron, F. *Artists in the making*. New York: Seminar Press, 1972.

Barron, F., & Welsh, G. S. Artistic perception as a possible factor in personality style: Its measurement by a figure preference test. *Journal of Psychology*, 1952, *33*, 199–203.

Barrows, H. S., & Mitchell, D. L. M. An innovative course in undergraduate neuroscience experiment in problem based learning with "problem boxes." *British Journal of Medical Education*, 1975, *9*, 223–230.

Barrows, H. S., & Tamblyn, R. M. *Problem-based learning: An approach to medical education*. Vol. I in Springer Series on Medical Education. New York: Springer, 1980.

Bartlett, F. C. *Remembering*. Cambridge: Cambridge University Press, 1932.

Bartlett, F. C. *Thinking: An experimental and social study*. London: Allen and Unwin, 1958.

Beardsley, M. C. *Aesthetics*. New York: Harcourt, Brace, & World, 1958.

Beardsley, M. C. *Thinking straight: Principles of reasoning for readers and writers*. Englewood Cliffs, NJ: Prentice-Hall, 1975.

Belmont, J. M., & Butterfield, E. C. The instructional approach to developmental cognitive research. In R. V. Kail, Jr. & J. W. Hagen (Eds.), *Perspectives on the development of memory and cognition*. Hillsdale, NJ: Lawrence Erlbaum Associates, 1977.

Belmont, J. M., Butterfield, E. C., & Borkowski, J. G. Training retarded people to generalize memorization methods across memory tasks. In M. M. Gruneberg, P. E. Morris, & R. N. Sykes (Eds.), *Practical aspects of memory*. New York: Academic Press, 1978.

Belmont, J. M., Butterfield, E. C., & Ferretti, R. P. To secure transfer of training instruct self-management skills. In D. K. Detterman & R. J. Sternberg (Eds.), *How and how much can intelligence be increased?* Norwood, NJ: Ablex, 1982.

Bereiter, C. Writing. In R. Tyler & S. White (Eds.), *Testing, teaching, and learning*. Washington, D.C.: National Institute of Education, 1979.

Bereiter, C. Development in writing. In L. W. Gregg & E. R. Steinberg (Eds.), *Cognitive processes in writing*. Hillsdale, NJ: Lawrence Erlbaum Associates, 1980.

Bereiter, C., & Engelmann, S. *Teaching disadvantaged children in the preschool*. Englewood Cliffs, NJ: Prentice-Hall, 1966.

Bereiter, C., & Scardamalia, M. Cognitive coping strategies and the problem of "inert knowledge." In S. F. Chipman, J. W. Segal, & R. Glaser (Eds.), *Thinking and learning skills, Volume 2: Research and open questions*. Hillsdale, NJ: Lawrence Erlbaum Associates, 1985.

Berliner, D. C., & Rosenshine, B. The acquisition of knowledge in the classroom. In R. C. Anderson & R. J. Spiro (Eds.), *Schooling and the acquisition of knowledge*. Hillsdale, NJ: Lawrence Erlbaum Associates, 1977.

Bernstein, B. *Class, codes and control. I. Theoretical studies towards a sociology of language*. St. Albans: Paladin, 1973.

Besel, G. Individualized training: Besel study (summary). El Segundo, CA: SOI Institute, 1980.

Binet, A., & Simon, T. Methodes nouvelles pour le diagnostic du nivean intellectual des anormaux. *Annee Psycologic*, 1905, *11*, 191–244.

Blank, M., & Solomon, F. A tutorial language program to develop abstract thinking in socially disadvantaged preschool children. *Child Development*, 1968, *39*, 379–389.

Blooberg, M. Introduction: Approaches to creativity. In M. Blooberg (Ed.), *Creativity: Theory and research*. New Haven, CT: College & University Press, 1973.

Bloom, B. S., & Broder, L. *Problem-solving process of college students*. Chicago: University of Chicago Press, 1950.

Bloom, B. S., Engelhart, M. D., Furst, E. J., Hill, W. H., & Krathwohl, D. R. *Taxonomy of* educational objectives: Handbook I—Cognitive domain. New York: David McKay, 1956.

Botkin, J. W., Elmandjra, M., & Malitza, M. *No limits to learning: Bridging the human gap*. England: Pergamon Press, 1979.

Bradley, J. V. Overconfidence in ignorant experts. *Bulletin of the Psychonomic Society*, 1981, *17*, 82–84.

Brainerd, C. J. *Piaget's theory of intelligence*. Englewood Cliffs, NJ: Prentice-Hall, 1978a.

Brainerd, C. J. The stage question in cognitive-developmental theory. *The Behavioral and Brain Sciences*, 1978b, *2*, 173–213.

Bransford, J. D. *Human cognition: Learning, understanding and remembering*. Belmont, CA: Wadsworth, 1979.

Bransford, J. D., & Johnson, M. K. Contextual prerequisites for understanding: Some investigations of comprehension and recall. *Journal of Verbal Learning and Verbal Behavior*, 1972, *11*, p. 717–726.

Bregman, A. S. Perception and behavior as compositions of ideals. *Cognitive Psychology*, 1977, *9*, 250–292.

Brody, N. The effect of commitment to correct and incorrect decisions on confidence in a sequential decision task. *American Journal of Psychology*, 1965, *78*, 251–256.

Bronowski, J. *Science and human values*. New York: Harper & Row, 1965.

Brown, A. L. The role of strategic behavior in retardate memory. In N. R. Ellis (Ed.), *International review of research in mental retardation*. Vol. 7. New York: Academic Press, 1974.

Brown, A. L. The development of memory: Knowing, knowing about knowing, and knowing how to know. In H. Reese (Ed.), *Advances in child development and behavior, 10*. New York: Academic Press, 1975.

Brown, A. L. Knowing when, where, and how to remember: A problem of metacognition. In R. Glaser (Ed.), *Advances in instructional psychology*. Hillsdale, NJ: Lawrence Erlbaum Associates, 1978.

Brown, A. L., & Barclay, C. R. The effects of training specific mnemonics on the metamnemonic efficiency of retarded children. *Child Development*, 1976, *47*, 71–80.

Brown, A. L., Bransford, J. D., & Chi, M. T. H. The development of expertise. Paper presented at the Michigan Conference on Experimental and Developmental Approaches to Memory Research, October 1979.

Brown, A. L., & Campione, J. C. Permissible inferences from the outcome of training studies in cognitive developmental research. *Quarterly Newsletter of the Institute for Comparative Human Development*, 1978, *2*, 46–53.

Brown, A. L., & Campione, J. C. Inducing flexible thinking: The problem of access. Center for the Study of Reading, Technical Report No. 156, January 1980.

Brown, A. L., & French, L. A. The zone of potential development: Implication for intelligence testing in the year 2000. *Intelligence*, 1979, *3*, 253–271.

Bruce, B. C., Rubin, A. D. & Loucks, S. *Quill Teacher's Guide*, Andover, MA: The Network, Inc., 1983.

Bruner, J. S. *On knowing—essays for the left hand*. Cambridge, MA: Harvard/Belknap Press, 1962.

Bruner, J. S. *Toward a theory of instruction*. Cambridge, MA: Harvard/Belknap Press, 1966; 7th Printing, 1975.

Bruner, J. S., Goodnow, J. J., & Austin, G. A. *A study of thinking*. New York: Wiley, 1956.

Buisman, J. SOI training related to achievement: Buisman study (summary). El Segundo, CA: SOI Institute, 1981.

Burkhart, R. C. *Spontaneous and deliberate ways of learning*. Scranton, PA: International Textbook, 1962.

Burns, B. The effect of self-directed verbal comments on arithmetic performance and activity level of urban hyperactive children. Unpublished doctoral dissertation, Boston College, 1972.

Campbell, T. C. *An evaluation of a learning cycle intervention strategy for enhancing the use of formal operational thought by beginning college physics students.* Unpublished doctoral dissertation, University of Nebraska, 1977.

Campbell, T. C., Fuller, R. G., Thornton, M. C., Petr, J. L., Peterson, M. Q., Carpenter, E. T., & Narveson, R. D. A teacher's guide to the learning cycle. A Piagetian-based approach to college instruction. In R. G. Fuller et al. (Eds.), *Piagetian programs in higher education.* Lincoln, NE: ADAPT, University of Nebraska-Lincoln, 1980, 27–46.

Campione, J. C., & Armbruster, B. B. Acquiring information from text: An analysis of four approaches. In J. W. Segal, S. F. Chipman, & R. Glaser (Eds.), *Thinking and learning skills, Vol. 1: Relating instruction to research.* Hillsdale, NJ: Lawrence Erlbaum Associates, 1985.

Campione, J. C., & Brown, A. L. The effects of contextual changes and degree of component mastery on transfer of training. In H. W. Reese (Ed.), *Advances in child development and behavior.* Vol. 9. New York: Academic Press, 1974.

Campione, J. C., & Brown, A. L. Memory and metamemory development in educable retarded children. In R. V. Kail, Jr. & J. W. Hagen (Eds.), *Perspectives on the development of memory and cognition.* Hillsdale, NJ: Lawrence Erlbaum Associates, 1977.

Campione, J. C., & Brown, A. L. Toward a theory of intelligence: Contributions from research with retarded children. *Intelligence*, 1978, *2*, 279–304.

Carmichael, J. W., Hassell, J., Hunter, J., Jones, L., Ryan, M., & Vincent, H. Project SOAR (Stress on Analytical Reasoning). *The American Biology Teacher*, 1980, *42*(3), 169–173.

Carpenter, E. T. Piagetian interviews of college students. In R. G. Fuller et al. (Eds.), *Piagetian programs in higher education.* Lincoln, NE: ADAPT, University of Nebraska-Lincoln, 1980, pp. 15–21.

Carroll, J. B. Psychometric tests as cognitive tasks: A new "structure of intellect." Princeton, NJ: Educational Testing Service, Research Bulletin 74–16, 1974.

Case, R. A developmentally based approach to the problem of instructional design. In S. F. Chipman, J. W. Segal, & R. Glaser (Eds.), *Thinking and learning skills, Vol. 2: Research and open questions.* Hillsdale, NJ: Lawrence Erlbaum Associates, 1985.

Cattell, J. M. K. Mental tests and measurements. *Mind*, 1890, *15, 373–380.*

Cattell, R. B. Theory of fluid and crystallized intelligence: A critical experiment. *Journal of Educational Psychology*, 1963, *18*, 165–244.

Chapman, L. J., & Chapman, J. P. Illusory correlation as an obstacle to the use of valid psychodiagnostic signs. *Journal of Abnormal Psychology*, 1969, *74*, 271–280.

Chi, M. T. H., Feltovich, P. J., & Glaser, R. Categorization and representation of physics problems by experts and novices. *Cognitive Science*, 1981, *5*, 121–152.

Chiapetta, E. L. A review of Piagetian studies relevant to science instruction at the secondary and college level. *Science Education*, 1976, *60*, 253–261.

Clark, H. H. Linguistic processes in deductive reasoning. *Psychological Review*, 1969, *76*, 387–404.

Clark, H. H. More about "adjectives, comparatives, and syllogisms": A reply to Huttenlocher and Higgins. *Psychological Review*, 1971, *78*, 487–504.

Clark, H. H., & Clark, E. V. *Psychology and Language*, New York: Harcourt Brace Jovanovich, 1977.

Cohen, J., Chesnick, E. I., & Harran, D. Confirmation of inertial – PSI effect in sequential choice and decision. *British Journal of Psychology*, 1972, *63*, 41–46.

Cole, M., Gay, J., Glick, J., & Sharp, D. *The cultural context of learning and thinking.* New York: Basic Books, 1971.

Collea, F. P., & Nummedal. S. G. Development of Reasoning in Science (DORIS): A course in abstract thinking. Progress Report No. 2. Fullerton, CA: California State University, School of Mathematics, Science and Engineering, 1979.

Collea, F. P., & Nummedal, S. G. Development of Reasoning in Science (DORIS): A course in abstract thinking. *Journal of College Science Teaching*, November 1980.

Collins, A. M., & Adams, M. J. A schema-theoretic view of reading. In R. Freedle (Ed.), *New directions in discourse processing*. Norwood, NJ: Ablex, 1982.

Collins, A. M., & Smith, E. E. Teaching the process of reading comprehension. In D. K. Detterman & R. J. Sternberg (Eds.), *How and how much can intelligence be increased?*. Norwood, NJ: Ablex, 1982.

Collins, A. M., & Stevens, A. L. *Goals and strategies of interactive teachers* (Report No. 4345). Cambridge, MA: Bolt Beranek and Newman Inc., 1980.

Connolly, A., Nachtman, W., & Pritchett, E. M. KeyMath diagnostic arithmetic test. Circle Pines, MN: American Guidance Service, 1971.

Copes, L. *Can college students reason?* Talk given at meeting of Seaway Section, Mathematical Association of America, York University, Toronto, Spring 1975.

Corzine, H. J. Piaget and social problems. In R. G. Fuller et al. (Eds.), *Piagetian programs in higher education*. Lincoln, NE: ADAPT, University of Nebraska-Lincoln, 1980.

Costa, A. L. Teaching for intelligent behavior. *Educational Leadership, 1981, 39*, 29–32.

Covington, M. V., Crutchfield, R. S., Davies, L., & Olton, R. M. *The productive thinking program: A course in learning to think*. Columbus, OH: Merrill, 1974.

Craik, F. I. M. A levels of analysis view of memory. In P. Pliner, L. Krames, & T. Alloway (Eds.), *Communication and affect: Language and thought*. New York: Academic Press, 1973.

Craik, F. I. M., & Lockhart, R. S. Levels of processing: A framework for memory research. *Journal of Verbal Learning and Verbal Behavior*, 1972, *2*, 671–684.

Crandall, V. C., Katkovsky, W., & Crandall, V. J. *Intellectual achievement responsibility questionnaire*. Chicago: University of Chicago Press, 1965.

Crockenberg, S. B. Creativity tests: A boon or boondoggle for education? *Review of Educational Research*, 1972, *42*(1), 27–45.

Crosslin, D. SOI readiness test related to achievement: Crosslin study (summary). El Segundo, CA: SOI Institute, 1978.

Crutchfield, R. S. Nurturing the cognitive skills of productive thinking. In L. J. Rubin (Ed.), *Life skills in school and society*. Association for Supervision and Curriculum Development, Yearbook 1969, 53–71.

Dacey, J. S. Programmed instruction in creativity and its effects on eighth grade students. *Dissertation Abstracts International*, 1971, *32*, 2479A. (University Microfilms No. 71–29, 252).

Davis, R. B., & McKnight, C. The influence of semantic content on algorithmic behavior. *The Journal of Mathematical Behavior*, 1980, *3*(1), 39–87.

DeAvila, E. A., & Duncan, S. The language minority child: A psychological, linguistic, and social analysis. In J. W. Segal, S. F. Chipman. & R. Glaser (Eds.). *Thinking and learning skills, Vol. 2: Research and open questions*. Hillsdale, NJ: Lawrence Erlbaum Associates, 1985.

de Bono, E. *The five-day course in thinking*. New York: Basic Books. 1967.

de Bono, E. *New think. The use of lateral thinking in the generation of new ideas*. New York: Basic Books, 1968.

de Bono, E. *Lateral thinking: Creativity step by step*. New York: Harper & Row, 1970.

de Bono, E. *CoRT thinking*. Blandford, Dorset, England: Direct Education Services Limited, 1973, 1974, 1975.

de Bono, E. *Teaching thinking*. London: Temple Smith, 1976.

de Bono, E. The cognitive research trust (CoRT) thinking program. In Maxwell. W. (Ed.), *Thinking: The expanding frontier*. Philadelphia: The Franklin Institute Press, 1983.

de Groot, A. D. *Thought and choice in chess*. The Hague: Mouton, 1965.

Denham, C., & Lieberman, A. (Eds.), *Time to learn*. Washington, DC: National Institute of Education, 1980.

Denney, D. The effects of exemplary and cognitive models and self-rehearsal on children's interrogative strategies. *Journal of Experimental Child Psychology*, 1975, *19*, 476–488.

Dermen, D., French, J. W., & Harman, H. H. Verification of self-report temperament factors. Educational Testing Service, Technical Report No. 6, 1974.

de Sanchez, M. A, & Astorga, M. *Proyecto aprendar a pensar: Estudio de sus efectos sobre una muestra de estudiantes venezolanos*. Caracas, Venezuela: Ministerio de Educacion, 1983.

Detterman, D. K. Introduction: Questions I would like to have answered. In D. K. Detterman & R. J. Sternberg (Eds.), *How and how much can intelligence be increased?* Norwood, NJ: Ablex, 1982.

Dewey, J. The child and the curriculum. In R. D. Archambault (Ed.), *John Dewey on education*. Chicago: University of Chicago Press, 1902.

Dickstein, L. S. Error processes in syllogistic reasoning. *Memory & Cognition*, 1978, *6*(5), 537–543.

Dickstein, L. S. Inference errors in deductive reasoning. *Bulletin of the Psychonomic Society*, 1980, *16*, 414–416.

diSessa, A. A. On 'learning' representations of knowledge: A meaning for the computational metaphor. In J. Lochhead & J. Clement (Eds.), *Cognitive process instruction*. Philadelphia: The Franklin Institute Press, 1979, 239–288.

Dulit, D. Adolescent thinking a la Piaget: The formal stage. *Journal of Youth and Adolescence*, 1972, *1*, 281–301.

Duly, L. C. ADAPT History: The inexpensive unification of Clio and Piaget. In *Multidisciplinary Piagetian-based programs for college freshman*, 3rd ed. Lincoln, NE: ADAPT Program, 1978, 59–64.

Duncker, K. On problem-solving. *Psychological Review*, 1945, *58*(5), (Whole No. 270).

Dunn, L. M., & Markwardt, F. C. Peabody individual achievement test. Circle Pines, MN: American Guidance Service, 1970.

Earley, C. E. Profiles of low achieving readers: Earley study (summary). *SOI research studies*. El Segundo, CA: SOI Institute, 1978.

Easterling, J., & Pasanen, J. *Confront, construct, complete: A comprehensive approach to writing*. Rochelle Park, NJ: Hayden Book Co., 1979.

Ebel, R. L. What are schools for? In H. F. Clarizo, R. C. Craig, & W. A. Mehrens (Eds.), *Contemporary issues in educational psychology* (2nd ed.). Boston: Allyn and Bacon, 1974.

Edwards, J., & Baldauf, R. B. Teaching thinking in secondary science. In W. Maxwell (Ed.), *Thinking: The expanding frontier*. Philadelphia: The Franklin Institute Press, 1983.

Edwards, W., Lindman, H., & Phillips, L. D. Emerging technologies for making decisions. *New directions in psychology II*. New York: Holt, Rinehart, & Winston, 1965, 261–325.

Ehrenberg, L. M., & Sydelle, D. *Basics thinking/learning strategies program: participant Manual*. Ohio: Institute for Curriculum and Instruction, 1980.

Einhorn, H. J., & Hogarth, R. M. Confidence in judgment: Persistence of the illusion of validity. *Psychological Review*, 1978, *95*(5), 395–416.

Ekstrom. R. B. *Cognitive factors: Some recent literature*. Princeton, NJ: Educational Testing Service, PR-73-30, 1973.

Ekstrom, R. B., French, J. W., & Harman, H. H. *Problems of replicating seven divergent production factors*. Princeton, NJ: Educational Testing Service, PR-74-14, 1974.

Ekstrom, R. B., French, J. W., & Harman, H. H. *An attempt to confirm five recently identified cognitive factors*. Princeton, NJ: Educational Testing Service, PR-75-17, 1975.

Ekstrom, R. B., French, J. W., Harman, H. H., & Dermen, D. *Manual for kit of factor-referenced cognitive tests*. Princeton, NJ: Educational Testing Service, 1976.

Feather, N. Acceptance and rejection of argument in relation to attitude strength, critical ability, and intolerance of inconsistency. *Journal of Abnormal and Social Psychology*, 1965, *57*, 239–245.

Feuerstein, R. A dynamic approach to the causation, prevention, and alleviation of retarded performance. In H.C. Haywood (Ed.), *Social-cultural aspects of mental retardation*. New York: Appleton-Century-Crofts, 1970.

Feuerstein, R. *The dynamic assessment of retarded performers*. Baltimore, MD: University Park Press, 1979.

Feuerstein, R., Miller, R., Hoffman, M. B., Rand, Y., Mintzker, Y., & Jensen, M.R. Cognitive modifiability in adolescence: Cognitive structure and the effects of intervention. *The Journal of Special Education*, 1981, *15*, 269–286.

Feuerstein, R., Miller, R., & Jensen, M. R. Can evolving techniques better measure cognitive change? *Journal of Special Education*, Symposium Edition, 1980.

Feuerstein, R., & Rand, Y. Mediated learning experiences: An outline of the proximal etiology for differential development of cognitive functions. *International Understanding*, 1974, *9, 10, 7–37.*

Feuerstein, R., Rand, Y., & Hoffman, M. B. *The dynamic assessment of retarded performers: The learning potential assessment device, theory, instruments, techniques*. Baltimore: University Park Press, 1979.

Feuerstein, R., Rand, Y., Hoffman, M. B., Hoffman, M., & Miller, R. Cognitive modifiability in retarded adolescents: Effects of instrumental enrichment. *American Journal of Mental Deficiency*, 1979, *83*, 539.

Feuerstein, R., Rand, Y., Hoffman, M., & Miller, R. *Instrumental enrichment*. Baltimore: University Park Press, 1980.

Feurzeig, W., Lukas, G., Faflick, P., Grant, R., Lukas, J. D., Morgan, C. R., Weiner, W. B., & Wexelblat, P. M. *Programming-languages as a conceptual framework for teaching mathematics, Vol. 1* (Report No. 2165). Cambridge, MA: Bolt Beranek and Newman Inc., 1971.

Feurzeig, W., Papert, S., Bloom, M., Grant, R., & Solomon, C. *Programming-languages as a conceptual framework for teaching mathematics* (Report No. 1889). Cambridge, MA: Bolt Beranek and Newman Inc., November 1969.

Fischer, K. W. A theory of cognitive development: The control of hierarchies of skill. *Psychological Review*, 1980, *87*, 477–531.

Fisher, C. W., Berliner, D. C., Filby, N. N., Marliave, R., Cahen, L. S., & Dishaw, M. M. Teaching behaviors, academic learning time, and student achievement: An overview. In C. Denham & A. Liberman (Eds.), *Time to learn*. Washington, DC: National Institute of Education, 1980.

Flanders, N. A. Quoted in "Teacher Effectiveness." In R. Ebel (Ed.), *Encyclopedia of Educational Research*, 4th ed. New York: Macmillan, 1969.

Flavell, J. H. *The development of metacommunication*. Paper presented at the Twenty-first International Congress of Psychology, Paris, July 1976.

Flavell, J. H. *Cognitive monitoring*. Paper presented at Conference on Children's Oral Communication Skills. University of Wisconsin, October, 1978.

Flavell, J. H. *Monitoring social-cognitive enterprises: Something else that may develop in the area of social cognition*. Paper prepared for the Social Sciences Research Council Committee on Social and Affective Development During Childhood, January 1979.

Flavell, J. H. Cognitive monitoring. In W.P. Dickson (Ed.), *Children's oral communication* skills. New York: Academic Press, 1981.

Flavell, J. H. Metacognition and cognitive monitoring: A new area of cognitive-developmental inquiry, undated.

Flavell, J. H., Friedrichs, A. G., & Hoyt, J. D. Developmental changes in memorization processes. *Cognitive Psychology*, 1970, *1*, 324–340.

Flavell, J. H., & Wellman, H. M. Metamemory. In R. V. Kail, Jr. & J. W. Hagen (Eds.), *Perspectives on the development of memory and cognition*. Hillsdale, NJ: Lawrence Erlbaum Associates, 1977.

Flower, L. S., & Hayes, J. R. The dynamics of composing: Making plans and juggling constraints. In L. W. Gregg & E. R. Steinberg (Eds.), *Cognitive processes in writing*. Hillsdale, NJ: Lawrence Erlbaum Associates, 1980.

Fredrick, W. C. The use of classroom time in high schools above or below the median reading score. *Urban Education*, 1977, 459–464.

French, J. W. *Toward the establishment of noncognitive factors through literature search and interpretation*. Princeton, NJ: Educational Testing Service, Technical Report No. 1, 1977.

French, J. W., & Dermen, D. *Seeking markers for temperament factors among positive and negative poles of temperament scales*. Princeton, NJ: Educational Testing Service, Technical Report No. 7, 1974.

French, J. W., Ekstrom, R. B., & Price, L. A. *Kit of reference tests for cognitive factors*. Princeton, NJ: Educational Testing Service, 1963.

Friedburg, D. Training in memory and cognition: St. Joseph study (summary). El Segundo, CA: SOI Institute, 1979.

Fuller, R. G. Active learning based upon the work of Piaget. In R. G. Fuller et al. (Eds.), *Piagetian programs in higher education*. Lincoln, NE: ADAPT Program, 1980, 23–25.

Fuller, R. G., Bergstrom, R. F., Carpenter, E. T., Corzine, H. J., McShane, J. A., Miller, D. W., Moshman, D. S., Narveson, R. D., Petr, J. L., Thornton, M. C., & Williams, V. G. (Eds.), *Piagetian programs in higher education*. Lincoln, NE: ADAPT Program, 1980.

Furth, H. G. *Piaget for teachers*. Englewood Cliffs, NJ: Prentice-Hall, 1970.

Gagne, R. M. *Science—A process approach: Purposes, accomplishments, expectations*. Commission on Science Education, Association for the Advancement of Science, 1967.

Gagne, R. M. *The conditions of learning*. New York: Holt, Rinehart, and Winston, 1970.

Galton, F. *Hereditary genius: An inquiry into its laws and consequences*. New York: Appleton, 1869.

Galton, F. *Inquiries into human faculty and its development*. London: Macmillan, 1883.

Garber, H., & Heber, R. Modification of predicted cognitive development in high-risk children through early intervention. In D. K. Detterman & R. J. Sternberg (Eds.), *How and how much can intelligence be increased?* Norwood, NJ: Ablex, 1982.

Geller, E. S., & Pitz, G. F. Confidence and decision speed in the revision of opinion. *Organizational Behavior and Human Performance*, 1968, *3*, 190–201.

Getzels, J., & Csikszentmihalyi, M. *The creative vision: A longitudinal study of problem finding in art*. New York: Wiley, 1976.

Gibson, R. S., & Nicol, E. H. The modifiability of decisions made in a changing environment. ESD-TR-64-657 Electronic Systems Division, U.S. Air Force, December, 1964.

Gick, M. L., & Holyoak, K. J. Analogical problem solving. *Cognitive Psychology*, 1980, *12*, 306–355.

Goldenberg, E. P. *Special technology for special children*. Baltimore: University Park Press, 1979.

Goldstein, I., & Papert, S. Artificial intelligence, language, and the study of knowledge. *Cognitive Science*, 1977, *1*, 84–124.

Good, T. L., & Beckerman, T. M. Time on task: A naturalistic study in sixth-grade classrooms. *The Elementary School Journal*, 1978, *73*, 193–201.

Goodman, N. *Ways of worldmaking*. Hassocks, Sussex, England: Harvester Press, 1978.

Goodnow, J. J. The nature of intelligent behavior: Questions raised by cross-cultural studies. In L.B. Resnick (Ed.), *The nature of intelligence*. Hillsdale, NJ: Lawrence Erlbaum Associates, 1976.

Goor, A., & Sommerfeld, R. A comparison of problem-solving processes of creative students and non-creative students. *Journal of Educational Psychology*, 1975, *67*, 495–505.

Gordon, R. Attitudes toward Russia on logical reasoning. *Journal of Social Psychology*, 1953, *37*, 103–111.

Gordon, W. J. J. *Synectics: The development of creative capacity*. New York: Harper, 1961.

Gordon, L. V. Student's environmental preference survey. In *Measures for psychological assessment: A guide to 3,000 original sources and their applications*. Ann Arbor, MI: Survey Research Center, Institute for Social Research, University of Michigan, 1975.

Gore, D. SOI training in memory and creativity: Gore study (summary). El Segundo, CA: SOI Institute, 1980.

Grabitz, H. J., & Jochem, H. An evaluation of confirming and disconfirming information in decision making. *Archive fur Psychologie*, 1972, *124*, 133–144.

Gray, R. L. Toward observing that which is not directly observable. In J. Lochhead & J. Clement (Eds.), *Cognitive process instruction*. Philadelphia: The Franklin Institute Press, 1979.

Greeno, J. G. Hobbits and orcs: Acquisition of a sequential concept. *Cognitive Psychology*, 1974, *6*, 270–292.

Greeno, J. G. Trends in the theory of knowledge for problem solving. In D. T. Tuma & F. Reif (Eds.), *Problem solving and education: Issues in teaching and research*. Hillsdale, NJ: Lawrence Erlbaum Associates, 1980, 9–23.

Groff, P. Children's oral language and their written composition. *Elementary School Journal*, 1978, *78*(3), 181–191.

Guilford, J. P. Intellectual resources and their values as seen by scientists. In C.W. Taylor & F. Barron (Eds.), *Scientific creativity: Its recognition and development*. New York: Wiley, 1963.

Guilford, J. P. *The nature of human intelligence*. New York: McGraw-Hill, 1967.

Guilford, J. P. Rotation problems in factor analysis. *Psychological Bulletin*, 1974, *81*(B), 498–501.

Guilford, J. P., & Hoepfner, R. *The analysis of intelligence*. New York: McGraw-Hill, 1971.

Harman, H. H. (Ed.). *Proceedings: Toward the development of more comprehensive sets of personality measures*. Princeton, NJ: Educational Testing Service, Technical Report No. 3, 1973.

Harpin, W. *The second "R": Writing development in the junior school)*. London: George Allen & Unwin Ltd., 1976.

Harvard University. *Project Intelligence: The development of procedures to enhance thinking skills.* Final Report, submitted to the Minister for the Development of Human Intelligence, Republic of Venezuela, October, 1983.

Harvey, O. J., Hunt, D., & Schroder, D. *Conceptual systems*. New York: Wiley, 1961.

Hayakawa, S. I. *Language in thought and action*. New York: Harcourt, Brace & World, 1964.

Hayes, J. R. Human data processing limits in decision making. In E. Bennett (Ed.), *Information system science and engineering. Proceedings of the First Congress on the Information Systems Sciences*. New York: McGraw-Hill, 1964.

Hayes, J. R. Three problems in Teaching General Skills. In S. F. Chipman, J. W. Segal, & R. Glaser (Eds.), *Thinking and learning skills Volume 2; Research and open questions*. Hillsdale, NJ: Lawrence Erlbaum Associates, 1985.

Hayes, J. R. *The complete problem solver*. Philadelphia, PA: The Franklin Institute Press, 1981.

Haywood, H. C. Individual differences in motivational orientation: A trait approach. In H. I. Day, D. E. Berlyne, & D. E. Hunt (Eds.), *Intrinsic motivation: A new direction in education*. Toronto: Holt, Rinehart & Winston, 1971.

Haywood, H. C., & Arbitman-Smith, R. Modification of cognitive functions in slow-learning adolescents. In P. Mittler (Ed), *Frontiers of knowledge in mental retardation Vol. 1: Proceedings of the Fifth Congress of IASSMD I—Social, educational, and behavioral aspects*, Baltimore: University Park Press, 1981.

Heller, J., & Greeno, J. Information processing analyses of mathematical problem solving. In *Testing, teaching and learning*. Washington, DC: The National Institute of Education, 1979.

Henle, M. On the relation between logic and thinking. *Psychological Review*, 1962, *69*, 366–378.

Henshaw, D. *Cognitive mediators in creative problem solving*. Unpublished doctoral dissertation, University of Waterloo, 1977.

Herrnstein, R. J. In defense of intelligence tests. *Commentary*, February 1980, 40–51.

Herrnstein, R. J., Nickerson, R. S., Sanchez, M., & Swets, J. A. Teaching thinking skills (submitted for publication).

Herron, J. D. Piaget for chemists. *Journal of Chemical Education*, 1975, *52*, 146–150.

Hoepfl, R. T., & Huber, G. P. A study of self-explicated utility models. *Behavioral Science*, 1970, *15*, 408–414.

Horn, J. L. Trends in the measurement of intelligence. In R.J. Sternberg & D.K. Detterman (Eds.), *Human Intelligence*. Norwood, NJ: Ablex, 1979.

Horn, J. L., & Knapp. J. R. On the subjective character of the empirical base of Guilford's structure-of-intellect model. *Psychological Bulletin*, 1973, *80*(1), 33–43.

Hutchinson, R. T. Teaching problem solving to developmental adults; a pilot project. In J. W. Segal, S. F. Chipman & R. Glaser (Eds), *Thinking and Learning Skills Volume 1: Relating Instruction to Research*. Hillsdale, NJ: Lawrence Erlbaum Associates, 1985.

Jackson, P. W., & Messick, S. The person, the product, and the response: Conceptual problems in the assessment of creativity. In M. Bloomberg (Ed.), *Creativity, theory, and research*. College and University Press, 1973

Jackson, S. The growth of logical thinking in normal and subnormal children. *British Journal of Educational Psychology*, 1965, *35*, 255–258.

Janis, I., & Frick, P. The relationship between attitudes toward conclusions and errors in judging logical validity of syllogisms. *Journal of Experimental Psychology*, 1943, *33*, 73–77.

Jastak, J., & Jastak, S. *The wide range achievement test*. Wilmington, DL: Jastak Associates, 1978.

Jennings, D., Amabile, T. M., & Ross, L. Informal covariation assessment: Data-based vs. theory-based judgements. In A. Tversky, D. Kahneman, & P. Slovic (Eds.), *Judgements under uncertainty: Heuristics and biases*, New York: Cambridge University Press, 1981.

Jones, O. SOI abilities training: Caster study (summary). El Segundo, CA: SOI Institute, 1980.

Johnson, D. M. *A systematic introduction to the psychology of thinking*. New York: Harper & Row, 1972.

Johnson-Laird, P. N. *Mental models*. Cambridge, MA: Harvard University Press, 1983.

Johnson-Laird, P. N. Logical thinking: Does it occur in daily life? Can it be taught? In S. F. Chipman, J. W. Segal, & R. Glaser (Eds.), *Thinking and learning skills, Vol. 2: Research and open questions*. Hillsdale, NJ: Lawrence Erlbaum Associates, 1985.

Johnston, S., & Moshman, D. *Evaluation of ADAPT, 1979-1980*. Lincoln, NE: University of Nebraska, 1980.

Kahneman, D., & Tversky, A. Subjective probability: A judgment of representativeness. *Cognitive Psychology*,1971, *3*, 430–454.

Kahneman, D., & Tversky, A. Subjective probability: A judgment of representativeness. *Cognitive Psychology*, 1972, *3*, 430–454.

Kahneman, D., & Tversky, A. On the psychology of prediction. *Psychological Review*, 1973, *80*, 237–251.

Kanarick, A. F., Huntington, J. M., & Petersen, R. C. Multi-source information acquisition with optional stopping. *Human Factors*, 1969, *11*, 379–386.

Karnes, M. B. Evaluation and implication of research with young handicapped and low-income children. In J. C. Stanley (Ed.), *Contemporary education for children, ages 2 to 8*. Baltimore: The Johns Hopkins University Press, 1973.

Karplus, R. *Science curriculum improvement study, teacher's handbook*. Berkeley, CA: University of California, Berkeley, 1974.

Karplus, R. Proportional reasoning in the People's Republic of China: A pilot study. In J. Lochhead & J. Clement (Eds.), *Cognitive process instruction*. Philadelphia, PA: The Franklin Institute Press, 1979.

Karweit, N. *The organization of time in schools: Time scales and learning*. Paper presented at the NIE Conference on Schooling, San Diego, California, 1976.

Kaufman, H., & Goldstein, S. The effects of emotional value of conclusions upon distortions in syllogistic reason. *Psycholonomic Science*, 1967, *7*, 367–368.

Keniston, A., & Flavell, J. H. The nature and development of intelligent retrieval. Research supported by National Institute of Child Health & Human Development Grants ND-05027 and HD-10429, 1980.

Kent, A. *SOI abilities related to reading: Kent study (summary)*. El Segundo, CA: SOI Institute, no date.

Kitzhaber, A. R. *Themes, theories, and therapy*. New York: McGraw-Hill, 1963.

Klaus, R. A., & Gray, S. W. The early training project for disadvantaged children: A report after five years. *Monographs of the Society for Research in Child Development*, 1968, *33*(4).

Klausmeier, H. J. with the assistance of Sipple, T.S. *Learning and teaching concepts—a strategy for testing applications of theory*. New York: Academic Press, 1980.

Klevin, A. *An investigation of a methodology for value clarification: Its relationship to consistency of thinking, purposefulness, and human relations*. Doctoral dissertation, New York University, 1958.

Koberg, D., & Bagnall, J. *The universal traveler: A soft-systems guide to creativity, problem-solving, and the process of reaching goals*. Los Altos, CA: William Kaufmann, 1974.

Koestler, A. *The act of creation*. New York: Dell, 1964.

Kohlberg, L., & Gilligan, C. The adolescent as a philosopher. *Daedalus*, 1971, *100*, 1051–1103.

Kolodiy, G. The cognitive development of high school and college science students. *Journal of College Science Teaching*, 1975, *13*, p. 20.

Kurland, D. M., & Pea, R. D. Children's mental models of recursive logo programs (Technical Report Number 10). New York: Center for Children and Technology, Bank Street College of Education, 1983.

Laboratory of Comparative Human Cognition, Culture, and Intelligence. In R. J. Sternberg (Ed.), *Handbook of human intelligence*. Cambridge, London: Cambridge University Press, 1982, 642–719.

Larkin, J. H. Teaching problem solving in physics: The psychological laboratory and the practical classroom. In D. T. Tuma & F. Reif (Eds.), *Problem solving and education: Issues in teaching and research*. Hillsdale, NJ: Lawrence Erlbaum Associates, 1980, 111–125.

Larkin, J. H. The role of problem representation in physics. In D. Gentner & A. S. Stevens (Eds.), *Mental models*. Hillsdale, NJ: Lawrence Erlbaum Associates, 1983.

Larkin, J. H., McDermott, J., Simon, D. P., & Simon, H. A. Expert and novice performance in solving physics problems. *Science*, 1980, *208*, 1335–1342.

Lawson, A. E. The development and validation of a classroom test of formal reasoning. *Journal of Research in Science Teaching*, 1978, *15*, 11–24.

Lawson, A. E., & Renner, J. W. A quantitative analysis of responses to Piagetian tasks and its implications for education. *Science Education*, 1974, *58*(4), 454–559.

Levine, H. *Vocabulary for the college-bound student*. New York: AMSCO School Publications, 1965.

Lichtenstein, S., Slovic, P., Fischhoff, B., Layman, M., & Coombs, B. Judged frequency of lethal events. *Journal of Experimental Psychology: Human Learning and Memory*, 1978, *4*, 551–578.

Link, F. R. Instrumental enrichment: The classroom perspective. *Educational Forum*, May 1980, *XLIV*, 425–428.

Lipman, M. Philosophy for children. *Metaphilosophy*, 1976, *7*(1).

Lipman, M., Sharp, A.M., & Oscanyan, F. *Philosophy in the classroom*. Philadelphia: Temple University Press, 1980.

Loevinger, J. *Ego development: Conceptions and theories*. San Francisco: Jossey-Bass, 1976.

Lorge, I., & Thorndike, R. L. *The Lorge-Thorndike intelligence tests: Examiner's Manual*. Boston: Houghton Mifflin, 1954.

Lovelle, K. A follow-up study of Inhelder and Piaget's growth of logical thinking. *British Journal of Psychology*, 1961, *52*, 143–154.

MacKinnon, D. W. The nature and nurture of creative talent. *American Psychologist*, 1962, *17*, 484–495.

Mackworth, N. H. Originality. *American Psychologist*, 1965, *20*, 51–66.

Mahoney, M. J. Publication prejudices: An experimental study of confirmatory bias in the peer review system. *Cognitive Therapy and Research*, 1977, *1*, 161–175.

Mahoney, M. J., & DeMonbreun, B. G. Psychology of the scientist: An analysis of problem-solving bias. *Cognitive Therapy and Research*, 1977, *1*, 229–238.

Manning, E. Training creativity: East Whitter study (summary). El Segundo, CA: SOI Institute, 1974.

Mansfield, R. S., & Busse, T. V. *The psychology of creativity and discovery*. Chicago: Nelson-Hall, 1981.

Mansfield, R. S., Busse, T. V., & Krepelka, E. J. The effectiveness of creativity training. *Review of Educational Research*, 1978, *48*(4), 517–536.

Markman, E. M. Realizing that you don't understand: A preliminary investigation. *Child Development*, 1977, *48*, 986–992.

Markman, E. M. Realizing that you don't understand: Elementary school children's awareness of inconsistencies. *Child Development*, 1979, *59*, 643–655.

McCabe, B. J. A program for teaching composition to pupils of limited academic ability. In M.F. Shugrue & G. Hillocks (Eds.), *Classroom practices in teaching English*. Washington, DC: National Council of Teachers of English, 1965.

McCarthy, D. A. *Differences in the performance of high-achieving and low-achieving gifted pupils in grades four, five, and six on measures of field dependence-field independence, creativity, & self-concept*. Doctoral Dissertation, University of Southern California, 1977.

McDermott, J., & Larkin, J. H. Re-representing textbook physics problems. *Proceedings of the 2nd National Conference of the Canadian Society for Computational Studies of Intelligence*. Toronto: University of Toronto Press, 1978.

McKinnon, J. W. Earth science, density, and the college freshman. *Journal of Geological Education*, 1971, *19*.

McKinnon, J. W., & Renner, J. W. Are colleges concerned with intellectual development? *American Journal of Physics*, 1971, *39*.

McQuillan, M. K. *A critical appraisal of James Moffett's theory of composition*. Special qualifying paper, Harvard Graduate School of Education, 1979.

McShane, J. A. Poetry, prose and Piaget. In R. G. Fuller et al. (Eds.), *Piagetian programs in higher education*. Lincoln, NE: ADAPT Program, 1980, 95–108.

Mednick, S. A. The associative basis of the creative process. *Psychological Review*, 1962, *69*, 220–232.

Meeker, M. N. *The structure of intellect: Its interpretation and uses*. Columbus, OH: Charles E. Merrill, 1969.

Meichenbaum, D. Enhancing creativity by modifying what subjects say to themselves. *American Educational Research Journal*, 1975, *12*, 129–145.

Meichenbaum, D. *Cognitive-behavior modification*. New York: Plenum Press, 1977.

Meichenbaum, D., & Goodman, J. Training impulsive children to talk to themselves: A means of developing self-control. *Journal of Abnormal Psychology*, 1971, *77*, 115–126.

Mendelsohn, G. A. Associative and attentional processes in creative performance. *Journal of Personality*, 1976, *44*, 341–369.

Miller, G. E. An inquiry into medical teaching. *Journal of Medical Education*, 1962, *37*, 185–191.

Miller, G. E. Continuing medical education for what? *MCV Quarterly*, 1967, *3*, 152–156.

Miller, L. A. *Programming by nonprogrammers* (Research Rep. No. RC–4280). IBM, 1973.

Minsky, M. A. A framework for representing knowledge. In P.H. Winston (Ed.), *The psychology of computer vision*. New York: McGraw-Hill, 1975.

Moffett, J. *Teaching the universe of discourse*. Boston: Houghton-Mifflin, 1968.

Moffett, J., & Wagner, B.J. *Student-centered language arts and reading, K-12: A handbook for teachers*, (2nd ed.). Boston: Houghton Mifflin, 1976.

Moreno, J. M., & Hogan, J. D. The influence of race and social-class level on the training of creative thinking and problem-solving abilities. *Journal of Educational Research*, 1976, *70*, 91–95.

Morgan, J., & Morton, J. The distortion of syllogistic reasoning produced by personal convictions. *Journal of Social Psychology*, 1944, *20* 39–59.

Morris, T. L., & Bergum, B. O. A note on the relationship between field-independence and creativity. *Perceptual and Motor Skills*, 1978, *46*, 1114.

Moshman, D. Piaget's theory and college teaching. In R. G. Fuller et al. (Eds.), *Piagetian programs in higher education*. Lincoln, NE: ADAPT Program, 1980, 1–13.

Moshman, D., Johnston, S., Tomlinson-Keasey, C., Williams, V., & Eisert, D. ADAPT: The first five years. In R. G. Fuller et al. (Eds.), *Piagetian programs in higher education*. Lincoln, NE: ADAPT Program, 1980, 115–121.

Narveson, R. D. Development and learning: Complementary or conflicting aims in humanities education? In R. G. Fuller et al. (Eds.), *Piagetian programs in higher education*. Lincoln, NE: ADAPT Program, 1980, 79–88.

Neisser, U. General, academic and artificial intelligence. In L. Resnick (Ed.), *The nature of intelligence*. Hillsdale, NJ: Lawrence Erlbaum Associates, 1976.

Neisser, U. The concept of intelligence. In R. J. Sternberg & D. K. Detterman (Eds.), *Human intelligence*. Norwood, NJ: Ablex, 1979.

Neisser, U., & Weene, P. Hierarchies in concept attainment. *Journal of Experimental Psychology*, 1962, *64*, 640–645.

Newell, A., & Simon, H. A. *Human problem solving*. Englewood Cliffs, NJ: Prentice-Hall, 1972.

Nickerson, R. S. Thoughts about teaching thinking. *Educational Leadership*, 1981, *39*(1), 21–24.

Nickerson, R. S. *Three uses of computers in education* (Report No. 5178). Cambridge, MA: Bolt Beranek and Newman Inc., 1982.

Nickerson, R. S. Computer programming as a vehicle for teaching thinking skills. *Thinking*, 1983, *4*(3 & 4), 42–48.

Nickerson, R. S. Understanding understanding. *American Journal of Education*, 1985, *93*, 201–239.

Nickerson, R. S., & Feehrer, C. E. Decision making and training: A review of theoretical and empirical studies of decision making and their implications for the training of decision makers. NAVTRAEQUIPCEN 73-C-0128-1, August 1975.

Nickerson, R. S, Salter, W., Shepard, S., & Herrnstein, J. *The teaching of learning strategies* (Report No. 5578). Cambridge, MA: Bolt Beranek and Newman Inc., 1984.

Nieman, H., & Gastright, F. *Preschool plus all-day-kindergarten: The cumulative effects of early childhood programs on the cognitive growth of four and five year old children.* Presented at the annual meeting of the American Educational ResearchAssociation, Washington, DC, March, 1975.

Nilsson, N. J. *Problem-solving methods in artificial intelligence*. New York: McGraw-Hill, 1971.

Nisbett, R., & Ross, L. *Human inference: Strategies and shortcomings of social judgment.* Englewood Cliffs, NJ: Prentice-Hall, 1980.

Nisbett, R., & Wilson, T. D. Telling more than we can know: Verbal reports on mental processes. *Psychological Review*, 1977, *84*, p. 231–259.

Noppe, L. D. *A neo-Piagetian cognitive styles analysis of creative problem solving*. Doctoral dissertation, Temple University, 1978.

Nowicki, S., & Strickland, B. R. A locus of control scale for children. *Journal of Consulting Clinical Psychology*, 1973, *40*, 148.

O'Brien, T. C. Logical thinking in college students. *Educational Studies in Mathematics*, 1973, *5*, 71–79.

Oehrn, A. Experimentelle Studien zur Re Dorpater Dissertation, 1889.

Olson, D. R. Culture, technology, and intellect. In L. B. Resnick (Ed.), *The nature of intelligence*. Hillsdale, NJ: Lawrence Erlbaum Associates, 1976.

Olton, R. M., & Crutchfield, R. S. Developing the skills of productive thinking. In P. Mussen, J. Langer, & M. Covington (Eds.), *Trends and issues in developmental psychology*. New York: Holt, Rinehart and Winston, 1969.

Osborn, A. F. *Applied imagination*. New York: Charles Scribner's Sons, 1963.

Palkes, H., Stewart, M., & Freedman, J. Improvement in maze performance on hyperactive boys as a function of verbal training procedures. *Journal of Special Education*, 1962, *5*, 337–342.

Papert, S. *Teaching children thinking*. Cambridge, MA: A.I. Laboratory M.I.T., October, 1971.

Papert, S. Teaching children thinking. *Programmed Learning and Educational Technology*, 1972, *9*.

Papert, S. *Mindstorms*. New York: Basic Books, 1980.

Papert, S., Watt, D., diSessa, A., & Weir, S. *Final report of the Brookline Logo project, Part II: Project summary and data analysis* (Logo Memo No. 53, A.I. Memo No. 545.) Cambridge, MA: Artifical Intelligence Laboratory, Massachusetts Institute of Technology, 1979.

Pea, R. Logo programming and problem solving. In *Chameleon in the classroom: Developing roles for computers* (Technical Report Number 22). New York: Center for Children and Technology, Bank Street College of Education, 1983.

Pelz, D. C., & Andrews, F.M. *Scientists in organizations: Productive climates for research and development*. New York: Wiley, 1966.

Perkins, D. N. Metaphorical perception. In E. Eisner (Ed.), *Reading, the arts and the creation of meaning*. Reston, VA: National Art Education Association, 1978.

Perkins, D. N. *The mind's best work*. Cambridge, MA: Harvard University Press, 1981.

Perkins, D. N. General cognitive skills: Why not? In S. F. Chipman, J. W. Segal, & R. Glaser (Eds.), *Thinking and learning skills, Vol. 2: Research and open questions*. Hillsdale,

NJ: Lawrence Erlbaum Associates, 1985.

Perkins, D. N., Allen, R., & Hafner, J. Difficulties in everyday reasoning. In W. Maxwell (Ed.), *Thinking*. Philadelphia: The Franklin Institute Press, 1983.

Perkins, D. N., & Gardner, H. *Analysis and training of processes and component skills in the arts* (Final report of NIE Project No. 3-1190). Cambridge, MA: Project Zero, Harvard Graduate School of Education, 1978.

Perkins, D. N., Ives, W., Meringoff, L., Silberstein, L., & Wolf, D. *Aesthetic development and arts education—a report from Harvard Project Zero*. St. Louis: CEMREL, Inc., 1979.

Perry, W. G., Jr. *Forms of intellectual and ethical development in the college years*. New York: Holt, Rinehart & Winston, 1970.

Perry, W. G. *Forms of intellectual and ethical development in the college years*. New York: Holt, Rinehart & Winston, 1970.

Peterson, J. *Early conceptions and tests of intelligence*. Yonkers-on-Hudson, New York: World Book Co., 1926.

Petr, J. L. Piaget and learning economics. In R. G. Fuller et al. (Eds.), *Piagetian programs in higher education*. Lincoln, NE: ADAPT Program, 1980, 49–65.

Piaget, J. Intellectual evolution from adolescence to adulthood. *Human Development*, 1972, *15*, 1–12.

Piers, E. V., & Harris, D. B. *The Piers-Harris children's self-concept scale*. Nashville: Counselor Recordings and Tests, 1969.

Pinter, R. *Intelligence testing*. New York: Henry Holt, 1931.

Pitz, G. F., Downing, L., & Reinhold, H. Sequential effects in the revision of subjective probabilities. *Canadian Journal of Psychology*, 1967, *21*, 381–393.

Pollard, P. F., & Evans, J. The influence of logic on conditional reasoning performance. *Quarterly Journal of Experimental Psychology*, 1980, *32*, 605–624.

Polya, G. *Induction and analogy in mathematics*. Princeton, NJ: Princeton University Press, 1954a.

Polya, G. *Patterns of plausible inference*. Princeton, NJ: Princeton University Press, 1954b.

Polya, G. *How to solve it* (2nd ed.). Princeton, NJ: Princeton University Press; New York: Doubleday, 1957.

Prosser, M. Cognitive analysis of physics textbooks at the tertiary or college level. *Science Education*, 1979, *63*, 677–683.

Pruitt, P. G. Informational requirements in making decisions. *American Journal of Psychology*, 1961, *74*, 433–439.

Pylyshyn, Z. W. When is attribution of beliefs justified? *Behavioral and Brain Sciences*, 1978, *1*, 592–593.

Ramey, C. T., MacPhee, D., & Yeates, K. O. Preventing developmental retardation: A general systems model. In Detterman, D. K. & Sternberg, R. J. (Eds.), *How and how much can intelligence be increased?* Norwood, NJ: Ablex, 1982.

Rand, Y., Tannenbaum, A. J., & Feuerstein, R. Effects of Instrumental Enrichment on the psychoeducational development of low-functioning adolescents. *Journal of Educational Psychology*, 1979, *71*, 751–763.

Raven, J. C. *Guide to the standard progressive matrices*. London: H. K. Lewis & Co., 1960.

Reif, F. Theoretical and educational concerns with problem solving: Bridging the gaps with human cognitive engineering. In D. T. Tuma & F. Reif (Eds.), *Problem solving and education: Issues in teaching and research*. Hillsdale, NJ: Lawrence Erlbaum Associates, 1980.

Renner, J. W., & Lawson, A. E. Promoting intellectual development through science teaching. *The Physics Teacher*, 1973, *11*.

Renner, J. W., & McKinnon, J. W. Are colleges concerned with intellectual development? *American Journal of Physics*, September 1971, *39*, 1047–1052.

Renner, J. W., & Stafford, D. G. *Teaching science in the secondary school*. New York: Harper and Row, 1972.

Resnick, L. B. Changing conceptions of intelligence. In L. B. Resnick (Ed.), *The nature of intelligence*. Hillsdale, NJ: Lawrence Erlbaum Associates, 1976a.

Resnick, L. B. Task analogies in instructional design: Some cases from mathematics. In D. Klahr (Ed.), *Cognition and instruction*. Hillsdale, NJ: Lawrence Erlbaum Associates, 1976b.

Resnick, L. B. The future of IQ testing in education. In R. J. Sternberg & D.K. Detterman (Eds.), *Human intelligence*. Norwood, NJ: Ablex, 1979.

Revlin, R., Leirer, V., Yopp, H., & Yopp, R. The belief-bias effect in formal reasoning: The influence of knowledge on logic. *Memory & Cognition*, 1980, *8*(6), 584–592.

Revlis, R. Syllogistic reasoning: Logical decisions from a complex data base. In R. Falmagne (Ed.), *Reasoning: Representation and process*. Hillsdale, NJ: Lawrence Erlbaum Associates, 1975a.

Revlis, R. Two models of syllogistic reasoning: Feature selection and conversion. *Journal of Verbal Learning and Verbal Behavior*, 1975b, *14*, 180–195.

Ridberg, E., Parke, R., & Hetherington, E. Modification of impulsive and reflective cognitive styles through observation of film mediated models. *Developmental Psychology*, 1971, *5*, 369–377.

Rigney, J. W., & DeBow, C. H. *Decision strategies in AAW: I. Analysis of air threat judgments and weapons assignments*. USN ONR Technical Report No. 47, 1966.

Ripple, R. E., & Dacey, J. The facilitation of problem solving and verbal creativity by exposure to programmed instruction. *Psychology in the Schools*, 1967, *4*, 240.

Robin, A., Armel, S., & O'Leary, D. The effects of self-instruction on writing deficiencies. *Behavior Therapy*, 1975, *6*, 178–187.

Robin, A., Schneider, M., & Dolnick, M. The turtle technique: An extended case study of self-control in the classroom. *Psychology in the Schools*, 1976, *12*, 120–128.

Roe, A. A psychologist examines 64 eminent scientists. *Scientific American*, 1952a, *187*(5), 21–25.

Roe, A. *The making of a scientist*. New York: Dodd, Mead & Co., 1952b.

Roe, A. Psychological approaches to creativity in science. in M. A. Coler & H. K. Hughes (Eds.), *Essays on creativity in the sciences*. New York: New York University, 1963.

Rosch, E. R. Human categorization. In N. Warren (Ed.), *Studies in cross-cultural psychology*. London: Academic Press, 1978.

Rosch, E. R., & Metuis, C. B. Family resemblance in studies in the internal structure of categories. *Cognitive Psychology*, 1975, *1*, 573–605.

Rosenberg, M. *Society and the adolescent self-image*. Princeton, NJ: Princeton University Press, 1965.

Ross, L., Lepper, M. H., & Hubbard, M. R. Perseverance in self perception and social perception: Biased attributional processes in the debriefing paradigm. *Journal of Personality and Social Psychology*, 1975, *32*, 880–982.

Rothenberg, A. *The emerging goddess: The creative process in art, science, and other fields*. Chicago: University of Chicago Press, 1979.

Rowe, M. B. Wait time and rewards as instructional variables: Their influence on language, logic, and fate control. *Journal of Research in Science Teaching*, 1974, *11*, 81–94.

Rozin, P. The evolution of intelligence and access to the cognitive unconscious. *Progression in Psychobiology and Physiological Psychology*, 1976, *6*, 245–280.

Rubenstein, M. F. *Patterns of problem solving*. Englewood Cliffs, NJ: Prentice-Hall, 1975.

Rubenstein, M. F. A decade of experience in teaching an interdisciplinary problem-solving course. In D. T. Tuma & F. Reif (Eds.), *Problem solving and education: Issues in teaching and research*. Hillsdale, NJ: Lawrence Erlbaum Associates, 1980, 25–38.

Rubin, A., & Bruce, B. C. QUILL: Reading and writing with a microcomputer. In B. A.

Huston (Ed.), *Advances in Reading/Language Research 3*. Greenwich, CT: JAI Press, 1983.

Sanders, J. R., & Sonnad, S. R. Research on the introduction, use and impact of the *ThinkAbout* instructional television series: Executive Summary. Agency for Instructional Television, January 1982.

Sanford, N. Personality development during college years. *Journal of Social Issues*, 1956, *12*.

Scardamalia, M., & Bereiter, C. Fostering the development of self-regulation in children's knowledge processing. In. S. F. Chipman, J. W. Segal, & R. Glaser (Eds.), *Thinking and learning skills, Vol. 2: Current research and open questions*. Hillsdale, NJ: Lawrence Erlbaum Associates, 1985.

Scardamalia, M., Bereiter, C., & Fillion, B. *The little red writing book: A source book of consequential writing activities*. Ontario, Canada: Pedagogy of Writing Project, O.I.S.E., 1979.

Schank, R., & Abelson, R. *Scripts, plans, goals, and understanding*. Hillsdale, NJ: Lawrence Erlbaum Associates, 1977.

Schermerhorn, L. L., Williams, L. D., & Dickison, A. K. *Project COMPAS: A design for change*. Sanford, FL: Seminole Community College, 1982.

Schoenfeld, A. H. Presenting a strategy for indefinite integration. *American Mathematical Monthly*, 1978, *85*(8), 673–678.

Schoenfeld, A. H. Can heuristics be taught? In J. Lochhead & J. Clement (Eds.), *Cognitive process instruction*. Philadelphia, PA: The Franklin Institute Press, 1979a.

Schoenfeld, A. H. Explicit heuristic training as a variable in problem solving performance. *Journal for Research in Mathematics Education*, 1979b, *10*(3), 173–187.

Schoenfeld, A. H. Teaching problem-solving skills. *American Mathematical Monthly*, 1980, 87(10), 794–805.

Schoenfeld, A. H. Measures of problem-solving performance and of problem-solving instruction. *Journal for Research in Mathematics Education*, 1982, 13(1), 31–49.

Schoenfeld, A. H. Episodes and executive decisions in mathematical problem solving. In R. Lesh & M. Landau (Eds.), *Acquisition of mathematical concepts and processes*. New York: Academic Press, 1983a.

Schoenfeld, A. H. *Theoretical and pragmatic issues in the design of mathematical "problem solving" instruction*. Paper presented at the 1983 Annual Meeting of the American Educational Research Association, Montreal, April 1983b.

Schoenfeld, A. H., & Herrmann, D. J. Problem perception and knowledge structure in expert and novice mathematical problem solvers. *Journal of Experimental Psychology: Learning, Memory, and Cognition*, 1982, 8(5), 484–494.

Schopenhauer, A. The art of controversy. Translated by J. B. Saunders and printed in *The essays of Arthur Schopenhauer*. New York: Wiley, undated.

Schuler, G. *The effectiveness of the Productive Thinking Program*. Ithaca, NY: Ithaca College, 1974. (ERIC Document Reproduction Service No. ED 103 479)

Scriven, M. Prescriptive and descriptive approaches to problem solving. In D. T. Tuma & F. Reif (Eds.), *Problem solving and education: Issues in teaching and research*. Hillsdale, NJ: Lawrence Erlbaum Associates, 1980, 127–139.

Searle, D. J. A study of classroom language activity of five selected high school students. *Research in the Teaching of English*, 1975, *9*, 267–289.

Sheldon, R. ADAPT: Teaching students to think. *Nebraska Alumnus*, 1978, *74*, 12–14.

Shweder, R. A. Likeness and likelihood in everyday thought: Magical thinking in everyday judgments about personality. In P. N. Johnson-Laird & P. C. Wason (Eds.), *Thinking: Readings in cognitive science*. Cambridge: Cambridge University Press, 1977.

Siegler, R. S. Developmental sequences within and between concepts. *Society for Research in Child Development Monograph*, 1981, *46*(2).

Siegler, R. S. Encoding and the development of problem solving. In S. F. Chipman, J. W. Segal, & R. Glaser (Eds.), *Thinking and learning skills, Vol. 2: Current research and open questions*. Hillsdale, NJ: Lawrence Erlbaum Associates, 1985.

Simon, H. A. Problem solving and education. In D. T. Tuma & F. Reif (Eds.), *Problem solving and education: Issues in teaching and research*. Hillsdale, NJ: Lawrence Erlbaum Associates, 1980, 81–96.

Simon, H. A., & Chase, W. Skill in chess. *American Scientist*, 1973, *61*, 394–403.

Simon, D. P., & Simon, H. A. Individual differences in solving physics problems. In R. S. Siegler (Ed.), *Children's thinking: What develops?*. Hillsdale, NJ: Lawrence Erlbaum Associates, 1978.

Simon, D. P., & Simon, H. A. A tale of two protocols. In J. Lochhead & J. Clement (Eds.), *Cognitive process instruction*. Philadelphia: The Franklin Institute Press, 1979.

Slavin, R. E. Cooperative learning in teams: State of the art. *Educational Psychologist*, 1980, *15*(2), 93–111.

Slovic, P. Value as a determiner of subjective probability. *IEEE Transactions on Human Factors in Electronics*, 1966, *HFE-7*, 22–28.

Slovic, P., Fischhoff, B., & Lichtenstein, S. Behavioral decision theory. *Annual Review of Psychology*, 1977, *28*, 1–39.

Slovic, P., & Lichtenstein, S. Comparison of Bayesian and regression approaches to the study of information processing in judgment. *Organizational Behavior and Human Performance*, 1971, *6*, 649–744.

Smith, E. E., & Medin, D. L. *Categories and concepts*. Cambridge, MA: Harvard University Press, 1981.

Smith, P., & Baranyi, H. *A comparison of the effectiveness of the traditional and audio-lingual approaches to foreign language instruction utilizing laboratory equipment* (Report on Project No. 7-0133 for the Office of Education, H.E.W.), October 1968.

Snyder, M., & Cantor, N. Testing theories about other people: Remembering all the history that fits. Unpublished manuscript, University of Minnesota, 1979.

Snyder, M., & Swann, W. B. Behavioral confirmation in social interaction: From social perception to social reality. *Journal of Experimental Social Psychology*, 1978, *14*, 148–162.

Soelberg, P. O. Unprogrammed decision making. *Industrial Management Review*, 1967, *8*, 19–29.

Spearman, C. *The nature of "intelligence" and the principles of cognition*. London: Macmillan, 1923.

Stallings, J. A., & Kaskowitz, D. *Follow-through classroom observation evaluation*, 1972-73. Menlo Park, California: Stanford Research Institute, 1974.

Stein, M. *Stimulating creativity: Individual differences, Vol. 2*. New York: Academic Press, 1975.

Steiner, A. Why a practicum in thinking? In D. D. Wheeler & W. N. Dember (Eds.), *A practicum in thinking*. Cincinnati: University of Cincinnati, Department of Psychology, 1979.

Sternberg, R. J. *Intelligence, information processing, and analogical reasoning: The componential analysis of human abilities*. Hillsdale, NJ: Lawrence Erlbaum Associates, 1977.

Sternberg, R. J. Intelligence as thinking and learning skills. *Educational Leadership*, 1981, *39*, 18–20.

Sternberg, R. J. Instrumental and componential approaches to the nature and training of intelligence. In S. F. Chipman, J. W. Segal, & R. Glaser *Thinking and learning skills (Vol. 2): Research and open questions*. Hillsdale, NJ: Lawrence Erlbaum Associates, 1985.

Sternberg, R. J., & Detterman, D. K. (Eds.), *Human Intelligence*. Norwood, NJ: Ablex, 1979.

Suchman, J. R. *The elementary school training program in scientific inquiry*. Urbana, IL: University of Illinois, 1962.

Suchman, J. R. A model for the analysis of inquiry. In *Analyses of concept learning*. New York: Academic Press, 1966.

Tamblyn, R. M., & Barrows, H. S. Bedside clinics in neurology: An alternate format for the one-day course in continuing medical education. *Journal of the American Medical Association*, 1980, *243*, 1448–1450.

Tamblyn, R. M., Barrows, H. S., & Gliva, G. An initial evaluation of learning units to facilitate problem solving in self-directed study (Portable Patient Problem Pack). *Medical Education*, 1980, *14*, 394–400.

Thomas, J. C., Jr. An analysis of behavior in the hobbits-orcs problems. *Cognitive Psychology*, 1974, *6*, 257–269.

Thomas, J. C., & Gould, J. D. *A psychological study of query by example* (Research Rep. No. RC–5124). IBM, 1974.

Thomas, J. W. *Varieties of cognitive skills: Taxonomies and models of the intellect.* (Pub. No. OP-407). Philadelphia: Humanizing Learning Program, Research for Better Schools, 1972.

Thorndike, E. L. *Measurement of intelligence*. New York: Teacher's College, Columbia University, 1926.

Thornton, M. C. Piaget and mathematics students. In R. G. Fuller et al., (Eds.), *Piagetian programs in higher education*, Lincoln, NE: ADAPT Program, 1980, 67–73.

Thurstone, L. L. *The nature of intelligence*. London: Routledge and Kegan Paul, Ltd., 1924. Reprinted: Paterson, NJ: Littlefield, Adams, 1960.

Thurstone, T. G. *Primary mental abilities, Rev. 1962*. (Technical report). Chicago: Science Research Associates, Inc., 1965.

Tomlinson-Keasey, C. Formal operations in females aged 11 to 66 years of age. *Developmental Psychology*, 1972, *6*, 364.

Tomlinson-Keasey, C., & Eisert, D. C. Can doing promote thinking in the college classroom? *Journal of College Student Personnel*, 1978, *19*, 99–105.

Torrance, E. P. Can we teach children to think creatively? *Journal of Creative Behavior*, 1972, *6*(2), 114–143.

Toulmin, S. E. *The uses of argument*. Cambridge, England: Cambridge University Press, 1958.

Toulmin, S. E., Rieke, R., & Janik, A. *An introduction to reasoning*. New York: Macmillan, 1979.

Towler, J. O., & Wheatley, G. Conservation concepts in college students: A replication and critique. *Journal of Genetic Psychology*, 1971, *118*.

Training creativity: Walnut Valley study. El Segundo, CA: SOI Institute, 1969.

Treffinger, D. J. *Improving children's creative problem solving ability: Effects of distribution of training, teacher involvement, and teacher's divergent thinking ability on instruction* (Final Report, Office of Education Bureau Number BR-8-A-042, Grant Number OEG-5-70-0029(509)). West Lafayette, Indiana: Purdue University, 1971. (ERIC Document Reproduction Service No. ED 063 268)

Treffinger, D. J., & Ripple, R. E. Developing creative problem solving abilities and related attitudes through programmed instruction. *Journal of Creative Behavior*, 1969, *3*, 105–110; 127.

Treffinger, D. J., & Ripple, R. E. Programmed instruction in creative problem solving: An interpretation of recent research findings. *Educational Leadership*, 1971, *28*, 667–675.

Treffinger, D. J., Speedie, S. M., & Bruner, W. D. Improving children's creative problem solving ability: The Purdue Creativity Project. *Journal of Creative Behavior*, 1974, *8*, 20–30.

Tulving, E. Episodic and semantic memory. In E. Tulving & W. Donaldson (Eds.), *Organization of memory*. New York: Academic Press, 1972, 381–403.

Tulving, E. Relation between encoding specificity and levels of processing. In L. S. Cermak & F. I. M. Craik (Eds.), *Levels of processing and human memory*. Hillsdale, NJ: Lawrence Erlbaum Associates, 1978.

Tulving, E., & Pearlstone, Z. Availability versus accessibility of information in memory for words. *Journal of Verbal Learning and Verbal Behavior*, 1966, *5*, 381–391.

Turnbull, W. W. Intelligence testing in the year 2000. In R. J. Sternberg & D. K. Detterman (Eds.), *Human intelligence: Perspectives on its theory and measurement*. Norwood, NJ: Ablex, 1979.

Tversky, A., & Kahneman, D. Belief in the law of small numbers. *Psychological Bulletin*, 1971, *76*, 105–110.

Tversky, A., & Kahneman, D. Availability: A heuristic for judging frequency and probability. *Cognitive Psychology*, 1973, *4*, 207–232.

Tversky, A., & Kahneman, D. Judgment under uncertainty: Heuristics and biases. *Science*, 1974, *185*, 1124–1131.

Tyler, L. E. The intelligence we test—an evolving concept. In L. B. Resnick (Ed.), *The nature of intelligence*. Hillsdale, NJ: Lawrence Erlbaum Associates, 1976.

Vice, N., & Gonzales, R. SOI training leading to arithmetic achievement: Mall study (summary). El Segundo, CA: SOI Institute, 1979.

Von Elek, T., & Oskarsson, M. *Teaching foreign language grammar to adults: A comparative study* (Gothenburg Studies in English, Vol. 26). Stockholm, Sweden: Almqvist & Wiksell, 1973.

Vygotsky, L. S. *Thought and language*. Cambridge, MA: M.I.T. Press, 1962.

Vygotsky, L. S. *Mind in society: The development of higher psychological processes*. Cambridge, MA: Harvard University Press, 1978.

Wallach, M. A. Psychology of talent and graduate education. In S. Messick & Associates (Eds.), *Individuality in learning*. San Francisco: Jossey-Bass, 1976a.

Wallach, M. A. Tests tell us little about talent. *American Scientist*, 1976b, *64*, 57–63.

Wardrop, J. L., Olton, R. M., Goodwin, W. L., Covington, M. V., Klausmeier, H. J., Crutchfield, R. S., & Ronda, T. The development of productive thinking skills in fifth-grade children. *Journal of Experimental Education*, 1969, *37*, 67–77.

Wason, P. C. Reasoning about a rule. *Quarterly Journal of Experimental Psychology*, 1968, *20*, 273–281.

Wason, P. C. T he psychology of deceptive problems. *New Scientist*, 1974, *63*, 382–385.

Wason, P. C., & Johnson-Laird, P. N. *Psychology of reasoning: Structure and content*. London: B. T. Batsford, 1972.

Watson, G., & Glaser, E. M. *Critical thinking appraisal manual*. New York: Harcourt, Brace & World, 1964.

Watt, D. *Final report of the Brookline Logo project, Part III: Profiles of individual student's work* (Logo memo No. 54, A. I. Memo NO. 546). Cambridge, MA: Artificial Intelligence Laboratory, Massachusetts Institute of Technology, 1979.

Welsh, G. S. Personality correlates of intelligence and creativity in gifted adolescents. In J. Stanley, W. George, & C. Solano (Eds.), *The gifted and the creative: A fifty-year perspective*. Baltimore: Johns Hopkins University Press, 1977.

Wertheimer, Max. In Michael Wertheimer (Ed.) *Productive thinking* (enlarged ed.). New York: Harper & Brothers, 1959.

Westcott, M. R. *Toward a contemporary psychology of intuition*. New York: Holt, Rinehart, & Winston, 1968.

Wheeler, D. D. A practicum in thinking. In D.D. Wheeler & W.N. Dember (Eds.), *A practicum in thinking*. Cincinnati: University of Cincinnati, Department of Psychology, 1979.

Wheeler, D. D., & Dember, W. N. (Eds.), *A practicum in thinking*. Cincinnati: University of

Cincinnati, Department of Psychology, 1979.
Whimbey, A. *Intelligence can be taught*. New York: E. P. Dutton, 1975.
Whimbey, A., Carmichael, J. W., Jones, L. W., Hunter, J. T., & Vincent, H. A. Teaching critical reading and analytical reasoning in Project SOAR. *Journal of Reading*, 1980, *24*, 5–10.
Whimbey, A., & Lochhead, J. *Problem solving and comprehension: A short course in analytic reasoning*. Philadelphia: The Franklin Institute Press, 1979.
Wickelgren, W. A. *How to solve problems: Elements of a theory of problems and problem solving*. San Francisco: Freeman, 1974.
Wiley, D. E. Another hour, another day: Quantity of schooling, a potent path for policy. In W.J. Sewel, R.M. Hauser, & D.L. Featherman (Eds), *Schooling and achievement in American society*. New York: Academic Press, 1976.
Wilkins, M. C. The effect of changed material on ability to do formal syllogistic reasoning. *Archives of Psychology*, 1928, *16*, No. 102.
Wingard, J. R., & Williamson, J. W. Grades as predictors of physician's career performance: An evaluative literature review. *Journal of Medical Education*, 1973, *48*, 311–332.
Witkin, H. A. Cognitive style in academic performance and in teacher-student relations. In S. Messick & Associates (Eds.), *Individuality in learning*. San Francisco: Jossey-Bass, 1976.
Wright, E. Effect of intensive instruction in cue attendance on solving formal operational tasks. *Science Education*, 1979, *63*, 381–393.
Young, R. E., Becker, A. L., & Pike, K. L. *Rhetoric: Discovery and change*. New York: Harcourt, Brace & World, 1970.

Author Index

A

Abelson, R., 255
Ackoff, R.L., 120
Adams, J.L., 84
Adams, M.J., 106, 185
Allen, R., 55, 113, 130, 136
Amabile, T.M., 128, 339
Anastasi, A., 23
Andre, T., 337
Andrews, F.M., 95
Arbitman-Smith, R., 151, 154, 155, 158, 159–60
Armbruster, B.B., 56
Armel, S., 267
Arnold, 233
Arons, A.B., 228
Astorga, M., 219
Austin, G.A., 115, 124, 126

B

Bacon, F., 133–34
Bagnall, J., 96
Baldauf, R.B., 217–18
Baranyi, H., 56
Barclay, C.R., 296
Bar-Hillel, M., 121
Baron, J., 52, 57, 92, 94
Barron, F., 95
Barrows, H.S., 102, 221–25
Bartlett, F.C., 46–48, 50, 61, 67, 122, 126, 132, 133, 255
Beardsley, M.C., 87, 293–94
Becker, A.L., 259
Beckerman, T.M., 334
Beilin, 34
Belmont, J.M., 296, 301, 335, 336
Bereiter, C., 15, 37–38, 53, 101, 252–53, 256–57, 259, 299–300
Bergum, B.O., 94
Berliner, D.C., 334
Bernstein, B., 261
Besel, G., 167
Bierman, M., 287
Binet, A., 26, 27
Blank, M., 37
Blooberg, M., 91
Bloom, B.S., 39, 328
Bloom, M., 269
Boas, 25
Bolton, 25
Borkowski, J.G., 301
Bradley, C.J., 132–33
Brainerd, C.J., 246
Bransford, J.D., 104, 117, 151, 154, 155, 159–60, 191
Bregman, A.S., 255
Broder, L., 39

Brody, N., 133
Bronowski, J., 98
Brown, A.L., 15, 101, 103–4, 105, 107, 108, 191, 295, 296, 297, 300–301
Bruce, B.C., 254
Bruner, J.S., 35–36, 50, 115, 124, 126, 314, 317
Bruner, W.D., 211, 212
Buisman, J., 167
Burkhart, R.C., 96
Burns, B., 267
Busse, T.V., 90–95, 209, 211, 214, 317
Butterfield, E.C., 296, 301, 335, 336
Bynum, 282, 283

C

Cahen, L.S., 334
Campbell, T.C., 227, 231, 242, 316, 317
Campione, J.C., 104, 107, 108, 295, 296, 297, 300–301
Cantor, N., 122
Carlson, 242
Carmichael, J.W., 240, 241, 316
Carpenter, E.T., 32, 227, 231
Carroll, J.B., 18
Case, R., 34, 53
Cattell, J.M.K., 25, 26, 27
Cattell, R.B., 15
Chapman, J.P., 128
Chapman, L.J., 128
Chase, W., 55, 57
Chi, M.T.H., 104, 191, 202
Chiapetta, E.L., 32, 227
Cholson, 34
Clapp, 242
Clark, E.V., 116
Clark, H.H., 115, 116
Cole, M., 22
Collea, F.P., 242, 244, 316–17
Collins, A.M., 106, 264, 296
Colvin, S.S., 14
Connolly, A., 158, 316
Coombs, B., 121
Copes, L., 30
Corzine, H.J., 31
Costa, A.L., 317, 336–37
Covington, M.V., 209, 211, 212
Craik, F.I.M., 265
Crandall, V.C., 316
Crandall, V.J., 316
Crockenberg, S.B., 90
Crosslin, D., 166
Crowley, 242
Crutchfield, R.S., 59, 209, 211, 212
Csikszentmihalyi, M., 53, 87, 92–95, 97, 305

D

Dacey, J.S., 212
Darwin, C., 27
Davies, L., 209
Davis, R.B., 102–3
DeAvila, E.A., 15, 102–3
De Bono, E., 50, 96–97, 214–19, 317, 325
DeBow, C.H., 120
De Groot, A.D., 97
Dember, W.N., 203
DeMonbreun, B.G., 133
Denney, D., 268
Dermen, D., 18
De Sanchez, M.A., 219
Detterman, D.K., 39
Dewey, J., 48
Dickison, A.K., 234–39
Dickstein, L.S., 113
DiSessa, A., 275–77
Dishaw, M.M., 334
Dolnick, M., 268
Donders, 26
Downing, L., 133
Dulit, D., 32
Duly, L.C., 30
Duncan, S., 15, 102–3
Duncker, K., 83–84
Dunn, L.M., 158, 316

E

Earley, C.E., 166
Easterling, J., 254–56
Ebbinghaus, 26
Ebel, R.L., 337
Eckstein, 233
Edwards, J., 217–18
Edwards, W., 124–25
Einhorn, H.J., 132
Eisert, D., 233–34
Ekstrom, R.B., 18, 20
Engelhart, M.D., 328
Engelmann, S., 15, 37–38
Evans, J., 114–15, 282

F

Faflick, P., 269
Feather, N., 112
Feehrer, C.E., 120
Feltovich, P.J., 104, 202
Ferretti, R.P., 336
Feuerstein, R., 20, 147, 148–57, 206, 207–8, 320
Feurzeig, W., 269
Filby, N.N., 334
Fillion, B., 256–57
Fischer, K.W., 246
Fischhoff, B., 121, 132
Fisher, C.W., 334
Flanders, N.A., 337
Flavell, J.H., 101–2, 105, 106, 108, 294, 295, 298–99, 301
Flower, L.S., 53, 252
Fredrick, W.C., 334
French, J.W., 18, 20
French, L.A., 15
Frick, P., 112
Friedburg, D., 167
Friedrichs, A.G., 105
Fuller, R.G., 30, 227, 228, 231
Furst, E.J., 328
Furth, H.G., 238

G

Gagne, R.M., 169, 170
Galton, F., 15, 25
Garber, H., 41
Gardner, H., 95
Gastright, F., 333
Gay, J., 22
Geller, E.S., 133
Getzels, J., 53, 87, 92–95, 97, 305
Gibson, R.S., 133
Gick, M.L., 76
Gilbert, J.A., 25
Gilligan, C., 32
Glaser, E.M., 233, 244, 245, 316, 317
Glaser, R., 104, 202
Glick, J., 22
Gliva, G., 224–25
Goldenberg, E.P., 273–74
Goldstein, I., 49
Goldstein, S., 112
Gonzales, R., 167
Good, T.L., 334
Goodman, J., 268
Goodman, N., 96
Goodnow, J.J., 22, 115, 124, 126
Goodwin, W.L., 211, 212
Goor, A., 266
Gordon, L.V., 316
Gordon, R., 112
Gordon, W.J.J., 98, 204
Gore, D., 167
Gould, 115
Grabitz, H.J., 133
Grant, R., 269
Gray, S.W., 37
Greeno, J.G., 49, 81
Groff, P., 264
Guilford, J.P., 16, 50, 53–54, 161–63, 164

H

Haas, 288, 289
Hafner, J., 55, 113, 130, 136
Haggerty, M.E., 14
Harman, H.H., 18
Harpin, W., 264
Harris, D.B., 158, 316
Harvey, O.J., 233
Hassell, J., 240, 241, 316
Hayakawa, S.I., 248–51
Hayes, J.R., 49, 53, 120, 252, 302–6
Haywood, H.C., 158, 316
Haywood, W.C., 151, 154, 155, 159–60
Heber, R., 41
Helmholtz, 26
Henle, M., 116
Henri, 27
Henshaw, D., 266
Herrmann, D.J., 200, 202
Herrnstein, J., 48, 145
Herrnstein, R.J., 28–29, 186, 317
Herron, J.D., 30
Hetherington, E., 268
Hiegel, 242
Hill, W.H., 328
Hoepfl, R.T., 120
Hoepfner, R., 53–54, 161, 163, 164
Hoffman, M., 147, 148, 149, 150–51, 152, 154
Hoffman, M.B., 148, 150–51, 154, 155, 157
Hogan, J.D., 212
Hogarth, R.M., 132
Holyoak, K.J., 76
Horn, J.L., 18, 22, 162
Hoyt, J.D., 105

Hubbard, M.R., 126
Huber, G.P., 120
Hunt, D., 233
Hunter, J., 240, 241, 316
Huntington, J.M., 120
Hutchinson, R.T., 206, 208, 209, 337

I

Ives, W., 95

J

Jackson, P.W., 87–88
Jackson, S., 32
Jaeger, 26
Janik, A., 290, 293, 294
Janis, I., 112
Jastak, J., 158, 316
Jastak, S., 158, 316
Jastrow, 25, 27
Jennings, D., 128
Jensen, M.R., 148, 149, 154, 155, 157
Jochem, H., 133
Johnson, D.M., 52, 90, 97
Johnson, M.K., 117
Johnson–Laird, P.N., 55, 112, 139, 204
Johnston, S., 231, 233–34
Jones, L., 240, 241, 316
Jones, O., 167

K

Kahneman, D., 119, 120, 121, 125, 139, 263
Kanarick, A.F., 120
Kans, 233
Karnes, M.B., 37
Karplus, R., 32, 227
Karweit, N., 333
Kaskowitz, D., 334
Katkovsky, W., 316
Kaufman, H., 112
Keniston, A., 298–99
Kent, A., 166
Kilpatrick, 242
Kitzhaber, A.R., 252
Klaus, R.A., 37
Klausmeier, H.J., 56–57, 170–72, 211, 212
Klevin, A., 337
Knapp, J.R., 162
Koberg, D., 96
Koestler, A., 98
Kohlberg, L., 32
Kolb, 242
Kolodiy, G., 32, 227
Korzybski, A., 249
Kraepelin, 18, 27
Krathwohl, D.R., 328
Krepelka, E.J., 209, 211, 214, 317
Kurland, D.M., 278

L

Lange, 26
Larkin, J.H., 57, 70, 104, 191
Lawson, A.E., 32, 227, 240, 316
Layman, M., 121
Leirer, V., 112, 117
Lepper, M.H., 126
Levine, H., 240
Lichtenstein, S., 120, 121, 132
Lindman, H., 124–25
Lipman, M., 280–81, 283, 286–89, 316
Lochhead, J., 206–9, 240, 268, 306
Lockhart, R.S., 265
Loevinger, J., 96, 233
Lonky, 233
Lorge, I., 158, 159, 316
Loucks, S., 254
Lovell, K., 32
Lukas, G., 269
Lukas, J.D., 269

M

McCarthy, D.A., 94
McDermott, J., 104
MacKinnon, D.W., 03
McKinnon, J.W., 32, 227
McKnight, C., 102–3
Mackworth, N.H., 95
MacPhee, D., 39–41
McQuillan, M.K., 264
McShane, J.A., 33
Mahoney, M.J., 133
Manning, E., 167
Mansfield, R.S., 90–95, 209, 211, 214, 317
Markman, E.M., 105–6, 107, 295
Markwardt, F.C., 158, 316
Marliave, R., 334
Matthews, 281
Medin, D.L., 115, 180

Mednick, S.A., 91
Meeker, M.N., 54, 163–64
Meichenbaum, D., 265–69
Mendelsohn, G.A., 91
Meringoff, L., 95
Messick, S., 87–88
Metuis, C.B., 16
Mill, J.S., 36–37
Miller, G.E., 102, 222
Miller, R., 147, 148, 149, 150–51, 152, 154, 155, 157
Ministerberg, H., 27
Minsky, M.A., 255
Mintzker, Y., 148, 154, 155, 157
Mitchell, D.L.M., 224
Moffett, J., 261–65
Moreno, J.M., 212
Morgan, C.R., 269
Morgan, J., 112
Morris, T.L., 94
Morton, J., 112
Moshman, D., 231, 233–34

N

Nachtman, W., 158, 316
Narveson, R.D., 32, 33, 121, 227, 231
Neisser, U., 16–17, 115, 255, 317
Newell, A., 67, 75, 79, 81, 96, 305
Nichol, E.H., 133
Nickerson, R.S., 33, 48, 120, 145, 186, 228, 269, 317, 323
Nieman, H., 333
Nilsson, N.J., 66, 71–72, 73
Nisbett, R., 53, 119, 126, 127, 128, 132, 250, 263, 293
Noppe, L.D., 94
Norsworthy, 25–26
Nowicki, S., 158, 316
Nummedal, S.G., 242, 244, 316–17

O

O'Brien, T.C., 116
Oehrn, A., 27
O'Leary, D., 267
Olson, D.R., 248, 258, 264
Olton, R.M., 209, 211, 212
Osborn, A.F., 99
Oscanyan, F., 287, 288, 289, 316
Oskarsson, M., 56

P

Pagni, 242
Papert, S., 49, 62, 269, 271, 272–73, 275–77, 336
Parke, R., 268
Pasanen, J., 254–56
Pea, R., 277, 278
Pearlstone, Z., 107
Pelz, D.C., 95
Perkins, D.N., 52, 55, 58, 88, 89, 90, 95–98, 113, 130, 136, 251, 255, 265
Perry, W.G., 96
Peterson, C.R., 120
Peterson, J., 14, 23
Peterson, M.Q., 227, 231
Petr, J.L., 227, 231–33
Phillips, L.D., 124–25
Piaget, J., 29–31, 32, 34, 35, 151, 170–71, 246, 261, 307
Piers, E.V., 158, 316
Pike, K.L., 259
Pintner, R., 14, 23
Pitz, G.F., 133
Pollard, P.F., 114–15
Polya, G., 50, 52, 55, 69, 74, 75–79, 82, 84, 327
Preyer, 27
Price, L. A., 20
Pritchett, E.M., 158, 316
Prosser, M., 32
Pruitt, P.G., 133
Pylyshyn, Z.W., 108, 109

R

Ramey, C.T., 39–41
Rand, Y., 147, 148, 149, 150–55, 157
Raven, J.C., 158, 316
Reinhold, H., 133
Renner, J.W., 32, 227
Resnick, L.B., 14, 29, 255
Revlin, R., 112, 117
Revlis, R., 116
Ridberg, E., 268
Rieke, R., 290, 293, 294
Rigney, J.W., 120
Ripple, R.E., 212
Robin, A., 267, 268
Roe, A., 95
Ronda, T., 211, 212
Rosch, E.R., 16
Rosenberg, M., 158, 316

Ross, L., 53, 119, 126, 127, 128, 250, 263, 293
Rothenberg, A., 94
Rowe, M.B., 337
Rozin, P., 108
Rubenstein, M.F., 191–95
Rubin, A.D., 254
Ryan, M., 240, 241, 316

S

Salter, W., 48, 145
Sanchez, M., 186, 317
Sanders, J.R., 175–76
Sanford, N., 233
Scardamalia, M., 101, 252, 253, 256–57, 299–300
Schank, R., 255
Schermerhorn, L.L., 234–39
Schneider, M., 268
Schoenfeld, A., 52, 68–69, 195–203, 220, 325
Schopenhauer, A., 37, 131
Schroder, D., 233
Schuler, G., 212
Scriven, M., 69
Searle, D.J., 264
Sharp, A.M., 287, 288, 289, 316
Sharp, D., 22
Sheldon, R., 233
Shepard, S., 48, 145
Shweder, R.A., 128
Siegler, R.S., 52, 53, 57
Silberstein, L., 95
Simon, D.P., 76, 104, 287, 288
Simon, H.A., 49, 55, 57, 67, 75, 76, 79, 81, 96, 104, 287, 288, 305, 316
Slovic, P., 120, 121, 132, 133
Smith, E.E., 7, 106, 115, 180, 296
Smith, P., 56
Snyder, M., 122–23
Solomon, C., 269
Solomon, F., 37
Sommerfeld, R., 266
Sonnad, S.R., 175–76
Spearman, C., 15
Speedie, S.M., 211, 212
Spencer, 15
Stallings, J.A., 334
Stein, M., 99
Steiner, A., 203
Sternberg, R.J., 20, 21, 29, 152, 162
Stevens, A.L., 264
Strickland, B.R., 158, 316
Suchman, J.R., 229, 230, 337
Swann, W.B., 122
Swets, J.A., 186, 317

T

Tamblyn, R.M., 102, 221–25
Tannenbaum, A.J., 153, 154, 155, 157
Terman, L., 14, 23, 26
Thomas, J.C., 81
Thomas, J.W., 22
Thorndike, R.L., 14
Thornton, M.C., 30, 31, 116, 227, 231
Thurstone, L.L., 15–16, 338
Thurstone, T.G., 158, 159, 316
Titchener, 26
Tomlinson-Keasey, C., 32, 227, 231, 233–34, 238
Torrance, E.P., 90
Toulmin, S.E., 290–94
Towler, J.O., 32, 227
Treffinger, D.J., 211, 212
Tulving, E., 107, 163
Turnbull, W.W., 29
Tversky, A., 119, 120, 121, 125, 139, 263
Tyler, L.E., 24

V

Vice, N., 167
Vincent, H., 240, 241, 316
Von Elek, T., 56
Vygotsky, L.S., 259, 292

W

Wagner, B.J., 262–63
Wallach, M.A., 90
Wardrop, J.L., 211, 212
Ware, 327–29
Wason, P.C., 32, 112, 114, 121, 204
Watson, G., 233, 244, 245, 316, 317
Watt, D., 275–77
Weene, P., 115
Weiner, W.B., 269
Weir, S., 275–77
Wellman, H.M., 301
Welsh, G.S., 87, 94, 95
Wertheimer, M., 272
Westcott, M.R., 91, 95, 100

Wexelblat, P.M., 269
Wheatley, G., 32, 227
Wheeler, D.D., 203, 205
Whimbey, A., 15, 37, 38–39, 206–9, 240, 241, 268, 306, 316
Wickelgren, W.A., 52, 79, 80–81
Wiley, D.E., 333
Wilkins, M.C., 112
Williams, L.D., 234–39
Williams, V., 231, 233–34
Williamson, J.W., 2
Wilson, T.D., 132
Wingard, J.R., 2
Witkin, H.A., 94
Wolf, D., 95
Woodrow, H., 14
Wright, E., 32, 104
Wundt, 26

Y

Yeates, K.O., 39–41
Yopp, H., 112, 117
Yopp, R., 112, 117
Young, R.E., 259

Subject Index

A

Abecedarian Program, 39–41, 42
Abilities, thinking. *See also* Reasoning
  calibration to level of, 339, 342
  creative, 89–93
  defining intelligence through, 8–14
  as limiting factor, 53–54
  as skill, 45–46, 48–50, 59–61
Abstract statistical information, 125–26
Abstract thinking, 231–34, 246
Accessibility, 107–9
Acquisition components of intelligence, 20–21
Adaptability, 9–10, 26
ADAPT (Accent on the Development of Abstract Processes of Thought), 231–34
Affective demands of learning tasks, 208
Agency for Instructional Television, 172
Algorithm, 74
Allocated time, 334
Alternatives, consideration of, 127
American Association for the Advancement of Science, 168
Analogy, 76, 98
Analysis, managerial strategy, 198, 199
Analytical reasoning, 239–41
Application phase of learning, 227, 228
Argument. *See also* Reasoning
  anatomy of, 290–94
  circularity in, 118
  validity of, 111–15
Argumentum ad hominem, 134–35
Assessability of instructional objectives, 330
Assessment. *See* Evaluation
Associates, remote, 90–91
Associational fluency, 19
Associative memory, 19
Associative writing, 253
"At-risk" children, 39–40
Attention, 26
Attitudes, 94–96, 208, 339–40, 343
Autism, use of computers in cases of, 274
Availability heuristic, 120–21, 129, 139
Availability of information, 300

B

Backing in argument, 291
Bank Street College of Education, 277
Barron–Welsh Art Scale, 95
BASICS, 176–80
BASICS TRAINERS, 176
Behavior
  ability to modify adaptively, 9–10
  impulsive, 15–16
  rule-based vs. model-based, 54–56
Biases. *See* Errors and biases

Blockbusting, 175
Bolt Beranek and Newman Inc., 181, 270
Brainstorming, 99, 174–75
Building and Applying Strategies for Intellectual Competencies in Students, 176–80

C

California, University of, 191, 194, 196
California Test of Mental Maturity, 288
Capabilities, assessing one's own, 104–7
Categories, conceptual, 9
Cattell Culture-Fair Test, 186
Causality, co-occurrence and, 129
CAUSE. *See* DORIS program
Cerebral palsy, LOGO program for, 274
Certainty, decisions under, 304
Chance, creativity and, 97
Children as natural philosophers, 281
Cincinnati, University of, 203
Circularity in argument, 118
Classroom, 282, 336–37
Classroom Participation Scale, 156
Clinical reasoning process, 222–23
Closure, 19, 321–22
Cognitive Behavior Modification (Meichenbaum), 265–69
Cognitive development, 29–36, 150–51, 231–33
Cognitive map, 149, 152
Cognitive modifiability, 149–51
Cognitive operations approaches, 147–89
  BASICS, 176–80
  focus of, 308
  in general, 187–89
  Instrumental Enrichment Program, 147–61, 316
  Project Intelligence, 181–87, 317, 331
  Science . . . A Process Approach, 56, 168–72
  Structure of Intellect Program, 53–54, 161–68
  Thinkabout, 172–76
"Cognitive Research Trust", 215–20
Cognitive structure, 151–52
Cognitive Studies Project, 206–9
Cognitive style, 52–53, 54, 57, 58, 93–94, 100
Combinatorial logic, 243
Commitment, creativity and, 95
Communicative writing, 252
COMPAS, 237–39
Competence, intellectual. *See* Intelligence
Competency, teacher, 326
Complete Problem Solver, The (Hayes), 302–6
"Complex extended problems", 211, 212
Complex representation, 279
Composition. *See* Writing
Comprehension, monitoring of, 105–7, 295–96
Comprehension, verbal, 20
Comprehensive Test of Basic Skills, 289
Computers, use of, 70–74, 79, 83, 269–78
Conceptual categories, 9
Conceptual models, 11–12
Concrete operations stage, 30, 31, 33, 232
Conducive environments, 336–37
Confirmation bias, 121–24, 129–30
Conflict, decisions under, 304
Confront, Construct, Complete (Easterling & Pasanen), 254–56
Consciousness, stream of, 266
Conservatism in use of probabilistic information, 124–25
Consistency, validity vs., 112–13
Consortium for Operating and Managing Program for the Advancement of Skills, 237–39
Context-boundedness, 57–59
Contradiction, 138, 139
Contrary antecedent, 137, 138, 139
Conversion, premise, 116–17
Co-occurrence, 129
Correlational reasoning, 128–29, 243
CoRT Program, 215–20
Cost-benefit analysis, 304
Costs, opportunity, 321
Counterexample, 138, 139
Counterproductive persistence, 126–27
Covariance, problems in detecting, 127–29
CREATE Program, 238
  Creativity, 86–100
  components of, 89–99, 100
  definitions of, 87–89, 304
  implications of, 99–100
  inner speech and, 266–67
  programs to teach, 163, 164, 209–20
  as skill, 142
  strategies, 304–5
"Critical" epistemologist, 130
Critical thinking, 88–89

Criticism, inhibiting effects of, 99
Crystallized intelligence, 15
Cues, 106, 295–96, 297
Culture, intelligence and, 22

D

Debugging, 273
Decentration, 261
Decision making, 304
Deductive reasoning, 10–11, 111–18
Deficient cognitive functions, 152
Deliberate personality, 96
Demands of writing, 251–54
Depth of processing, 297
Descent of Man, The (Darwin), 26
Design in managerial strategy, 198, 199
Development, cognitive, 29–36, 150–51, 231–33
Development of Operational Reasoning Skills, 234–37, 238
Development of Reasoning in Science, 241–45, 316–17
Dichotomies, 50–51
Differential intelligence, 14–22
Direct effects, 319
Disappointment, risk of, 344
Disconfirming evidence, neglect of, 122–23, 130
Disconnection, 138–39
Discourse, universe of, 260–65
"Discover the rule" type task, 121–22
Discovery, 283, 327
Discussion skills, 282
Disjunction, errors due to, 115
Divergent effects, hypothesis of, 157
DOORS program, 234–37, 238
DORIS program, 241–45, 316–17

E

Education
  cognitive development and, 32–34
  increasing intelligence through, 36–42
  informal reasoning and, 136–37
  objectives of, 49–50, 323–26, 329–31
Educational Testing Service, 18, 113, 228, 289
Effective Listening Program, 206
Effects, divergent, 157
Effects, program, 319–20, 321
"Ego–syntonic" mathematics, 272–73
Elaboration, failures of, 138–40
Elements of Psychophysics (Titchener), 26
Encoding, 51, 52, 116
Engagement, student, 332, 334
Environment, conducive, 336–37
"Episodic" memory, 163
Epistemic writing, 253, 259
Epistemologists, 130
Equivalence Class heuristic, 80
Errors and biases, 111–40
  in deductive reasoning, 111–18
  due to social factors, 130–35
  elaboration, failures at, 138–40
  in hypotheses, 124–35
  in inductive reasoning, 118–30
  in informal reasoning, 137–38
  in samples, 119–27, 129–30
Evaluation, 313–22
  of ADAPT program, 233–34
  of BASICS program, 179–80
  of COMPAS program, 238–39
  of CoRT program, 217–20
  of DOORS program, 235–37
  of DORIS program, 242–45, 316–17
  formative vs. summative, 314–15
  functions, 72–73, 80
  of heuristic instruction in mathematics, 200–203
  of Instrumental Enrichment Program, 155–61, 316
  of intelligence, 22–29
  of LOGO, 275–78
  LPAD, 148–49
  neglected issues of, 318–22
  obstacles to, 315–16
  of own knowledge and performance, 104–7, 132–33
  performance measures and tests, 316–18
  of Philosophy for Children Program, 286–90, 316
  of Practicum in Thinking course, 205–6, 317
  procedures for success, 332–33
  of Productive Thinking Program, 211–14, 317
  of Project Intelligence, 185–87, 317
  purposes of, 313–15
  of SOAR program, 240–41, 316
  of Structure of Intellect Program, 166–68
  of ThinkAbout Series, 175–76

Evaluation (*Cont.*)
of universe of discourse program, 263–65
Evidence, errors in use of, 122–23, 130, 133–34
"Executive review", 69
Exercises to aid in transfer, 335–36
Exhaustive search, 72
Expert problem solving, study of, 68–70
Explicit know–how, 56–57
Exploration, 198, 199, 227
Expository writing, 252
Expressional fluency, 19
Expression of Emotion in Man and Animals, The (Darwin), 26
Extensional meaning, 249
External factor objection, 138, 139
Extrapolation, 47

F

Factor analysis, 18–20, 162
Factor–referenced cognitive tests, 18–20
Failure, risk of, 343–44
Favoritism in evaluating hypothesis, 131–34
Feasibility of instructional objectives, 330
Feedback, creativity and attitude toward, 95–96
Field dependence/independence, 94
Figural flexibility, 20
Figural fluency, 19
Filtering, critical, 88, 89
"Flat associative hierarchy", 91
Flexibility, types of, 19, 20
Fluency, types of, 19, 89–90, 97
Fluid intelligence, 15
Formal operational stage, 30, 32, 33–34, 232–33, 246
Formal reasoning, 30, 34, 234–37
Formal thinking approaches, 227–47
ADAPT, 231–34
assumptions underlying, 229
COMPAS, 237–39
DOORS, 234–37, 238
DORIS, 241–45, 316–17
focus of, 308
SOAR, 239–41, 316
Formative evaluation, 314
Fractionation, 303

G

Gains, evidence of, 325–26
Gap–filling processes, 47
General Abilities Tests, 186
General Enrichment, 154, 156
Generalization, 10, 57–59, 78, 300–301
Generating process, 88–89. *See also* Creativity
Geometry, "turtle", 271–73, 276–77
Gestaltists, 83
Goals, 51, 52, 320–21
Grounds in argument, 291
Growth, intellectual, nature of, 35–36
Guidance Testing Associates' Tests of General Ability, 186
Guidance to teachers, 326–27

H

Handicapped persons, 273–75, 287–89
Harvard University, 181
Hereditary Genius: An Inquiry into its Laws and Consequences (Galton), 24
Heuristics, 74–86, 141
availability, 120–21, 129, 139
Complete Problem Solver, The (Hayes), 302–6
Equivalence Class, 80
general observations about, 82–85
hill–climbing, 80–81
metacomprehension, 106–7
representativeness, 125–26, 130
Heuristics–oriented approaches, 190–226
Cognitive Studies Program, 206–9
focus of, 308
in general, 225–26
lateral thinking and CoRT Program, 214–20
in mathematics, 195–203
Newell–Simon approach, 79–82
Patterns of Problem Solving course, 191–95
Polya approach, 75–79
Practicum in Thinking, 203–6, 317
problem-based self instruction, 220–25
Productive Thinking Program, 209–14, 317
Hill–climbing heuristics, 80–81
Hypothesis(-ses)
of divergent effects, 157
errors and biases in, 124–35
testing vs. generation, 50
Hypothetico–Deduction skills, 243

I

Ideational fluency, 19, 89–90, 97
Illinois Test of Psycholinguistic Abilities, 288
Images, inner speech and, 268
Implementation, managerial strategy, 198, 199
Implementation of program, 342–43
Implicit know–how, 56–57
Impulsive behavior, 15–16
Inconsistency cue, 295–96
Indefinite results, risk of, 344
Indirect effects, 319
Indirect proof, 81–82
Individual differences, measuring, 25
Inductive reasoning, 19. *See also* Heuristics
  ability, 10
  conceptual models and, 11
  deductive argument form vs., 114
  errors in, 118–30
"Inert knowledge", 253, 257
Inference, rules of, 249, 250
Inferences, pragmatic, 117
Informal reasoning, 135–40, 250
Information, availability of, 300
Information, use of, 115–16, 119–20, 124–26
Information–processing view, 34–35
Inhibition of impulsiveness, 15–16
Inner speech, 265–69
Inquiries into Human Faculty and its Development (Galton), 24
Inquiry, writing as process of, 259
Inquiry Training program, 229–31
Insight, 12, 79, 83
Institute for Curriculum and Instruction, 176
Institute for the Advancement of Philosophy for Children, 285
Instructional objectives, 329–31
Instructional procedures, 331–32
Instrumental Enrichment Program, 147–61
  cognitive modifiability, 149–51
  evaluation of, 155–61, 316
  mediated learning, 149–52
  specifics of, 153–55
  view of intelligence in, 148–49
Integrative processes, 19
"Intellectance" scale, 95
Intelligence, 8–43
  assessment of, 22–29
  cognitive development, 29–36, 150–51, 231–33
  components of, 20–21, 188
  defining, 8–14
  differential, conceptions of, 14–22
  fluid vs. crystallized, 15
  increase through training of, 36–42
  in Instrumental Enrichment Program, 148–49
  knowledge as distinct from, 22
  nature of, 14–15, 17–20
  as secondary issue, 141
  structure of, 16, 53–54
Intelligence quotient (IQ). *See* IQ
Intelligence (Taine), 26
Intensional meaning, 249, 250
Interdependence of knowledge and thinking, 48–50, 62, 324
Interpolation, 47
Intrinsic motivation, 339
Introduction to Reasoning, An (Toulmin, Rieke, & Janik), 290, 292, 293
Intuition, 91–92, 100
Invention phase of learning, 227–28. *See also* Creativity
Iowa Test of Basic Skills, 287
IQ
  introduction of, 26
  modeling inner speech and, 268
  tests, criticisms of, 28, 29, 148, 317
  training and modification of, 37, 40–42, 158–59

J

"Janusian thinking", 94
Journal of Education Psychology, 14

K

Know–how, 52, 54, 56–57
Knowledge, 101–9
  accessibility of, 107–9
  effective application of, 102–3
  to facilitate memory retrieval, 298
  "inert", 253, 257
  intelligence as distinct from, 22
  interdependence of thinking and, 48–50, 62, 324
  metacognitive, 101–3
  monitoring and evaluation of own, 104–7, 132–33
  need for content, 160
  -telling, 253, 257
  "working", 56

L

Language approach, 248–79
focus of, 309
in general, 278–79
inner speech and self instruction, 265–69
Language in Thought and Action program, 248–51
LOGO, 269–78
universe of discourse program, 260–65
writing, 251–60, 264
Language in Thought and Action (Hayakawa), 248–51
Lateral thinking, 214–20
Learning
ability of, 9–10
cognitive development and, 32-34
mediated, 149–52
problem-based, 220–25
slow, accretive nature of, 333
strategies, 304
Learning Cycle approach, 227–28, 229, 231, 238, 239. *See also* Formal thinking approaches
Learning–disabled emotionally–handicapped students, 287–89
Learning Potential Assessment Device, 148–49
Legitimacy of teaching thinking, 323–26
Levidal Self–concept Scale, 156
LIFT Program, 238
Limitations, assessing one's own, 104–7
Limits on thinking, 51–59, 62
Little Red Writing Book, The (Scardamalia, Bereiter, & Fillion), 256–57
Load, cognitive, 52, 54, 55, 130, 139, 255
Logic, combinatorial, 243. *See also* Reasoning
LOGO, 269–78
Long searches, 97–98
Long–term effects, 319–20
Low achiever, cognitive modifiability and, 150
Low–aptitude students, characteristics of, 39
LPAD, 148–49

M

Machado, Luis Alberto, 181
"Makes sense" epistemologist, 130
Managerial strategy, 197–200
Manhattan Community College, 206, 337
Map, cognitive, 149, 152
Massachusetts Institute of Technology, 271
Mastery, stages of, 170–72
Mathematics
"ego–syntonic", 272–73
heuristic instruction in, 195–203
LOGO for teaching, 269–78
Maturation, cognitive load limits and, 54
Meaning, intensional vs. extensional, 249, 250
Means-end analysis, 70, 303
Mediated learning, 149–52
Medical problem solving, 220–25
Memory, 19, 163, 258–59, 296–99
Mental act, phases of, 152
Mental testing, 17–18, 23–27, 148–49
Mental Tests and Measurements (Cattell), 25
Metacognition, 100–109
implications of, 109
program for fostering good, 210–11
skills, 142, 294–302
examples of, 103–9
metamemory, 296–99
self-monitoring for reading comprehension, 295–96
transfer of training, 265, 299–302, 334–36
Metacomponents of intelligence, 20–21
Metacomprehension heuristics, 106–7
Metalearning habits, 154
Metamemory, 296–99
Metaphor, inner speech and, 268
Metropolitan Achievement Tests, 289
Milwaukee Project, 41–42
Mind of a Child, The (Preyer), 26–27
Misunderstandings, 295
Modality, 291
Modeling inner speech, 265–69
Model(s)
-based behavior, 54–56
conceptual, 11–12
developmental, 34–35
of situation, failures to elaborate, 135–40
Modifiability, cognitive, 149–51
Modus ponens, 113
Modus tollens, 113
Monitoring, self, 104–7, 295–96, 300–301
Montclair State College, 285
Motivation, 274–75, 337–39
Multiple accessible knowledge, 108–9

N

National Science Foundation, 168
"Nature–nurture" question, 60–61

Nebraska, University of, 234
Negative effects, 321
Negative information, 115–16, 124
Neglected critical distinction, 138, 139
Nelson-Denny Reading Test, 241
Newell–Simon problem–solving approach, 79–82
Number facility, 19

O

Objections to informal reasoning, 137–38, 139
Objectives
  educational, 49–50, 323–26, 329–31
  need to assess, 320–21
  selection of programs and, 341, 342
Objectivity, failure at, 131–33
Obstacles to evaluation, 315–16
"One-shot thinking", 39
Openmindedness, failure at, 131–33
"Open-system" view, 148–49
Operational stage, 29–34, 232–33, 246
Operations as limiting factor, 51, 52
Opportunity costs, 321
Oral preparation for writing, 264
Origence, 94
Originality, predisposition toward, 94–95. *See also* Creativity
Otis Lennon School Ability Test, 186
Overload, 120

P

Partiality in assessment and use of evidence, 133–34
PATH Program, 238
Patterns, 9, 46
Patterns of Plausible Inference (Polya), 77
Patterns of Problem–Solving, 191–95
Patterns of Problem Solving (Rubenstein), 192–95
Penetrance, 72
Perceptual speed, 19
Performance
  components of intelligence, 20–21
  expert problem-solving, study of, 68–70
  measures, 316–18
  Milwaukee Project and school, 41–42
  monitoring and evaluation of own, 104–7
Persistence, 126–27, 210
Personality types, 96
Person metacognition, 108
Person variables, 101
Perspectives on thinking, 44–63
  abilities as skill, 45–46, 48–50, 59–61
  Bartlett's view, 46–48
  dichotomous distinctions, 50–51
  limits on thinking, 51–59, 62
Philosophy for Children Program, 280–90
Physical setting, 337
Plan, heuristics for executing and devising, 76–78, 80–82
Planning skills, 104, 278
Polarity, validity vs., 114–15
Portable Patient Problem Pack, 223–24
Potential, unactualized, 60–61
Practical significance, 318–19
Practice, 45–46, 48
Practicum in Thinking, A, 203–6, 317
Pragmatic inferences, 117
Precoded response sequences, 46
Predisposition toward originality, 94–95
Premature closure, 321–22
Premise conversion, 116–17
Pre-operational stage, 29
Preschoolers, programs for, 37–42
Prescriptive problem–solving model, 75–79
Primary effects, 319
Probabilistic information, 124–25
Problem(s)
  -based learning approach, 220–25
  calibration to ability level, 339
  "complex extended", 211, 212
  finding, 93
  formulation, 223
  representation, 71–72, 75–76, 79–80, 83–84
  selection of, 338
  "space", 96
  types of, 211, 212, 224, 299–300
Problem solving, 64–86. *See also* Creativity; Heuristics; Heuristics–oriented approaches
  ability to understand and, 12–13
  aspects of, 302–3
  availability of information and, 300
  characteristics of good, 207
  defined, 65–67
  guidelines to, 193–94
  implications for teaching of thinking, 85–86
  limits to, 52
  LOGO instruction and, 277
  mathematical, 195–203
  medical, 220–25
  metacognitive skill and, 104
  Patterns of Problem Solving course, 191–95

Problem Solving (*Cont.*)
prescriptive model of, 75–79
strategies, identification of, 68–74
Problem Solving and Comprehension (Whimbey & Lochhead), 206, 240, 268
"Procedural facilitation", 257–58
Procedural thinking, 269–78
Process concepts, 171–72
"Processor", 34–35
Productive Thinking Program, 209–14, 317
Programming with LOGO, 269–78
Programs. *See also* specific programs
implementation of, 342–43
for preschoolers, 37–42
selection of, 341–42
teacher acceptance of, 327–29
Project Achievement Battery, 156
Project Intelligence, 181–87, 317, 331
Promotional material, problem of, 344
Proof, indirect, 81–82
Proportional reasoning, 243
Prospects for teaching thinking, 323–45
ingredients for success, 326–40
legitimacy as objective, 323–26
recommendations on, 340–43
risks, 343–45
Proximity method, 303

R

Reading comprehension, self monitoring for, 295–96
"Reading in", problems with, 250
Reasoning
analogical, 76, 98
analytical, 239–41
anatomy of argument approach to, 290–94
clinical, 222–23
conceptual models and, 11
concrete, 30
correlational, 128–29, 243
deductive, 10–11, 111–18
DOORS program, 234–37, 238
errors and biases. *See*Errors and biases
formal, 30, 34, 234–37
inductive, 10, 11, 19, 74, 114, 118–30
informal, 135–40, 250
Language in Thought and Action approach, 248–51
logical, 19
model-based vs. rule-based behavior and, 55–56
Philosophy for Children Program and, 282–83
proportional, 243
in science, DORIS program for, 241–45, 316–17
syllogistic, 290, 293
ThinkAbout program for, 172–76
Rebuttal, 291
Recognition of utility of skill, 107
Recursion, 278
Reflective access to knowledge, 109
Reinterpretation, 47
Relationships, ability to "see", 13
Remedial training program, 39
Remote associates, 90–91
Representation
argument, altering of, 116–18
complex, language approach and, 279
problem, 71–72, 75–76, 79–80, 83–84
Representativeness heuristic, 125–26, 130
Resemblance, 128
Response sequences, precoded, 46
Restricted search, 72
Retention components of intelligence, 20–21
Retrieval, memory, 297–98
Rhetoric: Discovery and Change (Young, Becker, & Pike), 259
RISE Program, 238
Risk, decisions under, 304
Risks to teaching thinking, 343–45
"Rogerian argument", 259–60
Rule-based behavior, 54–56
"Rules of inference" approach, 249, 250

S

Sample errors and biases, 119–27, 129–30
Scanning, spatial, 20
Science . . . A Process Approach (SAPA) program, 56, 168–72
Science, programs for, 56, 168–72, 241–45, 316–17
Search techniques, 72–73, 97–98, 303
Secondary effects, 319, 321
Selection of programs, 341–42
Self-awareness, 203
Self instruction, 220–25, 265–69
Self-monitoring, 104–7, 295–96, 300–301
Sensori-motor stage, 29
Setting, physical, 337
Short-range objectives, 341
Short-term effects, 319–20
Short-term evaluation, 333

Significance, statistical vs. practical, 318–19
Simulated problems, 224
Skill(s)
  creativity as, 142
  discussion, 282
  Hypothetico-Deduction, 243
  intelligence as set of, 21
  metacognitive, 103–9, 142
  planning, 104, 278
  potential, 60–61
  recognition of utility of, 107
  thinking as, 45–46, 48–50, 59–61
Skills Essential to Learning Project, 172
SOAR, 239–41, 316
Social factors in reasoning errors, 130–35
SOI Institute, 161, 165, 166
SOI-LA, 164, 166–67
Spatial orientation and scanning, 20
Speech, inner, 265–69
Speed, perceptual, 19
Speed of closure, 19
Spontaneous personality, 96
Standardization in testing, 26
Stanford-Binet test, 26
STARS Program, 238
"State space" representation, 71–72
Statistical information, abstract, 125–26
Statistical significance, 318–19
STEPPE Program, 238
Stereotypes, 126
Strategies
  for BASICS, 177–78, 179, 180
  for conducive environment, 336–37
  as creativity component, 96–99
  learning, 304
  managerial, 197–200
  metacognitive skill and, 101, 104, 108
  problem-solving, identification of, 68–74
Stream of consciousness, 266
Stress on Analytical Reasoning program, 239–41, 316
Structural model of intelligence, 16
Structure of Intellect Program, 53–54, 161–68
Student–Centered Language Arts and Reading, K–12 (Moffett & Wagner), 261–63
Style, cognitive, 52–53, 54, 57, 58, 93–94, 100
Subgoal analysis, 81
Subgoal Analysis (Newell & Simon), 78
Success, ingredients of, 326–40
  attitudes, 339–40
  conducive environment, 336–37
  instructional objectives, procedures and evaluation, 329–33
  motivation, 337–39
  teacher, 326–29
  time on task, 333–34
  transfer, 265, 299–302, 334–36
Success rate, 334
Summative evaluation, 314–15
Syllogistic reasoning, 290, 293
Symbol manipulation. *See* Language approach
Synectics, 98

T

Target Abilities Tests (TATs), 186
Tasks
  appropriate, 333–34
  time on, 332, 333–34
  transforming, 265
  types of, 108, 121–22, 252
  variables, 101
Teacher(s)
  quality of, 315–16
  role of, 222, 338–40
  success of program and, 326–29
Teacher's Manual for Project Intelligence, 182–85
Teaching the Universe of Discourse (Moffett), 260–61
"Teaching to the test", 167, 168
Terms, errors due to difficult, 115–16
Tests. *See also* Evaluation
  criticism of, 28–29
  evaluation, 316–18
  factor-referenced cognitive, 18–20
  mental, 17–18, 23–27, 28, 29, 148–49, 317
ThinkAbout program, 172–76
Thinking–about–thinking approaches, 280–309
  anatomy of argument and, 290–94
  Complete Problem Solver, 302–6
  in general, 306–7
  metacognitive skills and, 294–302
  Philosophy for Children Program, 280–90
"Thinking aloud", 207
Thinking (periodical), 285
Thinking Straight (Beardsley), 293–94
Thurstone Primary Mental Abilities Test, 156
Time on task, 332, 333–34
Training. *See* Education
Transfer, issue of, 265, 299–302, 334–36
Transfer components of intelligence, 20–21
Transforming tasks, 265
Trial and error, 303
Truth, validity vs., 112
"Turtle geometry", 271–73, 276–77

U

Unactualized potential, 60–61
Uncertainty, decisions under, 304
Uncertainty principle, 123
Understanding, ability of, 12–14
Undistributed middle, fallacy of, 118
Unified writing, 253, 256
Universe of discourse, 260–65
Uses of Argument, The (Toulmin), 290

V

Validity, 111–15, 132, 329–30
Verbal closure, 19
Verbal comprehension, 20
Verification, managerial strategy, 198–200
Vertical thinking, 214–15
Vested interest in hypothesis, 131–34
Visualization, 20, 75–76
Visual memory, 19
Vocabulary for the College–Bound Student (Levine), 240
Vorslegen uber die Menschen un Tierseele (Lectures on the Human and Animal Mind) (Wundt), 26

W

Warrant, 291
Watson-Glaser Critical Thinking Appraisal, 244
Word fluency, 19
"Working knowledge", 56
World War I, mental testing during, 24
Writing, 251–60, 264
  as means of thinking, 258–60
  as occasion for thinking, 251–58
  types of, 252, 253, 256, 259

X

Xavier University, 239